CIMA

Paper C02

Fundamentals of Financial Accounting

Study Text

CIMA Certificate in Business Accounting

Published by: Kaplan Publishing UK

Unit 2 The Business Centre, Molly Millars Lane, Wokingham, Berkshire RG41 2QZ

Acknowledgements

The CIMA Publishing trade mark is reproduced with kind permission of CIMA.

Notice

British Library Cataloguing in Publication Data

A catalogue record for this book is available from the British Library

ISBN: 978-0-85732-958-5

Printed and bound in Great Britain

Contents

Paper Introduction

How to Use the Materials

These Official CIMA learning materials brought to you by CIMA Publishing and Kaplan Publishing have been carefully designed to make your learning experience as easy as possible and to give you the best chances of success in your Fundamentals of Financial Accounting computer based assessments.

The product range contains a number of features to help you in the study process. They include:

- a detailed explanation of all syllabus areas;
- extensive 'practical' materials;
- generous question practice, together with full solutions;
- a computer based assessments preparation section, complete with computer based assessments standard questions and solutions.

This Study Text has been designed with the needs of home-study and distance-learning candidates in mind. Such students require very full coverage of the syllabus topics, and also the facility to undertake extensive question practice. However, the Study Text is also ideal for fully taught courses.

The main body of the text is divided into a number of chapters, each of which is organised on the following pattern:

- **Detailed learning outcomes.** This is expected after your studies of the chapter are complete. You should assimilate these before beginning detailed work on the chapter, so that you can appreciate where your studies are leading.
- **Step-by-step topic coverage.** This is the heart of each chapter, containing detailed explanatory text supported where appropriate by worked examples and exercises. You should work carefully through this section, ensuring that you understand the material being explained and can tackle the examples and exercises successfully. Remember that in many cases knowledge is cumulative: if you fail to digest earlier material thoroughly, you may struggle to understand later chapters.
- **Activities.** Some chapters are illustrated by more practical elements, such as comments and questions designed to stimulate discussion.

- **Question practice.** The test of how well you have learned the material is your ability to tackle exam-standard questions. Make a serious attempt at producing your own answers, but at this stage do not be too concerned about attempting the questions in computer based assessments conditions. In particular, it is more important to absorb the material thoroughly by completing a full solution than to observe the time limits that would apply in the actual computer based assessments.
- **Solutions.** Avoid the temptation merely to 'audit' the solutions provided. It is an illusion to think that this provides the same benefits as you would gain from a serious attempt of your own. However, if you are struggling to get started on a question you should read the introductory guidance provided at the beginning of the solution, where provided, and then make your own attempt before referring back to the full solution.

Having worked through the chapters you are ready to begin your final preparations for the computer based assessments. The final section of this Study Text provides you with the guidance you need. It includes the following features:

- A brief guide to revision technique.
- A note on the format of the computer based assessments. You should know what to expect when you tackle the real computer based assessments and in particular the number of questions to attempt.
- Guidance on how to tackle the computer based assessments itself.
- Revision questions. These are of computer based assessments standard and should be tackled in computer based assessments conditions, especially as regards the time allocation.
- Solutions to the revision questions.
- Two mock computer based assessments.

You should plan to attempt the mock tests just before the date of the real computer based assessments. By this stage your revision should be complete and you should be able to attempt the mock computer based assessments within the time constraints of the real computer based assessments.

If you work conscientiously through this Official CIMA Study Text according to the guidelines above you will be giving yourself an excellent chance of success in your computer based assessments. Good luck with your studies!

Icon Explanations

Definition – these sections explain important areas of knowledge which must be understood and reproduced in an exam environment.

Key Point – identifies topics which are key to success and are often examined.

Supplementary reading – identifies a more detailed explanation of key terms, these sections will help to provide a deeper understanding of core areas. Reference to this text is vital when self studying.

Test Your Understanding – following key points and definitions are exercises which give the opportunity to assess the understanding of these core areas.

Illustration – to help develop an understanding of particular topics. The illustrative examples are useful in preparing for the Test Your Understanding exercises.

Exclamation Mark – this symbol signifies a topic which can be more difficult to understand, when reviewing these areas care should be taken.

Study technique

Passing exams is partly a matter of intellectual ability, but however accomplished you are in that respect you can improve your chances significantly by the use of appropriate study and revision techniques. In this section we briefly outline some tips for effective study during the earlier stages of your approach to the computer based assessments. Later in the text we mention some techniques that you will find useful at the revision stage.

Planning

To begin with, formal planning is essential to get the best return from the time you spend studying. Estimate how much time in total you are going to need for each subject you are studying for the Certificate in Business Accounting. Remember that you need to allow time for revision as well as for initial study of the material. You may find it helpful to read **'Pass First Time!'** second edition by David R. Harris, ISBN 978-1-85617-798-6. This book will provide you with proven study techniques. Chapter by chapter it covers the building blocks of successful learning and examination techniques. This is the ultimate guide to passing your CIMA exams, written by a past CIMA examiner and shows you how to earn all the marks you deserve, and explains how to avoid the most common pitfalls. You may also find "The E Word: Kaplan's Guide to Passing Exams" by Stuart Pedley-Smith ISBN: 978-0-85732-205-0 helpful. Stuart Pedley-Smith is a senior lecturer at Kaplan Financial and a qualified accountant specialising in financial management.

His natural curiosity and wider interests have led him to look beyond the technical content of financial management to the processes and journey that we call education. He has become fascinated by the whole process of learning and the exam skills and techniques that contribute towards success in the classroom. This book is for anyone who has to sit an exam and wants to give themselves a better chance of passing. It is easy to read, written in a common sense style and full of anecdotes, facts, and practical tips. It also contains synopses of interviews with people involved in the learning and examining process.

With your study material before you, decide which chapters you are going to study in each week, and which weeks you will devote to revision and final question practice.

Prepare a written schedule summarising the above and stick to it!

It is essential to know your syllabus. As your studies progress you will become more familiar with how long it takes to cover topics in sufficient depth. Your timetable may need to be adapted to allocate enough time for the whole syllabus.

Students are advised to refer to the notice of examinable legislation published regularly in CIMA's magazine (Financial Management), the students e-newsletter (Velocity) and on the CIMA website, to ensure they are up-to-date.

The amount of space allocated to a topic in the Study Text is not a very good guide as to how long it will take you. For example, the material relating to 'Conceptual and Regulatory Framework'accounts for 20 per cent of the syllabus, but there may be more pages in one because there are more illustrations or examples, which take up more space. The syllabus weighting is the better guide as to how long you should spend on a syllabus topic.

Tips for effective studying

(1) Aim to find a quiet and undisturbed location for your study, and plan as far as possible to use the same period of time each day. Getting into a routine helps to avoid wasting time. Make sure that you have all the materials you need before you begin so as to minimise interruptions.

(2) Store all your materials in one place, so that you do not waste time searching for items around your accommodation. If you have to pack everything away after each study period, keep them in a box, or even a suitcase, which will not be disturbed until the next time.

(3) Limit distractions. To make the most effective use of your study periods you should be able to apply total concentration, so turn off all entertainment equipment, set your phones to message mode, and put up your 'do not disturb' sign.

(4) Your timetable will tell you which topic to study. However, before diving in and becoming engrossed in the finer points, make sure you have an overall picture of all the areas that need to be covered by the end of that session. After an hour, allow yourself a short break and move away from your Study Text. With experience, you will learn to assess the pace you need to work at.

(5) Work carefully through a chapter, making notes as you go. When you have covered a suitable amount of material, vary the pattern by attempting a practice question. When you have finished your attempt, make notes of any mistakes you made, or any areas that you failed to cover or covered more briefly.

(6) Make notes as you study, and discover the techniques that work best for you. Your notes may be in the form of lists, bullet points, diagrams, summaries, 'mind maps' or the written word, but remember that you will need to refer back to them at a later date, so they must be intelligible. If you are on a taught course, make sure you highlight any issues you would like to follow up with your lecturer.

(7) Organise your notes. Make sure that all your notes, calculations etc can be effectively filed and easily retrieved later.

Computer based assessments

CIMA uses objective test questions in the computer based assessments. The most common types are:

- Multiple choice, where you have to choose the correct answer from a list of four possible answers. This could either be numbers or text.
- Multiple choice with more choices and answers, for example, choosing two correct answers from a list of eight possible answers. This could either be numbers or text.
- Single numeric entry, where you give your numeric answer, for example, profit is $10,000.
- Multiple entry, where you give several numeric answers.
- True/false questions, where you state whether a statement is true or false.
- Matching pairs of text, for example, matching a technical term with the correct definition.
- Other types could be matching text with graphs and labelling graphs/diagrams.

In every chapter of this Study Text we have introduced these types of questions, but obviously we have had to label answers A, B, C etc rather than using click boxes. For convenience we have retained quite a lot of questions where an initial scenario leads to a number of sub-questions. There will be questions of this type in the CBA but they will rarely have more than three sub-questions.

Guidance re CIMA online calculator

As part of the CIMA Certificate level computer based assessment software, candidates are now provided with a calculator. This calculator is onscreen and is available for the duration of the assessment. The calculator is available in each of the five Certificate level assessments and is accessed by clicking the calculator button in the top left hand corner of the screen at any time during the assessment.

All candidates must complete a 15 minute tutorial before the assessment begins and will have the opportunity to familiarise themselves with the calculator and practice using it.

Candidates may practise using the calculator by downloading and installing the practice exam at http://www.vue.com/athena/ The calculator can be accessed from the fourth sample question (of 12).

Please note that the practice exam and tutorial provided by Pearson VUE at http://www.vue.com/athena/ is not specific to CIMA and includes the full range of question types the Pearson VUE software supports, some of which CIMA does not currently use.

Fundamentals of Financial Accounting Syllabus

The computer based assessments for Fundamentals of Financial Accounting are 2 hour assessments comprising 50 compulsory questions, with one or more parts. There will be no choice and all questions should be attempted.

Additional CBA resources, including sample assessment questions are available online at www.cimaglobal.com/cba2011

Structure of subjects and learning outcomes

Each subject within the syllabus is divided into a number of broad syllabus topics. The topics contain one or more lead learning outcomes, related component learning outcomes and indicative knowledge content.

A learning outcome has two main purposes:

(a) To define the skill or ability that a well prepared candidate should be able to exhibit in the examination

(b) To demonstrate the approach likely to be taken in examination questions

The learning outcomes are part of a hierarchy of learning objectives. The verbs used at the beginning of each learning outcome relate to a specific learning objective e.g.

Calculate the break-even point, profit target, margin of safety and profit/volume ratio for a single product or service

The verb '**calculate**' indicates a level three learning objective. The following table lists the learning objectives and the verbs that appear in the syllabus learning outcomes and examination questions.

Certificate level verbs

CIMA VERB HIERARCHY

CIMA place great importance on the choice of verbs in exam question requirements. It is thus critical that you answer the question according to the definition of the verb used.

In Certificate level exams you will meet verbs from levels 1, 2, and 3. These are as follows:

Level 1: KNOWLEDGE

What you are expected to know

VERBS USED	DEFINITION
List	Make a list of.
State	Express, fully or clearly, the details of/facts of.
Define	Give the exact meaning of.

Level 2: COMPREHENSION

What you are expected to understand

VERBS USED	DEFINITION
Describe	Communicate the key features of.
Distinguish	Highlight the differences between.
Explain	Make clear or intelligible/state the meaning or purpose of.
Identify	Recognise, establish or select after consideration.
Illustrate	Use an example to describe or explain something.

Level 3: APPLICATION

How you are expected to apply your knowledge

VERBS USED	DEFINITION
Apply	Put to practical use.
Calculate	Ascertain or reckon mathematically.
Demonstrate	Prove with certainty or exhibit by practical means.
Prepare	Make or get ready for use.
Reconcile	Make or prove consistent/compatible.
Solve	Find an answer to.
Tabulate	Arrange in a table.

PAPER C02
FUNDAMENTALS OF FINANCIAL ACCOUNTING

Syllabus overview

The main objective of this paper is the preparation of financial statements for single entities. These statements are constructed within a conceptual and regulatory framework requiring an understanding of the various valuation alternatives, the role of legislation and of accounting standards. Being able to apply accounting techniques and systems enables the preparation of accounts for different types of operations and for specific transactions. There is an introduction to measuring financial performance with the calculation of basic ratios. The need to understand and apply necessary controls for accounting systems, looking at internal control and the nature of errors and fraud, is also covered.

Note: students are required to be aware of the format and content of published accounts but are not required to prepare them. No knowledge of any specific accounting treatment contained in the International Financial Reporting Standards (IFRSs) – including the International Accounting Standards (IASs), – is necessary, except in terms of how they influence the presentation of financial statements. IAS 1 and IAS 7 formats will form the basis of those statements. The terminology used for all entities will be that seen in the International Financial Reporting Standards. This will enable students to use a consistent set of accounting terms throughout their studies.

Also note that IAS1 allows the presentation of income in the form of a single statement of comprehensive income or as two separate statements, an income statement and a statement of comprehensive income. Because of the nature of the material dealt with at this level, the majority of questions on this topic will ask for income statement format. However students must be aware of the layout of the single statement of comprehensive income and be able to use it if required.

Syllabus structure

The syllabus comprises the following topics and study weightings:

A	Conceptual and regulatory framework	20%
B	Accounting systems	20%
C	Preparation of accounts for single entities	45%
D	Control of accounting systems	15%

Assessment strategy

There will be a two hour computer based assessment, comprising 50 compulsory questions, each with one or more parts.

A variety of objective test question styles and types will be used within the assessment.

C02 – A. CONCEPTUAL AND REGULATORY FRAMEWORK (20%)

Learning outcomes **On completion of their studies students should be able to:**			**Indicative syllabus content**
Lead	**Component**	**Level**	
1. explain the concepts of financial accounting.	(a) explain the need for accounting records; [1] (b) identify user groups and the characteristics of financial statements; [1] (c) distinguish between financial and management accounts; [1] (d) identify the underlying assumptions, policies and changes in accounting estimates; [10] (e) explain capital and revenue, cash and profit, income and expenditure, assets and liabilities; [2] (f) distinguish between tangible and intangible assets; [6] (g) explain the historical cost convention; [10] (h) identify alternative methods of valuing assets, and their impact on profit measures and statement of financial position values. [6], [10]	2 2 2 2 2 2 2 2	• Accounting records. [1] • Users of accounts and the objectives and the qualitative characteristics of financial statements. [1] • Functions of financial and management accounts; purpose of accounting statements; stewardship; the accounting equation. [1], [2] • Underlying assumptions, policies, changes in accounting estimates; capital and revenue; cash and profit; income, expenditure, assets and liabilities. [10] • Tangible and intangible assets. [6] • Historical cost convention. [10] • Asset valuation including current cost, fair value and value in use bases and their implications for profit measurement and the statement of financial position. [6], [10]
2. explain the regulatory and legal framework for financial accounting.	(a) explain the influence of legislation on published accounting information for organisations; [10] (b) explain the role of accounting standards in preparing financial statements; [10] (c) explain approaches to creating accounting standards. [10]	2 2 2	• Regulatory influence of company law (e.g. Companies Acts, EC directives); items in formats for published accounts. [10] • Role of accounting standards in financial statements. [10] • Principles and rules based approaches to creating accounting standards. [10]

C02 – B. ACCOUNTING SYSTEMS (20%)

Learning outcomes On completion of their studies students should be able to:			**Indicative syllabus content**
Lead	**Component**	**Level**	
1. prepare ledger accounts and supporting documents.	(a) explain the principles of double-entry bookkeeping; [3]	2	• Ledger accounts; double-entry bookkeeping. [3] • Accounts for cash and bank, bank reconciliations, imprest system for petty cash. [3] • Accounts for sales and purchases, including personal accounts and control accounts. [3], [8], [9] • Nominal ledger accounts and journal entries. [3], [8] • Trial balance. [4] • Accounts for indirect taxes e.g. value added tax, sales tax. [5] • Accounts for payroll. [5] • Non-current asset register. [6]
	(b) prepare cash and bank accounts, and bank reconciliation statements; [3], [9]	3	
	(c) prepare petty cash statements under an imprest system; [8]	3	
	(d) prepare accounts for sales and purchases, including personal accounts and control accounts; [3], [8], [9]	3	
	(e) prepare nominal ledger accounts, journal entries and a trial balance; [3], [4], [8]	3	
	(f) prepare accounts for indirect taxes; [5]	3	
	(g) prepare accounts for payroll; [5]	3	
	(h) prepare a non-current asset register. [6]	3	
2. explain the use of codes in accounting systems.	(a) explain the need for accounting codes; [9]	2	• Accounting codes and their uses. [9]
	(b) illustrate the use of simple coding systems. [9]	2	

C02 – C. PREPARATION OF ACCOUNTS FOR SINGLE ENTITIES (45%)

Learning outcomes **On completion of their studies students should be able to:**			**Indicative syllabus content**
Lead	**Component**	**Level**	
1. prepare accounts for transactions.	(a) prepare accounts using accruals and prepayments; [5] (b) prepare accounts for bad debts and allowances for receivables; [5] (c) prepare accounts using different methods of calculating depreciation and for impairment values; [6] (d) prepare accounts for inventories; [8] (e) prepare manufacturing accounts; [12] (f) prepare income and expenditure accounts; [11] (g) prepare accounts from incomplete records; [11] (h) prepare accounts for the issue and redemption of shares and debentures. [13]	3 3 3 3 3 3 3 3	• Adjustments to the trial balance; accruals and prepayments. [5] • Bad debts and allowances for receivables. [5] • Accounting treatment for depreciation (straight line, reducing balance and revaluation methods) and impairment. [6] • Accounts for inventories (excluding construction contracts); methods of inventory measurement (FIFO, LIFO and average cost). [8] • Manufacturing accounts. [12] • Income and expenditure accounts. [11] • Accounting statements from incomplete data. [11] • Accounts for the Issue and redemption of shares and debentures. [13]
2. prepare financial statements for a single entity.	(a) prepare financial statements from trial balance; [7], [13] (b) prepare a statement of cash flows. [13]	3 3	• Income statement, statement of comprehensive income and statement of financial position; statement of changes in equity. [13] • Statement of cash flows. [13]
3. demonstrate the use of basic ratios in financial performance.	(a) calculate basic ratios. [14]	3	• Ratios: return on capital employed; gross and net profit margins; asset turnover; trade receivables collection period and trade payables payment period; current and quick ratios; inventory turnover; gearing. [14]

C02 – D. CONTROL OF ACCOUNTING SYSTEMS (15%)

Learning outcomes **On completion of their studies students should be able to:**			**Indicative syllabus content**
Lead	**Component**	**Level**	
1. explain the need for external controls on a business.	(a) identify the requirements for external audit and the basic processes undertaken; [10] (b) explain the meaning of fair presentation; [10] (c) distinguish between external and internal audit. [10]	2 2 2	• External audit. [10] • Fair presentation. [10] • Distinction between external and internal audit. [10]
2. explain internal control techniques.	(a) explain the purpose and basic procedures of internal audit; [10] (b) explain the need for financial controls; [10] (c) explain the purpose of audit checks and audit trails; [10]	2 2 2	• Internal audit. [10] • Financial controls, audit checks and audit trails. [10]
3. demonstrate how accounting errors are corrected.	(a) explain the nature of accounting errors; [4] (b) prepare accounting entries for the correction of errors; [9]	2 3	• Errors including those of principle, omission, and commission. [4] • Journal entries and suspense accounts [9]
4. explain the nature of fraud.	(a) explain the nature of fraud; [10] (b) explain the basic methods of fraud prevention and detection. [10]	2 2	• Types of fraud. [10] • Methods for prevention of fraud including levels of authorisation, documentation and staff organisation. [10] • Methods of detection of fraud including spot checks, comparison with external evidence, reconciliations and control accounts. [10]

chapter

1

The Accounting Scene

Chapter learning objectives

When you have completed this chapter, you should be able to:

- explain the need for accounting records;
- identify user groups and the characteristics of financial statements;
- distinguish between financial and management accounts;
- identify the different types of business organisations.

1 Introduction

This chapter provides:

- an introduction to the accounting framework and
- introduces the function of accounting systems.

Much of the chapter relates to the first syllabus area 'conceptual and regulatory framework', which is also continued in chapter 15.

This chapter covers:

- the objectives of accounting;
- the financial statements;
- who uses the financial statements;
- the qualitative characteristics of financial statements;
- the difference between financial and management accounting and
- types of business organisations.

2 What is accounting?

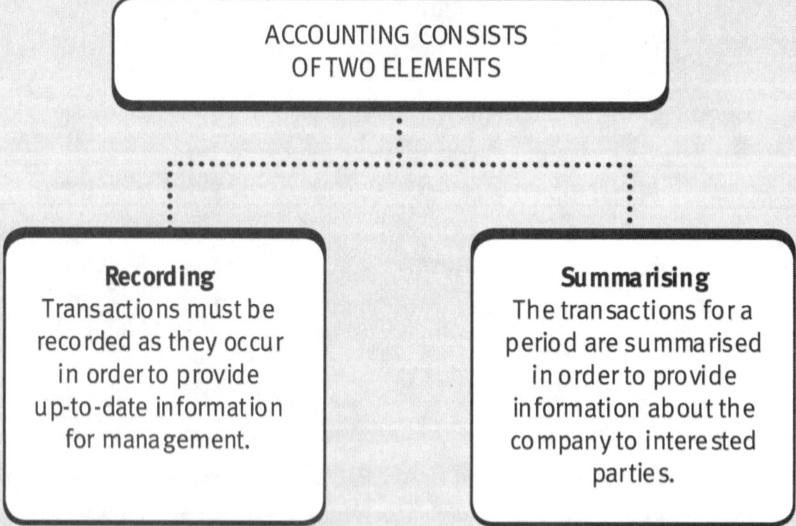

Further detail on accounting

Accounting can be described as being concerned with **measurement and management**. Measurement is largely concerned with the recording of past data, and management with the use of that data in order to make decisions that will benefit the organisation.

The measurement process is not always easy. One of the most common problems is that of when to recognise a transaction. For example, if we are to obtain goods from a supplier with payment to be due 60 days after the goods are received, when should the transaction be recorded?

The following possibilities may be considered:

- when we place the order;
- when we take delivery of the goods;
- when we receive the invoice from the supplier; or
- when we pay the supplier for the goods.

Accounting, therefore, involves the exercising of judgement by the person responsible for converting data into meaningful information. It is this that distinguishes accounting from bookkeeping.

Accounting may be defined as:

- the classification and recording of monetary transactions;
- the presentation and interpretation of the results of those transactions in order to assess performance over a period and the financial position at a given date;
- the monetary projection of future activities arising from the alternative planned courses of action.

Note the three aspects considered in this definition: recording, reporting and forecasting:

(1) Accounting is partly a matter of record-keeping. The monetary transactions entered into by a business need to be controlled and monitored, and for this a permanent record is essential. For an efficient system of record-keeping, the transactions must first be classified into categories appropriate to the enterprise concerned.

(2) At appropriate intervals, the individual transactions must be summarised in order to give an overall picture.

(3) Finally, accounting information can be the basis for planning and decision-making.

An alternative explanation is that accounting is part of the management information system (MIS) of an organisation. In this context, the accounting element is referred to as an accounting information system (AIS).

Accounting can thus be said to be a method of providing information to management (and other users) relating to the activities of an organisation. In order to do this it relies on the accurate collection of data from sources both internal and external to the organisation. The recording of this data is often referred to as bookkeeping.

3 The objectives of accounting

The objectives of accounting are to **provide financial information to the managers, owners and other parties interested in an organisation.** This is done by the production of financial statements.

You will see in chapter 15 that the International Accounting Standards Board (IASB) in their **Framework for the Preparation and Presentation of Financial Statements (Framework)** state that

Providing useful information to investors is the main objective of financial reporting.

4 What are financial statements?

There are three main financial statements:

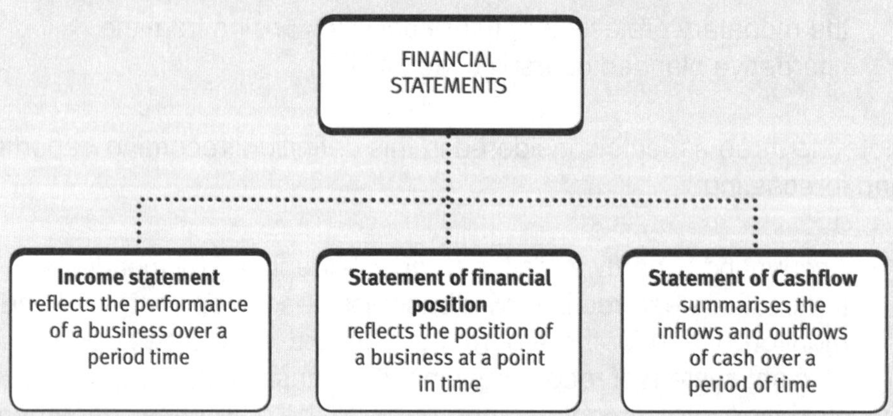

Financial statements are prepared so that we can examine and evaluate all information, in order to make key decisions.

5 Who uses financial statements?

Accounting information is used by many people, both by individuals and in organisations. To get a feel for the purpose of accounts it is useful to **classify these users into groups**, and to look at the reasons why they use accounts and what they hope to get from them.

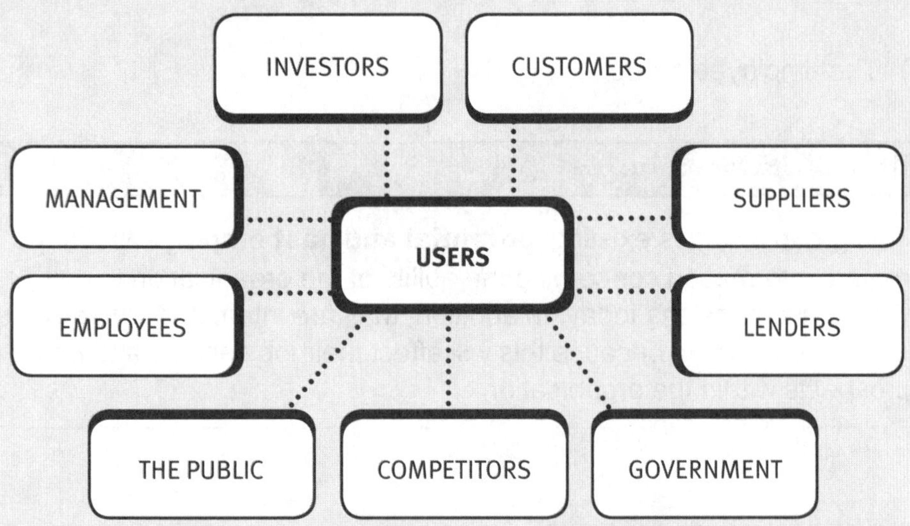

Any classification of this sort is somewhat arbitrary, and many users fall into more than one classification. However, the following groups are commonly recognised as having particular needs for accounting information:

(a) The investor group

What do they require?

This group includes **both existing and potential owners** of shares in companies. They require information concerning the performance of the company measured in terms of its profitability and the extent to which those profits are to be distributed to shareholders. They are also interested in the social/economic policies of the company so that they may decide if they wish to be associated with such an organisation.

(b) The lender group

What do they require?

This group includes both **existing and potential providers** of secured or unsecured, long or short-term loan finance. They require information concerning the ability of the organisation to repay the interest on such loans as they fall due; and the longer-term growth and stability of the organisation to ensure that it is capable of repaying the loan at the agreed time. In addition, if the loan is secured, the value of the appropriate secured assets is important as a means of recovering the amount due.

(c) The employee group

What do they require?

This group includes existing, **potential and past employees**. They require information concerning the ability of the organisation to pay wages and pensions today. In addition, they are interested in the future of the organisation because this will affect their job security and future prospects within the organisation.

(d) The analyst/adviser group

What do they require?

This group includes a range of **advisers to investors, employees and the general public**. The needs of these users will be similar to those of their clients. The difference is, perhaps, that in some instances, the members of this group will be more technically qualified to understand accounting reports.

(e) The business contact group

What do they require?

This group includes **customers and suppliers** of the organisation. Customers will be concerned to ensure that the organisation has the ability to provide the goods/services requested and to continue to provide similar services in the future. Suppliers will wish to ensure that the organisation will be capable of paying for the goods/services supplied when payment becomes due.

(f) The government

What do they require?

This group includes **taxation authorities, and other government agencies and departments**. The taxation authorities will calculate the organisation's taxation liability based upon the accounting reports it submits to them. Other departments require statistical information to measure the state of the economy.

(g) The public

What do they require?

This group includes **taxpayers, consumers and other community and special interest groups**. They require information concerning the policies of the organisation and how those policies affect the community. The public is increasingly interested in environmental issues.

(h) Internal users

What do they require?

The **management of the company** require information to assist them in the performance of their duties. Three different levels of management can be identified:

- **Strategic**. This is the level of management found at the top of organisations. In a commercial organisation it is referred to as the board of directors. These people require information to assist them in decisions affecting the long-term future of the organisation.
- **Tactical.** This is often referred to as middle management. These people require information to assist them in monitoring performance and making decisions to enable the organisation to achieve its short- to medium-term targets.
- **Operational.** This is the level of management responsible for decisions concerning the day-to-day activities of the organisation. It is common for the information provided to them to be quantified in non-monetary units, such as hours worked, number of components produced, and so on.

6 The qualitative characteristics of financial statements

All of the above user groups, both internal and external to the organisation, require the information provided to be useful. In this context, information should:

(a) enable its recipient to make effective decisions;

(b) be adequate for taking effective action to control the organisation or provide valuable details relating to its environment;

(c) be compatible with the responsibilities and needs of its recipient;

(d) be produced at optimum cost;

(e) be easily understood by its recipient;

(f) be timely;

(g) be sufficiently accurate and precise for the purpose of its provision.

The IASB's Framework also suggests that financial statements should have certain qualitative characteristics

The Framework splits qualitative characteristics into two categories:

(i) Fundamental qualitative characteristics

- Relevance;
- Faithful representation

(ii) Enhancing qualitative characteristics

- Comparability;
- Verifiability;
- Timeliness;
- Understandability.

Further detail

For decisions to be made, the information must be relevant to the decision and be clearly presented, stating any assumptions upon which the information is based, so that the user may exercise judgement as appropriate.

Often, better information may be provided at additional cost or after an additional time delay. The adequacy of information is important, and factors such as the cost of the information and the speed with which it is available may be more important than it being 100 per cent accurate.

The information provided must be communicated to the person responsible for taking any action in respect of the information provided. In this regard it is better to distinguish information between that which relates to controllable aspects of the business and that which relates to non-controllable aspects. The controllable aspects may then be further divided into those that are significant and an exception reporting approach applied.

Fundamental qualitative characteristics

(i) **Relevance** - Information is relevant when it influences the economic decisions of users by helping them evaluate past, present or future events or confirming or correcting their past evaluations.

The relevance of information can be affected by its nature and materiality. Some items may be relevant to users simply because of their nature whereas some items may only become relevant once they are material. Hence, materiality is a threshold quality of information rather than a primary characteristic.

According to the Framework, information is material if its omission or misstatement could influence the decisions of users.

Materiality - Materiality is an entity specific aspect of relevance and depends on the size of the item or error judged in the particular circumstances of its omission or misstatement.

Information is material if its omission or misstatement could influence the economic decisions of users taken on the basis of the financial statements.

(ii) **Faithful representation -**

If information is to represent faithfully the transactions and other events that it purports to represent, they must be accounted for and presented in accordance with their substance and economic reality and not merely their legal form.

To be a perfectly faithful representation, financial information would possess the following characteristics:

Completeness

To be understandable information must contain all the necessary descriptions and explanations.

Neutrality

Information must be neutral, i.e. free from bias. Financial statements are not neutral if, by the selection or presentation of information, they influence the making of a decision or judgement in order to achieve a predetermined result or outcome.

Free from error

Information must be free from error within the bounds of materiality. A material error or an omission can cause the financial statements to be false or misleading and thus unreliable and deficient in terms of their relevance.

Free from error does not mean perfectly accurate in all respects. For example, where an estimate has been used the amount must be described clearly and accurately as being an estimate.

Enhancing qualitative characteristics

Comparability

Users must be able to compare financial statements over a period of time in order to identify trends in financial position and performance. Users must also be able to compare financial statements of different entities to be able to assess their relative financial position and performance.

In order to achieve comparability, similar items should be treated in a consistent manner from one period to the next and from one entity to another. However, it is not appropriate for an entity to continue accounting for transactions in a certain manner if alternative treatments exist that would be more relevant and reliable.

Disclosure of accounting policies should also be made so that users can identify any changes in these policies or differences between the policies of different entities.

Verifiability

Verification can be direct or indirect. Direct verification means verifying an amount or other representation through direct observation i.e.counting cash. Indirect verification means checking the inputs to a model, formula or other technique and recalculating the outputs using the same methodology i.e. recalculating inventory amounts using the same cost flow assumption such as first-in, first-out method.

Timeliness

Timeliness means having information available to decision makers in time to be capable of influencing their decisions. Generally, the older the information is the less useful it becomes.

Understandability

Information needs to be readily understandable by users. Information that may be relevant to decision making should not be excluded on the grounds that it may be too difficult for certain users to understand.

Understandability depends on:

- the way in which information is presented; and
- the capabilities of users.

It is assumed that users:

- have a reasonable knowledge of business and economic activities; and
- are willing to study the information provided with reasonable diligence.

For information to be understandable users need to be able to perceive its significance.

Reporting

Exception reporting is the technique of reducing the size of management reports by including only those items that should be drawn to the manager's attention, rather than including all items.

Most organisations will set targets against which actual performance can be compared. You will learn more about the setting of such targets in your studies of management accounting. Their use enables exception reports to be produced to highlight the differences between the actual and target results. The use of exception reporting avoids wasting unnecessary management time reading reports that merely advise the management that no action is required and concentrates on those issues that do require management action.

In conclusion, therefore, internal information will be much more detailed than external information, and will be prepared on a more regular basis.

7 Terminology

Bookkeeping

Bookkeeping can be described as the recording of monetary transactions, appropriately classified, in the financial records of an entity, by either manual means or otherwise.

Further detail

Bookkeeping involves maintaining a detailed 'history' of transactions as they occur. Every sale, purchase or other transaction will be classified according to its type and, depending on the information needs of the organisation, will be recorded in a logical manner in the 'books'. The 'books' will contain a record or account of each item showing the transactions that have occurred, thus enabling management to track the individual movements on each record, that is, the increases and decreases.

Periodically a list of the results of the transactions is produced. This is done by listing each account and its final position or balance. The list is known as a **trial balance** and is an important step prior to the next stage of providing financial statements.

Financial accounting

Financial accounting can be described as the classification and recording of monetary transactions of an entity in accordance with established concepts, principles, accounting standards and legal requirements, and their presentation, by means of various financial statements, during and at the end of an accounting period.

Key characteristics of financial accounting are:

- Produced for external users.
- Prepared annually.
- Required by law.
- Reflect past performance and current position.
- Information prepared in accordance with international accounting standards.

Further detail

Two points in particular are worth noting about this description:

(1) Financial statements **must comply with accounting rules** published by the various advisory and regulatory bodies. In other words, an organisation does not have a completely free hand. The reason for this is that the end product of the financial accounting process – a set of financial statements – is primarily intended for the use of people outside the organisation. Without access to the more detailed information available to insiders, these people may be misled unless financial statements are prepared on uniform principles.

(2) Financial accounting is **partly concerned with summarising the transactions of a period and presenting the summary in a coherent form.** This again is because financial statements are intended for outside consumption. The outsiders who have a need for and a right to information are entitled to receive it at defined intervals, and not at the whim of management.

Management accounting

Management accounting can be described as the process of identification, measurement, accumulation, analysis, preparation, interpretation and communication of information used by management to plan, evaluate and control within an entity and to assure appropriate use of and accountability for its resources.

Key characteristics of management accounting are:

- Production of detailed accounts used by management to control the business and plan for the future (internal use).
- Often reflect budgets, forecasts in addition to past performance.
- Normally prepared monthly.
- Not required by law.
- Presented in a manner to suit the management needs.

Further detail

Management accounting also comprises the preparation of financial reports for non-management groups such as shareholders, lenders, regulatory agencies and tax authorities.

Although the needs of external users of accounts are addressed in this definition, it can be seen that the emphasis of management accounting is on **providing information to help managers in running the business**. The kind of information produced, and the way in which it is presented, are at the discretion of the managers concerned; they will request whatever information, in whatever format, they believe to be appropriate to their needs.

The differences between external and internal information

External information is **usually produced annually**, though in organisations listed (or quoted) on a stock exchange, information may be produced more frequently, for example quarterly. External information is provided mainly by limited companies, in accordance with the relevant company legislation. These may prescribe the layouts to be used and the information that is to be disclosed either on the face of the financial statements or in the notes that accompany them. For other organisations that are not regulated by such legislation, accounts may have to be provided for other interested parties such as those dealing with taxation and lenders. For these organisations, the requirements of legislation are not mandatory and may not be appropriate. However, these requirements are often considered to be good accounting practice.

External information is **often available publicly** and is therefore available to the competitors of the organisation as well as its owners and employees. Of necessity, therefore, it is important that the information provided does not allow the organisation's competitors to obtain detailed information concerning the working of the organisation. Thus external information is summarised in order to protect the organisation from losing any competitive edge that it may possess.

Internal information is **produced on a regular basis** in order for management to compare the organisation's performance with its targets and to make decisions concerning the future. Accounting information is usually produced on a monthly basis, although other non-financial performance measures may be produced more regularly. Whereas external information is almost exclusively measured in monetary terms, internal information will most likely involve reporting financial and non-financial measures together.

There is a very good reason for this: many managers, particularly those in control of operational matters, will not feel competent to understand accounting reports. They will understand differences in output levels and in usage of materials and labour much more readily than they will understand the implications of these same differences upon profit.

ACCOUNTING

Financial accounting	Management accounting
• Production of summary financial statements for external users.	• Production of detailed accounts, used by management to control the business and plan for the future.
• Prepared annually (six-monthly or quarterly in some countries).	• Normally prepared monthly, often on a rolling basis.
• Generally required by law.	• Not mandatory.
• Reflects past performance and current position.	• Includes budgets and forecasts of future activities, as well as reflecting past performance.
• Information calculated and presented in accordance with international accounting standards.	• Information computed and presented in order to be relevant to managers.

8 What is a business organisation?

A business is an **organisation that regularly enters into transactions that are expected to provide a reward measurable in monetary terms.** It is thus obvious from everyday life that many business organisations exist; what is less obvious is that their organisational (legal) structure and therefore their accounting requirements may differ.

There are two main reasons for the different organisational structures that exist – **the nature of their activities and their size.**

Profit-making organisations

Some organisations are formed with the intent of making profits from their activities for their owners:

(a) Sole traders (sole proprietors)

Who are they?

These are organisations that are **owned by one person**. They tend to be small because they are constrained by the limited financial resources of their owner.

(b) Partnerships

Who are they?

These are organisations **owned by two or more persons** working in common with a view to making a profit. The greater number of owners compared with a sole trader increases the availability of finance and this is often the reason for forming such a structure

(c) Limited companies

Who are they?

These are organisations **recognised in law as 'persons' in their own right**. Thus a company may own assets and incur liabilities in its own name.

The accounting of these organisations must meet certain minimum obligations imposed by legislation, for example, via company law and other regulations. Some of these requirements constitute recommended accounting practice for other types of organisation.

Two types of limited companies can be identified: **private limited companies**; and **public limited companies.**

Who are they?

Public limited companies are **'listed' on a stock exchange**. Listed companies may have many thousands of owners (shareholders) who are even further removed from the running of the business.

In private limited companies the **owners are actively involved in running the business**. In this way they are similar to sole traders and partnerships. This is rarely true of public companies, where the owners may not become involved in the day-to-day activities of the business.

These distinctions can be important when considering the accounting requirements.

Non-profit-making organisations

Other organisations are formed with the intent of providing services, without intending to be profitable in the long term:

(a) Clubs and societies

Who are they?

These organisations exist to provide facilities and entertainments for their members. They are often sports and/or social clubs and most of their revenue is derived from the members who benefit from the club's facilities. They may carry out some activities that are regarded as 'trading' activities, in which profits are made, but these are not seen as the main purpose of the organisation.

(b) Charities

Who are they?

These exist to provide services to particular groups, for example people with special needs and to protect the environment. Although they are regarded as non-profit-making, they too often carry out trading activities, such as running shops.

(c) Local and central government

Who are they?

Government departments are financed by members of society (including limited companies). Their finances are used to provide the infrastructure in which we live, and to redistribute wealth to other members of society. You will not look at the accounts of government bodies in this Learning System.

9 Chapter summary

In this chapter you have learnt:

- that 'accounting' involves recording, summarising and forecasting, to meet the information needs of different user groups;
- the qualitative characteristics of financial statements;
- the distinction between 'bookkeeping', 'financial accounting' and 'management accounting';
- the differences between internal and external information; the different types of business organisation.

Test your understanding questions

Test your understanding 1

The main aim of accounting is to:

A maintain ledger accounts for every transaction

B provide financial information to users of such information

C produce a trial balance

D record every financial transaction individually

Test your understanding 2

The main aim of financial accounting is to:

A record all transactions in the books of account

B provide management with detailed analyses of costs

C present the financial results of the organisation by means of recognised statements

D calculate profit

Test your understanding 3

Financial statements differ from management accounts in that they:

A are prepared monthly for internal control purposes

B contain details of costs incurred in manufacturing

C are summarised and prepared mainly for external users of accounting information

D provide information to enable the trial balance to be prepared

Test your understanding 4

Which **one** of the following does **not** apply to the preparation of financial statements?

A They are prepared annually

B They provide a summary of the outcome of financial transactions

C They are prepared mainly for external users of accounting information

D They are prepared to show the detailed costs of manufacturing and trading

Test your understanding 5

Which of the following statements gives the best definition of the objective of accounting?

A To provide useful information to users

B To record, categorise and summarise financial transactions

C To calculate the taxation due to the government

D To calculate the amount of dividend to pay to shareholders

Test your understanding 6

Which **one** of the following sentences does **not** explain the distinction between financial statements and management accounts?

A Financial statements are primarily for external users and management accounts are primarily for internal users

B Financial statements are normally produced annually, and management accounts are normally produced monthly

C Financial statements are more accurate than management accounts

D Financial statements are required by law and management accounts are not

Test your understanding 7

Match the following users with their information requirements.

1	Investors	A	Firm's ability to provide goods now and in future and pay debts
2	Lenders	B	Performance, profitability and dividends
3	Employees	C	Profit levels, tax liability and statistics
4	Business contacts	D	Firm's ability to pay interest and repay loans, the value of secured assets
5	Government departments	E	Firm's ability to pay wages, cash resources, future prospects, pay pensions

Test your understanding 8

Which **one** of the following is **not** an enhancing qualitative characteristic?

A Comparability

B Timeliness

C Understandability

D Relevance

Test your understanding answers

Test your understanding 1

B

Maintaining ledger accounts, producing a trial balance and recording transactions are all part of the bookkeeping system.

Test your understanding 2

C

Recording transactions is part of the bookkeeping function. This should be capable of providing management with internal information, but this is part of the management accounting function. The calculation of profit also results from the bookkeeping system and contributes towards the presentation of the financial results.

Test your understanding 3

C

Management accounts are prepared monthly (or more frequently) for internal control purposes; they also contain detailed information such as costing figures. The trial balance is prepared from the bookkeeping system and is used as a basis for the preparation of financial statements.

Test your understanding 4

D

Management accounts would provide detailed costs and other information regarding manufacturing and trading.

Test your understanding 5

A

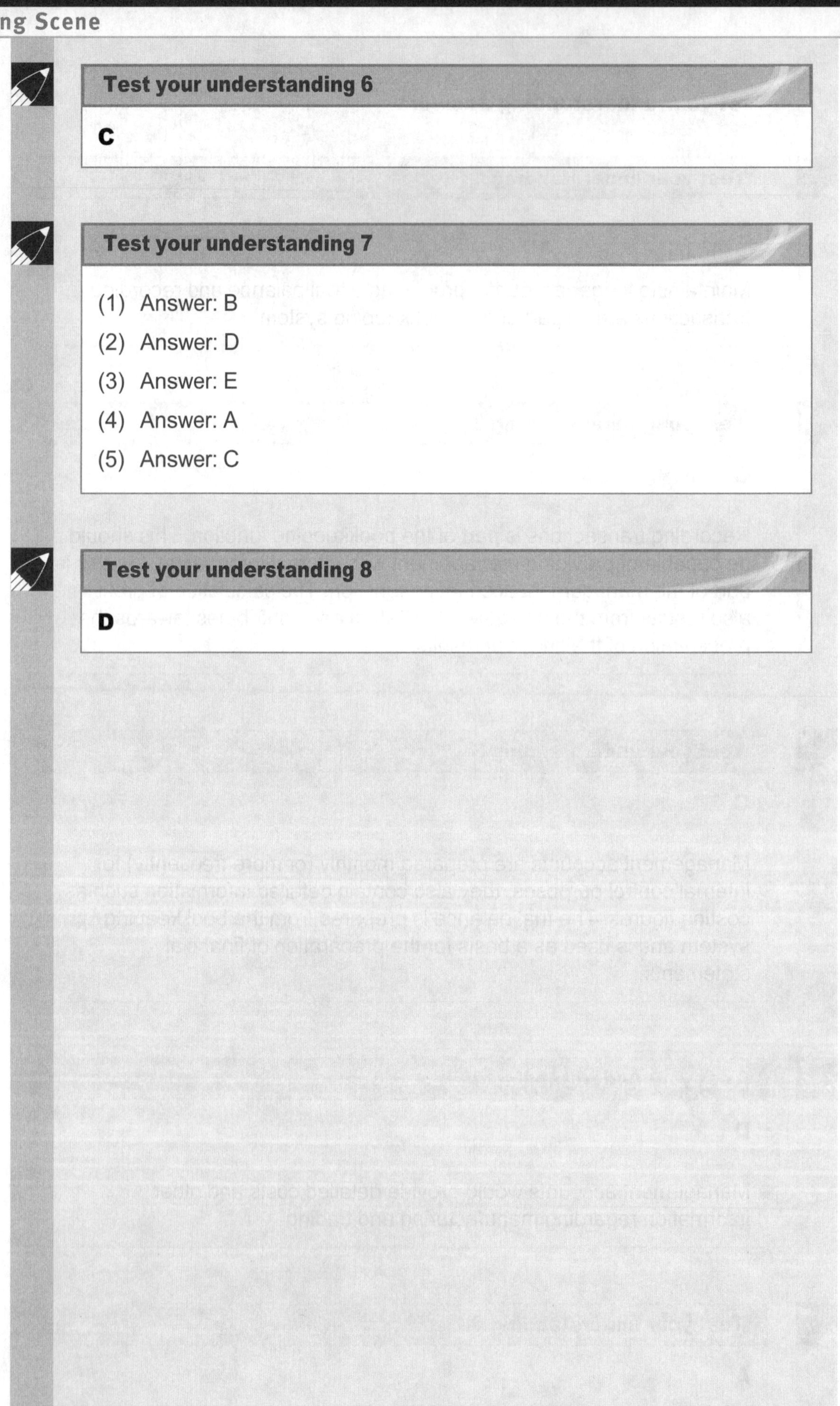

Test your understanding 6

C

Test your understanding 7

(1) Answer: B

(2) Answer: D

(3) Answer: E

(4) Answer: A

(5) Answer: C

Test your understanding 8

D

chapter

2

The Framework of Financial Statements

Chapter learning objectives

When you have completed this chapter, you should be able to:

- explain the seperate entity concept;
- explain and calculate the accounting equation;
- explain the difference between current and non-current assets and liabilities.
- explain assets, liabilities, capital, income and expenditure.
- explain gross and net profit;
- explain the difference between capital and revenue transactions;
- have a general appreciation of the income statement and the statement of financial position.

1 Introduction

In this chapter we begin to look at:

- what is contained in financial statements and
- how the information is compiled and presented.

The chapter also introduces some of the basic conventions of accounting, although these are covered in more depth in chapter 15.

In particular, the chapter looks at:

- the accounting equation and
- the single entity concept.

2 The separate entity convention

In discussing limited companies in chapter 1, it was mentioned that the law recognises **a company as a 'person' in its own right, distinct from the personalities of its owners** (known as shareholders).

Further detail

In other words, if a company runs up debts in its own name & then has difficulty in paying them, its suppliers may be entitled to seize the assets owned by the company. But they have no claim against the personal assets owned by the shareholders: it is the company that owes money, not its owners. In law, this distinction does not exist with other forms of business entity, such as the sole proprietor. If Bill Smith is in business as a plumber, trading under the name of 'Smith & Co. Plumbing Services', the law recognises no distinction between the business & the individual. If there are large debts outstanding for plumbing supplies, & the business assets of Smith & Co. are insufficient to pay them, the suppliers can demand payment from Bill Smith the individual, who may be forced to sell his personal assets – home, car, & so on. But in this respect accounting conventions do not correspond with the strict legal form of the business. It is an absolutely crucial concept in accounting that, regardless of the legal form of a business – limited company, sole trader, partnership or whatever – the business is treated as a separate entity from its owner(s). For accounting purposes, Bill Smith the individual is not the same as Smith & Co.

Plumbing Services. This reflects the fact that accounting information relates only to business transactions. What Bill Smith does as an individual is of no concern to the accountant, & his private activities must be kept quite separate from the business transactions of Smith & Co. Students often find this concept hard to grasp, particularly when they notice that, as a consequence of it, Bill Smith the individual can actually have business dealings with Smith & Co. For example, Bill may take some copper piping from the inventories held by Smith & Co. in order to repair the heating system in his own home. From the accounting point of view, a business transaction has occurred: Smith & Co. has supplied an individual called Bill Smith with some piping, & its value must be accounted for.

Despite its apparent artificiality, the importance of this convention will become apparent in the next section, where we look at an arithmetic relationship called the accounting equation.

3 The accounting equation

The accounting equation shows that

Assets = Liabilities + Capital

What do these terms mean?

Asset

A resource that may be used by a business or other organisation to derive revenue in the future.

Further detail on assets

Examples of assets are land, buildings, plant and machinery, motor vehicles, inventories of goods, receivables, bank balances and cash. Assets may be described as **tangible or intangible.** Tangible assets are those that can be physically seen or touched (e.g. land, buildings, equipment, inventories, etc.). Intangible assets cannot be physically seen or touched (e.g. goodwill, which represents the value of a business as a whole compared with the sum of the values of its individual assets and liabilities). As such, goodwill represents the value of the organisation's customer base, employee relationships, and so on. Other intangible assets might include patents and trademarks. You will learn more about intangible assets in chapter 11.

Liability

An entity's obligations to transfer economic benefits as a result of past transactions or events.

Further detail on liabilities

Thus a liability can be described as an amount owed by a business or organisation to an individual or other business organisation. Examples of liabilities are payables, loans received and bank overdrafts.

Capital

In this context, capital is difficult to define, but it can be regarded as a special kind of liability that exists between a business and its owner(s).

Further detail on capital

To return to the accounting equation, you can perhaps see that the assets of an organisation have been provided, or 'financed', by liabilities either to outsiders or to the owner. This emphasises the importance of the separate entity concept described above. Because we regard the owner as being separate from the business, we can regard the amount owed by the business to its owner as a kind of liability. Effectively, we can restate the accounting equation in an even simpler form:

Assets of the business = Liabilities of the business

This statement is always true no matter what transactions the business undertakes. Any transaction that increases or decreases the assets of the business must increase or decrease its liabilities by an identical amount.

You may be wondering exactly what is meant by saying that capital is an amount 'owed' by the business to its owner. How can the business 'owe' anything in this way? How has it incurred a debt? The answer is that when a business commences, it is common for the owners to 'invest' some of their private resources in the business. As the business operates it generates its own resources in the form of profits, which technically belong to the owner. Some of the profits may remain in the business, while some may be withdrawn by the owner in the form of goods or cash. This withdrawal of profits in simple organisation structures such as sole traders is known as 'drawings'.

The equation that states that

Assets = Liabilities + Capital

can thus be seen to demonstrate the relationships that exist within any business. The equation is the basis of one of the most common accounting statements to be prepared – **the statement of financial position.** It is worth noting here that the presentation of a statement of financial position is based on the accounting equation.

The accounting equation in action

To see how this works, study the following example.

Example 2.A

On 31 March, Ahmed's employment with Gigantic Stores Ltd came to an end and on 1 April, Ahmed sets up in business by himself, trading as 'Ahmed's Matches', and selling boxes of matches from a tray on a street corner.

Ahmed puts $100 into a bank account opened in the name of Ahmed's Matches. He persuades a supplier of matches to let him have an initial inventory of 400 boxes, costing 5¢ each, promising to pay for them next week.

During his first day of trading he sells 150 boxes at 12¢ each – $18 in all. Feeling pleased, he takes $5 from the cash tin and treats himself to supper at the local café.

He also writes a cheque for $5 to his supplier in part payment for the initial inventory of boxes.

Show what happens to the accounting equation as each of these transactions takes place.

Solution

To begin with, the only asset of the business is $100 in the business bank account. Capital invested by Ahmed also amounts to $100 and the accounting equation looks like this:

Assets		=	**Liabilities**	+	**Capital**	
Bank	$100	=	0	+	Capital	$100

The business then acquires matches worth $20 with a corresponding liability to the supplier. The accounting equation now looks like this:

Assets		=	**Liabilities**		+	**Capital**	
Bank	$100		Payables	$20		Capital	$100
Inventory	$20						
	$120	=		$20	+		$100

When Ahmed sells 150 boxes, he makes a profit of (150 x 7¢) = $10.50. His inventory falls to 250 boxes at 5¢ each ($12.50). He also acquires a further asset in the process: cash in hand of $18. The accounting equation now looks like this:

Assets		=	**Liabilities**		+	**Capital**	
Bank	$100		Payables	$20		Original capital	$100
Cash in hand	$18					Profit	$10.50
Inventory (20 – 7.50)	$12.50						
	$130.50	=		$20	+		$110.50

Don't forget that when Ahmed sells the inventory we must remove the **cost** from the inventory balance, i.e. 150 boxes x 5¢ = 7.50. We can see the sale has three effects on the accounting equation - the inventory reduces by the cost of the goods sold, i.e. $7.50, the cash increases by the amount the goods are sold for, i.e. $18 and the capital increases by the profit on the sale $10.50.

Then Ahmed withdraws $5 from the business for his private use. This amount (referred to as drawings) reduces the sum owed to him by the business. The accounting equation now looks like this:

Assets		=	**Liabilities**		+	**Capital**	
Bank	$100		Payables	$20		Original capital	$100
Cash in hand (18 – 5)	$13					Profit earned	$10.50
Inventory	$12.50					Less: drawings	($5)
	$125.50	=		$20	+		$105.50

Finally, Ahmed makes a payment to his supplier, reducing the funds in the business bank account, and also reducing the amount of his liability. The accounting equation now looks like this:

Assets		=	Liabilities		+	Capital	
Bank (100 – 5)	$95		Payables (20 – 5)	$15		Original capital	$100
Cash in hand	$13					Profit earned	$10.50
Inventory	$12.50					Less: drawings	($5)
	$120.50	=		$15	+		$105.50

Test your understanding 1

J Jones commenced business on 31 January 20X1, transferring $5,000 from her personal bank account into a business bank account. During the first week of February 20X1 the following transactions occurred:

1 Feb	Bought motor van costing $800 paying by cheque	
2 Feb	Bought goods on credit:	
		P Smith $400
		E Holmes $250
3 Feb	Sold goods for cash $600 (cost $400)	
4 Feb	Banked cash $600	
	Paid P Smith $400 by cheque	
5 Feb	Sold goods on credit (cost $200):	
		J Amos $200
		A Turner $300

You are required to:

Show the accounting equation at the end of each day's transactions.

4 The accounting equation and the statement of financial position

The statement of financial position is simply **a statement of the assets, liabilities and capital** of a business at a particular time.

It is thus nothing more than a detailed representation of the accounting equation.

The contents of a statement of financial position

In its simplest form the statement of financial position is presented horizontally with assets being shown on the left and liabilities and capital being shown on the right.

As a result the total of each side of the statement of financial position will be the same – hence the statement of financial position balances.

When we prepare statements of financial position, assets and liabilities are divided into two categories: **non-current and current.**

Non-current assets

Any asset acquired for retention by an entity for the purpose of providing a service to the business, and not held for resale in the normal course of trading.

Further detail on non-current assets

In other words, a non-current asset is a resource acquired by an organisation with the intention of using it to earn income for a long period of time. These non-current assets can be tangible, (in simple terms we can physically see and touch them), or intangible (we cannot physically see and touch them). Examples of tangible non-current assets include land, buildings, motor vehicles, machinery and equipment. Examples of intangible non-current assets include patents, development costs and goodwill. All of these assets will be discussed in more detail in later chapters.

Current assets

Cash or other assets – for example inventory, receivables and short-term investments – held for conversion into cash in the normal course of trading.

Receivables are a person or an entity owing money to an entity.

Further detail on current assets

In other words, a current asset is one that is either already cash, or will be converted into cash within a short period of time.

Receivables are assets to the business because they are eventually converted into cash, which is a resource that can be used by the business.

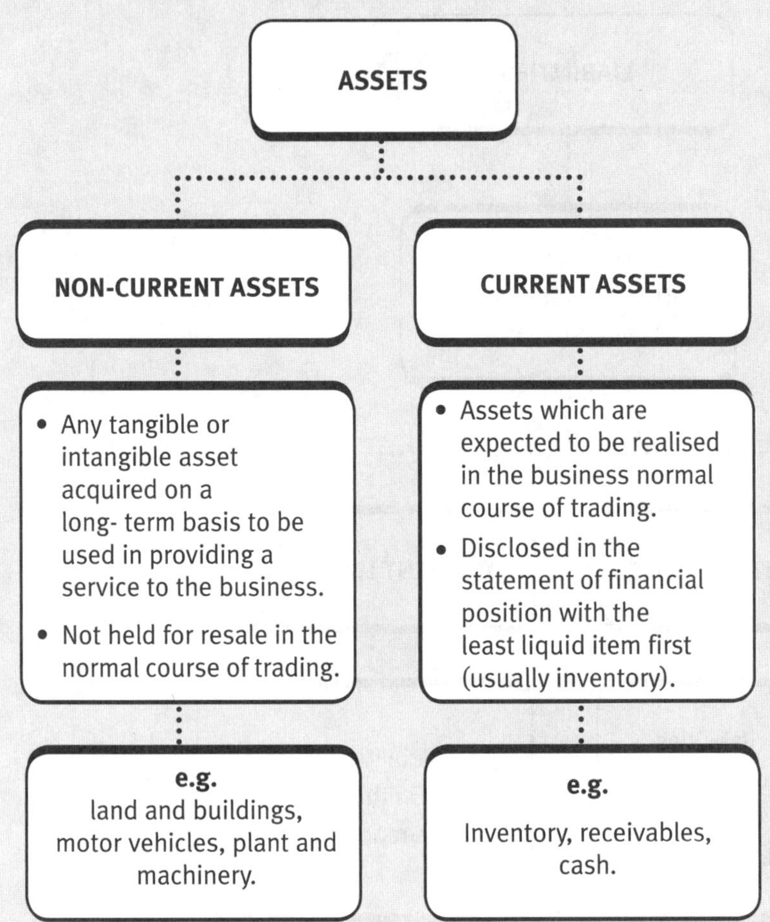

Liabilities are similarly divided into two categories, reflecting the time between the statement of financial position date and the date by which the liability should be settled. These categories are referred to as **current liabilities and non-current liabilities.**

Current liabilities

Liabilities that fall due for payment within 1 year. They include that part of non-current loans due for repayment within 1 year and payables.

Payables are a person or an entity to whom money is owed as a consequence of the receipt of goods or services in advance of payment, i.e. on credit.

Non-current liabilities

Liabilities that are due for repayment more than 1 year after the statement of financial position date.

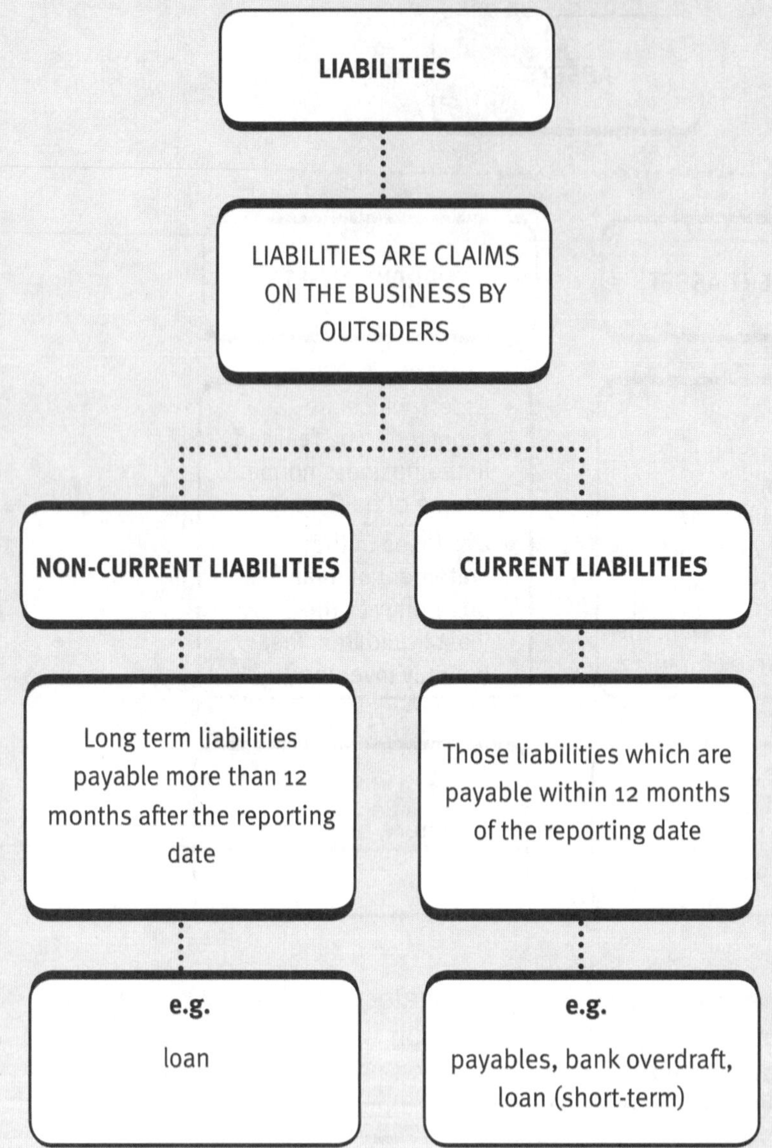

Further detail on payables

These are financial obligations or liabilities of a business until they are paid. These lists of assets and liabilities are not exhaustive, and you will encounter other examples as your studies progress.

Example 2.B

Nadim had the following assets and liabilities on 1 January:

	$
Land	200,000
Buildings	60,000
Inventory	10,000
Receivables	15,000
Bank balance	32,000
Cash in hand	5,000
	322,000
Payables	17,000
Bank loan	240,000
	257,000

We can calculate the value of Nadim's capital using the accounting equation.

The total value of Nadim's assets on 1 January is $322,000; his liabilities totalled $257,000. Therefore his capital must be $65,000, that is:

Assets	=	Liabilities	+	Capital
322,000		257,000		65,000

We can now prepare Nadim's statement of financial position.

Statement of financial position of Nadim as at 1 January

Assets	$000	$000	**Liabilities**	$000
Non-current asset			Capital	65
Land	200			
Buildings	60		Non-current liabilities	
		260	Bank loan	240

Current assets				
Inventory	10		Current liabilities	
Receivables	15		Payables	17
Bank balance	32			
Cash in hand	5			
		62		
		322		322

We can see from the above that the statement of financial position could be used to calculate the value of capital. If this method were used the capital value is the figure to make the statement of financial position balance.

You should also note the order in which the current assets are listed. This is referred to as the order of liquidity. **Liquidity is the measure of closeness of assets to being cash**, and it is usual for current assets to be listed from the least liquid to the most liquid (as above).

Returning to our example, let us assume that Nadim had the following transactions during the first week of January:

(1) Bought office equipment costing $7,000, paying $2,000 deposit by cheque, the balance to be paid at the end of March.

(2) Returned some of the above office equipment to his supplier because it was faulty. Nadim had originally been charged $3,000 for it.

(3) Received $8,000 from his receivables. They all paid him by cheque.

We can now see how these transactions affected his accounting equation.

(1) Assets (office equipment) increase by $7,000
Assets (bank balance) decrease by $2,000
Liabilities (payables) increase by $5,000
Nadim's accounting equation is amended to:

Assets	=	Liabilities	+	Capital
327,000		262,000		65,000

(2) Assets (office equipment) decrease by $3,000
Liabilities (payables) decrease by $3,000
Nadim's accounting equation becomes:

Assets	=	Liabilities	+	Capital
324,000		259,000		65,000

(3) Assets (receivables) decrease by $8,000
Assets (bank balance) increase by $8,000
This has no effect on Nadim's accounting equation.
Nadim's statement of financial position after these three transactions looks as follows:

Statement of financial position of Nadim as at 7 January

Assets	$000	$000	**Liabilities**	$000
Non-current asset			Capital	65
Land	200			
Buildings	60		Non-current liabilities	
Office equipment (7 – 3)	4		Bank loan	240
	—			
		264		
Current assets				
Inventory	10		Current liabilities	
Receivables (15 – 8)	7		Payables (17 + 5 – 3)	19
Bank balance (32 – 2 + 8)	38			
Cash in hand	5			
	—			
		60		
		—		—
		324		324
		—		—

Vertical presentation of a statement of financial position

The statement of financial position presentation used so far is known as the horizontal format. It may be thought of as representing a set of scales, whereby the amount on each side of the centre is equal. In this way it can be said to balance.

In practice, a vertical presentation is used more often and an example is given below.

Statement of financial position: vertical format

Assets	$000	$000
Non-current asset		
Land	200	
Buildings	60	
Office equipment	4	
		264
Current assets		
Inventory	10	
Receivables	7	
Bank balance	38	
Cash in hand	5	
		60
		324
Capital and liabilities		
Capital		65
Non-current liabilities		
Bank loan		240
Current liabilities		
Payables		19
		324

The difference between the current assets and the current liabilities is known as the net current assets, if positive, or net current liabilities, if negative; it is also known as the **working capital** of the business.

Key headings

In later studies you will learn that this is an important measure of the short-term liquidity of an organisation. In Nadim's statement of financial position above, the net current assets (working capital) is $41 (60−19). In order to prepare the above statement you should recognise that individual assets, capital and liabilities are grouped under five main headings as:

(1) non-current assets
(2) current assets
(3) capital
(4) non-current liabilities
(5) current liabilities.

5 The income statement

The income statement is a record of **income generated and expenditure incurred** to generate the income over a period of time, usually a year.

Income less expenditure = profit or loss for the period.

In the course of his business, Nadim will attempt to earn money by selling his goods to customers. The money earned in this way is referred to as the sales revenue (or simply the sales) of the business. To sell goods, he first has to buy them (or manufacture them – but we shall assume that Nadim is a retailer rather than a manufacturer). Obviously, there is a cost involved in the buying of the goods.

Running costs

He must buy fuel for his delivery van. He probably pays rent for the warehouse or shop premises in which he stores his goods. If he employs anyone to help him he will have to pay wages. All of these costs have to be paid for from the gross profit earned by selling goods.

Gross profit

This is calculated by taking the sales revenue and deducting the cost of goods sold.

Net profit

This is calculated by deducting any other running costs of the business from the gross profit.

Where does profit go?

What happens to this net profit once it has been earned?

- As a private individual, Nadim has living expenses like everyone else. He will need to withdraw some of the net profit from the business to pay for these; such a withdrawal is referred to as drawings.
- Any profit that Nadim does not need to withdraw simply remains in the business, increasing his capital.

In Example 2.A, you saw that Ahmed, trading as Ahmed's Matches, made a profit of $10.50, and withdrew $5 for himself, leaving the other $5.50 in the business to increase his capital.

Example 2.C

In the following month, Nadim sells goods on credit to his customers for $6,000. He already had some inventory , costing $10,000, so he used $1,000 worth of that existing inventory, and bought in another $3,000 worth of inventory that was all used to fulfil the order. He has not yet paid for this extra inventory.

His rent bill for the month is $500 and his van running costs are $300.

He withdraws $200 from the business for his private use.

Present an income statement for Nadim for this month, and a statement of financial position at the end of the month.

Solution

Income statement for the month

	$	$
Sales		6,000
Less: cost of goods sold (1,000 + 3,000)		(4,000)
Gross profit		2,000
Less: Rent	500	
Van running costs	300	
		(800)
Net profit earned		1,200

Notes:

(1) The cost of goods sold figure can be calculated as $1,000 from existing inventory, plus $3,000 bought specially. See later in the chapter for another way to calculate the cost of goods sold.

(2) Nadim's drawings are not business expenses, but are deducted from his capital on the statement of financial position below.

The part of the income statement which calculates gross profit is known as the trading account. The trading account is thus a sub-section of the income statement although its name does not appear within the income statement. Nevertheless, it is a very important part of the income statement and you may asked to prepare a trading account in your exam.

Statement of financial position at the end of the month

Assets	$	$
Non-current asset		
As before		264,000
Current assets		
Inventory (10,000 – 1,000)	9,000	
Receivables (7,000 + 6,000)	13,000	
Bank balance	38,000	
Cash in hand (5,000 – 500 – 300 – 200)	4,000	
		64,000
		328,000

Capital and liabilities	
Capital	66,000
Long-term liabilities	
Bank loan	240,000
Current liabilities	
Payables (19,000 + 3,000)	22,000
	328,000

Notice that the capital of the business has increased by $1,000 – the amount of net profit retained in the business. It is possible to prepare a statement of changes in capital, showing exactly how the figure of $65,000 has risen to $66,000.

Statement of changes in capital

	$	$
Capital at start of the month		65,000
Net profit earned in period	1,200	
Net profit withdrawn by Nadim	(200)	
Net profit retained in the business		1,000
Capital at end of month		66,000

You should see clearly from this statement how the income statement links up with the statement of financial position: the net profit earned, shown in the income statement, becomes an addition to capital in the statement of financial position, and Nadim's drawings are deducted from this.

In Chapter 19 we will learn more about the income statement and how it may be part of a statement of comprehensive income. However, until Chapter 19, we will just refer to the income statement.

The cost of goods sold

The calculation of the cost of goods sold is an important figure.

The cost of goods sold will be deducted from sales revenue when calculating the gross profit or loss in the income statement.

When calculating the cost of goods sold we can use the following formula:

	$
Cost of opening inventory at the start of the period	X
Cost of purchases during the period	X
	X
Less: cost of closing inventory at the end of the period	(X)
Cost of goods sold	X

Cost of goods sold

We shall be looking at the income statement in more detail later on, but at this stage it is worth noting one general point, which will be illustrated by the particular example of the cost of goods sold.

In computing the profit earned in a period the accountant's task is:

- first, to establish the sales revenue earned in the period;
- second, to establish the costs incurred by the business in earning this revenue.

This second point is not as simple as it might sound. For example, it would not be true to say that the costs incurred in an accounting period are equal to the sums of money expended in the period. This could be illustrated by many examples, some of which you will encounter later in the text. For now, we focus on one particular cost: **The cost of goods sold.**

A trader may be continually buying goods and selling them on to customers. At the moment he draws up his financial statements it is likely that he has inventories that have been purchased in the period but not yet sold. It would be wrong to include the cost of this closing inventory as part of the cost of goods sold, for the simple reason that these goods have not yet been sold.

Looking back to the beginning of the accounting period, it is likely that opening inventory was on hand. These have presumably been sold in this period and their cost must form part of the cost of goods sold, even though they were purchased in an earlier period.

What all this illustrates is that the cost of goods sold in an accounting period is not the same as the cost of goods purchased in the period. In fact, to calculate the cost of goods sold we need to do the following calculation (presented here using the figures from Nadim's business above):

	$
Cost of opening inventory at the start of the period	10,000
Cost of purchases during the period	3,000
	13,000
Less: cost of closing inventory at the end of the period	9,000
Cost of goods sold	4,000

It is this figure of $4,000 – not the purchases of $3,000 – that is matched with the sales revenue for the period in order to derive the figure of gross profit.

Test your understanding 2

Explain briefly what is meant by the following terms giving at least one example of each:

- assets
- liabilities
- capital
- revenue
- expense.

Test your understanding 3

On 1 June 20X1, J Brown started business as a gardener with a capital of $2,000 in cash. A list of figures extracted from his records on 31 May 20X2 shows the following:

	$
Cash purchases of seeds, plants, etc.	700
New motor van	1,100
Mowing machine	70
Hedge trimmer	250
Motor van expenses	300
Rent of garage	200
Paid to wife for clerical work	500
Insurance	200
Private expenses paid from bank	1,500
Cash in hand and bank	180
Cash sales made to customers	3,000
Capital at the start of the year	2,000
Inventory of seeds, plants, etc. at the end of the year	100

You are required to prepare:

(a) an account to show J Brown's profit or loss for the year ended 31 May 20X2,

(b) a statement of financial position as at 31 May 20X2.

Profit and cash

Note that in Example 2.C, Nadim's business made a profit of $1,200. But his bank balance remained unchanged and his cash holdings actually fell. This was because some of his transactions that affected profit did not affect cash at the same time. For example, his customers did not pay Nadim, nor did Nadim pay his suppliers, until after the end of the month. Also, there was a transaction that affected cash, but not profit – Nadim took $200 cash in drawings, which reduced his capital but not his profit. There are lots of other reasons why profit does not always result in an equal change in bank and cash balances. You will look at these in chapter 20.

6 Capital and revenue

All expenses incurred by an entity fall into one of two categories:

- capital transaction or
- revenue transaction.

Capital transactions

Capital transactions relate to expenses that will affect the organisation in the long term, i.e. more than a year.

For the purpose of this course we will assume this relates to purchases of non-current assets such as buildings, plant and machinery.

Capital expenses will **NOT** be shown as an expense in the income statement but as a non-current asset on the statement of financial position.

Revenue transactions

Revenue transactions relate to expenses that will only affect the organisation in the current year, for example wages, rent, vehicle running costs.

Revenue expenses will be shown as expenses in the income statement and **NOT** on the statement of financial position.

Capital transactions = statement of financial position

Revenue transactions = income statement

Capital versus Revenue

Capital transactions

The word 'capital' means different things in different contexts. You have already seen how the word is used to identify the investment by an owner in his business. Capital transactions are those that affect the organisation in the long term, as well as in the current period. Capital expenditure is expenditure on non-current assets, and capital receipts would result from the disposal of those assets. Other transactions that are regarded as capital transactions are the obtaining of, and repayment of, non-current finance. Capital transactions initially affect the figures in the statement of financial position. Of course, non-current assets are used up over a number of years, and so eventually they will be consumed. We account for this by including depreciation in the income statement. You will look at this in detail in chapter 10.

Revenue transactions

Revenue transactions are those that affect the organisation in the current period. Revenue receipts come from sales, and sometimes in the form of income from investments. Revenue expenditure is expenditure on items that are consumed in the period, for example the running expenses of the organisation, cost of sales and so on. Revenue transactions affect the figures in the income statement.

7 Chapter summary

In this chapter you have:

- seen how the separate entity convention works – for accounting purposes, a business is always regarded as an entity separate from its owners;
- seen how the accounting equation is defined as:

  Assets = Liabilities + Capital

  and how it changes as a result of financial transactions;

- learnt how to use the accounting equation to draw up a simple statement of financial position after certain transactions have occurred and how to prepare an income statement, including a calculation of cost of goods sold;
- learnt that profit does not always result in an equivalent change in bank and cash balances;
- that transactions can be classified as either 'capital' or 'revenue' according to whether they affect the statement of financial position or the income statement.

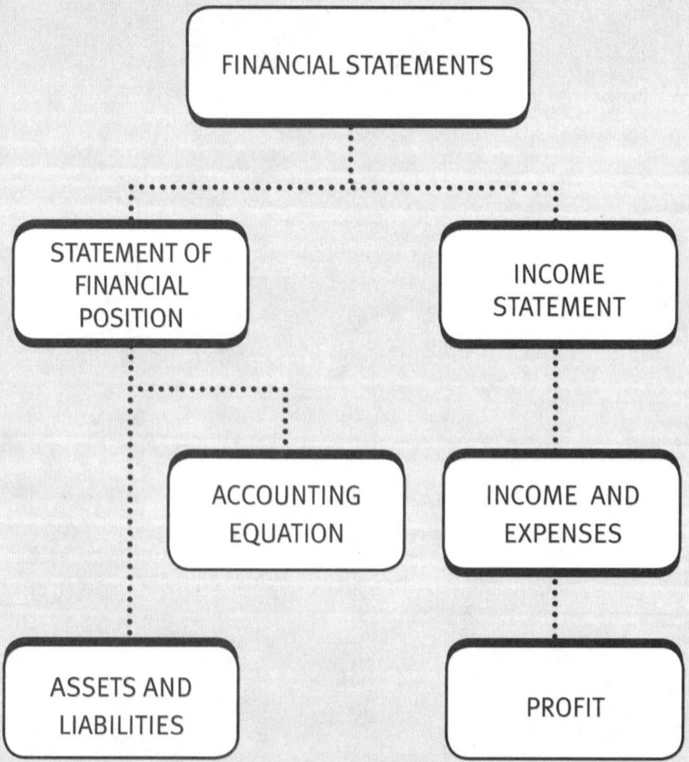

Test your understanding questions

Test your understanding 4

Gross profit for 20X1 can be calculated from:

A purchases for 20X1, plus inventory at 31 December 20X1, less inventory at 1 January 20X1

B purchases for 20X1, less inventory at 31 December 20X1, plus inventory at 1 January 20X1

C cost of goods sold during 20X1, plus sales during 20X1

D net profit for 20X1, plus expenses for 20X1

Test your understanding 5

The capital of a sole trader would change as a result of:

A a payable being paid into his account by cheque

B raw materials being purchased on credit

C non-current assets being purchased on credit

D wages being paid in cash

Test your understanding 6

The 'accounting equation' can be rewritten as:

A assets plus profit less drawings less liabilities equals closing capital

B assets less liabilities less drawings equals opening capital plus profit

C assets less liabilities less opening capital plus drawings equals profit

D opening capital plus profit less drawings less liabilities equals assets

Test your understanding 7

An increase in inventory of $250, a decrease in the bank balance of $400 and an increase in payables of $1,200 results in:

A a decrease in working capital of $1,350

B an increase in working capital of $1,350

C a decrease in working capital of $1,050

D an increase in working capital of $1,050

Test your understanding 8

A sole trader had opening capital of $10,000 and closing capital of $4,500. During the period, the owner introduced capital of $4,000 and withdrew $8,000 for her own use. Her profit or loss during the period was:

	Amount
	$

Test your understanding 9

The accounting equation at the start of the month was:

Assets $28,000 less liabilities $12,500

During the following month, the business purchased a non-current asset for $6,000,paying by cheque, a profit of $7,000 was made, and payables of $5,500 were paid by cheque.

Capital at the end of the month would be:
$.......

Test your understanding 10

The accounting equation can change as a result of certain transactions. Which one of the following transactions would not affect the accounting equation?

A Selling goods for more than their cost

B Purchasing a non-current asset on credit

C The owner withdrawing cash

D Receivables paying their accounts in full, in cash

Test your understanding 11

The profit of a business may be calculated by using which one of the following formulae?

A Opening capital + drawings + capital introduced − closing capital

B Closing capital + drawings − capital introduced − opening capital

C Opening capital + drawings − capital introduced − closing capital

D Closing capital − drawings + capital introduced − opening capital

Test your understanding 12

You are given the following information relating to a business for the month of May 20X1.

	$
Sales of goods for cash	17,000
Sales of goods on credit	28,000
Purchases of inventory on credit	19,500
Wages paid in cash	2,000
Non-current assets bought on credit	12,000
Cash withdrawn by the owner	1,600
Inventory of goods at the start of the period	5,000
Inventory of goods at the end of the period	6,250

Required:

Complete the following statement to determine the net profit for the period:

	$		$		$
Sales	....	+	....	=	....
Less: cost of sales					
Opening inventory			....		
Purchases			....		
			....		
Closing inventory			....		
Cost of goods sold					....
Gross profit					....
Less: expenses – wages					....
Net profit					....

Test your understanding 13

In addition to the information in Question TYU 12, you are given the following information regarding assets and liabilities at the start of the period.

	$
Non-current assets	37,000
Receivables	7,000
Bank and cash	12,000
Payables	7,300

Required:

Insert the missing figures below to prepare a statement of financial position at the end of the period.

	$
Capital at the start of the period:	
Non-current assets	....
Inventory	....
Receivables	....
Bank and cash	....
Total assets	....
Less: payables	....
Capital	....

Statement of financial position: vertical format

Assets	$	$
Non-current assets		....
Current assets		
Inventory	....	
Receivables	....	
Bank and cash	....	
Subtotal		....
Capital and liabilities		
Capital at the start of the period (as per above)		....
Net profit (as per TYU 12)		....
Subtotal		....
Less: drawings		....
Capital at the end of the period		....
Current liabilities: payables		....

Test your understanding answers

Test your understanding 1

Assets	=	Liabilities	+	Capital	
31 Jan					
Bank	5,000		Nil		5,000
1 Feb					
Bank	4,200				
Van	800				
	5,000		Nil		5,000
2 Feb					
Bank	4,200	P Smith	400		
Van	800	E Holmes	250		
Inventory	650				
	5,650		650		5,000
3 Feb					
Bank	4,200	P Smith	400	Original capital	5,000
Van	800	E Holmes	250	Profit earned	200
Inventory	250				
Cash	600				
	5,850		650		5,200
4 Feb					
Bank	4,400			Original capital	5,000
Van	800			Profit earned	200
Inventory	250	E Holmes	250		
	5,450		250		5,200

5 Feb

Bank	4,400	E Holmes	250	Original capital	5,000
Van	800			Profit earned	500
J Amos	200			(200 + (200 + 300 – 200)	
A Turner	300				
Inventory (250 – 200)	50				
	5,750		250		5,500

Test your understanding 2

- **Assets.** Items possessed by an organisation, which may be used to provide income in the future. Includes non-current assets (land, buildings, machinery, etc.) and current assets (inventories, receivables, cash, etc.).
- **Liabilities**. Financial obligations or amounts owed by an organisation. Includes loans, overdrafts and payables.
- **Capital**. The amount of investment made by the owner(s) in the organisation, and not yet withdrawn. The amount includes initial and subsequent amounts introduced by the owner(s), plus any profits earned that have been retained in the organisation.
- **Revenue**. Amounts earned by the activities of the organisation, which eventually result in receiving money. Includes sales revenue, interest received and so on. Revenue increases profit.
- **Expense**. Costs used up in the activities of the organisation. Includes heat, light, local business tax, inventories consumed, wages and so on. Expenses reduce profit.

Test your understanding 3

Income statement of J Brown for the year ended 31 May 20X2

	$	$
Sales		3,000
Purchases of seeds, plants	700	
Less: closing inventory of seeds, plants	(100)	
Cost of goods sold		600
Gross profit		2,400
Less: Motor van expenses	300	
Rent of garage	200	
Wife's wages	500	
Insurance	200	
		1,200
Net profit		1,200

Statement of financial position of J Brown as at 31 May 20X2

	$	$
Assets		
Non-current assets		
Motor van		1,100
Mowing machine		70
Hedge trimmer		250
		1,420
Currents assets		
Inventory of seeds and plants	100	
Cash in hand and at bank	180	
		280
		1,700

Capital

Capital introduced	2,000
Add: net profit for the year	1,200
	3,200
Less: drawings	(1,500)
Capital at the end of the period	1,700

Test your understanding 4

D

Working backwards often confuses candidates. Try drawing up a short example of an income statement using simple figures of your own, to prove or disprove the options given.

For example:

	$	$
Sales		20,000
Inventory at 31.12.20X0	2,000	
Purchases during 20X1	8,000	
	10,000	
Less: Inventory at 31.21.20X1	(1,000)	
Cost of goods sold		9,000
Gross profit		11,000
Less: expenses		(4,000)
Net profit		7,000

Make all the figures different or you will make mistakes.

You can now see that options A, B and C will not give the correct answer.

Test your understanding 5

D

Transactions that affect only assets and liabilities do not affect capital. Therefore, options A, B and C are irrelevant.

Test your understanding 6

C

The 'standard' accounting equation is

Assets = Liabilities + Capital

and capital equals opening capital plus profits less drawings. The only rearrangement of this equation that maintains the integrity of the accounting equation is C.

Test your understanding 7

A

The effect on working capital is calculated as:

	$
Increase in inventory = increase in working capital	250
Decrease in bank = decrease in working capital	(400)
Increase in payables = decrease in working capital	(1,200)
Overall decrease in working capital	(1,350)

Test your understanding 8

Answer:

	$
Opening capital	10,000
Introduced	4,000
Drawings	(8,000)
Loss – balancing figure	(1,500)
Closing capital	4,500

Test your understanding 9

Only the profit affects the capital at the end of the month. The capital at the start was $15,500 ($28,000 assets less $12,500 liabilities), so a profit of $7,000 increases this to $22,500. The purchase by cheque of a non-current asset affects only assets, and the payment of payables by cheque affects assets and liabilities, but neither affects capital.

Test your understanding 10

D

The accounting equation changes when one or more of assets, liabilities or capital changes. Selling goods at a profit would change capital; purchasing a non-current asset on credit would change assets and liabilities; the owner withdrawing cash would change assets and capital; receivables paying their accounts in cash would not affect any of these.

Test your understanding 11

B

Test your understanding 12

May 20X1	$	$
Sales ($17,000 + 28,000)		45,000
Less: cost of sales		
Opening inventory	5,000	
Purchases	19,500	
	24,500	
Closing inventory	(6,250)	
Cost of goods sold		(18,250)
Gross profit		26,750
Less: expenses – wages		(2,000)
Net profit		24,750

Test your understanding 13

First of all calculate the capital at the start of the period (not forgetting the inventory balance given in TYU 12), then adjust the opening assets and liabilities for the changes given in TYU 12. Finally, add the profit to the opening capital, and deduct drawings.

	$
Non-current assets	37,000
Inventory	5,000
Receivables	7,000
Bank and cash	12,000
	61,000
Less: payables	(7,300)
Capital	53,700

Statement of financial position as at 31.5.X1

	$	$
Assets		
Non-current assets (37,000 + 12,000)		49,000
Current assets		
Inventory	6,250	
Receivables (7,000 + 28,000)	35,000	
Bank and cash (12,000 + 17,000 – 2,000 – 1,600)	25,400	
		66,650
		115,650
Capital and liabilities		
Capital at the start of the period (as per above)		53,700
Net profit (as per TYU 12)		24,750
		78,450
Less: drawings		(1,600)
Capital at the end of the period		76,850
Current liabilities: payables (7,300 + 19,500 +12,000)		38,800
		115,650

chapter

3

Double Entry Bookkeeping

Chapter learning objectives

When you have completed this chapter, you should be able to:

- explain the principles of double-entry bookkeeping;
- prepare simple ledger accounts;
- prepare bookkeeping entries for income and expenditure;
- prepare bookkeeping entries for assets, liabilities and capital.

1 Introduction

In the last chapter, you were able to draw up a simple income statement and statement of financial position after considering a small number of transactions.

Imagine an organisation with hundreds or thousands of transactions in a period, and how difficult (impossible, even) it would be to draw up the financial statements from just a list of transactions.

This chapter introduces you to the system of maintaining ledger accounts, to enable the income statement and statement of financial position to be prepared. It is known as the system of **bookkeeping**. Although nowadays most organisations maintain their accounts on computer, the basic principles of bookkeeping have remained unchanged for centuries, and are still important if you are to understand how such systems work, especially if adjustments need to be made to the system or its records.

Some of these topics will also be covered in more detail in subsequent chapters.

2 What is a ledger account?

An **account** is a record of the transactions involving a particular item.

A ledger account may be thought of as a record kept as a page in a book. The book contains many pages – many accounts – and is referred to as a ledger.

In this chapter we are concerned with the **nominal ledger**, which is the ledger containing all of the accounts necessary to summarise an organisation's transactions and prepare a statement of financial position and income statement.

Each account comprises two sides: the left-hand side is referred to as the **debit** side, and the right-hand side is referred to as the **credit** side. The format is shown below:

Debit (Dr)			**Credit (Cr)**		
Date	Details	$	Date	Details	$

3 What is double-entry bookkeeping?

According to the **CIMA Official Terminology:**

Double-entry bookkeeping: The most commonly used system of bookkeeping based on the principle that every financial transaction involves the simultaneous receiving and giving of value, and is therefore recorded twice.

Duality concept

Earlier in this text we saw how some transactions affected the accounting equation and the statement of financial position. We saw that each transaction had two effects: this is referred to as the **dual aspect** or **duality** concept. For example, receiving payment from a receivable increases the asset 'cash', while reducing the asset 'receivables'; paying a supplier reduces the asset 'cash' while reducing the liability 'payables'; In both cases, the accounting equation remains intact. The fact that every transaction has two effects – equal and opposite –means that each transaction must be recorded in two ledger accounts. This is double-entry bookkeeping.

Bookkeeping is the technique of recording financial transactions as they occur so that summaries may be made of the transactions and presented as a report to the users of accounts. The double-entry bookkeeping technique applies to the recording of transactions in ledger accounts.

Test your understanding 1

Explain what is meant by the term 'double-entry bookkeeping'.

In the previous chapter, you learned the following terms:

- assets
- liabilities
- capital
- revenues
- expenses.

These **five items** can be put into **two categories**, according to whether they appear on the **statement of financial position** or in the **income statement**.

- Assets, liabilities and capital appear on the statement of financial position.
- Expenses and revenue appear in the income statement.

If you compare these pairs you will see that they are, in effect, two pairs of opposites.

Each type of asset, liability, capital, expense or income is recorded separately. This is achieved by using **separate ledger** accounts for each of them.

4 Bookkeeping entries for the statement of financial position

We shall look first of all at recording assets, liabilities and capital. Transactions are recorded on either the debit or the credit side of a ledger account according to the following table:

Debit (Dr)	**Credit (Cr)**
Increases in assets	Decreases in assets
Decreases in liabilities	Increases liabilities
Decreases in capital	Increases in capital

Entering transactions in ledger accounts is also called **posting** the transactions.

Examples of debit and credit entries

Examples of debit entries:

- Increase in assets, e.g. purchase of inventory, non-current assets, increase in cash/bank
- Decreases in liabilities, e.g. payment of suppliers/loans
- Decreases in capital, e.g. drawings

Examples of credit entries:

- Decrease in assets, e.g. sale of non-current assets, payment of receivables, decreases in cash/bank
- Increases in liabilities, e.g. purchase of goods on credit, new loans purchased
- Increase in capital, e.g. introduce new capital into the business

In the previous chapter, we saw how transactions would affect the accounting equation and the statement of financial position. Example 2.B is reproduced here so that the double-entry bookkeeping entries (or postings) may be compared with the solution given in chapter 2.

Example 3.A

Nadim had the following assets and liabilities on 1 January:

	$
Land	200,000
Buildings	60,000
Inventory	10,000
Receivables	15,000
Cash in hand	5,000
Bank balance	32,000
	322,000
Payables	17,000
Bank loan	240,000
	257,000

First of all, we enter the opening balances into the ledger accounts. **Assets have debit balances**, and **liabilities and capital have credit balances.** These balances are shown as b/d on the appropriate side of the ledger but may also be shown as b/fwd or b/f in questions.

Land

Dr	$	Cr	$
1 Jan Balance b/d	200,000		

Buildings

Dr	$	Cr	$
1 Jan Balance b/d	60,000		

Inventory

Dr	$	Cr	$
1 Jan Balance b/d	10,000		

Receivables

Dr	$	Cr	$
1 Jan Balance b/d	15,000		

Cash in hand

Dr	$	Cr	$
1 Jan Balance b/d	5,000		

Bank balance

Dr	$	Cr	$
1 Jan Balance b/d	32,000		

Payables

Dr	$	Cr	$
		1 Jan Balance b/d	17,000

Bank loan

Dr	$	Cr	$
		1 Jan Balance b/d	240,000

Capital

Dr	$	Cr	$
		1 Jan Balance b/d	65,000

Notes:

(1) The capital account balance is the difference between assets and liabilities ($322,000 – $257,000).

(2) 'Balance b/d' is short for 'balance brought down'. It is sometimes also called 'balance brought forward' or 'balance b/fwd'.

Assume that Nadim had the following transactions during the first week of January:

(1) Bought office equipment costing $7,000, paying $2,000 deposit by cheque, the balance to be paid at the end of March.

(2) Returned some office equipment to his supplier because it was faulty. Nadim had originally been charged $3,000 for it.

(3) Received $8,000 from his receivables. They all paid him by cheque.

We now want to enter the January transactions into the ledger accounts. First, though, let us look at each transaction to determine how we are going to record it.

(1) Office equipment is an asset, and is increasing. Therefore we want to **debit the office equipment** account.

A cheque for $2,000 has been paid. The bank account, an asset, is decreasing, so we want to credit the bank account. $5,000 is still owing to the supplier (payable), so liabilities are increasing, leading us to **credit payables**.

(2) Office equipment is being returned, so the asset of office equipment is decreasing. Therefore we want to **credit the office equipment** account.

As Nadim has not yet paid for the goods, the amount will be included in the payables figure. If we return goods, the amount owed to payables decreases and, as payables are liabilities, we therefore want to **debit the payables** account.

(3) Receivables are assets. If they pay their debts, the amount owed decreases, so we want to **credit receivables**.

Bank is an asset. Paying money in increases the balance, so we want to **debit bank**.

These transactions can now be entered into the ledger accounts, as follows:

Land

Dr		$	Cr		$
1 Jan	Balance b/d	200,000			

Buildings

Dr		$	Cr		$
1 Jan	Balance b/d	60,000			

Inventory

Dr		$	Cr		$
1 Jan	Balance b/d	10,000			

Receivables

Dr		$	Cr		$
1 Jan	Balance b/d	15,000	Jan	Bank	8,000

Cash in hand

Dr		$	Cr		$
1 Jan	Balance b/d	5,000			

Bank balance

Dr		$	Cr		$
1 Jan	Balance b/d	32,000	Jan	Office equipment	2,000
Jan	Receivables	8,000			

Payables

Dr		$	Cr		$
Jan	Office equipment	3,000	1 Jan	Balance b/d	17,000
			Jan	Office equipment	5,000

Bank loan

Dr		$	Cr		$
			1 Jan	Balance b/d	240,000

Capital

Dr		$	Cr		$
			1 Jan	Balance b/d	65,000

Office equipment

Dr		$	Cr		$
Jan	Bank	2,000	Jan	Payables	3,000
	Payables	5,000			

5 Bookkeeping entries for expenses and revenue

An expense is a cost connected with the day-to-day activities of the organisation. Examples of expenses include rent, local business tax, light and heat, wages and salaries, postage, telephone and the cost of items bought for resale, i.e. running costs.

Revenue is the term used to describe the activities that will eventually lead to the organisation receiving money. The most common source of revenue is that derived from the sale of its goods or services, but others include the receipt of interest on bank deposits. This is often referred to as income.

Transactions are recorded on either the debit or the credit side of a ledger account according to the following table:

Debit	**Credit**
Increases in expenses	Decreases in expenses
Decreases in revenue	Increases in revenue

Examples of debit and credit entries

Examples of debit entries:

- Increases in expenses, e.g. purchase of materials, rent, wages, electricity costs
- Decreases in revenue, e.g. sales returns

Examples of credit entries:

- Decreases in expenses, e.g. purchase returns
- Increases in revenue, e.g. sales of goods for cash or credit

6 Summary of bookkeeping entries

You may find it easier to remember the mnemonic **PEARLS** to remember the debit and credit rule for transactions.

Debit (Dr)		Credit (Cr)	
Increase in	$	Increase in	$
Purchases		**R**evenue	
Expenses		**L**iabilities	
Assets		**S**hareholder's equity (capital)	

Summary of steps to record a transaction:

(1) Identify the items that are affected.

(2) Consider whether they are being increased or decreased.

(3) Decide whether each account should be debited or credited.

(4) Check that a debit entry and a credit entry have been made and they are both for the same amount.

Bookkeeping entries for purchases and sales

We keep separate ledger accounts for the different types of inventory movement. Purchases and sales of inventory must always be kept in separate accounts, because one is at cost price and the other at selling price. You might have difficulty in determining how to classify purchases and sales. You could regard purchases as being assets, or you could regard them as being expenses. It all depends on whether they are consumed during the period, and that is unknown at the time they are bought. Similarly, sales could be regarded as decreases in inventory or as revenues. The fact is that it does not matter how you regard them. Both will result in the correct entry being made. For example, if you regard the purchase of inventory as an increase in an asset, you will make a debit entry; if you regard it as an increase in an expense, you will still make a debit entry. The same applies to sales – a decrease in inventory results in a credit entry, as does an increase in revenue. So, you will choose the right side for the entry, whichever way you classify these. The most important thing is to use the correct account – and never use the inventory account for purchases and/or sales as the inventory account is used only at the beginning and end of the accounting period.

Also note that you should **never** use either the purchases account or the sales account for anything other than the goods in which the business trades. Purchases of non-current assets, stationery and so on should all be recorded in their own ledger accounts.

Test your understanding 2

Tick the correct box for each of the following:

		Debit	Credit
1	Increases in assets	....	....
2	Increases in liabilities	....	....
3	Increases in income	....	....
4	Decreases in liabilities	....	....
5	Increases in expenses	....	....
6	Decreases in assets	....	....
7	Increases in capital	....	....
8	Decreases in income	....	....

Illustration 1

The following illustration includes transactions involving all the above types of accounts.

You are required to prepare ledger entries.

It might help you to determine the correct ledger entries by completing a table before you start, like this (the first item is done for you):

Date	Names of accounts involved	Type of accounts	Increase/decrease	Debit/credit
1 May	Capital	Capital	Increase	Credit
	Cash	Asset	Increase	Debit

1 May	BR starts business as a sole proprietor with $20,000 in cash
2 May	Pays $15,000 cash into a business bank account
4 May	Purchases goods on credit from JM for $2,000
6 May	Purchases goods from ERD on credit for $3,000
7 May	Pays wages in cash $60
10 May	Pays rent by cheque $80
12 May	Sells goods for cash $210
16 May	Buys furniture for $1,500 paying by cheque
19 May	Sells goods on credit to SP for $580
22 May	Buys goods for cash $3,900
24 May	Buys fittings for cash $600
25 May	Pays wages by cash $110
	Sells goods for cash $430
27 May	Receives part payment from SP of $330 by cheque
28 May	Pays advertising by cheque $25
	Sells goods for cash $890
29 May	Sells goods on credit to KM for $8,090
30 May	Withdraws $100 cash for his personal use

Solution

Capital

Dr		$	Cr		$
			1 May	Cash	20,000

Cash

Dr		$	Cr		$
1 May	Capital	20,000	2 May	Bank	15,000
12 May	Sales	210	7 May	Wages	60
25 May	Sales	430	22 May	Purchases	3,900
28 May	Sales	890	24 May	Fittings	600
			25 May	Wages	110
			30 May	Drawings	100

Bank

Dr		$	Cr		$
2 May	Cash	15,000	10 May	Rent	80
27 May	SP	330	16 May	Furniture	1,500
			28 May	Advertising	25

Purchases

Dr		$	Cr		
4 May	JM	2,000			
6 May	ERD	3,000			
22 May	Cash	3,900			

JM

Dr			Cr		$
			4 May	Purchases	2,000

ERD

Dr			Cr		$
			6 May	Purchases	3,000

Wages

Dr		$	Cr		$
7 May	Cash	60			
25 May	Cash	110			

Rent

Dr		$	Cr		$
10 May	Bank	80			

Sales

Dr			Cr		$
			12 May	Cash	210
			19 May	SP	580
			25 May	Cash	430
			28 May	Cash	890
			29 May	KM	8,090

Furniture

Dr		$	Cr		$
16 May	Bank	1,500			

SP

Dr		$	Cr		$
19 May	Sales	580	27 May	Bank	330

Fittings

Dr		$	Cr		$
24 May	Cash	600			

Advertising

Dr		$	Cr		$
28 May	Bank	25			

KM

Dr		$	Cr		$
29 May	Sales	8,090			

Drawings

Dr		$	Cr		$
30 May	Cash	100			

Test your understanding 3

A Thompson commenced business on 1 February 20X1, paying $500 into a business bank account.

During the next month the following transactions took place. All payments are made by cheque and all receipts are banked.

		$
1 Feb	Bought goods for resale	150
5 Feb	Paid rent	50
10 Feb	Business takings to date	290
22 Feb	Paid for advertising	25
26 Feb	A Thompson's drawings	100
27 Feb	Business takings	240

You are required to:

(i) write up the bank account;

(ii) write up all the other accounts.

Note: When you draw up your accounts, leave ten extra lines after the bank account, and four extra lines after all other ledger accounts – this exercise is continued in the next chapter.

Nominal ledger accounts

At this stage in your studies, all your ledger accounts are kept in a single 'book'. In later chapters you will see how the ledger accounts can be divided into several books. The main book used is called the **nominal ledger.**

7 Chapter summary

In this chapter you have:

- seen how financial transactions are recorded in ledger accounts, using double-entry principles;
- learned how to calculate the balance on an account at a point in time.

Double entry is the cornerstone of the entire accounting process. You will not get far in your studies of this subject unless you have a thorough grasp of its principles. Make sure you can follow the steps involved in the examples given in this chapter, and memorise the table:

Debit	**Credit**
Increases in assets	Decreases in assets
Decreases in liabilities	Increases liabilities
Decreases in capital	Increases in capital
Increases in expenses	Decreases in expenses
Decreases in revenue	Increases in revenue

It is important that you fully understand the double-entry system, as it will enable you to understand how to record more complex transactions later on in your studies.

Try not to analyse the reason for the 'left and right' system for recording transactions. It is simply a rule that, if everyone abides by it, leads to a common system. It can be likened to the rule for driving a car. If the rule in a country is to drive on the left, then the system works as long as everyone abides by the rule.

Practise the examples in the chapter several times until you feel competent in them.

Test your understanding questions

Test your understanding 4

Which one of the following statements is correct?

A Assets and liabilities normally have credit balances

B Liabilities and revenues normally have debit balances

C Assets and revenues normally have credit balances

D Assets and expenses normally have debit balances

Test your understanding 5

Alice had the following assets and liabilities at 1 January:

	$
Inventory	350
Payables	700
Receivables	400
Bank overdraft	125
Motor vehicles	880

Her capital at 1 January was: $...............

Test your understanding 6

The correct entries needed to record the return of office equipment that had been bought on credit from P Young, and not yet paid for, are:

	Debit	**Credit**
A	Office equipment	Sales
B	Office equipment	P Young
C	P Young	Office equipment
D	Cash	Office equipment

Test your understanding 7

Which of the following is the correct entry to record the purchase on credit of inventory intended for resale?

	Debit	**Credit**
A	Inventory	Receivable
B	Inventory	Payable
C	Purchases	Payable
D	Payable	Purchases

Test your understanding 8

A receives goods from B on credit terms and A subsequently pays by cheque. A then discovers that the goods are faulty and cancels the cheque before it is cashed by B. How should A record the cancellation of the cheque in his books

	Debit	**Credit**
A	Payables	Returns outwards
B	Payables	Bank
C	Bank	Payables
D	Returns outwards	Payables

Test your understanding 9

The table below shows a selection of financial transactions. Complete the columns to identify the accounts and the debit/credit entries to be made in the ledger to record each of the transactions.

	Transaction description	Account to be debited	Account to be credited
1	Sold goods on credit to Bashir		
2	Bought goods for sale on credit from P Walker		
3	Returned goods to P Walker		
4	Bought office machinery on credit from W Print		
5	Returned office machinery to W Print		
6	Received a cheque from P Wright		
7	Received payment from T Wilkes by cheque		
8	Owner's private car brought into the business		
9	Cheque received from P Wright dishonoured		

Test your understanding answers

Test your understanding 1

Double-entry bookkeeping is a system of keeping records of transactions in ledger accounts such that every transaction requires debit and credit entries of equal value. For example, there might be a debit entry of $100 equalled by two credit entries of $90 and $10, respectively. The result of this method is that the total of debit balances on ledger accounts equals the total of credit balances.

Test your understanding 2

The order of boxes should be debit; credit; credit; debit; debit; credit; credit; debit.

Test your understanding 3

Bank

20X1		$	20X1		$
1 Feb	Capital	500	1 Feb	Purchases	150
10 Feb	Sales	290	5 Feb	Rent	50
27 Feb	Sales	240	22 Feb	Advertising	25
			26 Feb	Drawings	100

Capital

			20X1		$
			1 Feb	Bank	500

Purchases

20X1		$			
1 Feb	Bank	150			

Rent

20X1		$			
5 Feb	Bank	50			

Advertising

20X1		$			
22 Feb	Bank	25			

Drawings

20X1		$			
26 Feb	Bank	100			

Sales

			20X1		$
			10 Feb	Bank	290
			27 Feb	Bank	240

Test your understanding 4

D

Test your understanding 5

Capital	= Assets	– Liabilities
	= ($350 + $400 + $880)	– ($700 + $125)
	= $805	

Test your understanding 6

C

Test your understanding 7

C

The inventory account is never used to record purchases.

Test your understanding 8

C

Test your understanding 9

- This question tests your ability to determine the debit and credit entries of a range of simple transactions.
- It is common for students to reverse the entries at this stage in their studies. Keep referring to the table until you are sure of your accuracy.

Debit	**Credit**
Increases in assets	Decreases in assets
Decreases in liabilities	Increases liabilities
Decreases in capital	Increases in capital
Increases in expenses	Decreases in expenses
Decreases in revenue	Increases in revenue

	Account to be debited	**Account to be credited**
1	Bashir	Sales
2	Purchases	P Walker
3	P Walker	Purchase returns
4	Office machinery	W Print
5	W Print	Office machinery
6	Bank	P Wright
7	Bank	T Wilkes
8	Car	Capital
9	P Wright	Bank

chapter

4

From Trial Balance to Financial Statements

Chapter learning objectives

When you have completed this chapter, you should be able to:

- balance off ledgers;
- prepare the trial balance;
- identify and prepare the entries to be made in the income statement and statement of financial position;
- identify the form and content of the trading account and the income statement;
- close off accounts;
- explain the nature of accounting errors.

1 Introduction

In this chapter, you will learn how to:

- balance off the ledger accounts;
- prepare a trial balance;
- prepare the financial statements from the trial balance and
- close off the ledger accounts.

2 Balancing the accounts

From time to time it is necessary to determine the end result of the transactions recorded in each ledger account. For example, the cash account will contain a number of debit and credit entries, but no clear indication of how much cash is remaining. The same applies to other accounts: receivables and payables accounts will have a number of debit and credit entries, but no indication of what is currently owed as a result of these entries.

Calculating the balance on the account

Once the transactions for a period have been recorded, it will be necessary to find the balance on the ledger account:

(1) Total both sides of the T account and find the larger total.

(2) Put the larger total in **the total box** on the debit **and** credit side.

(3) Insert a balancing figure to the side of the T account which does not currently add up to the amount in the total box. Call this balancing figure 'balance c/f' (carried forward) or 'balance c/d' (carried down).

(4) Carry the balance down diagonally and call it 'balance b/f' (brought forward) or 'balance b/d' (brought down).

As an example, look at the cash account that was produced in illustration 1, chapter 3:

Cash

Dr		$	Cr		$
1 May	Capital	20,000	2 May	Bank	15,000
12 May	Sales	210	7 May	Wages	60
25 May	Sales	430	22 May	Purchases	3,900
28 May	Sales	890	24 May	Fittings	600
			25 May	Wages	110
			30 May	Cash	100

(1) Add both sides of the ledger and enter the highest balance in the total for both the debit and credit side. In this example the debit side totals $21,530 (meaning that that amount has been received) and the credit side totals $19,770 (meaning that that amount has been paid out).

(2) We should therefore take the higher figure of $21,530 and enter it into **both** totals.

(3) Now find the difference required to make the lighter side of the ledger agree with the total. In this example the credit side only added upto $19,770 and will therefore need an entry of $1,760 to make it agree with the total. This entry is called the balance carried down.

(4) Finally enter the amount called the balance carried down on the opposite side of the ledger after the total and call it the balance bought down. This represents the opening amount on the account for the following period. In this example we will have a balance bought down on the debit side of $1,760 which represents an asset.

The ledger will now look like this:

Cash

Dr		$	**Cr**		$
1 May	Capital	20,000	2 May	Bank	15,000
12 May	Sales	210	7 May	Wages	60
25 May	Sales	430	22 May	Purchases	3,900
28 May	Sales	890	24 May	Fittings	600
			25 May	Wages	110
			30 May	Cash	100
			31 May	Balance c/d	1,760
		21,530			21,530
1 June	Balance b/d	1,760			

Test your understanding 1

Work out the balances on the other accounts in illustration 1, chapter 3.

Test your understanding 2

Work out the balances on the accounts from TYU 3 in chapter 3.

3 Preparing the trial balance

One way of checking the accuracy of the ledger entries is by listing the balances on each account, and totalling them. Because of the 'double-entry' rule that has been employed, the total of all the accounts with **debit balances should equal the total of all the accounts with credit balances**. This list is known as a trial balance.

Using TYU 1 above, the trial balance at 31 May would appear as follows:

Trial Balance

	Debit ($)	**Credit ($)**
Capital		20,000
Cash	1,760	
Bank	13,725	
Purchases	8,900	
JM		2,000
ERD		3,000
Wages	170	
Rent	80	
Sales		10,200
Furniture	1,500	
SP	250	
Fittings	600	
Advertising	25	
KM	8,090	
Drawings	100	
	35,200	35,200

Notice that the accounts with **debit balances are either assets or expenses**, while the accounts with **credit balances are liabilities, capital or revenue** accounts (except for drawings, which represents a reduction in capital).

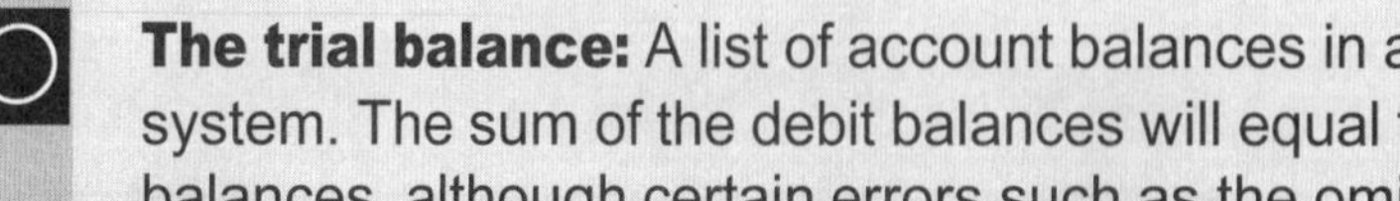

The trial balance: A list of account balances in a double-entry accounting system. The sum of the debit balances will equal the sum of the credit balances, although certain errors such as the omission of a transaction or erroneous entries will not be disclosed by a trial balance.

What if it doesn't balance?

The trial balance is thus a list of the balances on the ledger accounts. If the totals of the debit and credit balances entered on the trial balance are not equal, then an error or errors have been made either:

(1) in the posting of the transactions to the ledger accounts; or

(2) in the balancing of the accounts; or

(3) in the transferring of the balances from the ledger accounts to the trial balance.

Does the trial balance prove the accuracy of the ledger accounts?

Just because the trial balance totals agree does not mean that there are no errors within the ledger accounts. There are a number of errors that might have been made that do not prevent the trial balance from agreeing. These are:

- Errors of **omission**, where a transaction has been completely omitted from the ledger account.
- Errors of **commission**, where one side of the transaction has been entered in the wrong account (but of a similar type to the correct account, for example, entered in the wrong receivable's account, or in the wrong expense account). An error of commission would not affect the calculation of profit, or the position shown by the statement of financial position.
- Errors of **principle**, where the correct and incorrect accounts are of different types, for example, entered in the purchases account instead of a non-current asset account. This type of error would affect the calculation of profit, and the position shown by the statement of financial position.
- Errors of **original entry**, where the wrong amount has been used for both the debit and credit entries.
- **Reversal** of entries, where the debit has been made to the account that should have been credited and vice versa.
- **Duplication** of entries, where the transaction is posted twice.
- **Compensating errors**, where two or more transactions have been entered incorrectly, but cancelling each other out, for example, electricity debited $100 in excess, and sales credited with $100 excess.

In all these cases, an account has been debited and an account has been credited with the same amount, so the trial balance will still be in agreement, even though it contains incorrect entries. You will learn more about errors, and how to correct them, in chapter 14.

Test your understanding 3

Explain the purpose of a trial balance.

Test your understanding 4

Prepare a trial balance from the ledger accounts in TYU 3, chapter 3.

4 Closing off accounts

At the year-end, the ledger accounts must be closed off in preparation for the recording of transactions in the next accounting period.

Income statement

Once the trial balance has been completed we can now prepare the income statement.

This will contain any balances relating to **revenue or expense** accounts.

- At the end of a period any amounts that relate to that period are transferred out of the income and expenditure accounts into another ledger account called the income statement.
- This is done by closing the account.
- Do not show a balance c/f or balance b/f but instead put the balancing figure on the smallest side and label it 'income statement'.

Once the trial balance has been produced all items belonging to the income statement will be transferred from their individual ledgers to an account called the income statement account. This is used to summarise the profit or loss for the period. It is important to remember that any income statement ledgers **MUST NOT** have any balances on them at the end of the period.

The trading account

When the trial balance has been successfully completed, it is reasonably safe to assume that profit can now be accurately calculated. This is referred to as 'the income statement'. You should recall from chapter 2 that the part of the income statement which calculates gross profit is known as the 'trading account'. This comprises sales, less cost of goods sold, equals gross profit. The trading account is thus a sub-section of the income statement although its name does not appear within the income statement. Nevertheless, it is a very important part of the income statement.

The trading account

The trading account is part of the double-entry bookkeeping system of an organisation that buys and sells goods with the intention of making a profit. It is part of the income statement and is regularly produced by such an organisation during the year, often on a monthly basis.
The trading account compares the revenue derived from selling the goods with the costs of obtaining the goods sold.

A typical trading account is as follows:

Trading account for the year ending 31 December 20X1

	$		$
Opening inventory	500	Sales	9,400
Purchases	6,400	Less: sales returns	(300)
	6,900		
Less: closing inventory	(430)		
Cost of goods sold	6,470		
Gross profit	2,630		
	9,100		9,100

This presentation, as a ledger account, is known as the **horizontal format**.

Transferring the balances to the trading account

The trading account is a ledger account in the normal sense, and must conform to the double-entry rule. Therefore, every entry in it must have an opposite entry elsewhere in the ledger accounts. For example, the credit in the trading account for 'sales' of $9,400 will also be debited in the sales account. In effect, the balance on the sales account is transferred into the trading account. In the example above, the sales account might have appeared as follows:

Sales

			20X1		$
			10 Jan	B Nevitt	1,000
			13 Mar	A Turner	5,400
			6 Jun	G Fletcher	2,600
			5 Dec	P Bajwa	400

Once the balance has been transferred to the trading account, the sales account will appear as follows:

Sales

20X1		$	20X1		$
31 Dec	Trading account	9,400	10 Jan	B Nevitt	1,000
			13 Mar	A Turner	5,400
			6 Jun	G Fletcher	2,600
			5 Dec	P Bajwa	400
		9,400			9,400

Note that there is now no balance on the sales account, and so the two sides can be totalled to confirm that fact, and ruled off to prevent including them in the figures for the following year. The account is now said to be 'closed', although it can still be used to record the sales for the next period, below the totals.

This process is repeated with all the other figures that appear in the trading account, but there are some transfers that are worthy of special mention.

(a) **The inventory account**. In chapter 3, you were told never to use the inventory account for the purchase, sale or return of inventory, but that it was used only at the beginning and the end of the period.

In a business that has been trading in the past, there will be a balance on the inventories account at the start of the period, which will be a debit balance (representing an asset). In the example above, the inventory account at the start of the period would appear as follows:

Inventory

20X1		$			$
1 Jan	Balance	500			

As the trading account is being prepared, this balance is transferred into it, by crediting the inventory account and debiting the trading account. The inventory account then appears as follows:

Inventory

20X1		$			$
1 Jan	Balance	500	31Dec	Trading account	500

The inventory account now has no balance, so it can be 'closed off' as with the sales account you saw earlier.

As the preparation of the trading account continues, it will be necessary to determine the value of the inventory at 31 December. This is often done by referring to a separate inventory control system, which is maintained outside the bookkeeping system (you will learn more about the valuation of inventory in chapter 9). The figure is passed to the bookkeeper, who then debits the inventory account with the new value, and credits the trading account.

The inventory account now appears as follows:

Inventory

20X1		$	20X1		$
1 Jan	Balance	500	31 Dec	Trading account	500
31 Dec	Trading account	430			

However, notice that in the trading account above, the closing inventory does not appear to have been credited to it, instead it has been deducted on the debit side of the account. This is not normal practice for most ledger accounts, but is commonplace when the trading account is being prepared, because it is then possible to show the cost of goods sold figure. An item deducted on the debit side of an account is equivalent to making a credit entry.

(b) **Sales and purchase returns**. The same type of entry is used with sales and purchase returns. In the trading account above, the sales returns have been deducted from the sales figure on the credit side of the account. This is the equivalent of making a debit entry. The opposite entry would be to credit the sales returns account.

The trading account thus brings together the revenue and costs of the trading function for a specified period of time, and by comparing them calculates the **gross profit**. It is common for the gross profit to be expressed as a percentage of the sales value, when it is known as the gross profit margin, or as a percentage of the cost of sales, when it is known as the gross profit mark-up.

The balance on the trading account

We have seen that the revenue from the sale of goods is compared with the cost of those goods in the trading account and the resulting difference is referred to as gross profit. This figure is the balance on the trading account. This balance is then transferred to the income statement account.

Vertical presentation of the trading account

An alternative presentation of the trading account is shown below. This is known as the vertical format, and is used when producing an income statement.

Trading account for the year ended 31 December 20X1

	$	$
Sales		9,400
Less: sales returns		(300)
		9,100
Opening inventory	500	
Purchases	6,400	
	6,900	
Less: closing inventory	(430)	
		6,470
Gross profit		2,630

Illustration

Prepare the trading account (in horizontal format) for illustration 1, chapter 3, given that closing inventory was $1,200, and make the necessary entries in the ledger accounts.

Solution

Trading account for the month ended 31 May

	$		$
Opening inventory	Nil	Sales	10,200
Purchases	8,900		
	8,900		
Less: closing inventory	(1,200)		
Cost of goods sold	7,700		
Gross profit	2,500		
	10,200		10,200

Note: The company commenced trading only on 1 May.

Sales

		$			$
			12 May	Cash	210
			19 May	SP	580
			25 May	Cash	430
			28 May	Cash	890
31 May	Trading account	10,200	29 May	KM	8,090
		10,200			10,200

Purchases

		$			$
4 May	JM	2,000			
6 May	ERD	3,000			
22 May	Cash	3,900	31 May	Trading account	8,900
		———			———
		8,900			8,900
		———			———

Inventory

		$			$
31 May	Trading account	1,200			

Illustration

Prepare the trading account for TYU 2, chapter 4, (in vertical format), given that closing inventory was $50.

Solution

Trading account for the month ended 28 February 20X1

	$	$
Sales		530
Opening inventory	–	
Purchases	150	
	———	
	150	
Less: closing inventory	(50)	
	———	
		100
		———
Gross profit		430
		———

The income statement

A typical income statement, in horizontal format, is shown below:

Income statement for the year ended 31 December 20X1

	$		$
Rent	120	Gross profit c/d	2,630
Local business tax	80		
Light and heat	75		
Wages	1,120		
Printing and stationery	14		
Telephone	37		
Net profit	1,184		
	2,630		2,630

The income statement thus summarises all the costs and revenues of the business for a specified period of time. The various expenses (and sundry revenues, if there are any) are transferred out of the nominal ledger, and into the income statement. Those accounts are then closed off.

The resulting balance on the income statement is referred to as a **net profit** (if it is a credit balance), or **net loss** (if it is a debit balance).

It is common for the net profit (or loss) to be expressed as a percentage of the sales value shown in the trading account, and this is known as the **net profit percentage**.

The income statement is presented in a **vertical** format when it is presented as part of the financial statements. This is shown below:

Income statement for the year ended 31 December 20X1

	$	$
Gross profit		2,630
Less: Rent	120	
Local business tax	80	
Light and heat	75	
Wages	1,120	
Printing and stationery	14	
Telephone	37	
		(1,446)
Net profit		1,184

Illustration

Prepare the income statement in **horizontal** format for illustration 1, chapter 3, and make the necessary entries in the ledger accounts.

Solution

Income statement for the month ended 31 May

	$		$
Wages	170	Gross profit b/d	2,500
Rent	80		
Advertising	25		
Net Profit	2,225		
	2,500		2,,500

Wages

		$			$
7 May	Cash	60			
25 May	Cash	110	31 May	Income statement	170
		170			170

Rent

		$			$
10 May	Bank	80	31 May	Income statement	80

Advertising

		$			$
28 May	Bank	25	31 May	Income statement	25

Illustration

Prepare the income statement in horizontal format for TYU 3, chapter 3.

Solution

Income statement of A Thompson for the month ended 28 February 20X1

	$		$
Rent	50	Gross profit b/d	430
Advertising	25		
Net Profit	355		
	—		—
	430		430
	—		—

The balance on the income statement

The balance on the income statement represents the owner's profit, which has the effect of increasing his investment in the business. At the end of the year this is transferred to the owner's capital account, by debiting the income statement and crediting the capital account. If the balance on the income statement is a debit balance, this represents a net loss, and the entries are reversed.

The capital account from illustration 1, chapter 3, would now appear as follows:

Capital

	$			$
		1 May	Bank	20,000
		31 May	Income statement	2,225

Dealing with drawings

The balance on the capital account is increased by the net profit (or decreased by a net loss). The balance is also affected by any drawings that have occurred, and that have been debited to a separate drawings account. The balance on this account now needs to be transferred to the capital account, by means of the following entries:

- credit the drawings account;
- debit the capital account.

Using illustration 1, chapter 3 again, the drawings and capital account would now look like this:

Capital

		$			$
31 May	Drawings account	100	1 May	Bank	20,000
			31 May	Income statement	2,225

Drawings

		$			$
30 May	Cash	100	31 May	Capital	100

The statement of financial position

The next stage is to prepare the statement of financial position. The statement of financial position shows the **assets, liabilities and capital** that exist at the date at which it is drawn up. It will include **ALL** the ledger accounts that still have balances on them.

- Assets/liabilities at the end of a period = Assets/liabilities at start of the next period, e.g. the cash at bank at the end of one day will be the cash at bank at the start of the following day.
- Balancing the account will result in: – a balance c/f (being the asset/liability at the end of the accounting period) – a balance b/f (being the asset/liability at the start of the next accounting period).

The statement of financial position

It should be noted that the statement of financial position is not an 'account'. Its name is not the statement of financial position 'account' and it is not part of the double-entry bookkeeping system. The statement of financial position, is a list of all the balances in the ledger accounts.

The ledger accounts for expenses and revenues will all have no balance remaining, as they have been transferred to the income statement (but see the next chapter for occasions when this is not the case). The inventory account will have a new balance, and the capital account will have had the net profit or net loss and drawings entered. The balances on the other assets and liabilities will be those used in order to prepare the trial balance.

These, plus the inventory account and revised capital account balance can be presented in the statement of financial position.

Refer to chapter 2 for the presentation of the statement of financial position.

Test your understanding 5

Prepare the statement of financial position for illustration 1, chapter 3. Assume closing inventory of $1,200.

Balancing off the ledger accounts

The final task is to tidy up the remaining accounts in order to clearly show the final balance on each, in readiness for commencing posting the next period's transactions. This process is known as **balancing off** the accounts. In the previous chapter you saw how the balance is mathematically calculated in order to produce the trial balance, and to determine the amounts to be transferred to the income statement and included in the statement of financial position. Some accounts will now have no balance remaining, but those that appear on the statement of financial position will have, and this needs to be clearly identified.

The procedure can be shown in the following steps:

Step 1. Calculate the balance (or take the figure already used in the trial balance).

Step 2. Enter the balance on the **opposite side** of the account, for example, if there is a debit balance, enter it on the credit side. (Imagine the account as a pair of scales that was out of balance; entering the item on the opposite side brings the scales into balance.) Use the date at which the statement of financial position is prepared, and describe the balance as 'balance carried down', abbreviated to 'balance c/d'. This is, of course, making an entry in the ledger accounts, therefore an opposite entry needs to be made to conform to the double-entry rule – see step 4 for this.

Step 3. Total up each side, to confirm that the two sides now agree, and rule them off.

Step 4. Enter the balance on its **correct** side, beneath the totals. This completes the double entry from Step 2. Date the item as the first day of the next accounting period, for example, 1 January 20X2, and describe the balance as 'balance brought down', abbreviated to 'balance b/d'.

Step 5. Check that all accounts with debit balances are assets, and that all accounts with credit balances are either liabilities or capital, and compare them with the statement of financial position figures.

Illustration

Balance off the asset, liability and capital accounts, from illustration 1 in chapter 3.

Solution

Capital

		$			$
31 May	Drawings	100	1 May	Cash	20,000
	Balance c/d	22,125	31 May	Net Profit	2,225
		22,225			22,225
			1 Jun	Balance b/d	22,125

Cash

		$			$
1 May	Capital	20,000	2 May	Bank	15,000
12 May	Sales	210	7 May	Wages	60
25 May	Sales	430	22 May	Purchases	3,900
28 May	Sales	890	24 May	Fittings	600
			25 May	Wages	110
			30 May	Drawings	100
			31 May	Balance c/d	1,760
		21,530			21,530
1 Jun	Balance b/d	1,760			

Bank

		$			$
2 May	Cash	15,000	10 May	Rent	80
27 May	SP	330	16 May	Furniture	1,500
			28 May	Advertising	25
			31 May	Balance c/d	13,725
		15,330			15,330
1 Jun	Balance c/d	13,725			

JM

		$			$
			4 May	Purchases	2,000

ERD

		$			$
			6 May	Purchases	3,000

Furniture

		$			$
16 May	Bank	1,500			

SP

		$			$
19 May	Sales	580	27 May	Bank	330
			31 May	Balance c/d	250
		580			580
1 Jun	Balance b/d	250			

Fittings

		$			$
24 May	Cash	600			

Sales

		$			$
			12 May	Cash	210
			19 May	SP	580
			25 May	Cash	430
			28 May	Cash	890
31 May	Balance c/d	10,200	29 May	KM	8,090
		10,200			10,200
			1 June	Balance b/d	10,200

Note: the question only asks for the asset, liability and capital accounts but all accounts have been shown for completeness.

You should notice that the accounts that only have one entry have not been balanced off; this is because the balance on the account can easily be seen without balancing it. However, it is a good practice to balance off in the standard way at least once a year, to confirm that the account has been considered and included in the appropriate financial statement.

For example, the fittings account above would appear as follows:

Fittings

		$			$
24 May	Cash	600	31 May	Balance c/d	600
		600			600
1 Jun	Balance b/d				

The balances brought down then become the first entries in each account for the following accounting period.

Illustration

Balance off the asset, liability and capital ledger accounts from TYU 3, chapter 3, after transferring the net profit of $355 and the balance on the drawings account into the capital account. Remember that you also need to open an inventories account.

Advertising

		$			$
28 May	Bank	25			

KM

		$			$
29 May	Sales	8,090			

Rent

		$			$
10 May	Bank	80			

Purchases

		$			$
4 May	JM	2,000			
6 May	ERD	3,000			
22 May	Cash	3,900	31 May	Balance c/d	8,900
		8,900			8,900
1 June	Balance b/d	8,900			

Wages

		$			$
7 May	Cash	60			
25 May	Cash	110	31 May	Balance c/d	170
		170			170
1 June	Balance b/d	170			

Solution

Bank

20X1		$	20X1		$
1 Feb	Capital	500	1 Feb	Purchases	150
10 Feb	Sales	290	5 Feb	Rent	50
27 Feb	Sales	240	22 Feb	Advertising	25
			26 Feb	Drawings	100
			28 Feb	Balance c/d	705
		1,030			1,030
1 Mar	Balance b/d	705			

Capital

20X1		$	20X1		$
28 Feb	Drawings	100	1 Feb	Bank	500
28 Feb	Balance c/d	755	28 Feb	Net Profit	355
		855			855
			1 Mar	Balance b/d	755

Inventory

20X1		$			$
28 Feb	Trading account	50			

Ilustration

Continue with the ledger accounts from TYU 3, chapter 3, at 1 March, and enter the following transactions for March:

2 Mar	Bought goods for resale, on credit from J Smith	100
5 Mar	Paid rent	50
14 Mar	Received a loan from L Lock	450
16 Mar	Business sales	330
23 Mar	A Thompson's drawings	75
24 Mar	Paid J Smith by cheque	80
26 Mar	Business sales, on credit to A Pitt	180
29 Mar	Paid for advertising leaflets	30

Solution

Bank

20X1		$	20X1		$
1 Mar	Balance b/d	705	5 Mar	Rent	50
14 Mar	Loan	450	23 Mar	Drawings	75
16 Mar	Sales	330	24 Mar	J Smith	80
			29 Mar	Advertising	30
			31 Mar	Balance c/d	1,250
		1,485			1,485
1 Apr	Balance b/d	1,250			

Capital

			20X1		$
			1 Mar	Balance b/d	755

Inventory

20X1		$			
1 Mar	Trading account	50			

Purchases

20X1		$			
2 Mar	J Smith	100			

J Smith

20X1		$	20X1		$
24 Mar	Bank	80	2 Mar	Purchases	100

Rent payable

20X1		$			
5 Mar	Bank	50			

L Lock

			20X1		$
			14 Mar	Bank	450

Sales

			20X1		$
			16 Mar	Bank	330
			26 Mar	A Pitt	180

Drawings

20X1		$			
23 Mar	Bank	75			

A Pitt

20X1		$			
26 Mar	Sales	180			

Advertising

20X1		$			
29 Mar	Bank	30			

Test your understanding 6

Oreo sets up a business on 1st January. In the first two weeks of trading Oreo has the following transactions:
January

1st Introduces $15,000 into a business bank account by cash.
2nd Buys goods for resale worth $5,000 and pays by cheque.
2nd Pays rent of $400 by cheque.
3rd Buys a delivery van for $2,000 and pays by cheque.
6th Buys $1,000 of goods for resale on credit.
8th Sells good for $1,500 and receives a cheque for that amount.
10th Sells all of his remaining goods for $8,000 on credit.
12th Pays $800 to his supplier by cheque.
14th Withdraws $500 for personal living expenses from the business bank account.

(a) Complete the relevant ledger accounts for the above transactions.

(b) Extract a trial balance at 14th January.

(c) Prepare the income statement for the first two weeks of trading.

(d) Prepare the statement of financial position as at 14th January.

Note: On 12th January Oreo sold his remaining goods so there will be no closing inventory at 14th January.

5 Chapter summary

In this chapter you have looked at:

- the balancing off the ledger accounts at the end of the period;
- the preparation of the trial balance;
- the form and content of the trading account within the income statement;
- the form and content of the income statement;
- the ledger entries needed to prepare an income statement;
- the entries needed to record profit and drawings in the capital account;
- the preparation of the statement of financial position.

This chapter is one of the most 'technical' chapters you will study. Do practise the techniques you have learned here to ensure that you have a thorough understanding of them.

Test your understanding questions

Test your understanding 7

An error of commission is one where:

A a transaction has not been recorded

B one side of a transaction has been recorded in the wrong account, and that account is of a different class from the correct account

C one side of a transaction has been recorded in the wrong account, and that account is of the same class as the correct account

D a transaction has been recorded using the wrong amount

Test your understanding 8

A credit balance of $917 brought down on Y Ltd's account in the books of X Ltd means that

A X Ltd owes Y Ltd $917

B Y Ltd owes X Ltd $917

C X Ltd has paid Y Ltd $917

D X Ltd is owed $917 by Y Ltd

Test your understanding 9

On 1 January, a business had a customer, J King, who owed $400. During January, J King bought goods for $700 and returned goods valued at $250. He also paid $320 in cash towards the outstanding balance. The balance on J King's account at 31 January is:

A $530 debit

B $530 credit

C $270 debit

D $270 credit

Test your understanding 10

Which one of the following statements regarding the balance on a ledger account is not correct?

A A credit balance exists where the total of credit entries is more than the total of debit entries

B A debit balance exists where the total of debit entries is less than the total of credit entries

C A credit balance exists where the total of debit entries is less than the total of credit entries

D A debit balance exists where the total of debit entries is more than the total of credit entries

Test your understanding 11

Where a transaction is credited to the correct ledger account, but debited incorrectly to the repairs and renewals account instead of to the plant and machinery account, the error is known as an error of:

A omission

B commission

C principle

D original entry

Test your understanding 12

If a purchase return of $48 has been wrongly posted to the debit side of the sales returns account, but has been correctly entered in the supplier's account, the total of the trial balance would show:

A the credit side to be $48 more than the debit side

B the debit side to be $48 more than the credit side

C the credit side to be $96 more than the debit side

D the debit side to be $96 more than the credit side

Test your understanding 13

The debit side of a trial balance totals $50 more than the credit side. This could be due to:

A a purchase of goods for $50 being omitted from the payables account

B a sale of goods for $50 being omitted from the receivables account

C an invoice of $25 for electricity being credited to the electricity account

D a receipt for $50 from a debtor being omitted from the cash book

Test your understanding 14

An invoice from a supplier of office stationery has been debited to the rent account. This error is known as:

A an error of commission

B an error of original entry

C a compensating error

D an error of principle

Test your understanding 15

The double-entry system of bookkeeping normally results in which of the following balances on the ledger accounts?

	Debit balances	Credit balances
A	Assets and revenues	Liabilities, capital and expenses
B	Revenues, capital and liabilities	Assets and expenses
C	Assets and expenses	Liabilities, capital and revenues
D	Assets, expenses and capital	Liabilities and revenues

Test your understanding 16

Which one of the following is an error of principle?

A A gas bill credited to the gas account and debited to the bank account

B The purchase of a non-current asset credited to the asset at cost account and debited to the payables account

C The purchase of a non-current asset debited to the purchases account and credited to the payables account

D The payment of wages debited and credited to the correct accounts, but using the wrong amount

Test your understanding 17

Recording the purchase of computer stationery by debiting the computer equipment at cost account would result in:

A an overstatement of profit and an overstatement of non-current assets

B an understatement of profit and an overstatement of non-current assets

C an overstatement of profit and an understatement of non-current assets

D an understatement of profit and an understatement of non-current assets

Test your understanding 18

S Smart commenced in business as a decorator on 1 January.

1 Jan Commenced business by putting $1,000 of his own money into a business bank account.

3 Jan Bought a motor van on credit from AB Garages for $3,000.

4 Jan Bought decorating tools and equipment on credit from B & P Ltd for $650.

8 Jan Bought paint for $250, paying by cheque.

10 Jan Received $400 cash from a customer for work done.

12 Jan Bought paint for $150, paying in cash.

14 Jan Issued an invoice to a customer, K Orme, for $750 for work done.

18 Jan Returned some of the decorating tools, value $80, to B & P Ltd.

23 Jan Took $50 of the cash to buy a birthday present for his son.

28 Jan K Orme paid $250 by cheque towards his bill.

Required:

Calculate the balance on each account at 31 January, by completing the ledger accounts provided below:

Capital

	$		$

Bank

	$		$

Motor van

	$		$

AB Garages

	$		$

Tools and equipment

	$		$

B and P Ltd

$	$

Purchases

$	$

Sales

$	$

Cash

$	$

K Orme

$	$

Drawing

$	$

The balances on the accounts are as follows:

	$	Debit/Credit
Capital		
Bank		
Motor van		
AB Garges		
Tools and Equipment		
B and P Ltd		
Purchases		
Sales		
Cash		
K Orme		
Drawings		

Test your understanding 19

B Baggins commenced in business as a market gardener on 1 March. Record the following transactions in the ledger accounts:

1 Mar	Paid $70 rent for land for the month of March, from his own funds.
3 Mar	Bought equipment on credit for $400 from JK Ltd.
4 Mar	Bought plants for $2,000, paying from his own funds.
8 Mar	Received $100 cash for a talk to the local horticultural society.
10 Mar	Sold plants for $1,200, being paid by cheque. He opened a business bank account with this amount.
12 Mar	Paid wages of $50 in cash.
14 Mar	Bought plants for $800 on credit from BH Horticultural Ltd
18 Mar	Sold Plants for $500 on Credit to PB.
23 Mar	Paid $100 local business tax by cheque.
28 Mar	Paid wages of $20 in cash.
31 Mar	Sold plants for $240, being paid in cash.

Calculate the balance on each account at 31 March by completing the ledger accounts provided below:

Rent Expense

	$		$

Capital

	$		$

JK Ltd

	$		$

Equipment

	$		$

Purchases

	$		$

Sales

	$		$

Cash

	$		$

Bank

$	$

Wages

$	$

BH Horticultural Ltd

$	$

PB

$	$

Local business tax

$	$

The balances on the accounts are as follows:

	$	Debit/credit
Rent Expense		
Capital		
Equipment		
JK Ltd		
Purchases		
Sales		
Cash		
Bank		
Wages		
BH Horticultural Ltd		
PB		
Local business tax		

Test your understanding 20

On 1 January, P Roberts starts a business with $2,500 in the bank and $500 cash. The following transactions occur:

2 Jan	He buys raw materials on credit for $700 from J Martin.
3 Jan	He sells goods for $300 on credit to G Goddard.
7 Jan	He sells goods for $1,100 to K Lemon on credit.
12 Jan	He buys equipment for $3,000, paying by cheque.
18 Jan	He pays wages of $50 by cheque.
20 Jan	He buys raw materials for $350, paying by cheque.
	He takes $80 from the cash box for himself.
28 Jan	He pays J Martin $250 by cheque.
30 Jan	He transfers $200 cash into the bank from his cash box.

Required:

(a) Record the above transactions in the ledger accounts provided below.

Capital

		$			$
31 Jan	Drawings	.....	1 Jan	Bank	.....
	Balance c/d	.....		Cash	.....
			31 Jan	Net profit	.....
		.....			.....
			1 Feb	Balance b/d	.....

Bank

		$			$
1 Jan	Capital	.....	12 Jan	Equipment	.....
30 Jan	Cash	.....	18 Jan	Wages	.....
31 Jan	Balance c/d	.....	20 Jan	Purchases	.....
			28 Jan	J Martin	.....
		.....			.....
			1 Feb	Balance b/d	.....

Cash

		$			$
1 Jan	Capital	.....	20 Jan	Drawings	.....
			30 Jan	Bank	.....
			31 Jan	Balance c/d	.....
		.....			.....
1 Feb	Balance b/d	.....			

Purchases

		$			$
2 Jan	J Martin	.....	31 Jan	Trading a/c	.....
20 Jan	Bank	.....			
		.....			.....

J Martin

		$			$
28 Jan	Bank	.....	2 Jan	Purchases	.....
31 Jan	Balance c/d	.....			
		.....			.....
			1 Feb	Balance b/d	.....

Sales

		$			$
31 Jan	Trading a/c	.....	3 Jan	G Goddard	.....
			7 Jan	K Lemon	.....
		.....			.....

G Goddard

		$			$
3 Jan	Sales	.....			.....

K Lemon

		$			$
7 Jan	Sales	.....			

Equipment

		$			$
12 Jan	Bank	.....			

Wages

		$			$
18 Jan	Bank	.....	31 Jan	Income statement	.....
		.....			.....

Drawings

		$			$
20 Jan	Cash	.....	31 Jan	Capital account	.....
		.....			.....

(b) Insert the missing figures into the following trial balance.

Trial balance of P Roberts as at 31 January

	Debit ($)	Credit ($)
Capital		.....
Bank		.....
Cash	.....	
Purchases	.....	
Payables		.....
Sales		.....
Receivables	.....	
Equipment	.....	
Wages	.....	
Drawings	.....	
	.....	.....

(c) Insert the missing figures into the income statement for January, given that closing inventory was $200.

Income statement of P Roberts for the month ended 31 January

	$	$
Sales		.....
Less: cost of goods sold		
Purchases	.....	
Closing inventory	.....	
	——	
		.....
		——
Gross profit		.....
Less: expenses – wages		.....
		——
Net profit		
		——

(d) Insert the missing figures into the statement of financial position at 31 January.

Statement of financial position of P Roberts as at 31 January

	$	$
Assets		
Non-current assets		
Equipment		.....
Current assets		
Inventory	.....	
Receivables	.....	
Cash	.....	
		.....
		.....
Capital and liabilities		
Opening capital		.....
Add: net profit		.....
		.....
Less: drawings		.....
Current liabilities		
Payables	.....	
Bank overdraft	.....	.....
		.....

Test your understanding answers

Test your understanding 1

Capital	$20,000	credit
Cash	$1,760	debit
Bank	$13,725	debit
Purchases	$8,900	debit
JM	$2,000	credit
ERD	$3,000	credit
Wages	$170	debit
Rent	$80	debit
Sales	$10,200	credit
Furniture	$1,500	debit
SP	$250	debit
Fittings	$600	debit
Advertising	$25	debit
KM	$8,090	debit
Drawings	$100	debit

Test your understanding 2

Bank	$705	debit
Capital	$500	credit
Purchases	$150	debit
Rent	$50	debit
Advertising	$25	debit
Drawings	$100	debit
Sales	$530	credit

Test your understanding 3

The purpose of a trial balance is to check the arithmetical accuracy of the entries made to the ledger accounts, that is, that the total of debit entries equals the total of credit entries.

Test your understanding 4

Bank	$705	debit
Capital	$500	credit
Purchases	$150	debit
Rent	$50	debit
Advertising	$25	debit
Drawings	$100	debit
Sales	$530	credit

Trial balance of A Thompson as at 28 February 20X1

	Debit ($)	Credit ($)
Bank	705	
Capital		500
Purchases	150	
Rent	50	
Advertising	25	
Drawings	100	
Sales		530
	1,030	1,030

Test your understanding 5

Statement of Financial Position as at 31 May

Assets	$	$
Non-current assets		
Furniture		1,500
Fittings		600
		2,100
Current assets		
Inventory	1,200	
Receivables	8,340	
Bank balance	13,725	
Cash in hand	1,760	
		25,025
		27,125
Capital and liabilities		
Capital		20,000
Net profit for the month		2,225
		22,225
Less: drawings		(100)
		22,125
Current liabilities		
Payables		5,000
		27,125

Test your understanding 6

(a)

Bank

		$			$
1 Jan	Capital	15,000	2 Jan	Rent	400
8 Jan	Sales	1,500	2 Jan	Purchases	5,000
			3 Jan	Van	2,000
			12 Jan	Payables	800
			14 Jan	Drawings	500
			14 Jan	Balance c/d	7,800
		16,500			16,500
15 Jan	Balance b/d	7,800			

Capital

		$			$
14 Jan	Balance c/d	15,000	1 Jan	Bank	15,000
		15,000			15,000
			15 Jan	Balance b/d	15,000

Rent

		$			$
2 Jan	Bank	400	14 Jan	Balance c/d	400
		400			400
15 Jan	Balance b/d	400			

Purchases

		$			$
2 Jan	Bank	5,000			
6 Jan	Payables	1,000	14 Jan	Balance c/d	6,000
		6,000			6,000
15 Jan	Balance b/d	6,000			

Van

		$			$
3 Jan	Bank	2,000	14 Jan	Balance c/d	2,000
		2,000			2,000
15 Jan	Balance b/d	2,000			

Payables

		$			$
12 Jan	Bank	800	6 Jan	Purchases	1,000
14 Jan	Balance c/d	200			
		1,000			1,000
			15 Jan	Balance b/d	200

Sales

		$			$
			8 Jan	Bank	1,500
14 Jan	Balance c/d	9,500	10 Jan	Receivables	8,000
		9,500			9,500
			15 Jan	Balance b/d	9,500

Receivables

		$			$
10 Jan	Sales	8,000	14 Jan	Balance c/d	8,000
		8,000			8,000
15 Jan	Balance b/d	8,000			

Drawings

		$			$
14 Jan	Bank	500	14 Jan	Balance c/d	500
		500			500
15 Jan	Balance b/d	500			

(b) **Trial balance of Oreo at 14 January**

	Debit ($)	Credit ($)
Bank	7,800	
Capital		15,000
Rent	400	
Purchases	6,000	
Van	2,000	
Payables		200
Sales		9,500
Receivables	8,000	
Drawings	500	
	24,700	24,700

(c) **Oreo Income Statement for the two weeks ending 14th January**

	$	$
Sales		9,500
Opening inventory	–	
Purchases	6,000	
	6,000	
Less: closing inventory	–	
		(6,000)
Gross profit		3,500
Expenses: Rent		(400)
Net profit		3,100

(d) **Oreo Statement of Financial Position as at 14 January**

Assets	$	$
Non-current assets		
Van		2,000
Current assets		
Inventory	–	
Receivables	8,000	
Bank balance	7,800	
		15,800
		17,800
Capital and liabilities		
Capital		15,000
Net profit for the period		3,100
Drawings		(500)
		17,600
Current liabilities		
Payables		200
		17,800

Test your understanding 7

C

A is incorrect as this is an error of omission. B is incorrect as an error of principle occurs where the two accounts are of different classes. D is an example of an error of original entry.

Test your understanding 8

A

A credit balance in the books of X Ltd indicates that it owes money; none of the other distractors would result in a credit balance.

Test your understanding 9

A

The ledger account would be as follows:

J King

		$			$
1 Jan	Balance b/d	400	Jan	Returned Goods	250
Jan	Sales	700		Cash	320
			31 Jan	Balance c/d	530
		1,100			1,100
1 Feb	Balance b/d	530			

Test your understanding 10

B

Test your understanding 11

C

This is a straightforward test of your knowledge of the types of errors that can exist. If the wrong account is used, and this results in an incorrect statement of profit, then an error of principle has been made. Debiting the repairs and renewals account results in an extra charge for expenses in the income statement, when the item should be included as a non-current asset on the statement of financial position.

Test your understanding 12

D

A purchase return should be credited to the purchase returns account. If it has been debited to an account (whether the correct account or not), and also debited to the supplier's account (which is correct), then two debit entries will have been made with no corresponding credit. $96 (2 x $48) will have been debited, and nothing credited. Thus, the debit side will exceed the credit side by $96.

Test your understanding 13

A

B and D are incorrect as they would give a lower debit side. C is incorrect because it would give a higher credit side.

Test your understanding 14

A

An error of commission occurs where an entry is made in the wrong account, but that account is the same category as the correct account. Office stationery is an expense, so too is rent. Profit will be correct but the individual totals will be incorrect.

Test your understanding 15

C

Assets and expenses have debit balances; liabilities, capital and revenue have credit balances.

Test your understanding 16

C

An error of principle is where one side of an entry has been recorded in the wrong account, and where that account is classified differently to the correct account. In this case, debiting a non-current asset to the purchases account would result in the profit calculation being incorrect, and the value of assets shown on the statement of financial position being incorrect.

Test your understanding 17

A

Stationery is an expense and should be used to reduce profits; therefore profits would be overstated. Computer equipment is shown in the statement of financial position, and therefore the figure for non-current assets would be overstated.

Test your understanding 18

Capital

		$			$
			1 Jan	Bank	1,000

Bank

		$			$
1 Jan	Capital	1,000	8 Jan	Purchases	250
28 Jan	K Orme	250	31 Jan	Balance c/d	1,000
		1,250			1,250
1 Feb	Balance b/d	1,000			

Motor van

		$			$
3 Jan	AB Garages	3,000			

AB Garages

		$			$
			3 Jan	Motor van	3,000

Tools and Equipment

		$			$
4 Jan	B & P Ltd	650	18 Jan	B & P Ltd	80
			3 Jan	Balance c/d	570
		650			650
1 Feb	Balance b/d	570			

B & P Ltd

		$			$
18 Jan	Tools	80	4 Jan	Tools	650
31 Jan	Balance c/d	570			
		650			650
			1 Feb	Balance b/d	570

Purchases

		$			$
8 Jan	Bank	250			
12 Jan	Cash	150	31 Jan	Balance c/d	400
		400			400
1 Feb	Balance b/d	400			

Sales

		$			$
			10 Jan	Cash	400
31 Jan	Balance c/d	1,150	14 Jan	K Orme	750
		1,150			1,150
			1 Feb	Balance b/d	1,150

Cash

		$			$
10 Jan	Sales	400	12 Jan	Purchases	150
			23 Jan	Drawings	50
			31 Jan	Balance c/d	200
		400			400
1 Feb	Balance b/d	200			

K Orme

		$			$
14 Jan	Sales	750	28 Jan	Bank	250
			31 Jan	Balance c/d	500
		750			750
1 Feb	Balance b/d	500			

Drawings

		$			$
23 Jan	Cash	50			

The balances on the accounts are as follows:

	$	
Capital	1,000	credit
Bank	1,000	debit
Motor van	3,000	debit
AB Garages	3,000	credit
Tools and equipment	570	debit
B & P Ltd	570	credit
Purchases	400	debit
Sales	1,150	credit
Cash	200	debit
K Orme	500	debit
Drawings	50	debit

Test your understanding 19

Rent Expense

		$			$
1 Mar	Capital	70			

Capital

		$			$
			1 Mar	Rent	70
31 March	Balance c/d	2.070	4 Mar	Purchases	2,000
		2,070			2,070
			1 Apr	Balance b/d	2,070

JK Ltd

		$			$
			3 Mar	Equipment	400

Equipment

		$			$
3 Mar	JK Ltd	400			

Purchases

		$			$
4 Mar	Capital	2,000			
14 Mar	BH Horticultural Ltd	800	31 Mar	Balance c/d	2,800
		2,800			
1 Apr	Balance b/d	2,800			

Sales

		$			$
			8 Mar	Cash	100
			10 Mar	Bank	1,200
			18 Mar	PB	500
31 Mar	Balance c/d	2,040	31 Mar	Cash	240
		2,040			2,040
			1 Apr	Balance b/d	2,040

Cash

		$			$
8 Mar	Sales	100	12 Mar	Wages	50
31 Mar	Sales	240	28 Mar	Wages	20
			31 Mar	Balance c/d	270
		340			340
1 Apr	Balance b/d	270			

Bank

		$			$
10 Mar	Sales	1,200	23 Mar	Local business tax	100
			31 Mar	Balance c/d	1,100
		1,200			1,200
1 Apr	Balance b/d	1,100			

Wages

		$			$
12 Mar	Cash	50			
28 Mar.	Cash	20	31 Mar	Balance c/d	70
		70			70
1 Apr	Balance b/d	70			

BH Horticultural Ltd

		$			$
			14 Mar	Purchases	800

PB

	$		$
18 Mar Sales	500		

Local business tax

	$		$
23 Mar Bank	100		

The balances on the accounts are as follows:

	$	
Rent expense	70	debit
Capital	2,070	credit
Equipment	400	debit
JK Ltd	400	credit
Purchases	2,800	debit
Sales	2,040	credit
Cash	270	debit
Bank	1,100	debit
Wages	70	debit
BH Horticultural Ltd	800	credit
PB	500	debit
Local business tax	100	debit

Test your understanding 20

(a)

Capital

		$			$
31 Jan	Drawings	80	1 Jan	Bank	2,500
	Balance c/d	3,420		Cash	500
			31 Jan	Net profit	500
		3,500			3,500
			1 Feb	Balance b/d	3,420

Bank

		$			$
1 Jan	Capital	2,500	12 Jan	Equipment	3,000
30 Jan	Cash	200	18 Jan	Wages	50
31 Jan	Balance c/d	950	20 Jan	Purchases	350
			28 Jan	J Martin	250
		3,650			3,650
			1 Feb	Balance b/d	950

Cash

		$			$
1 Jan	Capital	500	20 Jan	Drawings	80
			30 Jan	Bank	200
			31 Jan	Balance c/d	220
		500			500
1 Feb	Balance b/d	220			

Purchases

		$			$
2 Jan	J Martin	700	31 Jan	Trading a/c	1,050
20 Jan	Bank	350			
		1,050			1,050

J Martin

		$			$
28 Jan	Bank	250	2 Jan	Purchases	700
31 Jan	Balance c/d	450			
		700			700
			1 Feb	Balance b/d	450

Sales

		$			$
31 Jan	Trading a/c	1,400	3 Jan	G Goddard	300
			7 Jan	K Lemon	1,100
		1,400			1,400

G Goddard

		$			$
3 Jan	Sales	300			

K Lemon

		$			$
7 Jan	Sales	1,100			

Equipment

		$			$
12 Jan	Bank	3,000			

Wages

		$			$
18 Jan	Bank	50	31 Jan	Income statement	50
		50			50

Drawings

		$			$
20 Jan	Cash	80	31 Jan	Capital account	80
		80			80

(b) Trial balance of P Roberts as at 31 January

	Debit ($)	*Credit* ($)
Capital		3,000
Bank		950
Cash	220	
Purchases	1,050	
Payables		450
Sales		1,400
Receivables (300 + 1,100)	1,400	
Equipment	3,000	
Wages	50	
Drawings	80	
	5,800	5,800

(c) Income statement of P Roberts for the month ending 31 January

	$	$
Sales		1,400
Less: cost of goods sold		
Purchases	1,050	
Closing inventory	(200)	
		(850)
Gross profit		550
Less: expenses – wages		(50)
Net profit		500

(d) Statement of financial position of P Roberts as at 31 January

	$	$
Assets		
Non-current assets		
Equipment		3,000
Current assets		
Inventory	200	
Receivables	1,400	
Cash	220	
		1820
		4,820
Capital and liabilities		
Opening capital		3,000
Add: net profit		500
		3,500
Less: drawings		(80)
		3,420
Current liabilities		
Payables	450	
Bank overdraft	950	1,400
		4,820

chapter

5

Accounting for Returns, Carriage and Discounts

Chapter learning objectives

When you have completed this chapter, you should be able to:

- record sales and purchase returns;
- account for carriage inwards and outwards;
- calculate and account for trade and cash discounts.

1 Introduction

In this chapter we continue looking at ledger accounts, and focus on ones of special significance. These are:

- returns inwards;
- returns outwards;
- carriage inwards;
- carriage outwards;
- discounts received;
- discounts allowed.

2 Sales and Purchase Returns

- It is normal for customers to return unwanted goods to a business; equally the business will occasionally have cause to return unwanted goods to their suppliers.
- The double entries arising will depend upon whether the returned goods were initially purchased on credit:

	Originally a credit transaction	**Originally a cash transaction**
Sales returns	Dr Sales returns	Dr Sales returns
(returns inwards)	Cr Receivables	Cr Cash
Purchase returns	Dr Payables	Dr Cash
(returns outwards)	Cr Purchase returns	Cr Purchase returns

3 Carriage costs

Organisations may pay for carriage and delivery charges on items that they buy and/or sell.

Non-current assets

Carriage and delivery charges on non-current assets are included with the cost of the non-current asset, and are debited to that non-current asset's account, along with the cost of the item.

Carriage charges on the purchase and sale of goods in which the organisation trades are recorded separately as follows.

Carriage outwards

- This relates to carriage on goods sold by the organisation.
- This should be treated as an expense against gross profit (similar to wages costs).

Carriage inwards

- This relates to carriage charged by the supplier on purchases made by the organisation.
- This should be treated as an expense in cost of sales (similar to purchases).

The following illustration (using imaginary figures) shows how the income statement may look:

	$	$	$
Sales revenue			20,000
Opening inventory		2,600	
Purchases	18,500		
Carriage inwards	500		
	19,000		
Less: purchase returns	(1,700)		
		17,300	
		19,900	
Less: closing inventory		(2,150)	
Cost of goods sold			17,750
Gross profit			2,250
Less: expenses			
Carriage outwards			(1,000)
Net profit			1,250

Although both carriage inwards and outwards are a cost to the company they must be presented differently. **Carriage inwards must be shown as part of the cost of sales** calculation and **carriage outwards must be shown as a normal expense below gross profit.**

Test your understanding 1

The following is an extract from the trial balance of a business for its most recent year.

	Debit ($)	Credit ($)
Opening Inventory	28,000	
Sales		310,000
Purchases	225,000	
Returns	22,000	26,000
Carriage inwards	7,000	
Carriage outwards	8,000	

You are also told that closing inventory was $23,000.

Using some or all of the figures above, the correct gross profit is:

$...............

4 Discounts

A discount is a reduction in the amount paid for goods and services. Discounts may be received from suppliers or allowed to customers. There are two types of discount: trade discounts and cash discounts.

Trade discounts

- Trade discounts are given to try and increase the volume of sales being made by the supplier.
- By reducing the selling price, buying items in bulk then becomes more attractive. If you are able to source your products cheaper, you can then also sell them on to the consumer cheaper too. For example, if we were to buy over 1000 items, the supplier might be able to drop the price of those items by 5%.
- The trade discount should be deducted from the quoted price and will **NOT** be accounted for, i.e. only the net amount will be recorded.

Trade discount

A trade discount may be offered to customers who are also traders, which is where the term 'trade discount' originates. However, nowadays it might be offered for a variety of other reasons, such as to existing customers, new customers, customers buying in bulk and so on. Once the discount has been offered, it cannot be taken away for whatever reason, so it simply means that a lower price is being charged. Trade discount is deducted from the quoted price (sometimes referred to as a 'list' price, or a 'catalogue' price), and only the net amount is recorded in the ledger accounts.

Example 5.A

On 1 January, AB buys goods for resale on credit from XY, with a list price of $250, subject to trade discount of 20 per cent. The trade discount is $50, and therefore the net amount payable is $200. The purchases account is debited with $200, and the account of XY is credited with $200.

Once this net figure has been agreed, any further calculations (see later for cash discounts and sales tax) are based on the **net** figure.

Test your understanding 2

Oliver sells goods with a book value of $1,000 to Sam on a cash basis and allows her a trade discount of 10%.

Required:

Show how the above should be recorded in both the books of Oliver and Sam.

Cash discounts

- This type of discount encourages people to pay for items much quicker. If you pay for the goods within a set time limit, then you will receive a % discount.
- These are often referred to as 'settlement discounts.' For example, a cash discount of 3% is offered to any customers who pay within 14 days.
- Whilst offering this discount makes the cash flow in quicker, it is still a 'lost cost' to the business who offers such a discount and therefore **must be** accounted for.
- If a organisation is given a trade discount in addition to a cash discount, the trade discount must be applied first before the cash discount is calculated.

Accounting for cash discounts

Discount allowed – this is a discount the organisation allows a customer to take for prompt payment.

Debit	Discounts allowed	X
Credit	Receivables	X

The expense is shown beneath gross profit in the income statement, alongside other expenses of the business.

Discount received – this is a discount the organisation is given by the supplier for paying promptly.

Debit	Payables	X
Credit	Discounts received	X

The income is shown beneath gross profit in the income statement.

Cash discount

A cash discount may be offered to encourage prompt payment. The term used to apply only to payments made in cash at the time of sale, but nowadays it applies to payments by many different methods, provided that payment is made within a certain time. If the payment is not made within that time, the discount is withdrawn.

The difficulty is that, at the time of sale, it will not be known whether the payment will be made in time (unless, of course, it is made at once), but the transaction still needs to be entered in the ledger accounts. Thus, at the time of sale, no account is taken of the cash discount.

Example 5.B

Continuing with Example 5.A, suppose that XY also offers cash discount of 5 per cent for payment within ten days. At the time of purchase, AB is not certain to pay within the 10 days, so the transaction is entered ignoring the cash discount (but after adjusting for the trade discount). The ledger accounts would appear as follows:

Purchases

20X1		$			$
1 Jan	XY	200			

XY

		$	20X1		$
			1 Jan	Purchases	200

If the account is not settled in the 10 days, the full amount of $200 is payable.

Let us suppose, however, that AB pays on 7 January. Five per cent is deductible, so only $190 is paid (by cheque). The bank account will be credited with $190, and the account of XY will be debited, thus:

XY

20X1		$	20X1		$
7 Jan	Bank	190	1 Jan	Purchases	200

The account has been settled, and yet there is still a balance of $10 credit in the ledger account, which gives the impression that there is still $10 owing to XY. This is not the case. The account needs to be cleared, to give a true impression, by debiting it with a further $10, and a credit is made to 'discounts received' account.

The ledger accounts after recording the cash discount are as follows:

XY

20X1		$	20X1		$
7 Jan	Bank	190	1 Jan	Purchases	200
	Discount received	10			

Discount received

		$	20X1		$
			7 Jan	XY	10

The discount received account is a form of revenue, and will be transferred to the income statement at the end of the period, to increase profit.

The discount allowed is treated like any other expense and transferred to the income statement at the end of the period, to reduce profit.

Using imaginary figures these will appear in the income statement as follows:

	$	$
Sales		26,600
Opening inventory	1,500	
Purchases	5,000	
	6,500	
Less: closing inventory	(1,700)	
Cost of goods sold		(4,800)
Gross profit		21,800
Plus: discounts received		200
Less: expenses		
Wages		(500)
Discounts allowed		(100)
Net profit		21,400

Test your understanding 3

George owes a supplier, Herbie, $2,000 and is owed $3,400 by a customer, Iris. George offers a cash discount to his customers of 2.5% if they pay within 14 days and Herbie has offered George a cash discount of 3% for payment within ten days.

George pays Herbie within ten days and Iris takes advantage of the cash discount offered to her.

What ledger entries are required to record these discounts?

A	Dr Payables	60	Dr	Discount allowed	85
	Cr Discount received	60	Cr	Receivables	85
B	Dr Discount allowed	60	Dr	Payables	85
	Cr Receivables	60	Cr	Discount received	85
C	Dr Payables	50	Dr	Discount allowed	102
	Cr Discount received	50	Cr	Receivables	102
D	Dr Discount allowed	50	Dr	Payables	102
	Cr Receivables	50	Cr	Discount received	102

Test your understanding 4

A business had a balance at the bank of $2,500 at the start of the month. During the following month, it paid for materials invoiced at $1,000 less trade discount of 20 per cent and cash discount of 10 per cent. It received a cheque from a receivable in respect of an invoice for $200, subject to cash discount of 5 per cent. The balance at the bank at the end of the month was:

$..................

5 Chapter summary

In this chapter you have looked at the bookkeeping and accounting treatment of a number of different transactions.

- returns;
- carriage costs;
- discounts.

All of these are likely to appear in every computer-based assessment involving either the preparation of ledger accounts or, more commonly, the preparation of financial statements.

Test your understanding answers

Test your understanding 1

Draw up the following:

	$	$	$
Sales			
Less: returns			310,000
			(22,000)
Less: cost of sales			288,000
Opening inventory		28,000	
Purchases	225,000		
Carriage inwards	7,000		
	232,000		
Less: returns	(26,000)		
Net purchases		206,000	
		234,000	
Less: closing inventory		(23,000)	
			211,000
Gross profit			77,000

Common errors include:

- reversing returns;
- not adding carriage inwards to the cost of purchases (or deducting it);
- adding carriage outwards to the cost of purchases.

Test your understanding 2

Oliver's books:

Debit	Cash	900
Credit	Sales	900

(Net purchase = $1,000 – 10%)

Sam's books:

Debit	Purchases	900
Credit	Cash	900

(Net purchase = $1,000 – 10%)

Test your understanding 3

A

Payables

	$		$
Cash (97% × 2,000)	1,940	Balance b/d	2,000
Discount received	60		
	2,000		2,000

Receivables

	$		$
Balance b/d	3,400	Cash (97.5% × 3,400)	3,315
		Discount allowed	85
	3,400		3,400

Discount received

	$		$
		Payables	60

Discount allowed

	$		$
Receivables	85		

Test your understanding 4

The answer is $1,970

Bank

	$		$
Balance b/d	2,500	Payment (1,000 – 20%) – 10%	720
Receipt (200 – 5%)	190	Balance c/d	1970
	2,690		2,690

chapter

6

Accounting for Indirect Taxes and Payroll

Chapter learning objectives

When you have completed this chapter, you should be able to:

- prepare accounts for indirect taxes;
- prepare accounts for payroll.

1 Introduction

In this chapter we continue looking at ledger accounts, and look at ones of special significance. These are:

- sales tax (e.g. VAT in UK, TVA in France),
- wages and salaries.

2 Accounting for sales tax

In many countries certain organisations are required to charge a sales tax. In the UK this is 'VAT', and in France 'TVA'. In this section we shall use the generic name 'sales tax'.

- As a consequence the amount that they charge their customers for goods and services supplied will increase by the addition of sales tax – this is known as output tax.
- The organisation may also have to pay sales tax itself on goods and services that it buys - this is known as input tax.
- This sales tax paid can normally be reclaimed.
- Even though the organisation has to pay the supplier the full amount, if the sales tax is reclaimable then it does not affect the value of the item purchased.
- The difference between output tax and input tax will be paid to the local tax authority.

Sales tax

The rate of sales tax varies between countries and will also vary between the nature of the goods and services supplied. The sales tax collected does not belong to the organisation that charges and collects it and the tax must therefore be remitted to the tax authorities on a regular basis. It is a tax that ultimately must be paid to the tax authorities. Because it does not belong to the organisation collecting it, it does not affect the value of its sales. However, it does mean that customers will have to pay to the organisation the full amount, including sales tax.

Therefore, an organisation may be charging sales tax to customers as well as paying sales tax on purchases. Such organisations will, as a consequence, be both receiving and paying sales tax. The organisation may offset sales tax paid against the sales tax received from customers, and only the difference is payable to/by the tax authority. The sales tax paid to suppliers is therefore an asset (receivable) and the amount received from customers is a liability (payable), until they are offset when a net asset or (more likely) a net liability arises.

The double-entry bookkeeping records need to show the goods and sales tax values separately so that the purchases, expenses and sales are posted net (i.e. without the addition of sales tax) and the sales tax amounts are posted to a separate sales tax account.

When making a sale the double entry will be:

Debit receivables/cash account	Gross amount (amount including sales tax)
Credit sales tax account	Sales tax
Credit sales account	Net amount (amount excluding sales tax)

When making a purchase the double entry will be:

Debit purchases account	Net amount (amount excluding sales tax)
Debit sales tax account	Sales tax
Credit payables/cash account	Gross amount (amount including sales tax)

If the organisation offers a discount the sales tax must be calculated after **all discounts** have been deducted, i.e. trade and cash discounts. This is done even if the cash discount is not taken.

Illustration 1

During October, W had the following credit transactions:

1 Oct	Purchased goods from H $360 subject to 20 per cent trade discount
3 Oct	Sold goods to HG for $80
5 Oct	Sold goods to PL for $15
8 Oct	Bought goods from KJ for $4,000 subject to 10 per cent cash discount if payment is made within 30 days
12 Oct	Received a credit note from H for goods returned valued at $120 list price
15 Oct	Sold goods to RW for $2,000
18 Oct	Issued credit note for $500 to RW for goods returned

All of these transactions are subject to sales tax at the rate of 20 per cent.

You are required to:

Prepare the sales tax account to record the above transactions.

Solution

Before entering these items in the ledger accounts, first calculate the relevant figures and determine the entries to be made. The following table illustrates this:

Date	Calculations	Debit entries	$	Credit entries	$
1 Oct	Trade discount $72 (deduct from list price)				
	Net goods value	Purchases	288		
	$360 – $72 = $288				
	Sales tax	Sales tax	57.60	H	345.60
	20% × $288 = $57.60				
3 Oct	Sales tax	HG	96	Sales	80
	20% × $80 = $16			Sales tax	16
5 Oct	Sales tax	PL	18	Sales	15
	20% × $15 = 3			Sales tax	3
8 Oct	Cash discount $4,000 (deduct from list price)				
	Net goods value	Purchases	4,000.00		
	$4000 – $400 = $3,600				
	Sales tax	Sales tax	720.00	KJ	4,720
	20% × 3,600 = $720				
12 Oct	Trade discount $24 (deduct from list price)				
	Net goods value			Purchases returns	96
	$120 – $24 = $96				
	Sales tax	H	115.20	Sales tax	19.20
	20% × $96 = $19.20				
15 Oct	Sales tax	PQ	2,400	Sales	2,000
	20% × $2,000 = $400			Sales tax	400
18 Oct	Sales tax	Sales returns	500	RW	600
	20% × $500 = $100	Sales tax	100		

Notice how the cash discount is deducted on 8 October **before** calculating the sales tax but the full list price is still entered into the purchases account. We are unable to enter the discounted amount of $3,600 into the books because unlike the trade discount, this discount is not guaranteed. We will only receive this discount if we pay in 30 days. However, the sales tax will not be altered if the cash discount is not taken.

The sales tax account would appear as follows:

Sales Tax

20X1		$	20X1		$
1 Oct	H	57.60	3 Oct	HG	16.00
8 Oct	KJ	720.00	5 Oct	PL	3.00
18 Oct	RW	100.00	12 Oct	H	19.20
			15 Oct	PQ	400.00
			31 Oct	Balance c/d	439.40
		877.60			877.60
1 Nov.	Balance b/d	439.40			

The balance on the account is now $439.40 debit, which signifies that a refund of this amount is due from the tax authorities. This amount will be shown as a current asset on the statement of financial position at 31 October.

Notice that the amounts debited and credited to sales, purchases and returns accounts exclude the sales tax. Profit is always based on net amounts.

Make sure you **always** round down sales tax, i.e. $616.875 = $616.87.

Test your understanding 1

The following transactions relate to Patel & Sons during December 20X1.

2 Dec	Bought goods on credit from R Williams, list price $350, trade discount 20 per cent
8 Dec	Bought goods on credit from Samuel Ltd, list price $750, trade discount 30 per cent
10 Dec	Sold goods on credit to Mary Smythe for $400, no discount, payment terms 30 days
18 Dec	Bought goods on credit from Amir, list price $1,000, trade discount 25 per cent
26 Dec	Sold goods on credit John Blair, $800, no discount

All transactions are subject to sales tax at 20 per cent.

You are required to:

Show the entries in the ledger accounts of Patel & Sons.

Sales tax on non-current assets and expenses

Input sales tax is also suffered on the purchase of non-current assets and expenses, and can be reclaimed in the normal way. There are, however, generally some items on which input sales tax cannot be reclaimed, although the detail will vary between countries. Examples in the UK are:

- Sales tax on passenger cars;
- Sales tax on entertainment expenses.

In both the above cases, the sales tax cannot be reclaimed, so it is included with the cost of the item. For example, the purchase of a passenger car, costing $10,000, plus sales tax of 20 per cent, in effect costs $12,000, and so the motor cars account would be debited with that amount.

Sales tax in separate ledger accounts

When completing the sales tax return to the tax authorities, it is necessary to provide separate totals of input and output sales tax. Therefore, some organisations may keep separate ledger accounts for these.

Non-registered businesses

Some businesses may not be required to account for sales tax; this may be because of their small size or because of the nature of the goods/services they provide. Such businesses are referred to as 'non-registered' businesses for sales tax purposes. In this case, they are not allowed to add sales tax to their sales, but on the other hand they cannot reclaim the sales tax on their purchases, either. Thus, where input sales tax is paid it is included with the cost of the item in the ledger accounts.

For example, if a non-registered business purchases goods costing $100, plus sales tax at 20 per cent, it will debit the purchases account with the full $120.00.

Zero-rated and exempt supplies

Supplies of some goods and services are **zero-rated**, which means that although they are taxable, the rate used is zero. Common examples in the UK include basic foodstuffs and children's clothing. Businesses that make such supplies add zero sales tax to their outputs, but are still able to reclaim the sales tax on inputs in full.

Yet other goods and services are **exempt** from sales tax. Businesses supplying such goods cannot reclaim the sales tax on their inputs.

Consider three businesses: A, B and C. All three make monthly cash sales of $10,000, before adding any applicable sales tax. Company A's supplies are all standard-rated, B's supplies are all zero-rated and C's supplies are all exempt. All three make monthly cash purchases of $4,000, plus sales tax at 20 per cent. Their results for a month will be as follows:

	A ($)	**B ($)**	**C ($)**
Sales	10,000	10,000	10,000
Sales tax	2,000	–	–
Cash received	12,000	10,000	10,000
Purchases	4,000	4,000	4,000
Sales tax	800	800	800
Cash paid	4,800	4,800	4,800
Sales tax payable	2,000	–	–
Sales tax reclaimable	(800)	(800)	–
Net payment/(refund)	1,200	(800)	–
Net cash in	6,000	6,000	5,200

You can see that C is at a disadvantage compared with A and B. This is because it has suffered sales tax that he cannot reclaim. This will affect its profit. A and B can both reclaim their sales tax, so their profit is not affected by the charging or suffering of sales tax.

A and B's profit can be calculated as sales (excluding sales tax), minus purchases (excluding sales tax), that is, $10,000 – $4,000 = $6,000, whereas C's profit is sales minus purchases (including sales tax), that is $10,000 – $4,800 = $5,200.

3 Accounting for wages and salaries

In this section we shall see how the wages cost is recorded in the ledger accounts of an organisation.

Gross pay and net pay

Example 6.A

George is paid $5.50 per hour for a basic 36-hour week. Any overtime is paid at basic rate plus 50 per cent.

During a particular week, George worked for 42 hours.

The first step is to calculate the amount of George's gross earnings:

		$
36 hours @ $5.50 per hour	=	198.00
6 hours @ $8.25 per hour	=	49.50
		247.50

Unfortunately for George, he will have to pay income tax, and also in some countries a social security tax, which will be deducted from his gross earnings of $247.50. Let us assume that he will be liable to pay income tax at 25 per cent on all his weekly earnings in excess of $75, and in addition he will be liable to pay social security tax (SS) of 9 per cent of his total earnings. In addition to George's SS, assume his employer is also liable to a further 10.5 per cent SS contribution based on George's gross earnings. The revised position is therefore:

	$	$
George's gross earnings		247.50
Less: income tax 25% × ($247.50 – $75.00)	43.12	
SS (9% × $247.50)	22.27	
		(65.39)
George's net earnings		182.11
Employer's SS contribution: 10.5% × $247.50		25.98

George's employer will deduct George's income tax and SS and pay George his net earnings. The employer will then pay George's income tax and all of the SS contributions over to the government. Thus it can be seen that the total cost of employing George during the week amounted to $273.48 (the total of George's gross earnings $247.50 and the employer's SS contributions $25.98).

This wages cost will be recorded in the employer's ledger accounts as follows:

Gross wages expense

	$		$
Wages payable	247.50		

SS and Income Tax payable

	$		$
		Wages payable	65.39
		Employer's SS	25.98

Employer's SS Expense

	$		$
SS & Income tax payable	25.98		

Wages payable

	$		$
Income tax payable	65.39	Gross wages	247.50

The liability on the wages payable account will be eliminated when the wages are paid. The liability to pay the income tax and SS will be eliminated when the employer pays the government.

The balance on the gross wages expense account and the employers SS expense account will be transferred to the income statement as an expense against gross profit.

Social security tax is referred to national insurance in the UK.

Other deductions

The deduction of income tax and SS from George's gross wages by his employer are statutory deductions. George is required to pay these by law. However, George may also authorise his employer to make other deductions from his wages – these voluntary deductions are made from George's net earnings, as they do not affect his liability to income tax and SS.

For example, George's employers may have a sports and social club with a weekly membership fee of $1.25. George may also ask his employer to pay $20.00 a week directly into a savings plan (SP) scheme. The deductions will have the following effect:

	$	$
George's net earnings		182.11
Less:		
Sports and social club	1.25	
SP scheme	20.00	
		(21.25)
Net pay to be received by George		160.86

The wages payable account would appear as follows:

Wages payable

	$		$
Income tax payable	65.39	Gross wages	247.50
Sports club payable	1.25		
SP scheme payable	20.00		

Two further payable accounts would be required:

Sports club payable

	$		$
		Wages payable	1.25

SP scheme payable

	$		$
		Wages payable	20.00

The liability to pay the sports club and SP scheme will be eliminated when the employer pays them, which may be weekly or monthly.

Pension contributions

Many employees contribute to pension schemes by allocating a percentage of their gross pay to the pension fund, for example 5 or 6 per cent. This amount is deducted from the employee's gross pay, and is payable to the pension-fund company.

Example 6.B

Lesley earns $200 gross in week 21. Pension contributions are 5 per cent. The ledger entries to record this are:

- debit wages payable with $10;
- credit pension company with $10.

Test your understanding 2

List the ledger entries required to record the following pay details, and the subsequent payment to the employee by cheque:

Gross pay	$1,200
Social security tax – employee's	9% of gross pay
Pension	6% of gross pay
Income tax	$185
Social security tax – employer's	10% of gross pay
Trade union subscription	$5

4 Chapter summary

In this chapter you have looked at the bookkeeping and accounting treatment of the following transactions.

- sales tax
- wages and salaries.

Both of these are likely to appear in every computer-based assessment involving either the preparation of ledger accounts or, more commonly, the preparation of financial statements. In particular you should pay attention to sales tax.

Remember, this is an international exam and the sales tax rate will be given, most likely to be 20 per cent. However, make sure you practice how to calculate the tax using other rates.

Test your understanding questions

Test your understanding 3

At the end of the month, an organisation needs to accrue for one week's wages. The gross wages amount to $500, tax amounts to $100, employer's social security tax is $50, employees' social security tax is $40, and employees' contributions to a pension scheme amount to $30. The ledger entries to record this accrual would be:

		$		$
A	Debit wages expense	500	Credit social security tax payable	90
			Credit income tax payable	100
			Credit pension scheme payable	30
			Credit wages accrued	280
		$		$
B	Debit wages expense	550	Credit social security tax payable	90
			Credit income tax payable	100
			Credit wages accrued	330
			Credit pension payable	30
C	Debit wages expense	280	Credit wages accrued	500
	Debit social security tax expense	90		
	Debit income tax expense	100		
	Debit pension scheme expense	30		
D	Debit wages expense	330	Credit wages accrued	550
	Debit social security tax expense	90		
	Debit income tax expense	100		
	Debit pension scheme expense	30		

Test your understanding 4

The sales account is:

A credited with the total of sales made, including sales tax

B credited with the total of sales made, excluding sales tax

C debited with the total of sales made, including sales tax

D debited with the total of sales made, excluding sales tax

Test your understanding 5

A business commenced with capital in cash of $1,000. Inventories costing $800 is purchased on credit (no sales tax), and half is sold for $1,000 plus sales tax of 20%, the customer paying in cash at once.

The accounting equation after these transactions would show:

A assets $1,800 less liabilities $200 equals capital $1,600

B assets $2,600 less liabilities $1,400 equals capital $1,200

C assets $2,600 less liabilities $800 equals capital $1,800

D assets $2,600 less liabilities $1,000 equals capital $1,600

Test your understanding 6

A sole trader's business made a profit of $32,500 during the year ended 31 March 20X8. This figure was after deducting $100 per week wages for himself. In addition, he put his home telephone bill through the business books, amounting to $400 plus sales tax at 20 per cent. He is registered for sales tax, and therefore has charged only the net amount to his income statement.

His capital at 1 April 20X7 was $6,500. His capital at 31 March 20X8 was:

$..................

Test your understanding 7

An employee is paid at the rate of $3.50 per hour. Earnings of more than $75 a week are taxed at 20 per cent. Employees' social security tax is 7 per cent, and employer's social security tax is 10 per cent. During week 24, the employee works for 36 hours. The amounts to be charged to the income statement and paid to the employee are:

	Income statement	Paid to employee
A	$126.00	$94.38
B	$126.00	$106.98
C	$138.60	$94.38
D	$138.60	$106.98

Test your understanding 8

An employee has a gross monthly salary of $1,000. In September the tax deducted was $200, the employee's social security tax was $60, and the employer's social security tax was $100. What was the charge for salaries in the income statement?

$..................

Test your understanding 9

A business purchases a machine on credit terms for $15,000 plus sales tax at 15 per cent. The business is registered for sales tax. How should this transaction be recorded in the books?

		Debit ($)	Credit ($)
A	Machinery	15,000	
	Payables		15,000
B	Machinery	17,250	
	Payables		17,250
C	Machinery	15,000	
	Sales tax	2,250	
	Payables		17,250
D	Machinery	17,250	
	Sales tax		2,250
	Payables		15,000

Test your understanding 10

B is a builder with a staff of ten employees. In April 20X1, he paid the following amounts:

	$
Net salaries after tax and social security tax	14,000
Tax and employee's social security tax for March	5,000
Employer's social security tax for March 20X1	1,400

He owes the following amounts in respect of tax and social security tax for April 20X1:

	$
Tax and employee's social security tax	6,000
Employer's social security tax	1,500

The correct expense for employee costs to be shown in the income statement for April 20X1 is

$..................

Test your understanding answers

Test your understanding 1

Purchases

20X1		$			
2 Dec	R Williams	280.00			
8 Dec	Samuel Ltd	525.00			
18 Dec	Amir	750.00			

Sales Tax

20X1		$	20X1		$
2 Dec	R Williams	56.00	10 Dec	Mary Smythe	80.00
8 Dec	Samuel Ltd	105.00	26 Dec	John Blair	160.00
18 Dec	Amir	150.00			

R Williams

		$	20X1		$
			2 Dec	Purchases	336.00

Samuel Ltd

		$	20X1		$
			8 Dec	Purchases	630.00

Amir

		$	20X1		$
			18 Dec	Purchases	900.00

Sales

		$	20X1		$
			10 Dec	Mary Smythe	400.00
			26 Dec	John Blair	800.00

Mary Smythe

20X1		$			$
10 Dec	Sales	480.00			

John Blair				
20X1		$		$
26 Dec	Sales	960.00		

Test your understanding 2

Gross wages	
Debit wages expense account	$1,200
Credit wages payable account	$1,200
SS employee's (9% x $1,200)	
Debit wages payable account	$108
Credit SS/tax payable account	$108
Pension (6% x $1,200)	
Debit wages payable account	$72
Credit pension payable account	$72
Income tax	
Debit wages payable account	$185
Credit SS/tax payable account	$185
SS employer's (10% x $1,200)	
Debit employers expenses account	$120
Credit SS/tax payable account	$120
Trade union expenses	
Debit wages payable account	$5
Credit trade union payable account	$5
Net pay ($1,200 – $108 – $72 – $5 – $185)	
Debit wages payable account	$830
Credit bank	$830

Test your understanding 3

B

A is incorrect as the employer's social security tax has been deducted from the net wages accrued. C is incorrect as there has been no deduction from wages accrued for tax, social security tax or pension contributions. Nor is there any record of liability for these items. D is similar, with the added error of employer's SS being included with wages accrued.

Test your understanding 4

B

Sales tax is excluded from sales and purchases accounts, so A and C are incorrect.

Sales is revenue, and therefore the sales account is credited.

Test your understanding 5

D

Opening statement of financial position and adjustments required:

	$		$
Assets (cash)	1,000	Liabilities (capital)	1,000
Transaction 1 (inventory)	800	Payables	800
Transaction 2 (cash)	1,200	Sales tax owing	200
Inventories	(400)	Profit (add to capital)	600
Closing balance	2,600		2,600

Assets ($2,600) less liabilities ($1,000) = capital ($1,600)

Test your understanding 6

The answer is $38,920.	$
Capital at 1/4/ X7	6,500
Add: profit (after drawings)	32,500
Less: sales tax element	(80)
Capital at 31/5/ X8	38,920

Test your understanding 7

D

Income statement	$	Paid to employee	$
36 × $3.50	126.00	Gross pay	126.00
Employer's SS (10%)	12.60	7% SS	(8.82)
	———		
Gross wages cost	138.60	Tax	(10.20)
	———		———
		Net pay	106.98
			———

Test your understanding 8

The answer is $1,100.

The charge for the salary in the income statement is the gross salary plus the employer's social security tax contribution. This is $1,000 plus $100, a total of $1,100.

Test your understanding 9

C

Test your understanding 10

The answer is $21,500

This is calculated using the April figures for salary ($14,000), tax and SS for the employee ($6,000) and SS for the employer ($1,500).

The income statement is always charged with the gross salary plus and additional costs to the employer, i.e. SS in this question.

chapter

7

Accounting for Accruals and Prepayments

Chapter learning objectives

When you have completed this chapter, you should be able to:

- prepare accounts using accruals and prepayments for expenses and income.

1 Introduction

In this chapter we continue looking at ledger accounts, and look at ones of special significance. These are:

- accrued and prepaid expenses;
- accrued and prepaid income.

2 Accruals and prepayments

The accruals basis of accounting means that to calculate the profit for the period, we must include all the income and expenditure relating to the period, whether or not the cash has been received or paid or an invoice received.

Profit is therefore:

Income earned	X
Expenditure incurred	(X)
	—
Profit	X

Accrued expenditure

An accrual arises where expenses of the business for the current period have not been paid at the end of the year.

In this case, it is necessary to record the extra expense relevant to the year and create a corresponding statement of financial position liability (called an accrual):

Debit	Expense account	X
Credit	Accrual account	X

An accrual therefore reduces profit.

Illustration 1

Draw up the heat and light account from the following information:

Bills received and paid during 20X1:

28 Feb	$460
31 May	$440
30 Aug	$390
30 Nov	$420
Bill received on 28 Feb 20X2	$450 (for the period 1 Dec. 20X1 to 28 Feb 20X2)

The year end is 31 December 20X1.

Solution

Heat and light

20X1		$	20X1		$
28 Feb	Bank	460			
31 May	Bank	440			
30 Aug	Bank	390			
30 Nov	Bank	420			
31 Dec	Accrual	150	31 Dec	Income statement	1,860
		1,860			1,860

The accrual of $150 represents one-third of the bill received on 28 February 20X2 (i.e. the amount applicable to the month of December 20X1). This amount will be credited to the accrual expenses account which will appear on the statement of financial position under current liabilities.

This ensures the correct amount is charged to the income statement for the year 20X1.

At the beginning of the following year, 20X2, the accrual will be reversed, i.e. debit accrual account and credit heat and light account. This would mean the heat and light account would look as follows:

Heat and light

20X1		$	20X1		$
28 Feb	Bank	460			
31 May	Bank	440			
30 Aug	Bank	390			
30 Nov	Bank	420			
31 Dec	Accrual c/d	150	31 Dec	Income statement	1,860
		1,860			1,860
			20X2	Accrual b/d	150

Test your understanding 1

Fred has a business which incurs electricity charges for the year ended 31 December 20X1 of $24,000. Fred has paid $18,000 during the year but will not pay the final quarter until January 20X2.

Show the entries in the electricity expense account.

Prepaid expenditure

A prepayment arises where expenses of the business, relating to the following year, have been paid in advance at the year end. In this case, it is necessary to remove the extra expense relevant to the following year and create a corresponding statement of financial position asset (called a prepayment):

Debit	Prepayment account	X
Credit	Expense account	X

A prepayment therefore increases profit.

Illustration 2

Draw up the rent expense account from the following information for a business commencing 1 March 20X1.

Rent is payable quarterly in advance on 1 March, June, September and December. The current annual rental is $4,800.

	$
1 Mar	1,200
1 Jun	1,200
1 Sep	1,200
1 Dec	1,500

The annual rental is increased to $6,000 per annum with effect from 1 December 20X1, and the year end is 31 December.

Solution

Rent expense

20X1		$	20X1		$
1 Mar	Bank	1,200			
1 Jun	Bank	1,200			
1 Sep	Bank	1,200	31 Dec	Prepayment	1,000
1 Dec	Bank	1,500	31 Dec	Income statement	4,100
		5,100			5,100

The prepayment is for January and February 20X2, which is at the new rate of $500 per month. This amount will be debited to the prepayment expenses account which will appear on the statement of financial position under current assets. The charge to the income statement can be confirmed as being 9 months at the old rate of $400 per month, and one month at the new rate of $500 per month, that is, $4,100.

At the beginning of the following year, 20X2, the prepayment will be reversed, i.e. debit prepayment account and credit rent payable account. This would mean the rent payable account would look as follows:

Rent expense

20X1		$	20X1		$
1 Mar	Bank	1,200			
1 Jun	Bank	1,200			
1 Sep	Bank	1,200	31 Dec	Prepayment c/d	1,000
1 Dec	Bank	1,500	31 Dec	Income statement	4,100
		5,100			5,100
20X2					
1 Jan	Prepayment b/d	1,000			

Test your understanding 2

The annual insurance charge for Asif is $24,000. Asif paid $30,000 on 1 January 20X1.

Show the entries in the insurance expense account for the year ended 31 December 20X1.

A proforma expense account would look like:

Expense

	$		$
Prepayment b/d (opening prepaid expense)	X	Accrual b/d (opening accrued expense)	X
Bank (amount paid in the year)	X	Income statement	X
Accrual c/d (closing accrued expense)	X	Prepayment c/d (closing prepaid expense)	X
	X		X
Prepayment b/d (opening prepaid expense)	X	Accrual b/d (opening accrued expense)	X

Accrued and prepaid income

Accrued and prepaid income can arise in the same way as accrued and prepaid expenses.

Accrued income arises when income is owing at the year end, e.g. rent due from renting out a warehouse has not been paid.

The double entry will be:

Debit	Accrued income account	X
Credit	Income account	X

The accrued income account will show as a current asset on the statement of financial position.

Accrued income increases the profit figure.

Prepaid income arises when income is paid advance at the year end.

The double entry will be:

Debit	Income account	X
Credit	Prepaid income account	X

The prepaid income account will show as a current liability on the statement of financial position.

Prepaid income reduces the profit figure.

3 Chapter summary

In this chapter you have looked at the bookkeeping and accounting treatment of the following transactions:

- accruals and prepayments relating to expenses;
- accruals and prepayments relating to income.

Both of these (especially accruals and prepayments relating to expenses,) are likely to appear in every computer-based assessment involving either the preparation of ledger accounts or, more commonly, the preparation of financial statements.

The topics in this chapter are very important. The principles involved are discussed in more detail in chapter 15.

In particular, the adjustments made for accruals and prepayments, and allowances for receivables, involve the **accruals and matching concepts**. The idea is that the revenue earned during a period is 'matched' in the income statement with the expense incurred in earning that revenue. So, the mere fact that something has been paid for during a period does not necessarily mean that it has been consumed during that period in earning revenue, and therefore some adjustment is needed to the ledger accounts to fairly reflect what has been consumed.

Another important concept is the **realisation** concept, which states that we 'recognise' (i.e. account for) revenue when it is earned, not necessarily when it is received. An important convention that affects accounting is the **prudence** concept, which states that revenue and assets should not be recognised unless it is probable that they can be valued reliably. This is also the case for expenses and losses, but a degree of caution should be exercised in making any judgement, such that revenue/assets are not overstated and expenses/liabilities are not understated. Perhaps it is this philosophy that has earned accountants the reputation of being 'miserable'!

Some of the topics contained in this chapter involve a degree of 'judgement', rather than hard evidence and fact, and it is important that accountants have sufficient guidance as to how to exercise that judgement when drawing up the financial statements. In other words, some items dealt within the financial statements are 'subjective', that is, subject to different measurement and interpretation: as accountants are human beings they may well differ in their degree of subjectivity. For this reason, chapter 15 discusses various sources of guidance for accountants, and their importance. Some of these ideas will also be encountered in the next chapter.

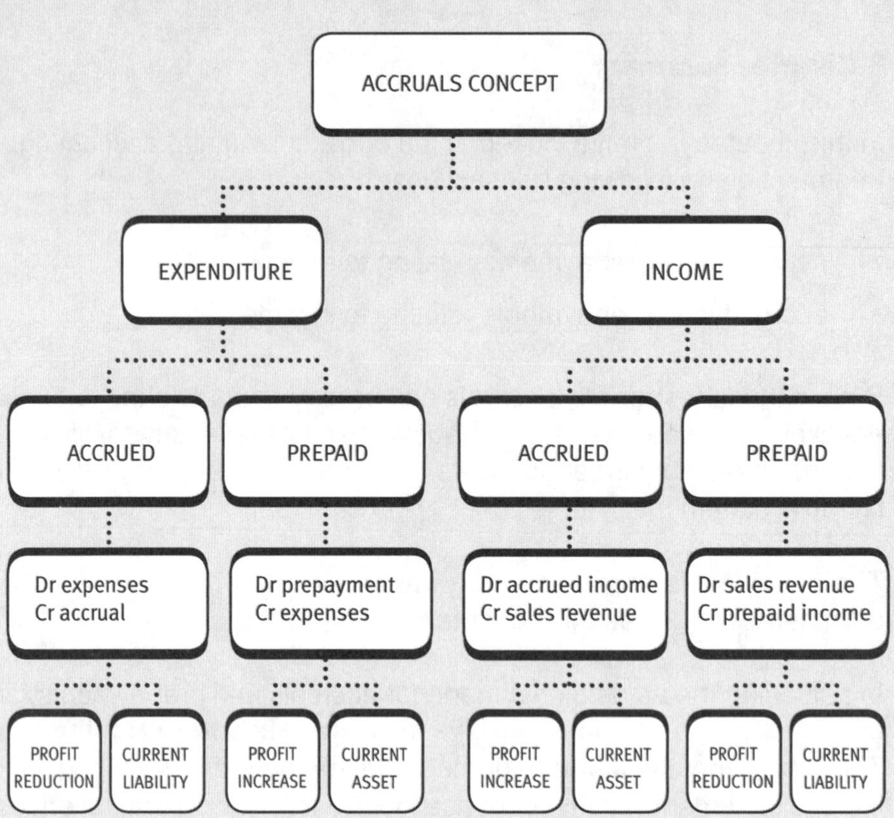
ACCRUALS CONCEPT
EXPENDITURE
INCOME
ACCRUED
PREPAID
ACCRUED
PREPAID
Dr expenses
Cr accrual
Dr prepayment
Cr expenses
Dr accrued income
Cr sales revenue
Dr sales revenue
Cr prepaid income
PROFIT REDUCTION
CURRENT LIABILITY
PROFIT INCREASE
CURRENT ASSET
PROFIT INCREASE
CURRENT ASSET
PROFIT REDUCTION
CURRENT LIABILITY

Test your understanding questions

Test your understanding 3

Rent paid on 1 October 20X2 for the year to 30 September 20X3 was $1,200 and rent paid on 1 October 20X3 for the year to 30 September 20X4 was $1,600. Rent payable, as shown in the income statement for the year ended 31 December 20X3, would be:

A $1,200

B $1,600

C $1,300

D $1,500

Test your understanding 4

Stationery paid for during 20X5 amounted to $1,350. At the beginning of 20X5 there were inventories of stationery on hand of $165 and an outstanding stationery invoice for $80. At the end of 20X5, there were inventories of stationery on hand of $140 and an outstanding stationery invoice for $70. The stationery figure to be shown in the income statement for 20X5 is:

$...................

Test your understanding 5

An organisation's year end is 30 September. On 1 January 20X6, the organisation took out a loan of $100,000 with annual interest of 12 per cent. The interest is payable in equal instalments on the first day of April, July, October and January, in arrears. How much should be charged to the income statement for the year ended 30 September 20X6, and how much should be accrued on the statement of financial position?

Income statement	Statement of financial position
$.........................	$.........................

Test your understanding 6

On 1 May 20X0, A Ltd pays a rent bill of $1,800 for the period to 30 April 20X1. What is the charge to the income statement and the entry in the statement of financial position for the year ended 30 November 20X0?

Income statement	Statement of financial position	Accrual or Prepayment
$	$	

Test your understanding answers

Test your understanding 1

Electricity

20X1		$	20X1		$
	Bank	18,000			
31 Dec	Accrual c/d	6,000	31 Dec	Income statement	24,000
		———			———
		24,000			24,000
		———			———
			20X2	Accrual b/d	6,000

The charge to the income statement must reflect the cost of electricity for the year, not the amount paid, i.e. $24,000. Therefore, we must make an accrual for $6,000 ($24,000 – $18,000).

To make the accrual we will:

Debit Electricity expense account
Credit Accrual account

An accrual therefore increases the expense account, thus reduces profit. The accrual account will be shown on the statement of financial position as a current liability.

Test your understanding 2

Insurance expense

20X1		$	20X1		$
1 Jan	Bank	30,000	31 Dec	Prepayment c/d	6,000
			31 Dec	Income statement	24,000
		30,000			30,000
20X2					
1 Jan	Prepayment b/d	6,000			

The charge to the income statement must reflect the cost of insurance for the year, not the amount paid, i.e. $24,000. Therefore, we must make a prepayment for $6,000 ($30,000 – $24,000).

To make the prepayment we will:

Debit Prepayment account
Credit Insurance expense account

A prepayment therefore decreases the expense account, thus increases profit. The prepayement account will be shown on the statement of financial position as a current asset.

Test your understanding 3

C

The year to 31 December 20X3 includes 3/4th of the rent for the year to 30 September 20X3 and 1/4th of the rent for the year to 30 September 20X4, that is:

(9/12 × $1,200) + (3/12 × $1,600) = $1,300

Test your understanding 4

The answer is $1,365.

The stationery ledger account would appear as:

Stationery

	$		$
Opening inventories b/d	165	Outstanding invoice at 1.1.20X5	80
Paid during year	1,350	Closing inventories c/d	140
Outstanding invoice at 31.12.20X5	70	Income statement	1,365
	1,585		1,585

Test your understanding 5

The answer is:

Income statement $9,000

Statement of financial position $3,000.

The charge to the income statement is $9,000 for 9 months' interest, at an annual rate of $12,000 (12 per cent of $100,000). The payment for the third quarter ending 30 September 20X6 is not paid until 1 October 20X6, so 3 months' interest is accrued, that is, $3,000.

Test your understanding 6

The answer is:

Income statement $1,050

Statement of financial position $750; Prepayment

chapter

8

Accounting for Irrecoverable Debts and Allowances for Receivables

Chapter learning objectives

When you have completed this chapter, you should be able to:

- account for irrecoverable debts;
- calculate allowances for receivables;
- account for increases and decreases in the allowance for receivables;
- account for irrecoverable debts recovered.

1 Introduction

When a business sells goods on credit, it assumes that the customer will pay up in full. However, it sometimes happens that a customer does not pay in full, or even at all, and thus it is incorrect to retain his balance as an asset, or to treat the sale as having created profit.

There may also be occasions when an organisation feels that a proportion of receivables may fail to pay their debts, but is not certain who they are, or the amount that may become unpaid.

Both of these situations need to be considered in preparing the financial statements.

2 Accounting for irrecoverable debts

When it becomes known that a customer is unlikely to pay, the receivable balance must be removed (since it is no longer an asset of the business) and transferred to the income statement as an expense of the period in which the irrecoverable debt arises. This may also be referred to as a bad debt.

The double entry will be:

Debit	Irrecoverable debts expense account	X
Credit	Receivables account	X

Example 8.A

X sold goods to Y on credit on 1 January 20X1 valued at $350. On 30 November 20X1, X was advised that Y was unable to pay the debt.

Prior to X receiving this information Y's account was as follows:

Y

		$			$
1 Jan	Sales	350			

However, now it is necessary to remove the asset and instead treat the outstanding balance as an expense. The entries are shown below:

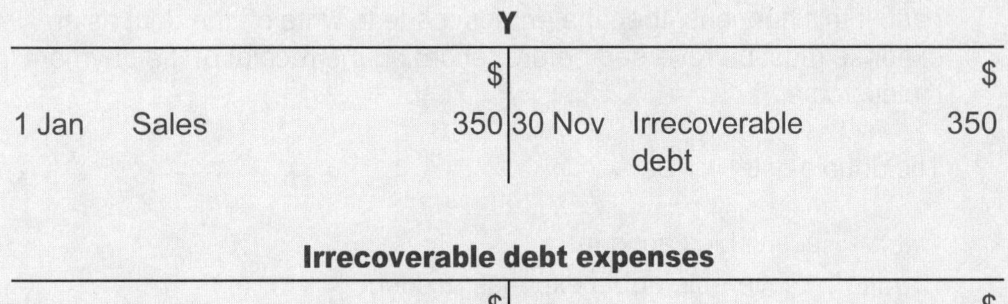

Y

		$			$
1 Jan	Sales	350	30 Nov	Irrecoverable debt	350

Irrecoverable debt expenses

		$			$
30 Nov	Y	350			

There may be circumstances where only part of the debt needs to be written off as an expense. For example, if Y had paid $200 on 30 June 20X1 and only the balance was to be written off, then the accounts would appear as follows:

Y

		$			$
1 Jan	Sales	350	30 June	Bank	200
			30 Nov	Irrecoverable debts	150
		350			350

Irrecoverable debts

		$			$
30 Nov	Y	150			

One irrecoverable debts account is used to record all bad debts occurring during a year. At the end of the year the balance on the irrecoverable debts expense account is transferred to the income statement.

3 Irrecoverable debts recovered

It is possible that debts that have previously been written off may later be paid. If this happens, then the entries made to write off the debt as an expense must be reversed before recording the receipt of the payment from the customer.

The double entry will be:

Debit	Receivables account	X
Credit	Irrecoverable debts expense account	X

This entry re-instates the debt to enable the business to allocate the cash received from the customer.

The payment can then be allocated to the receivables account as follows:

Debit	Bank account	X
Credit	Receivables account	X

We have now made a debit and credit entry to the receivables account of equal amounts. Therefore, we could take a shortcut double entry as follows:

Debit	Bank account	X
Credit	Irrecoverable debts account	X

Example 8.B

P sold goods to Q on credit valued at $500. Q did not pay and his debt was written off in 2X10. The original ledger account entries were as follows:

Q

2X10	$	2X10	$
Balance b/d	500	Irrecoverable debts	500

Irrecoverable debt expenses

2X10	$	2X10	$
Q	500	Income statement	500
	___		___

On 31 December 2X11, Q paid the debt in full. The entries required to record this in the ledger accounts are shown below:

Q

2X10	$	2X10	$
Balance b/d	500	Irrecoverable debts	500
	___		___
2X11		2X11	
Irrecoverable debts	500	Bank	500
	___		___

Irrecoverable debt expenses

	$	2X11	$
		Q	500
			___

The credit balance on the irrecoverable debts expense account will be credited to the income statement at the end of 2X11.

Sometimes a part payment of a debt previously written off is made. If Q had paid $200 as full and final settlement, then the entries made would have been:

Q

	$	2X10	$
Balance b/d	500	Irrecoverable debts	500
	___		___
Irrecoverable debts	500	Bank	200
		Irrecoverable debts	300
			___
	500		500
	___		___

Irrecoverable debts

2X11	$	2X11	$
Q	300	Q (bad debt brought back)	500
			___

The reason for reinstating the full amount of the original debt and then writing off the resulting $300 is so that if P were to trade with Q again in the future it would be clear that an irrecoverable debt arose from their previous trading activities. If only the part of the debt settled were reinstated it may appear that no irrecoverable debt occurred.

4 Allowance for receivables

While some debts are definitely irrecoverable – it is known for certain that the customer will not pay – others may be only **doubtful**. In this case it would not be appropriate to eliminate the receivable balance because he/she may pay after all. But we have to recognise that the value of the asset 'receivables' is probably less than it appears to be. The technique used is to create an **allowance for receivables.**

The double entry will be:

Debit	Irrecoverable debts expense account	X
Credit	Allowance for receivables account	X

Prudence concept

Both writing off irrecoverable debts and allowances for receivables are in accordance with the concept of **prudence**, which you will learn more about in chapter 15. Adopting a prudent approach is simply ensuring that profits and assets are not overstated, by estimating likely losses and decreases in assets as soon as they become apparent.

This estimate can be made using a number of different techniques. For example:

(1) using experience and knowledge of customers and the economic climate;

(2) listing all receivables and scrutinising them individually for their ability to pay;

(3) calculating an overall percentage of the outstanding receivable balances;

(4) preparing a schedule of receivables according to the length of time that their debt has been outstanding, and using different percentages depending on the age of the debt. This is known as an aged receivables schedule.

Example 8.C

Age of debt	Amount ($)	%	Allowance ($)
Less than 1 month	8,000	1	80
1–2 months	3,000	2	60
2–3 months	700	5	35
More than 3 months	140	20	28
	11,840		203

Irrecoverable debt expenses

20X1	$	20X1	$
Allowance for receivables	203		

Allowance for receivables

20X1	$	20X1	$
		Irrecoverable debts	203

This technique is based on the belief that the older the debt the more likely it is to become a bad debt.

When the allowance for receivables is first created, the ledger account entries are as shown above:

The balance on the irrecoverable debts account is transferred to the income statement at the end of the period. Thus the balance on this account will be reduced to nil.

The balance on the allowances account is used to decrease the value of receivables shown on the statement of financial position at the end of the period. The net balance on the statement of financial position will be receivables less the allowance for receivables. This balance on allowance for receivables will remain in the ledger accounts.

Note that no entries are made in the receivables accounts for the allowance.

Once the allowance has been created it must be reviewed and increased or decreased depending on the circumstances of the business.

For example, if the above allowance were to be decreased to $130 in 20X2, then the entries would appear as follows:

Irrecoverable debt expenses

		20X2	$
		Allowance for receivables	73

Allowance for receivables

20X2	$	20X2	$
Irrecoverable debts	73	Balance b/d	203
Balance c/d	130		
	203		203
		20X3	
		Balance b/d	130

Note that it is possible to avoid the use of the irrecoverable debts account if the entry is only being made once a year, since the income statement can be debited directly, but most modern accounting systems provide monthly profit statements for internal management use, and in these circumstances it is common to use the ledger accounts shown.

It is important to remember that only the **movement** on the allowance account will be transferred to the irrecoverable debts expense account.

Always remember to write off all irrecoverable debts before the allowance is calculated.

Test your understanding 1

The following receivables balances are given *before* the adjustments for irrecoverable debts:

Receivables at 31 December 20X0	$30,000
Receivables at 31 December 20X1	$25,000
Receivables at 31 December 20X2	$35,000
Receivables at 31 December 20X3	$40,000

The allowance at each year end is to be 5 per cent of receivables, after writing off irrecoverable debts.

Irrecoverable debts to be written off are as follows:

31 December 20X1	$3,000
31 December 20X2	$2,000

You are required to:

Write up the allowance for receivables account for the years 20X0 to 20X3.

Test your understanding 2

On 31 August 20X4, the sundry receivables of Henry Higgins stood at $10,000 and the balance on the allowance for receivables account at that date was $200. Of the receivables it was considered that $500 were irrecoverable and should be written off. It was decided that the allowance for receivables should be made equal to 5 per cent of the outstanding accounts.

At 31 August 20X5, the receivables balances had fallen to $8,000, of which $100 were considered to be irrecoverable and should be written off. The allowance for receivables was to be at the same rate as in 20X4.

You are required to:

(1) Show the irrecoverable debts account at 31 August 20X4 and 20X5;

(2) Show the allowance for receivables account at 31 August 20X4 and 20X5;

(3) Show the relevant figures in the statements of financial position for the 2 years 20X4 and 20X5.

Futher detail

In this and the previous examples, both the irrecoverable debts and the change in the allowance for receivables have been charged to a irrecoverable debts account in the income statement. In some organisations (and in some assessment questions) you may be asked to show these in separate ledger accounts. In this case, there would be a 'irrecoverable debts' account and a 'change in allowance for receivables' account. As the latter name implies, the expense in the income statement shows the change in the allowance; the statement of financial position shows the actual allowance. In the year that an organisation first creates an allowance for receivables, the full amount will be charged to the income statement. (This is logical as the change is from NIL to the first allowance, which must equal the first allowance.)

Thus in the example above, the irrecoverable debts account would show debits of $500 and $100 in 20X4 and 20X5, respectively.

The change in allowance for receivables account would show a debit $275 in 20X4 and a credit of $80 in 20X5.

The 'allowance for receivables' account would not be affected.

Payments received from 'doubtful' receivables

Because there is no adjustment made in the account of the receivable when an allowance is made there is no need to make any particular entries if that receivable eventually pays. The adjustment to the previous period's allowance will take place when the current year's receivables are assessed for the likelihood of being paid, and that debt will be ignored in the calculation of the allowance for the current year. It is accepted that, in making allowances, there is some doubt as to the absolute accuracy of the estimates made. An over allowance or an under allowance can occur, but provided that these do not make a significant (material) difference to the view portrayed by the financial statements, no action is taken.

Specific allowances

In some situations a 'specific allowance' is made. This is where the identity of the receivable is known, but the amount of the likely bad debt is unknown. It particularly arises where a receivable is known to be in difficulties, but is making efforts to repay his or her debt. He might have agreed to pay in instalments, and he has paid some, but missed others. It is prudent to write off any known bad receivables, but in this situation it is also prudent to consider the likelihood of only part of the debt being repaid. A specific allowance is treated in the same way as a general allowance, that is, it is debited to the irrecoverable debts account, and credited to the allowance for receivables account.

5 Chapter summary

In this chapter you have looked at the bookkeeping and accounting treatment of a number of the following transactions:

- irrecoverable debts,
- allowances for receivables.

Both of these are likely to appear in every computer-based assessment involving either the preparation of ledger accounts or, more commonly, the preparation of financial statements.

The topics in this chapter are very important. The principles involved are discussed in more detail in chapter 15.

An important convention that affects accounting is the **prudence** convention, which states that revenue and assets should not be recognised unless it is probable that they can be valued reliably. This is also the case for expenses and losses, but a degree of caution should be exercised in making any judgement, such that revenue/assets are not overstated and expenses/liabilities are not understated. Perhaps it is this philosophy that has earned accountants the reputation of being 'miserable'!

Some of the topics contained in this chapter involve a degree of 'judgement', rather than hard evidence and fact, and it is important that accountants have sufficient guidance as to how to exercise that judgement when drawing up the financial statements. In other words, some items dealt within the financial statements are 'subjective', that is, subject to different measurement and interpretation: as accountants are human beings they may well differ in their degree of subjectivity. For this reason, chapter 15 discusses various sources of guidance for accountants, and their importance. Some of these ideas will also be encountered in the next chapter.

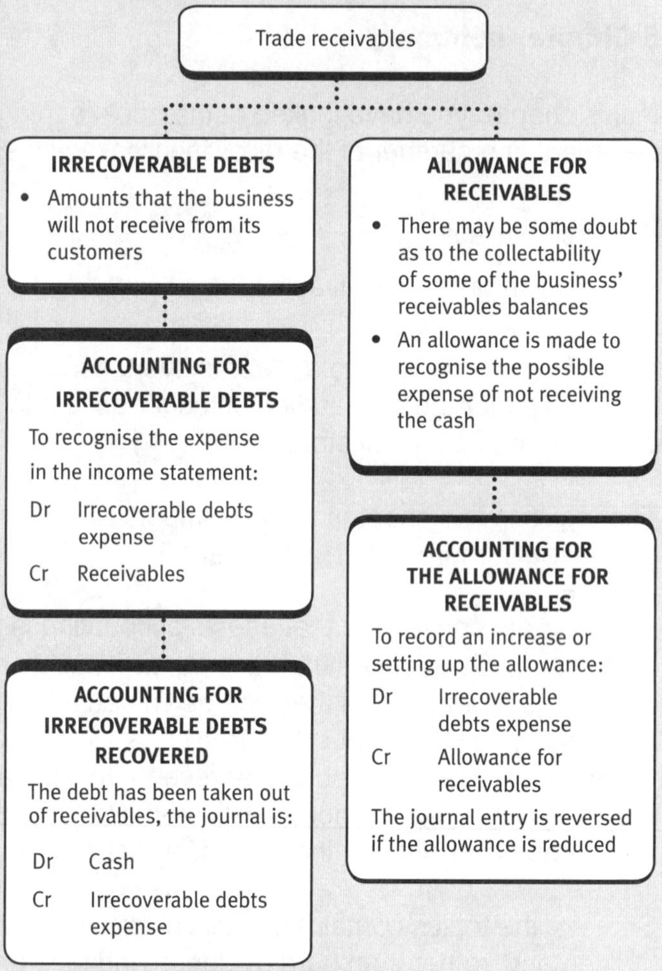

Trade receivables

IRRECOVERABLE DEBTS

- Amounts that the business will not receive from its customers

ACCOUNTING FOR IRRECOVERABLE DEBTS

To recognise the expense in the income statement:

Dr Irrecoverable debts expense

Cr Receivables

ACCOUNTING FOR IRRECOVERABLE DEBTS RECOVERED

The debt has been taken out of receivables, the journal is:

Dr Cash

Cr Irrecoverable debts expense

ALLOWANCE FOR RECEIVABLES

- There may be some doubt as to the collectability of some of the business' receivables balances
- An allowance is made to recognise the possible expense of not receiving the cash

ACCOUNTING FOR THE ALLOWANCE FOR RECEIVABLES

To record an increase or setting up the allowance:

Dr Irrecoverable debts expense

Cr Allowance for receivables

The journal entry is reversed if the allowance is reduced

Test your understanding questions

Test your understanding 3

Which of the following transactions would result in an increase in capital employed?

A Selling inventories at a profit

B Writing off an irrecoverable debt

C Paying a payable in cash

D Increasing the bank overdraft to purchase a non-current asset

Test your understanding 4

A decrease in the allowance for receivables would result in:

A an increase in liabilities

B a decrease in working capital

C a decrease in net profit

D an increase in net profit

Test your understanding 5

The turnover in a company was $2 million and its receivables were 5 per cent of turnover. The company wishes to have an allowance of 4 per cent of receivables, which would make the allowance of 33 and 1 third per cent higher than the current allowance. What figure would appear in the income statement for irrecoverable debts?

Debit or Credit	$
....	....

Test your understanding answers

Test your understanding 1

Allowance for receivables account

		$			$
20X0			20X0		
31 Dec	Balance c/d	1,500	31 Dec	Increase in allowance	1,500
		–––––			–––––
20X1			20X1		
31 Dec	Decrease in allowance	400	1 Jan	Balance b/d	1,500
	Balance c/d	1,100			
		–––––			–––––
		1,500			1,500
		–––––			–––––
20X2			20X2		
			1 Jan	Balance b/d	1,100
31 Dec	Balance c/d	1,650	31 Dec	Increase in allowance	550
		–––––			–––––
		1,650			1,650
		–––––			–––––
20X3			20X3		
			1 Jan	Balance b/d	1,650
31 Dec	Balance c/d	2,000	31 Dec	Increase in allowance	350
		–––––			–––––
		2,000			2,000
		–––––			–––––
			20X4		
			1 Jan	Balance b/d	2,000

Calculation of allowance:

20X0 – $30,000 x 5% = $1,500
20X1 – ($25,000 – $3,000) x 5% = $1,100
20X2 – ($35,000 – $2,000) x 5% = $1,650
20X3 – $40,000 x 5% = $2,000

Test your understanding 2

Irrecoverable debts

20X4		$	20X4		$
31 Aug	Receivables	500	31 Aug	Income statement	775
31 Aug	Allowance for receivables	275			
					775
		775			
20X5		$	20X5		$
31 Aug	Receivables	100	31 Aug	Allowance for receivables	80
				Income statement	20
		100			100

Allowance for receivables

20X4		$	20X4		$
			1 Sept	Balance b/d	200
31 Aug	Balance c/d	475	31 Aug	Irrecoverable debts	275
		475			475
20X5		$	20X5		
31 Aug	Irrecoverable debt	80	1 Sep	Balance b/d	475
31 Aug	Balance c/d	395			
		475			475
			20X6		$
			1 Sep	Balance b/d	395

Statement of Financial Position extracts

20X4	$	
Receivables	9,500	
Less: allowance	(475) (9,500 x 5%)	
Net receivables		9,025
20X5	$	
Receivables	7,900	
Less: allowance	(395) (7,900 x 5%)	
Net receivables		7,505

Test your understanding 3

A

Capital employed is increased by making a profit, or by adding more capital. Writing off an irrecoverable debt is clearly the opposite of making a profit; transactions such as B and C merely adjust the split of assets and liabilities but do not add anything overall.

Test your understanding 4

D

The change in allowance for receivables is taken to the income statement – an increase is debited and therefore decreases net profit, while a decrease is credited and therefore increases net profit. The resultant balance on the allowance for receivables account is deducted from receivables (current assets), which in turn affects working capital. A decrease in the allowance would increase net profit, and would also increase current assets. The latter is not one of the options, therefore D is the answer.

Test your understanding 5

The answer is Debit $1,000

Receivables = 5% × $2,000,000 = $100,000

Allowance now = $100,000 × 4% = $4,000

This allowance is 33 1/3 higher than before, i.e. represents 133.33333%.

The allowance was therefore previously $4,000/133.3333 × 100 = $3,000

This represents an increase of $1,000 and a charge to the income statement.

chapter

9

Inventory

Chapter learning objectives

When you have completed this chapter, you should be able to:

- record the adjustments for opening and closing inventory;
- apply the principles of inventory valuation in accordance with IAS 2;
- recognise the costs that should be included in inventory;
- calculate inventory cost using the FIFO and AVCO methods;
- understand and identify the impact of inventory valuation on reported profits and assets.

1 Introduction

Inventory consists of:

- goods purchased for resale;
- consumable stores (such as oil);
- raw materials and components (used in the production process);
- partly finished goods (usually called work in progress – WIP);
- finished goods (which have been manufactured by the business).

2 Inventory in the financial statements

We saw in chapter 4 how opening and closing inventory are used to calculate the cost of sales in the income statement and therefore directly affect the level of profit or loss made in an accounting period.

Measurement of inventory is also important, as we have already considered, as it is one of the assets in the statement of financial position at each reporting date.

This ability to alter the profit of an organisation by changing its inventory measurement explains the need to regulate the methods that can be used when valuing inventory.

- When calculating gross profit we match the revenue generated from the sales of goods in the year with the costs of purchasing or manufacturing those goods. You should understand that the costs of the unused inventory should not be included in this figure. These costs are carried forward into the next accounting period where they will be used to manufacture goods that are sold in that period.
- The goods carried forward are classified as assets on the statement of financial position.

Matching concept

The carrying forward of unused inventory is the application of the matching concept. This is an extension of the accruals concept. Inventory costs are matched the revenues they help generate.

3 Year-end adjustments

At the end of the year two basic adjustments are required to recognise opening and closing inventory correctly in the financial statements:

(1) Inventory brought forward from the previous year is assumed to have been used to generate assets for sale. It must be removed from inventory assets and recognised as an expense in the current year:

Dr	Opening inventory in costs of sales
Cr	Inventory assets

(2) The unused inventory at the end of the year is removed from purchase costs and carried forward as an asset into the next year:

Dr	Inventory assets
Cr	Closing inventory in cost of sales

Once these entries have been completed, cost of sales is correctly stated by including the opening inventory and excluding the closing inventory. **The inventory ledger account shows the closing inventory for the asset remaining at the end of the year.**

Ledger accounts

In a business that has been trading for more than one year, there will be a balance on the inventory account at the start of the period, which will be a debit balance (representing an asset). Let us assume opening inventory of $500. The inventory account at the start of the period would appear as follows:

Inventory

20X1		$			$
1 Jan	Balance	500			

At the end of the year the trading account is being prepared, the opening inventory is transferred into it, by crediting the inventory account and debiting the trading account. The inventory account then appears as follows:

Inventory

20X1		$			$
1 Jan	Balance	500	31Dec	Trading account	500

The inventory account now has no balance, so it can be 'closed off'.

As the preparation of the trading account continues, it will be necessary to determine the value of the inventory at the end of the year. The figure is passed to the bookkeeper, who then debits the inventory account with the new value, and credits the trading account. Let us assume an example of closing inventory of $430.

The inventory account now appears as follows:

Inventory

20X1		$	20X1		$
1 Jan	Balance	500	31 Dec	Trading account	500
31 Dec	Trading account	430			

The trading account would now look as follows:

Trading account

20X1		$	20X1		$
1 Jan	Opening inventory	500	31 Dec	Sales	X
31 Dec	Purchases	X		Closing inventory	430

The trading account thus brings together the revenue and costs of the trading function for a specified period of time, and by comparing them calculates the **gross profit**, being the balance remaining on the trading account.

We have seen that the revenue from the sale of goods is compared with the cost of those goods in the trading account and the resulting difference is referred to as gross profit. This figure is the balance on the trading account.

This balance is then transferred to the income statement account.

Here is an example of a trading account using assumed amounts for sales, returns and purchases in addition to the above mentioned opening and closing inventory.

Trading account for the year ended 31 December 20X1		
	$	$
Sales		9,400
Less: returns inwards		(300)
		9,100
Opening inventory	500	
Purchases	6,400	
	6,900	
Less: closing inventory	(430)	
		6,470
Gross profit		2,630

4 Valuing inventory

Inventory should be **valued at the lower of cost and net realisable value** (NRV).

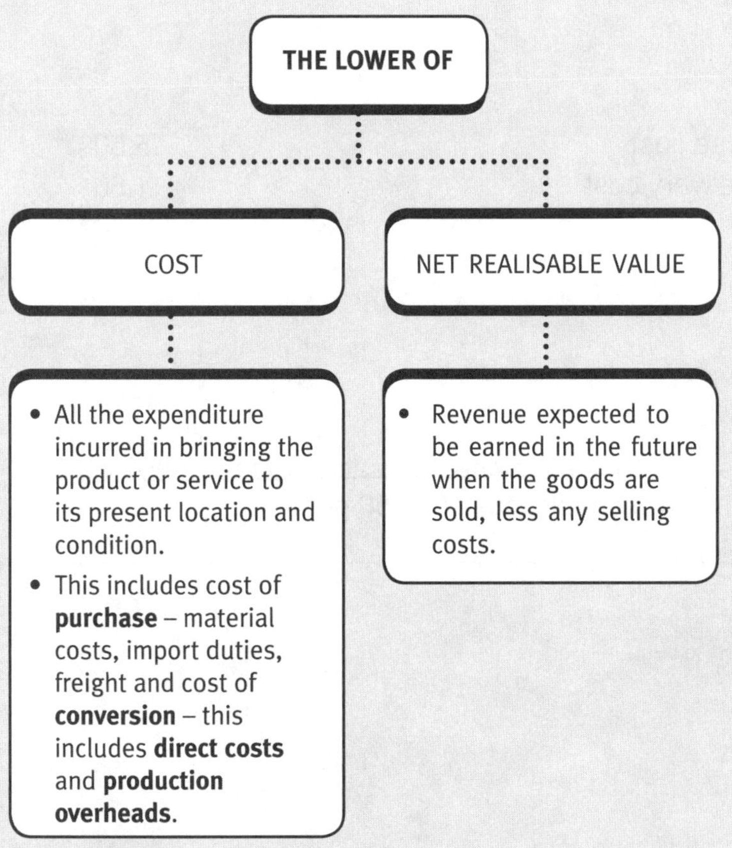

Costs which must be **excluded** from the cost of inventory are:

- overheads (with the exception of production overheads);
- selling costs;
- storage costs;
- abnormal waste of materials, labour or other costs;
- administrative overheads.

Cost versus NRV

For example, if some items have been bought at a cost of $5 each but, owing to market conditions, they can be sold for just $6 each and the cost of packaging and delivering them to customers is $1.50 each, it can be seen that

Cost	$5.00
Net realisable value ($6 – $1.50)	$4.50

In other words, when the items are eventually sold for $6 each there will be a loss of $0.50 per item.

	$	$
Selling price		6.00
Less: Purchase cost	5.50	
Packaging/delivery cost	1.50	
		(6.5)
Loss		(0.5)

By valuing the inventory at their net realisable value of $4.50 we are recognising the foreseeable loss of $0.50 per item.

The fall in value should be recognised as soon as it is known about. Suppose that we bought 100 units of the above item, and sold 60 in the first month, with the remainder being carried forward to the next month. The calculation of the loss in the first month would be as follows:

	$	$
Sales (60 × $6.00)		360
Less: cost of sales		
Purchases (100 × $5.00)	500	
Packaging costs (60 × $1.50)	90	
	590	
Less: closing inventory (40 × $4.50)	(180)	(410)
Loss		(50)

The whole of the loss is accounted for in the first month, not just the loss on those sold. In the second month, assuming the remaining items were all sold, the calculation would be as follows:

	$	$
Sales (40 × $6.00)		240
Less: cost of sales		
Opening inventory (as above)	180	
Packaging costs (40 × $1.50)	60	
		(240)
Profit/(Loss)		–

This treatment is an example of applying the convention of '**prudence**', which is explained more fully in chapter 15.

Test your understanding 1

S & Co. sells three products – Basic, Super and Luxury. The following information was available at the year end:

	Basic $ per unit	Super $ per unit	Luxury $ per unit
Original cost	6	9	18
Estimated selling price	9	12	15
Selling and distribution costs	1	4	5

	Units	Units	Units
Units in inventories	200	250	150

The value of inventory at the year end should be:

$............

5 Methods of calculating the cost of inventory

IAS 2 allows inventory to be calculated using either of the following methods:

- Unit cost;
- FIFO (first in first out);
- AVCO (average cost).

IAS 2 does not allow the use of LIFO (last in first out) but students should be aware of this method.

Further detail

UNIT COST

This is the actual cost of purchasing identifiable units of inventory.

FIFO

With this method of costing it is assumed that the oldest inventory are sold first, thereby leaving the business with a higher quantity of recently purchased goods, i.e. the first goods bought in are assumed to be the first goods sold. This provides an up-to-date costing method for existing inventory as it uses a recent purchase price to value the majority of goods.

AVCO

With this costing method we work out an average cost per unit prior to the sale of goods and use that to cost the remaining inventory.

LIFO

With this method of costing it is assumed that the newest inventory are sold first, thereby leaving the business with a higher quantity of oldest purchased goods. This provides an out of date costing method for existing inventory as it uses the oldest purchase price to value the majority of goods.

The value of inventory is obtained at a particular point in time – there are two ways to achieve this: either physically measure the quantity of inventory held at that time and then value it, or record the movement of inventory on a regular basis and verify such records randomly over a period of time. These inventory records are then used as the basis of the measurement.

Physical inventory count

The physical measurement of the quantity of inventory held at a particular time is known as a physical inventory count or stock-taking. It is not always possible to count inventory at the time required and in these circumstances cut-off procedures are applied to ensure that inventory movements between the date of the count and the year end are allocated to the correct accounting period.

Example 9.A

On 3 June, a physical inventory count was carried out that revealed that XYZ Ltd held 405 units of inventory. According to the company's records they had received a delivery of 250 units on 2 June and had sold 110 units since 31 May.

Solution

The inventory that existed on 31 May were therefore:

	Units
Quantity as per physical inventory count	405
Add: units sold/used before physical inventory count	110
Less: units received before the physical inventory count	(250)
Inventory on 31 May	265

The cost measurement of these items is then obtained by multiplying the quantity by the cost per unit.

This technique is most common in small organisations. Larger organisations keep records of the movement of inventory using bin cards or stores ledger cards, but even so they should physically check their inventories from time to time and compare it with the inventory recorded on the bin or stores ledger card, and make any necessary investigations and/or adjustments.

A bin card is a document, traditionally made of cardboard, on which is manually recorded the movement of inventory. It is called a bin card because in storekeeping terminology a 'bin' is the location of an item in the stores. This record is usually kept with the items in the stores so that any movement of the inventory is recorded as it occurs.

The stores ledger card is similar except that in addition to recording quantities, cost values are also recorded so that the value of inventory can be seen at any time.

Each item of inventory has its own inventory reference code and bin card/stores ledger card.

Application of methods of inventory measurement (also known as cost formulas)

Consider the following information regarding the movements of inventory during March:

1 Mar	Opening inventory Nil
2 Mar	Bought 10 units @ $3 each
7 Mar	Bought 20 units @ $4 each
10 Mar	Sold 15 units @ $8 each
13 Mar	Bought 20 units @ $5 each
17 Mar	Sold 5 units @ $8 each

Using these figures we can calculate that the inventory remaining after these transactions had occurred was 30 units. The difficulty is in measuring those units. Are the remaining inventory made up of items bought recently, or is it made up of items bought earlier? Or is a mixture of the two? How do we know?

Well, in practice, we do not know. It is up to the storekeeper to exercise good management of inventory, but it is up to the accountant to determine the cost of those inventory. Three cost formulas (or methods) are commonly used in financial accounting. Each of them gives different measurements of the closing inventory. Each of these methods will now be considered.

FIFO - This cost formula assumes that the items bought earliest are those used (or sold) first. This assumption is made only for cost purposes, it does not have any connection with the physical usage of the inventory.

Stores ledger card FIFO

Date	Units	Receipts $/unit	$	Units	Issues $/unit	$	Units	Balance $/unit	$
1 Mar							Nil		Nil
2 Mar	10	3	30				10	3	30
7 Mar	20	4	80				20	4	80
10 Mar				10	3	30			
				5	4	20	15	4	60
13 Mar	20	5	100				20	5	100
17 Mar				5	4	20	10	4	40
							20	5	100
Totals	50		210	20		70	30		140

Note that the card is 'ruled off' each time there is an 'issue' of inventory.

This cost formula gives a closing inventory cost of $140 and the cost of sales (obtained by totalling the cost of each issue) amounted to $70. Using this cost formula, the trading account would be as follows:

	$	$
Sales (20 units @ $8)		160
Opening inventory	Nil	
Purchases	210	
	210	
Closing inventory	(140)	
Cost of sales		(70)
Gross profit		90

LIFO - This cost formula assumes that the items bought most recently are those used first. Again, this assumption is made only for cost purposes, it does not have any connection with the physical usage of the inventory.

Using the earlier information regarding movement of inventory in March, the LIFO method would produce the following results:

Stores ledger card – LIFO

Date	Units	Receipts $/unit	$	Units	Issues $/unit	$	Units	Balance $/unit	$
1 Mar							Nil		Nil
2 Mar	10	3	30				10	3	30
7 Mar	20	4	80				20	4	80
10 Mar				15	4	60	10	3	30
							5	4	20
13 Mar	20	5	100				20	5	100
17 Mar				5	5	25	10	3	30
							5	4	20
							15	5	75
Totals	50		210	20		85	30		125

This cost formula gives a closing inventory cost of $125 and the cost of sales (obtained by totalling the cost of each issue) amounted to $85. Using this cost formula, the trading account would be as follows:

	$	$
Sales (20 units @ $8)		160
Opening inventory	Nil	
Purchases	210	
	210	
Closing inventory	(125)	
Cost of sales		(85)
Gross profit		75

You can see that this results in a **higher cost of sales** total than with the FIFO cost formula, and hence a **lower gross profit**, in times of inflation. It also results in a lower closing inventories figure, as the inventories are valued at earlier prices. **The cost formula is not acceptable when preparing financial statements for external reporting although it may be useful for management accounts**. It can be argued that the profit is more realistic than with the FIFO cost formula, as it values cost of sales at a value nearer to the current cost of replacing the inventory sold with new inventory.

AVCO - This cost formula recalculates a new weighted average cost each time a new delivery of units is received using the formula:

$$\frac{\text{Previous balance value} + \text{new receipts value}}{\text{Previous units} + \text{new units}}$$

Issues are then valued at the new weighted average cost.

Using the earlier information regarding movement of inventory in March, the AVCO method would produce the following results:

Stores ledger card – Weighted average

Date	Units	Receipts $/unit	$	Units	Issues $/unit	$	Units	Balance $/unit	$
1 Mar							Nil		Nil
2 Mar	10	3	30				10	3	30
7 Mar	20	4	80				30	3.6	110
10 Mar				15	3.6	55	15	3.6	55
13 Mar	20	5	100				35	4.4	155
17 Mar				5	4.4	22	30	4.4	133
Totals	50		210	20		77			

This cost formula gives a closing inventory cost of $133 and the cost of sales (obtained by totalling the cost of each issue) amounted to $77.

Using this cost formula the trading account would be as follows:

	$	$
Sales (20 units @ $8)		160
Opening inventory	Nil	
Purchases	210	
Closing inventory	(133)	
Cost of sales		(77)
Gross profit		83

You can see from this example that, in times of rising prices, the weighted average cost formula gives a lower closing inventory cost than FIFO and, consequently, a lower profit, but a higher closing inventory cost than the LIFO cost formula, and consequently a higher profit. It is an acceptable cost formula for reporting in financial statements.

It might be useful for you to see the profit calculation of the three cost formulas together, to compare them:

	FIFO	LIFO	AVCO
	$	$	$
Sales	160	160	160
Less: cost of sales			
Opening inventory	Nil	Nil	Nil
Purchases	210	210	210
Less closing inventory	(140)	(125)	(133)
	(70)	(85)	(77)
Gross profit	90	75	83

Issues and receipts

The three examples above used the words 'receipts' to mean 'purchases' and 'issues' to mean 'sales', but note that 'receipts' could also include inventory returned by customers, and 'issues' could also include inventory returned to suppliers. 'Issues' could also mean inventory taken out of the general store and sent to another department, for example, a production department.

Take care when doing exercises that require you to calculate cost of sales and purchases, as well as the closing cost of inventory, if your receipts and issues columns contain items other than sales and purchases. Remember also that the sales column indicates the cost of sales, not the selling price.

Test your understanding 2

M Lord had inventory on 1 January 20X1 consisting of 400 articles bought at $4 each. His purchases during the month of January consisted of 800 at $4.20 each purchased on 8 January, and 2,000 at $3.80 each on 18 January. He sold 2,400 at $5.00 each on 28 January. Forty of those sold were returned in perfect condition on 31 January.

Required:

(a) to ascertain, by means of an inventory account:

- the number of articles held in inventory on 31 January 20X1;
- the unit price and total cost of the inventory.

(b) to show the trading account for the month ended 31 January 20X1;

Note: Lord uses the FIFO cost formula.

6 Chapter summary

In this chapter you have been introduced to the importance of inventory in the financial statements. In particular we have looked at:

- year-end adjustments;
- inventory in the financial statements;
- inventory valuation;
- inventory records.

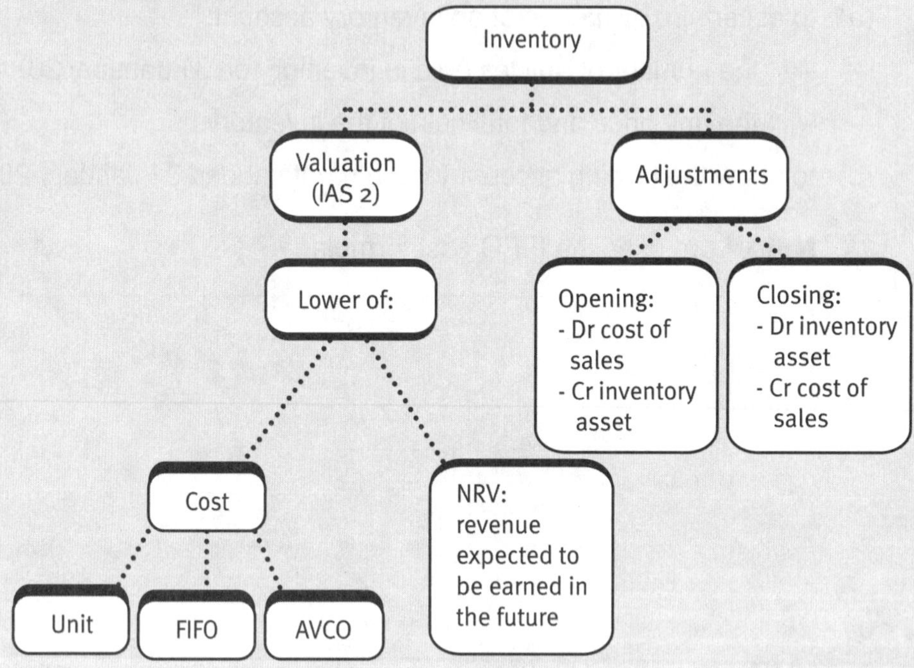

Test your understanding questions.

Test your understanding 3

The following totals appear in the daybooks for March 20X8:

	Goods exc. sales tax	Sales tax
	$	$
Sales daybook	40,000	7,000
Purchases daybook	20,000	3,500
Returns inwards daybook	2,000	350
Returns outwards daybook	4,000	700

Both opening and closing inventory are $3,000. The gross profit for March 20X8 is:

$...........

Test your understanding 4

Inventory is valued using FIFO. Opening inventory was 10 units at $2 each. Purchases were 30 units at $3 each, then issues of 12 units were made, followed by issues of 8 units. Closing inventory was:

$...........

Test your understanding 5

In times of rising prices, the FIFO cost formula for inventories cost, when compared with the average cost method, will usually produce:

A a higher profit and a lower closing inventory value

B a higher profit and a higher closing inventory value

C a lower profit and a lower closing inventory value

D a lower profit and a higher closing inventory value

Test your understanding 6

Your firm uses the weighted average cost formula for inventory. On 1 October 20X8, there were 60 units in inventory valued at $12 each. On 8 October, 40 units were purchased for $15 each, and a further 50 units were purchased for $18 each on 14 October. On 21 October, 75 units were sold for $1,200. The value of closing inventory at 31 October 20X8 was:

$............

Test your understanding 7

A firm uses the LIFO cost formula. Information regarding inventory movements during a particular month are as follows:

1	Opening balance	200 units valued at $1,600
10	Purchases	800 units for $8,000
14	Sales	400 units for $4,800
21	Purchases	800 units for $10,000
23	Sales	600 units for $9,000

The cost of inventory at the end of the month would be:

$............

Test your understanding 8

The inventory record card shows the following details:

1 Feb	50 units in inventory at a cost of $40 per unit
7 Feb	100 units purchased at a cost of $45 per unit
14 Feb	80 units sold
21 Feb	50 units purchased at a cost of $50 per unit
28 Feb	60 units sold

What is the cost of inventory at 28 February using the FIFO cost formula?

$............

Test your understanding 9

When measuring inventory at cost, which of the following shows the correct method of arriving at cost?

	Include inward transport costs	Include production overheads
A	Yes	No
B	No	Yes
C	Yes	Yes
D	No	No

Test your understanding answers

Test your understanding 1

	Cost ($)	Net realisable value ($)	Lower of cost & NRV ($)	Units	Cost ($)
Basic	6	8	6	200	1,200
Super	9	8	8	250	2,000
Luxury	18	10	10	150	1,500
					4,700

Test your understanding 2

Date	Units	Receipts $/unit	$	Units	Issues $/unit	$	Units	Balance $/unit	$
1 Jan							400	4.00	1,600
8 Jan	800	4.20	3,360				800	4.20	3,360
18 Jan	2,000	3.80	7,600				2,000	3.80	7,600
28 Jan				400	4.00	1,600			
				800	4.20	3,360			
				1,200	3.80	4,560	800	3.80	3,040
31 Jan	40	3.80	152				840	3.80	3,192

(a) Inventory at 31 January – 840 articles.

Unit price $3.80, total cost $3,192.

(b) Trading account for January:

	$	$
Sales (2,400 x $5)		12,000
Less: returns (40 x $5)		(200)
		11,800
Opening inventory	1,600	
Purchases	10,960	
	12,560	
Less: closing inventory	(3,192)	
Cost of sales		(9,368)
Gross profit		2,432

Test your understanding 3

Reconstruction of the trading account

	$	$
Sales		40,000
Less: Returns inwards		(2,000)
		38,000
Less: Opening inventory	3,000	
Purchases	20,000	
Returns outwards	(4,000)	
Closing inventory	(3,000)	
		(16,000)
Gross Profit		22,000

Test your understanding 4

FIFO means the oldest inventory will be issued first leaving the most recent purchases in stock. The first issues (12 units) would use up the opening inventory of 10 units and 2 units of the purchases at $3 each, leaving 28 units at $3 each. The next issues would be of $3 units, leaving closing inventory of 20 units at $3 each, valued at $60.

Test your understanding 5

B

The closing inventory figure reduces the cost of goods sold figure, which in turn increases the gross profit.

Therefore, a higher closing inventory figure means a lower cost of goods sold figure, and hence a higher gross profit. In times of rising prices, the FIFO cost formula will produce higher closing inventory values, and therefore a higher gross profit figure.

Test your understanding 6

Purchases	Cumulative Quantity	Cumulative Value ($)
1 October (60 × $12)	60	720
8 October (40 × $15)	100	1,320
14 October (50 × $18)	150	2,220
Issues		
21 October (75 × $14.80*)	75	1,110
	–––––	––––––
Closing inventory	75	1,110

(i.e. average cost $2,220/1502 = $14.80*)

Test your understanding 7

LIFO means the newest inventory will be issued first leaving the oldest purchases in stock.The sale of 400 units on the 14th will take up 400 of those purchased on the 10th, leaving 400 of those (valued at $4,000) and the opening inventory of 200 (valued at $1,600). Value of inventory remaining at that point is $5,600. The sale of 600 units on the 23rd will take up 600 units of those purchased on the 21st, leaving 200 of those (valued at $2,500), plus the previous balance of $5,600: total valuation of $8,100.

Test your understanding 8

FIFO means the oldest inventory will be issued first leaving the most recent purchases in stock. There are 60 units in inventory at 28 February (50 + 100 – 80 + 50 – 60) . These are deemed to comprise the 50 units purchased on 21 February at cost $50 per unit = $2,500, and 10 units from the units purchased on 7 February at $45 per unit = $450, which is $2,950 in total.

Test your understanding 9

C

chapter

10

Non-current Assets: Acquisition and Depreciation

Chapter learning objectives

When you have completed this chapter, you should be able to:

- define tangible and intangible non-current assets;
- clasify expenditure as capital or revenue;
- prepare accounting entries to record the acquisition and depreciation of tangible non-current assets;
- prepare accounts using different methods of calculating depreciation;
- prepare accounting entries to record the acquisition and amortisation of intangible non-current assets;
- prepare extracts of financial statements dealing with non-current assets.

1 Introduction

In this chapter we will look at non-current assets in relation to:

- accounting for the purchase of a tangible non-current asset;
- depreciation;
- the important distinction between capital expenditure and revenue expenditure;
- distinction between tangible and intangible non-current assets.
- amortisation;
- purchased and non-purchased goodwill.

2 Non-current assets

Non-current assets are distinguished from current assets because they:

- are a resource acquired by an organisation with the intention of using it to earn revenue for more than one accounting period;
- are not normally acquired for resale;
- could be tangible or intangible;
- are used to generate income directly or indirectly for a business;
- are not normally liquid assets (i.e. not easily and quickly converted into cash without a significant loss in value).

Examples of tangible non-current assets include land, buildings, motor vehicles, machinery and equipment.

Examples of intangible non-current assets include goodwill, development, licences and patents.

3 Capital and revenue expenditure

A business's expenditure may be classified as one of two types:

- capital expenditure – expenditure likely to increase the future earning capability of the organisation or
- revenue expenditure – expenditure associated with maintaining the organisation's present earning capability.

CAPITAL EXPENDITURE	REVENUE EXPENDITURE
• Expenditure on the acquisition of non-current assets required for use in the business, not for resale. • Expenditure on existing non-current assets aimed at increasing their earning capacity.	• Expenditure on current assets. • Expenditure relating to running the business (such as administration costs). • Expenditure on maintaining the earning capacity of non-current assets e.g. repairs and renewals.
Capital expenditure is long-term in nature as the business intends to receive the benefits of the expenditure over a long period of time.	Revenue expenditure relates to the current accounting period and is used to generate revenue in the business.

Capital and revenue expenditure

Business expenditure maybe classified as either:

Capital expenditure

- expenditure on the acquisition of non-current assets required for the use in the business, not for resale;
- expenditure on existing non-current assets aimed at increasing their earning capacity;
- capital expenditure is long-term in nature as the business intends to receive benefits of the expenditure over a long period of time.

Revenue expenditure

- expenditure on current assets;
- expenditure relating to running the business, e.g. electricity costs;
- expenditure on maintaining non-current assets, e.g. repairs;
- revenue expenditure relates to the current accounting period and is used to generate revenue in the business.

Illustration 1

Consider the situation where a computer is repaired by replacing a faulty floppy disk drive and a faulty hard drive. The replacement floppy disk drive is identical to that which it replaced. The faulty hard drive had a storage capacity of 500 megabytes, its replacement is a 5 gigabyte (i.e. 5,000 megabyte) unit. At the same time a CD-ROM drive is fitted. How should these 'repair' costs be classified?

Solution

The replacement of the faulty floppy disk drive with an identical unit is clearly a repair, and as such will be treated as an expense.

The fitting of the CD-ROM drive is clearly not a repair because the computer did not have a CD-ROM drive previously. This is an addition to the asset, which should be capitalised.

It is the cost of the hard disk drive that presents the classification problem. To the extent that it replaced the original hard drive it is a repair, but the new drive has ten times the capacity of the original. As it enhances the storage capacity of the computer it is capital expenditure. Thus this cost must be divided, part of it is treated as an expense and the remainder as capital expenditure.

The distinction between capital and revenue expenditure is important because of the implications for the financial statements. Revenue expenditure will be reflected in full in the measurement of profit in the period in which it is incurred. In contrast, capital expenditure will be reflected in an increase in asset values in the statement of financial position. This will diminish over the life of the asset as it is depreciated (see later), with a corresponding reduction in the profit reported.

Test your understanding 1

Classify each of the following transactions into capital or revenue expenditure transactions:

- Complete repaint of existing building.
- Installation of a new central heating system.
- Repainting of a delivery van.
- Providing drainage for a new piece of water-extraction equipment.
- Legal fees on the acquisition of land.
- Carriage costs on a replacement part for a piece of machinery.

4 Acquisition of a non-current asset

The cost of a non-current asset is any amount incurred to acquire the asset and bring it into working condition.

Includes

Capital expenditure such as:

- purchase price
- delivery costs
- legal fees
- subsequent expenditure which enhances the asset
- trials and tests

Excludes

Revenue expenditure such as:

- repairs
- renewals
- repainting
- administration
- general overheads
- wastage
- training costs

The correct double entry to record the purchase is:

Debit	Non-current asset account	X
Credit	Cash/bank/payable account	X

A separate cost account should be kept for each category of non-current asset, e.g. motor vehicles, fixtures and fittings.

Subsequent expenditure

Subsequent expenditure on the non-current asset can only be recorded as part of the cost (or capitalised), if it enhances the benefits of the asset, i.e. increases the revenues capable of being generated by the asset.

An example of subsequent expenditure which meets this criterion, and so can be capitalised, is an extension to a shop building which provides extra selling space.

An example of subsequent expenditure which does not meet this criterion is repair work. Any repair costs must be debited to the income statement, i.e. expensed.

5 Depreciation

- The cost of the non-current asset will contribute to the organisation's ability to earn revenue for a number of accounting periods. It would be unfair if the total cost was treated as an expense in the income statement in the year of acquisition.
- Instead, the cost is spread over all of the accounting periods in which the asset is expected to be making a contribution to earnings (this is known as the asset's **useful life**).
- The process by which this is achieved is called **depreciation.**
- **IAS 16 Property, Plant and Equipment**, defines depreciation as 'the measure of the cost or revalued amount of the economic benefits of the tangible non-current asset that has been consumed during the period'.
- In simple terms, depreciation spreads the cost of the asset over the period in which it will be used.
- Depreciation matches the cost of using a non-current asset to the revenues generated by that asset over its useful life.
- Depreciation must also be matched to the pattern of use of the asset.
- This must be regularly reviewed and may be changed if the method no longer matches the usage of the asset.
- This is achieved by recording a depreciation charge each year, the effect of which is two-fold ('the dual effect'), i.e. reduce the statement of financial position value of the non-current asset by cumulative depreciation to reflect the wearing out. Record the annual depreciation charge as an expense in the income statement to match to the revenue generated by the non-current asset.

Further detail on depreciation

We shall look at the calculation of depreciation in detail in the next section. For now, we shall just focus on the main principles.

- When we acquire a non-current asset, we credit cash (or payables), and debit an account called 'non-current assets' or 'plant and machinery' or another suitable description.
- If we were to prepare a set of financial statements immediately afterwards we would display the balance on the asset account – the cost of the asset – on the statement of financial position. It would not appear as an expense in the income statement at all, because we have not yet begun to 'consume' it in earning revenue.
- During the periods that the asset is in use – its useful life – we must allocate its original cost on some fair basis. An appropriate proportion of the cost must be recorded as an expense – called depreciation charge – in the income statement of each period concerned.
- We achieve this by, in effect, changing the balance in the asset account. Each year we decide that some proportion of the original cost has now been 'consumed' in operating the business. This proportion is transferred to the income statement, where it is shown as an expense, and the amount remaining on the statement of financial position is correspondingly reduced. (This remaining balance is referred to as the **carrying amount or carrying value of the asset.**)
- Eventually we reach a point where the whole of the original cost has been consumed and the carrying amount or carrying value for the asset on the statement of financial position has declined to zero (or perhaps to some small residual value may be realised on disposal).

It is extremely important to understand this basic notion of depreciation as a means of allocating the cost of a non-current asset over a number of accounting periods. It has nothing whatever to do with 'valuing' the asset, in the sense of estimating what its fair value might be at the end of each accounting period. (Fair value is the estimated amount for which an asset could be sold.) Indeed, it is not likely, in general, that the carrying amount or value of a non-current asset is anything like an approximation to its fair value. Nor does depreciation have anything to do with providing a fund for replacing the non-current asset when it is consumed. The process of transferring amounts from statement of financial position to income statement each year does not in any sense generate funds for the business. It may indeed be desirable to plan ahead for asset replacement by setting aside cash for the purpose, but this is an exercise quite separate from the process of charging depreciation.

6 Calculating depreciation

There are a number of methods that accountants use to depreciate a non-current asset. The two most common methods that are used are:

- straight-line and
- reducing balance.

In this section of the chapter we will use the same basic information about a single non-current asset:

Cost – 1 January 20X5	$50,000
Estimated useful life	10 years
Estimated residual value at the end of its life (residual value)	$1,280

The straight-line method

- This method allows an equal amount to be charged as depreciation to each accounting period over the expected useful life of the asset.
- If the depreciation charge were to be shown on a graph it would be a straight line parallel to the horizontal axis (hence the name of the method).
- Buildings are commonly depreciated using this method because businesses will commonly get the same usage out of a building every year.
- The amount to be charged to each accounting period is given by the formula:

$$\text{Depreciation per annum} = \frac{\text{Original cost} - \text{estimated residual value}}{\text{Estimated useful life}}$$

OR

% × Cost

Residual value: the estimated disposal value of the asset at the end of its useful life.

Useful life: the estimated number of years during which the business will use the asset.

Using the data above, the annual depreciation charge would be

$$\frac{\$50,000 - \$1,280}{10} = \$4,872$$

Futher detail

The effect of the above would be that the carrying amount of the asset shown in the organisation's statement of financial position would be reduced by $4,872 each year. The corresponding effect would be to reduce profits in the income statement by charging depreciation as an expense.

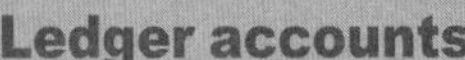

Ledger accounts

The example above shows the depreciation account in respect of the single asset used in the example; however, each asset would not normally have a separate ledger account. While it is necessary to calculate the depreciation of each asset separately, it is usual for the ledger accounts to summarise the depreciation charge and the accumulated depreciation in respect of different categories of assets such as buildings, motor vehicles, and plant and equipment.

The reducing-balance method

- Some assets give a greater service – and therefore depreciate more – in their early years than they do in later years. For this reason, it is considered sensible to charge a higher amount of depreciation in the earlier years. This method of depreciation is known as the reducing-balance method.
- Depreciation charge = X % × carrying value (CV).
- The reducing balance method results in a constantly reducing depreciation charge throughout the life of the asset. This is used to reflect the expectation that the asset will be used less and less as it ages.
- This is a common method of depreciation for vehicles, where it is expected that they will provide less service to the business as they age because of the increased need to service/repair them as their mileage increases.

CV: original cost of the non-current asset less accumulated depreciation on the asset to date.

This can be illustrated using the data from the previous example. For the purposes of the illustration this will be 31%.

	$	
Original cost	50,000	
Year 1 depreciation	15,500	(31% of 50,000)
	34,500	
Year 2 depreciation	10,695	(31% of 34,500)
	23,805	
Year 3 depreciation	7,380	(31% of 23,805)
	16,425	

Further detail

At the end of the asset's useful life the remaining amount should equal its estimated residual value of $1,280 subject to any difference caused by rounding the percentage to be used for the amounts of annual depreciation.

The double-entry bookkeeping will be the same in principle as that illustrated earlier for the straight-line method. Clearly, though, the amount charged as an expense and the corresponding reduction in the value of the asset will be different depending on the method of depreciation used, until the end of the asset's useful life.

We can summarise the two methods as follows:

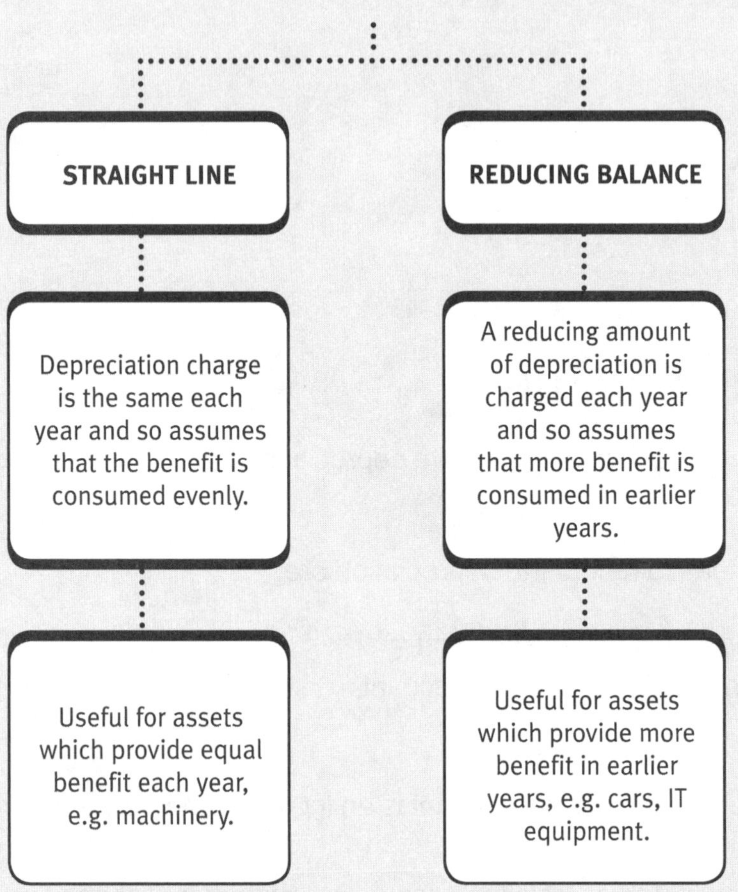

Test your understanding 2

Kalem has been running a successful pizza business since 20X1.

He bought the following assets as the pizza business grew:

- a new oven for the kitchen at a cost of $2,000 (purchased 1 December 20X4).
- a van for deliveries for $18,000 (purchased 1 June 20X4).

He depreciates the oven at 10% straight line and the van at 25% reducing balance. A full year's depreciation is charged in the year of purchase and none in the year of disposal.

What is the total depreciation charge for the year ended 31 October 20X6?

A $2,531

B $2,700

C $4,231

D $2,731

7 Accounting for depreciation

Whichever method is used to calculate depreciation, the accounting remains the same.

The ledger entries to record the depreciation are:

Debit	Depreciation expense account	X
Credit	Accumulated depreciation account	X

- The depreciation expense account is an income statement account and therefore is not cumulative.
- The accumulated depreciation account is a statement of financial position account and as the name suggests is cumulative, i.e. reflects all depreciation to date.
- On the statement of financial position it is shown as a reduction against the cost of non-current assets:

	$
Cost	X
Accumulated depreciation	(X)
Carrying value (CV)	X

Using the straight-line method example as each year passes, the balance on the accumulated depreciation account will increase as follows:

	Accumulated depreciation	
		$
31 Dec X5	Income statement	4,872
31 Dec X6	Income statement	4,872
		9,744
31 Dec X7	Income statement	4,872
		14,616

and the asset would be shown on the statement of financial position as follows:

	Cost ($)	**Accum. depreciation ($)**	**Carrying amount ($)**
(31 Dec 20X5) NCA	50,000	(4,872)	45,128
(31 Dec 20X6) NCA	50,000	(9,744)	40,256
(31 Dec 20X7) NCA	50,000	(14,616)	35,384

The depreciation expense account will be transferred to the income statement and should only reflect the depreciation for the **current year**.

The accumulated depreciation account will be shown on the statement of financial position and netted off against the cost of non-current assets. The accumulated depreciation account should always reflect the **cumulative** depreciation on the asset.

Test your understanding 3

A machine is purchased on 1 May 20X0 for $1,000 cash. The financial year ends on 30 April each year.

Show the account or accounts in the ledger for the first 3 years assuming that the machine is depreciated by 20 per cent per annum on the reducing-balance method.

Income statement and statement of financial position entries are not required.

The machine-hour method/units of production method

Some non-current assets depreciate according to their usage. If the asset has a measurable 'life' in terms of the number of hours it is likely to be used, or the number of units of output it is likely to produce, it can be depreciated according to that rate.

For example, a computer printer might have an expected total output of 50,000 sheets. If it produces 10,000 sheets in a year, it can be said to have used up one-fifth of its cost in that year.

Depreciation in the year of acquisition and disposal

If a non-current asset is bought or sold in the period, there are two ways in which the depreciation could be accounted for:

- provide a full year's depreciation in the year of acquisition and none in the year of disposal, or
- monthly or pro-rata depreciation, based on the exact number of months that the asset has been owned.

8 Accounting for intangible non-current assets

An intangible asset : An asset that does not have a physical substance, for example trademarks and patents.

- Intangibles can be purchased or internally generated, e.g. brand names.
- Generally purchased intangibles are capitalised and internally generated are not.
- Amortisation must be charged on intangibles capitalised which is a reflection of the wearing out of the asset.

Amortisation is really the same as depreciation but a term we use for intangible assets. The asset cost will be reduced by amortisation on the statement of financial position and the amortisation will be charged as an expense each year to the income statement.

Examples of intangibles are:

- development costs;
- goodwill;
- brands;
- copyrights;
- licences;
- trademarks.

What is goodwill?

Goodwill: The difference between the fair value of a business as a whole and the aggregate of the fair values of the separable and identifiable assets and liabilities. This implies that it is not possible to identify goodwill separately from the business, and this is largely because it is an intangible asset.

The definition above explains that goodwill is the value placed upon a business in excess of the sum of its individual assets; thus goodwill represents the value of the business continuing as a going concern, as compared with its assets being sold individually.

However, it could be said to be more than that. All established businesses have some goodwill. Goodwill comprises business contacts, good staff relations, the right to occupy certain pieces of land and so on. All of these have a value – the difficulty lies in placing a value on them.

Purchased and non-purchased goodwill

When a business first starts, it is either created by its owners or purchased from an existing business. In the latter case there will have been a certain amount of negotiation over the purchase price. The vendors will obviously seek to obtain the highest price possible, whereas the purchaser will seek to minimise the price. It is likely, however, that the final price will be greater than the purchaser's valuation of the tangible assets taken over. This is accepted because the price includes the rights to the existing business's customer base, possibly its name, its staff, and their experience and expertise, and so on. This difference is the goodwill and, more precisely, is said to be **purchased goodwill.**

However, whether the business is created as a new start-up business or is the result of the acquisition of another business, new goodwill is earned or created by the new owners over a period of time. This is known as **non-purchased goodwill**.

Accounting treatment

- The accounting treatment of purchased goodwill is for the purchaser to place a fair value on the net tangible assets (i.e. assets–liabilities) of the business acquired and to consider the difference between the sum of these values and the total purchase price to be goodwill.
- This amount is debited to the goodwill ledger account. The purchaser will hope that the value of the goodwill will at least be maintained and that, if he were to sell the business, he would be paid for its goodwill.

However, it is important to note, when applying the concept of prudence, that assets should not be overstated. It could be that the factors which caused goodwill to exist in the past, for example location and customer base, no longer apply and that the value of the goodwill is now less than the price paid for it.

- It is therefore necessary to estimate, on an annual basis, the value of the goodwill.
- If the current estimated value is less than the amount in the statement of financial position, then the goodwill is said to be 'impaired'.
- Impairment occurs when the value of a non-current asset is less than its carrying amount in the statement of financial position.
- In this situation, the goodwill is reduced to its new lower value and the difference (the 'impairment') is charged to the income statement as an expense.

It may be noted that impairment can also apply to tangible and other non-tangible non-current assets and will occur at any time that the carrying amount of an asset in a statement of financial position is overstated.

Non-purchased goodwill

Non-purchased (or 'internal') goodwill is **not recognised** in the statement of financial position. The reason for this is that it is not possible to obtain a reliable measurement of its value. In the case of purchased goodwill, the fact that someone has paid for goodwill does mean that it has a value and that this can be measured by the price paid. In the case of internal goodwill, there has been no such external transaction and there is no basis on which the internal goodwill can be valued.

Illustration 2

X Ltd has recently acquired the assets and liabilities of A Ltd for $1,500,000. The assets and liabilities acquired were valued by X Ltd as follows:

	$
Land and buildings	750,000
Plant and equipment	240,000
Inventories	65,000
Receivables	38,000
Payables	(41,000)
	1,052,000

Required:

Calculation the value of goodwill on the purchase of X Ltd.

Solution

The difference between the sum of the individual net assets $1,052,000 and the purchase price $1,500,000 is goodwill. In this illustration the value of goodwill is $448,000.

If in the future X Ltd values the goodwill at only $400,000, then the impairment of $48,000 will be charged to the income statement and the goodwill in the statement of financial position will be reduced to $400,000.

9 The valuation of intangible assets

Intangible assets affect the value of a business and challenge our use of the historical cost convention. They are all items that cause accountants difficulty in their valuation, mainly because of the subjective nature of the value of such items. The general principle on which all intangibles are valued is whether or not they have the potential to earn profits in the future. In other words, do they provide an economic benefit to the business, and can it be quantified with a reasonable degree of accuracy?

We shall look at one of the intangibles above in order to appreciate the difficulties involved and the approach to be taken in their valuation.

The valuation of research and development costs

Some businesses spend money on research and development (R&D), and this gives difficulties for accountants.

Research

- All research expenditure should be written off to the income statement as it is incurred.
- This is in compliance with the prudence concept.
- Research expenditure may or may not directly lead to future benefits and therefore it is not possible to follow the matching concept. Research is often too remote to predict with any certainty. It may lead to a development project or it may not, the results may be that the project is not possible, or at least not for a long period of time.
- Any capital expenditure on research equipment should be capitalised and depreciated as normal.

Development

- Development expenditure must be capitalised as an intangible asset on the statement of financial position provided that certain criteria are met:
  - **S**eparate project;
  - **E**xpenditure identifiable and reliably measured;
  - **C**ommercially viable;
  - **T**echnically feasible;
  - **O**verall profitable;
  - **R**esources available to complete;
- Any development expenditure capitalised must be then amortised over its useful life when the product or production method commences.
- If the above criteria are not met, development expenditure must be written off to the income statement as it is incurred.
- Once expenditure has been treated as an expense, it cannot be reinstated as an asset.

Amortisation

If the useful life of an intangible asset is finite, its capitalised development costs must be amortised once commercial exploitation begins.

The amortisation method used should reflect the pattern in which the asset's economic benefits are consumed by the enterprise. If that pattern cannot be determined reliably, the straight-line method should be used.

An intangible asset with an indefinite useful life should not be amortised.

An asset has an indefinite useful life if there is no foreseeable limit to the period over which the asset is expected to generate net cash inflows for the business.

10 Chapter summary

In this chapter, we have looked at the accounting issues associated with non-current assets. These issues can be summarised as:

- the classification of expenditure as capital or revenue;
- the difference between tangible and intangible non-current assets;
- the allocation of non-current asset cost to accounting periods using depreciation;
- accounting entries to record the acquisition and depreciation of tangible non-current assets;
- the calculation of depreciation using both the straight-line and reducing balance method;
- accounting entries to record the acquisition and amortisation of intangible non-current assets;
- the distinction between purchased and non-purchased goodwill;
- research and development.

Test your understanding questions.

Test your understanding 4

The most appropriate definition of depreciation is:

A a means of determining the decrease in fair value of an asset over time

B a means of allocating the cost of an asset over a number of accounting periods

C a means of setting funds aside for the replacement of the asset

D a means of estimating the fair value of the asset

Test your understanding 5

The phrase 'carrying amount or value' when applied to non-current assets means that

A the assets are shown in the statement of financial position at their original cost

B the assets are valued at their likely selling price

C the assets have been depreciated using the reducing-balance method

D the assets are shown in the statement of financial position at their cost less accumulated depreciation

Test your understanding 6

W Ltd bought a new printing machine from abroad. The cost of the machine was $80,000. The installation costs were $5,000 and the employees received training on how to use this particular machine, at a cost of $2,000. Before using the machine to print customers' orders, a test was undertaken and the paper and ink cost $1,000. What should be the cost of the machine in the company's statement of financial position.

$. . . . .

Test your understanding 7

Which one of the following should be accounted for as capital expenditure?

A The cost of painting a building

B The replacement of windows in a building

C The purchase of a car by a garage for resale

D Legal fees incurred on the purchase of a building

Test your understanding 8

Which of the following statements regarding goodwill is not correct?

A Goodwill is classed as an intangible non-current asset

B Goodwill is the excess of the value of a business as a whole over the fair value of its separable net assets

C Purchased goodwill may be shown on the statement of financial position and may be reduced by impairment

D Non-purchased goodwill is a liability

Test your understanding answers

Test your understanding 1

- Complete repaint: revenue expenditure.
- Installation of new heating system: capital expenditure.
- Repainting van: revenue expenditure.
- Drainage for new equipment: capital expenditure.
- Legal fees on acquisition of land: capital expenditure.
- Carriage costs on replacement part: revenue expenditure.

Test your understanding 2

D

	20X6 $
Oven	
$2,000 × 10%	200
Van	
20X4: $18,000 × 25% = $4,500	
20X5: ($18,000 – $4,500) × 25% = $3,375	
20X6: ($18,000 – $4,500 – $3,375) × 25% = $2,531	2,531
Total	2,731

Test your understanding 3

Machine at cost

		$			$
20X0					
1 May	Cash	1,000			

Accumulated depreciation for machinery

		$			$
20X1			20X1		
30 Apr	Balance c/d	200	30 Apr	Income statement	200
		——			——
			20X2		
20X2			1 May	Balance b/d	200
30 Apr	Balance c/d	360	30 Apr	Income statement	160
		——			——
		360			360
		——			——
			20X3		
20X3			1 May	Balance b/d	360
30 Apr	Balance c/d	488	30 Apr	Income statement	128
		——			——
		488			488
		——			——
			20X4		
			1 May	Balance b/d	488

Workings:

20X1 – $1,000 × 20% = $200
20X2 – ($1,000 – $200) × 20% = $160
20X3 – ($1,000 – $200 – $160) × 20% = $128

Test your understanding 4

B

Depreciation never provides a fund for the replacement of the asset, nor does it aim to show assets at their fair values.

Test your understanding 5

D

Non-current assets should, except in certain circumstances, be depreciated over their expected useful life. Answer A would almost never be appropriate. Assets are rarely valued at their expected selling price – if this is more than their cost, this would be imprudent, and if less than cost would contravene the 'going concern' convention, which is discussed in a later chapter. The method of depreciation is irrelevant.

Test your understanding 6

	$
Cost of machine	80,000
Installation	5,000
Testing	1,000
	86,000

Test your understanding 7

D

Test your understanding 8

D

A, B and C are all correct, in most situations.

chapter

11

Non-current Assets: Disposal and Revaluation

Chapter learning objectives

When you have completed this chapter, you should be able to:

- prepare accounting entries to record the disposal of tangible non-current assets, including part exchange transactions;
- calculate the profit or loss on the disposal of an asset;
- account for a revaluation of a non-current asset;
- prepare a non-current asset register;
- prepare accounts using impairment values.

1 Introduction

In this chapter we will look at non-current assets in relation to:

- disposal of an asset;
- revaluation of an asset;
- impairment of an asset;
- the non-current asset register.

2 Accounting for the disposal of a non-current asset

- At the end of the asset's life it will be either abandoned or sold. This is known as a 'disposal' in accounting terminology.
- A comparison is made of the difference between the carrying amount or value of the asset at the date of its disposal and the proceeds received (if any).
- The difference is referred to as the **profit or loss arising on the disposal of the asset**. It effectively represents the extent to which the depreciation charged during the life of the asset was incorrect.
- The profit or loss on disposal will be treated as an income statement item.

If the **proceeds** received on disposal are **less than the carrying amount** at that date the difference is a **loss** on disposal, which is treated as an expense when calculating the organisation's profitability.

If the **proceeds** received on disposal are **greater than the carrying amount** or value at that date the difference is a **profit** on disposal, which is treated as an income when calculating the organisation's profitability.

There is a three step approach to making a disposal:

Step 1 – remove the cost from the books and transfer to the disposal account.

Debit	Disposal account	X
Credit	Non-current asset cost account	X

Step 2 – remove the accumulative depreciation from the books and transfer to the disposal account.

Debit	Accumulative depreciation account	X
Credit	Disposal account	X

Step 3 – record the cash proceeds

Debit	Cash account	X
Credit	Disposal account	X

The balance on the disposal account represents the profit or loss on disposal and should be transferred to the income statement:

Disposal account

	$		$
Original cost	X	Accumulated depreciation	X
		Bank/cash	X
Profit ß (to income statement)	X	Loss ß (to income statement)	X
	X		X

Illustration 1

X purchased a van on 1 January 20X5 for $10,000. He estimated that its resale value on 31 December 20Y0 after 6 years' use would be $400, and depreciated it on a straight-line basis using the pro-rata basis in the year of acquisition and disposal.

He sold it on 30 June 20X7 for $5,500.

Required:

Calculate the profit or loss on disposal of the van.

Solution

The amount of depreciation to be charged each year was:

$$\frac{\text{Original cost – estimated residual value}}{\text{Estimated useful life}} = \frac{\$10{,}000 - \$400}{6} = \$1{,}600$$

X owned the asset for 2 years and 6 months, thus the total depreciation charged since acquisition is $1,600 × 2.5 = $4,000. This means that the carrying amount or value at the date of the disposal was $10,000 – $4,000 = $6,000.

Since the sale proceeds only amounted to $5,500 there has been a 'loss on disposal' of $500.

The bookkeeping entries related to this example are as follows:

Van at cost

20X5		$	20X5		$
1 Jan	Bank	10,000	31 Dec	Balance c/d	10,000
		10,000			10,000
20X6			20X6		
1 Jan	Balance b/d	10,000	31 Dec	Balance c/d	10,000
		10,000			10,000
20X7			20X7		
1 Jan	Balance b/d	10,000	30 Jun	Disposal	10,000

Accumulated depreciation – van

		$	20X5		$
			31 Dec	Depreciation	1,600
			20X6		
			31 Dec	Depreciation	1,600
20X7			20X7		
30 Jun	Disposal	4,000	30 Jun	Depreciation	800
		4,000			4,000

Non-current asset disposal – van

20X7		$	20X7		$
30 Jun	Van at cost	10,000	30 Jun	Accumulated depreciation – van	4,000
				Bank	5,500
				Loss (to income statement)	500
		10,000			10,000

Test your understanding 1

Write up the relevant accounts for a non-current asset that was purchased on 23 March 20X1 for $3,500. Its residual value is expected to be $200, and its expected useful life is 4 years. The asset is sold on 18 January 20X4 for $1,300. A full year's depreciation is to be charged in the year of purchase. The organisation's year end is 31 December.

A comprehensive example

A business bought the following machines:

- Machine A on 3 February 20X1, costing $1,000,
- Machine B on 18 March 20X2, costing $1,200,
- Machine C on 27 June 20X3, costing $2,000.

None of the machines has any expected residual value, and all are depreciated on the straight-line basis over 10 years, with a full year's depreciation in the year of purchase. Machine A is sold for $720 on 30 June 20X4. The business's year end is 31 December.
Annual depreciation is:

- Machine A $100,
- Machine B $120,
- Machine C $200.

Because there are three machines bought at different times, it is a good idea to tabulate the depreciation as follows:

Year	Machine A	Machine B	Machine C	Total
	$	$	$	$
20X1	100	Nil	Nil	100
20X2	100	120	Nil	220
20X3	100	120	200	420
20X4	Nil	120	200	320

The total column gives the depreciation to be charged each year. Remember to dispose of Machine A in 20X4. The ledger accounts are as follows:

Machines at cost

20X1		$	20X1		$
3 Feb	Cash	1,000	31 Dec	Balance c/d	1,000
20X2			20X2		
1 Jan	Balance b/d	1,000			
18 Mar	Cash	1,200	31 Dec	Balance c/d	2,200
		2,200			2,200
20X3			20X3		
1 Jan	Balance b/d	2,200			
27 Jun	Cash	2,000	31 Dec	Balance c/d	4,200
		4,200			4,200
20X4			20X4		
1 Jan	Balance b/d	4,200	30 Jun	Disposals a/c	1,000
			31 Dec	Balance c/d	3,200
		4,200			4,200
20X4					
1 Jan	Balance b/d	3,200			

Accumulated depreciation on machines

20X1		$	20X1		$
31 Dec	Balance c/d	100	31 Dec	Income statement	100
		———			———
20X2			20X2		
			1 Jan	Balance b/d	100
31 Dec	Balance c/d	320	31 Dec	Income statement	220
		———			———
		320			320
		———			———
20X3			20X3		
			1 Jan	Balance b/d	320
31 Dec	Balance c/d	740	31 Dec	Income statement	420
		———			———
		740			740
		———			———
20X4			20X4		
30 Jun	Disposals a/c	300	1 Jan	Balance b/d	740
31 Dec	Balance c/d	760	31 Dec	Income statement	320
		———			———
		1,060			1,060
		———			———
			20X5		
			1 Jan	Balance b/d	760

Non-current asset disposals

20X4		$	20X4		$
30 Jun	Machines at cost	1,000	30 Jun	Accumulated depreciation	300
31 Dec	Income statement	20	30 Jun	Cash	720
		———			———
		1,020			1,020
		———			———

The profit on disposal is credited to the income statement.

3 Disposal through a part exchange agreement (PEA)

A part exchange agreement arises where an old asset is provided in part payment for a new one, the balance of the new asset being paid in cash or a payable created for the outstanding liability.

The procedure to record the transaction is very similar to the three-step process seen for a cash disposal. The first two steps are identical, however steps 3 and 4 are as follows:

Step 3 – record the **part exchange proceeds**

Debit	Non-current asset cost account	X
Credit	Disposal account	X

Step 4 – record the **cash proceeds** (if any)

Debit	Non-current asset cost account	X
Credit	Cash/Payable	X

If the balance on the part exchange agreement was not paid cash and the entity was given credit then the credit entry to the journal in step 4 would be to the payables account instead of the cash account.

The balance on the disposal account still represents the profit or loss on disposal and should be transferred to the income statement.

Test your understanding 2

Tyrone runs a business repairing cars. When he started business on 1 January 20X2, he bought a compressor machine for $5,000. He depreciates machines using the straight-line method at a rate of 20% pa, and he charges a full year of depreciation in the year of acquisition and none in the year of disposal.

The business has now grown such that he needs a more up to date machine, and he will upgrade on 18 December 20X5. The salesman has offered him a part exchange deal as follows:

Part exchange allowance for old machine $2,500
Balance to be paid in cash for new machine $6,000

Required:

Show the ledger entries for the year ended 31 December 20X5 to reflect this transaction.

4 The non-current asset register

Most organisations will own a number of non-current assets and in large organisations their control is vital to the efficient running of the organisation.

Management will need to be aware of:

(1) the location of each asset;

(2) the extent to which it is being used;

(3) the repairs that have been carried out on the asset and the cost of those repairs;

(4) the expiry dates of any licences permitting the organisation to use the asset.

In addition, for accounting purposes, the following information is required:

(1) the date of purchase;

(2) the name and address of the asset's supplier;

(3) the cost of the asset;

(4) the estimated useful life of the asset;

(5) the estimated residual value of the asset at the end of its useful life;

(6) a description of the asset;

(7) a code number for the asset so that it can be found easily on a computerised system;

(8) the method of depreciation to be used for the asset;

(9) whether any government grants have been obtained to assist in the purchase of the asset;

(10) the accumulated depreciation of the asset;

(11) details of the disposal of the asset when it has occurred.

This information is normally recorded in a non-current asset register.

The non-current asset register should agree with the accounting ledgers at all times!

The non-current asset register

The efficiency of the organisation can be greatly improved if the register is stored on a computer. Specialist computer packages exist for the recording of an organisation's non-current assets, but much the same effect can be obtained by using a spreadsheet or database program, particularly in smaller organisations or where the information is recorded within each department.

In the context of a non-current asset register, each asset would be given a code number. There would be a separate record on the computer file for each non-current asset, and within each record there would be a field for each data item to be recorded. The asset code would normally be used as the key field so that the record of any particular asset could be located easily.

The use of a computerised non-current asset register would allow the calculation of depreciation to be automated and various reports could be produced showing, for example:

- the depreciation charge for the accounting period analysed by asset and by department as required;
- a list of assets requiring servicing;
- a list of assets at a particular location;
- the extent of any repair expenditure on each asset;
- a list of assets continuing in use beyond their estimated useful life.

The use of a computerised system greatly improves the speed and accuracy of reporting and allows management to design different reports specific to their needs. These needs will vary for different managers and the use of a computerised system means that the basic data needs to be entered only once, and the computer can then sort it in different ways in order to produce the report required.

Test your understanding 3

A non-current asset register showed a carrying amount of $67,460. A non-current asset costing $15,000 had been sold for $4,000, making a loss on disposal of $1,250. No entries had been made in the non-current asset register for this disposal. The balance on the non-current asset register is:

A $42,710

B $51,210

C $53,710

D $62,210

5 The revaluation of tangible assets

In accordance with accounting rules an entity can carry its non-current assets at either cost or fair value.

The fair value of assets is usually the market value.

If an asset is revalued, any accumulated depreciation at the date of the revaluation should be written off to the revaluation reserve. **The revaluation reserve appears in the capital section of the statement of financial position and represents an unrealised profit.** This will be seen in more detail in later chapters.

Depreciation will then be calculated based on the **revalued amount** using the remaining useful life of the asset at the revaluation date.

Revaluations must be made for the whole class of assets, i.e. if we revalue one building we must revalue the whole class of buildings at the same time.

The frequency of revaluations will depend upon the market conditions but must be carried out by a professional valuer.

Steps to account for a revaluation:

(1) Restate the asset cost to the revalued amount and transfer the increase to the revaluation reserve.

(2) Remove any accumulated depreciation provision at the revaluation date and transfer to the revaluation reserve.

(3) Recalculate the current year's depreciation on the revalued amount.

Illustration 2

A building with an original cost of $100,000 and a current carrying value of $70,000, was revalued to $120,000 on 31 December 20X2. The remaining life of the building is considered to be 12 years at the revaluation date and the building is depreciated on a straight-line basis.

Required:

Show the accounting entries required to revalue the building and calculate the future depreciation charge.

Solution

First we must revalue the asset cost the revalued amount. This would involve an increase of $20,000 ($100,000 increases to $120,000). The accounting entry would be to debit the asset cost account and credit the revaluation reserve.

The next step would be to remove the accumulated depreciation from the books at the revaluation date. As the original cost of the asset was $100,000 and the carrying value in the accounts is currently $70,000, this would be depreciation of $30,000. To remove this we must debit the accumulated depreciation account and credit the revaluation reserve.

The revaluation reserve now has two credit entries, $20,000 and $30,000. This $50,000 represents the increase in value of the building from the carrying value in the accounts before the revaluation of $70,000, to the revalued amount of £120,000. This reserve is part of the capital of the business and shown in the capital section of the statement of financial position. You will learn more about it when you study a later chapter dealing with limited companies.

The bookkeeping entries related to this example are as follows:

Building at cost

20X2		$	20X2		$
1 Jan	Balance b/d	100,000	31 Dec	Balance c/d	120,000
31 Dec	Revaluation	20,000			
		———			———
		120,000			120,000
		———			———
20X3					
1 Jan	Balance b/d	120,000			

Accumulated depreciation – building

20X2		$	20X2		$
31 Dec	Revaluation	30,000	1 Jan	Balance b/d	30,000
		———			———
		30,000			30,000
		———			———

Revaluation reserve

20X2		$	20X2		$
31 Dec	Balance c/d	50,000	31 Dec	Building cost	20,000
				Accum depn	30,000
		50,000			50,000
			20X3		
			1 Jan	Balance b/d	50,000

The future depreciation charge will be based on the revalued amount of $120,000, i.e. $120,000/12 years remaining life = £10,000 p.a.

Test your understanding 4

Navdeep owns a restaurant. The premises were purchased on 1 January 20X1 for $900,000 and depreciation charged at 2% pa straight-line.

Navdeep now wishes to revalue the restaurant to $1,600,000 on 1 January 20X7 to reflect the market value.

Required:

What is the balance on the revaluation reserve after this transaction?

A $750,000

B $790,000

C $808,000

D $826,000

6 Impairment of tangible assets

Tangible assets maybe impaired if the recoverable amount is less than the carrying value in the financial statements.

The recoverable amount is the higher of:

- net selling price (fair value less costs to sell) or
- value in use (given in the question).

If we identify that an asset has been impaired we must reduce the asset value to the recoverable amount and transfer the difference to the income statement as an expense against profit, (think of it as an extra depreciation charge in the year).

The journal entry would look as follows:

Debit	Income statement expense account	X
Credit	Non-current asset cost account	X

7 Chapter summary

this chapter, we have looked at the accounting issues associated with non-current assets. These issues can be summarised as:

- accounting entries to record the disposal of non-current assets with cash and part exchange proceeds;
- accounting entries to record the revaluation of non-current assets;
- impairment of non-current assets;
- the control of tangible non-current assets.

Test your understanding questions.

Test your understanding 5

Your firm bought a machine for $5,000 on 1 January 20X1, which had an expected useful life of 4 years and an expected residual value of $1,000; the asset was to be depreciated on the straight-line basis using the pro-rata basis in the year of acquistion and disposal. On 31 December 20X3, the machine was sold for $1,600. The amount to be entered in the 20X3 income statement for profit or loss on disposal is:

$ . . . .

Test your understanding 6

An organisation's non-current asset register shows a carrying amount or value of $135,600. The non-current asset account in the nominal ledger shows a carrying amount or value of $125,600. The difference could be due to a disposed asset not having been deducted from the non-current asset register:

A with disposal proceeds of $15,000 and a profit on disposal of $5,000

B with disposal proceeds of $15,000 and a carrying amount or value of $5,000

C with disposal proceeds of $15,000 and a loss on disposal of $5,000

D with disposal proceeds of $5,000 and a carrying amount or value of $5,000

Test your understanding 7

A machine costs $9,000. It has an expected useful life of 6 years, and an expected residual value of $1,000. It is to be depreciated at 30 per cent per annum on the reducing-balance basis. A full year's depreciation is charged in the year of purchase, with none in the year of sale. During year 4, it is sold for $3,000. The profit or loss on disposal is:

$ . . . .

Test your understanding 8

A non-current asset was disposed of for $2,200 during the last accounting year. It had been purchased exactly 3 years earlier for $5,000, with an expected residual value of $500, and had been depreciated on the reducing-balance basis, at 20 per cent per annum. The profit or loss on disposal was:

$ . . . .

Test your understanding 9

A car was purchased by a newsagent business in May 20X0 for:

	$
Cost	10,000
Annual vehicle licence tax	150
Total	10,150

The business adopts a date of 31 December as its year end.

The car was traded in for a replacement vehicle in August 20X3 at an agreed value of $5,000.

It has been depreciated at 25 per cent per annum on the reducing-balance method, charging a full year's depreciation in the year of purchase and none in the year of sale.

What was the profit or loss on disposal of the vehicle during the year ended December 20X3?

$ . . . .

Test your understanding 10

The carrying amount of a company's non-current assets was $200,000 at 1 August 20X0. During the year ended 31 July 20X1, the company sold non-current assets for $25,000 on which it made a loss of $5,000. The depreciation charge for the year was $20,000. What was the carrying amount or value of non-current assets at 31 July 20X1?

$ . . . .

Test your understanding 11

A car was purchased for $12,000 on 1 April 20X0 and has been depreciated at 20 per cent each year, straight line, assuming no residual value. The company policy is to charge a full year's depreciation in the year of purchase and no depreciation in the year of sale. The car was traded in for a replacement vehicle on 1 August 20X3 for an agreed figure of $5,000. What was the profit or loss on the disposal of the vehicle for the year ended 31 December 20X3?

$ . . . .

Test your understanding 12

A non-current asset register is:

A an alternative name for the non-current asset ledger account

B a list of the physical non-current assets rather than their financial cost

C a schedule of planned maintenance of non-current assets for use by the plant engineer

D a schedule of the cost and other information about each individual non-current asset

Test your understanding answers

Test your understanding 1

Non-current assets at cost

20X1		$	20X4		$
23 Mar	Cash	3,500	18 Jan	Disposals	3,500

Accumulated depreciation

		$	20X1		$
			31 Dec	Income statement	825
			20X2		
			31 Dec	Income statement	825
20X4			20X3		
18 Jan	Disposals a/c	2,475	31 Dec	Income statement	825
		2,475			2,475

Non-current asset disposals

20X4		$	20X4		$
18 Jan	Cost	3,500	18 Jan	Accumulated depreciation	2,475
31 Dec	Profit on disposal	275		Proceeds	1,300
		3,775			3,775

Workings:

$$\frac{\text{Original cost} - \text{estimated residual value}}{\text{Estimated useful life}} = \frac{\$3,500 - \$200}{4} = \$825\text{pa}$$

The depreciation policy is to charge full depreciation in the year of acquisition (20X1) and nothing in the year of disposal (20X4), hence three year's depreciation has been charged.

Note: The cost account amount of $3,500 and the accumulative depreciation account would be carried forward each year as a balance on the account, until the year of disposal 20X4. This has not been done in this question, simply to make the ledger account look neater for presentation purposes. However, it is important to remember this would be done in practice.

Test your understanding 2

Non-current assets at cost

20X2		$	20X4		$
1 Jan	Cash	5,000	31 Dec	Balance c/d	5,000
		5,000			5,000
20X5			20X5		
1 Jan	Balance b/d	5,000	18 Dec	Disposals	5,000
18 Dec	PEA	2,500			
	Cash	6,000	31 Dec	Balance c/d	8,500
		13,500			13,500
20X6					
1 Jan	Balance b/d	8,500			

Accumulated depreciation

		$			$
			20X2		
			31 Dec	Income statement	1,000
			20X3		
			31 Dec	Income statement	1,000
20X4			20X4		
31 Dec	Balance c/d	3,000	31 Dec	Income statement	1,000
		3,000			3,000
20X5			20X5		
18 Dec	Disposals a/c	3,000	1 Jan	Balance b/d	3,000
31 Dec	Balance c/d	1,700	31 Dec	Income statement	1,700
		4,700			4,700
			20X6		
			1 Jan	Balance b/d	1,700

Non-current asset disposals

		$			$
20X5			20X5		
18 Dec	Cost	5,000	18 Dec	Accumulated depreciation	3,000
31 Dec	Profit on disposal	500		PEA	2,500
		5,500			5,500

Workings:

Old compressor depreciation = $5,000 × 20% = $1,000 p.a. The depreciation policy is to charge full depreciation in the year of acquisition (20X2) and nothing in the year of disposal (20X5), hence three year's depreciation has been charged.

New compressor depreciation = $8,500 × 20% = $1,700 p.a. The depreciation policy is to charge full depreciation in the year of acquisition (20X5).

Test your understanding 3

D

The non-current asset register balance of $67,460 must be reduced by the carrying value of the asset disposed, i.e. $5,250 = $62,210. The register represents the carrying value of all assets held by the business.

If the asset is sold for $4,000 and made a loss of $1,250, the asset must have a carrying value of $5,250.

Test your understanding 4

C

The bookkeeping entries related to this example are as follows:

Building at cost

20X7		$	20X7		$
1 Jan	Balance b/d	900,000	1 Jan	Balance c/d	1,600,000
1 Jan	Revaluation	700,000			
		1,600,000			1,600,000
20X7					
1 Jan	Balance b/d	1,600,000			

Accumulated depreciation – building

20X7		$	20X7		$
1 Jan	Revaluation	108,000	1 Jan	Balance b/d	108,000
		108,000			108,000

Revaluation reserve

20X7		$	20X7		$
31 Dec	Balance c/d	808,000	1 Jan	Building cost	700,000
				Accum depn	108,000
		808,000			808,000
			20X8		
			1 Jan	Balance b/d	808,000

The accumulated depreciation at the revaluation date = 6 years, i.e. $900,000 × 2% × 6 = $108,000. This represents the depreciation from the purchase date 20X1 upto and including 20X6. The future depreciation charge for 20X7 will be based on the revalued amount of $1,600,000.

Test your understanding 5

The answer is: $400

The profit or loss on disposal is the difference between the carrying amount at the time of disposal and the disposal proceeds. An excess of disposal proceeds over carrying amount indicates a profit on disposal, while an excess of carrying amount over disposal proceeds indicates a loss on disposal.
The annual depreciation on the machine is calculated as:

$$\frac{\text{Cost} - \text{residual value}}{\text{Useful life}} = \frac{5{,}000 - 1{,}000}{4 \text{ years}} = 1{,}000 \text{ per year}$$

Depreciation by 31 December 20X3 would be 3 × $1,000 = $3,000, therefore the carrying amount of the machine at the date of disposal would be $2,000. Disposal proceeds were $1,600, therefore there was a loss on disposal of $400.

Test your understanding 6

A

The difference between the two records is $10,000, therefore the disposed asset must have had a carrying amount or value of this amount. B and D are clearly wrong, and C would produce a carrying amount or value of $20,000.

Test your understanding 7

	$	
$9,000 × 0.7 × 0.7 × 0.7 =	3,087	(carrying amount or value)
Proceeds of sale	(3,000)	
Loss on disposal	87	

Test your understanding 8

	$	
$5,000 × 0.8 × 0.8 × 0.8 =	2,560	(carrying amount or value)
Receipt	(2,200)	
Loss on disposal	360	

Test your understanding 9

	$
Cost	10,000
20X0 Depreciation	(2,500)
	7,500
20X1 Depreciation	(1,875)
	5,625
20X2 Depreciation	(1,406)
	4,219
20X3 Part-exchange	(5,000)
Profit	781

Test your understanding 10

	$	$
Carrying amount at 1 August 20X0		200,000
Less: depreciation		(20,000)
Proceeds	25,000	
Loss	5,000	
Therefore carrying amount or value		(30,000)
		150,000

Test your understanding 11

	$
Cost	12,000
20X0 Depreciation	(2,400)
	9,600
20X1 Depreciation	(2,400)
	7,200
20X2 Depreciation	(2,400)
	4,800
20X3 Part-exchange	(5,000)
Profit	200

Test your understanding 12

D

chapter

12

Preparation of Financial Statements with Adjustments

Chapter learning objectives

When you have completed this chapter, you should be able to :

- prepare financial statements from trial balances and adjustments.

1 Introduction

This chapter looks at the preparation of financial statements (i.e. income statement and statement of financial position) from a trial balance, with various adjustments to be made.

These adjustments include:

- closing inventory at the end of the period,
- accruals,
- prepayments,
- irrecoverable debts and allowance for receivables,
- depreciation.

The trial balance is often extracted from the ledger accounts prior to the consideration of adjustments for accruals and prepayments, depreciation and allowance for receivables, and so on, and these are given as notes following the trial balance.

This chapter summarises all of what we have learnt in the previous chapters.

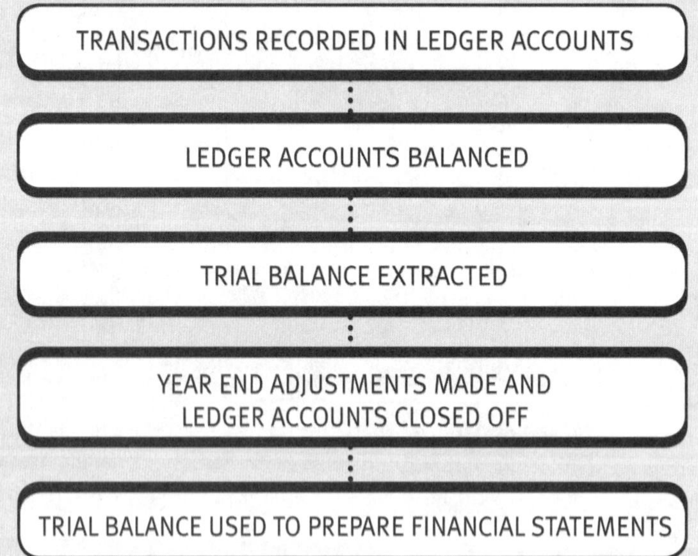

2 The trial balance

The following trial balance extracted from the nominal ledger of Yusuf on 30 November 20X3.

Trial balance of Yusuf as at 30 November 20X3

	$	$
Sales		125,658
Returns inwards/outwards	6,341	1,902
Receivables and payables	11,257	7,983
Office equipment		
Cost	10,000	
Acc. Depreciation at 1 December 20X2		1,550
Vehicles		
Cost	3,500	
Acc. Depreciation at 1 December 20X2		700
Purchases	64,726	
Inventory at 1 December 20X2	5,000	
Carriage inwards	908	
Carriage outwards	272	
Vehicle expenses	1,349	
Electricity	1,803	
Wages and salaries	11,550	
Rent and local business tax	8,800	
Stationery and postages	2,081	
Bank deposit account	10,000	
Bank	4,797	
Discount allowed and received	5,652	3,765
Sales tax payable		1,325
Employee income tax payable		453
Capital at 1 December 20X2		4,300
Finance cost	600	
Drawings	15,000	
Loan		16,000
	163,636	163,636

3 The adjustments

Following the extraction of the above trial balance from the ledgers and an examination of the accounting records, the following additional information was obtained:

(1) The value of the inventory on hand at 30 November 20X3 was $5,700.

(2) The bank deposit was made on 1 June 20X3. This account earns interest at 8 per cent per annum. The balance shown in the ledgers is the only deposit made into this account. Interest is credited on 31 December annually.

(3) Bank charges incurred to 30 November 20X3 are estimated to be $60.

(4) The balance of the rent and local business tax account includes a payment of rent for the 3 months to 31 December 20X3 of $1,200 and a payment of local business tax for the 6 months to 31 March 20X4 of $4,000.

(5) Following a review of receivables at the year end, it is decided that a irrecoverable debt of $1,207 should be written off, and an allowance for receivables made, of 2 per cent of receivables.

(6) Office equipment is to be depreciated at 10 per cent per annum on cost, and motor vehicles are to be depreciated at 20 per cent per annum on cost.

Required:

Using the above information, prepare an income statement of Yusuf for the period ended 30 November 20X3 together with his statement of financial position at that date.

Step 1: Labelling the trial balance

The trial balance contains all of the account balances from the ledger of Yusuf. It, therefore, includes assets, liabilities, capital, expenses and revenue. You should remember that the assets, liabilities and capital are shown in the statement of financial position, and the expenses and revenue in the income statement where they are used to calculate net profit, which is then also transferred to the statement of financial position. If you are unsure about the correct category for any of the items in the trial balance it might help to remember the following:

Debit balances usually represent either assets or expenses and these are always shown in the left-hand column of a trial balance. Therefore, credit balances (shown in the right-hand column) are usually revenue, liabilities or capital.

You should also remember that values shown in the trial balance have, by definition, been posted to the ledger accounts and that, therefore, the double entry is complete.

Other pieces of information given by way of a note have not been recorded in the ledger accounts and consequently will require both a debit and a credit entry (which is usually effected by entering them in both the income statement and the statement of financial position).

Step 2: Preparing workings

Each of the notes should be considered in turn, and you should head up a page entitled 'workings' on which any calculations and adjustments should be clearly shown and labelled.

(1) Closing inventory of $5,700 is to be entered in the income statement (trading account part) and the statement of financial position.

(2) There will be an entry in the income statement for accrued interest received and the outstanding amount will be shown on the statement of financial position as an asset. The deposit was made on 1 June 20X3, so that the interest earned to 30 November is: $10,000 × 8% × 6/12 =$400 (income statement/statement of financial position asset).

(3) The bank charges will be shown as an additional expense to the income statement and as a liability in the statement of financial position.

(4) Rent and local business tax includes prepayments as follows:

Rent: 1 month, therefore $1,200	× 1/3	= $400
Local Business Tax: 4 months, therefore $4,000	× 4/6	= $2,667

	$	
Rent and local business tax as per trial balance	8,800	
Less: prepayments (400 + 2,667)	(3,067)	(Statement of financial position: assets)
Income statement	5,733	

(5) Irrecoverable debts to be written off: $1,207 (income statement)

The double entry will be:

Debit	Irrecoverable debts expense account	$1,207
Credit	Receivables account	$1,207

New receivables figure: $11,257 – $1,207 written off = $10,050.
Allowance for receivables to be made: 2% × $10,050 = $201

The double entry will be:

Debit	Irrecoverable debts expense account	$201
Credit	Allowance for receivables account	$201

Total to the income statement for irrecoverable debts and allowances $1,408 ($1,207 + $201)

The allowance of $201 will be deducted from receivables figure on the statement of financial position.

(6) Depreciation on office equipment

	$	
10% × $10,000	1,000	(Income statement)
Accumulated depreciation as per the trial balance	1,550	
Accumulated depreciation	2,550	(Statement of financial position)

Depreciation on Vehicle

	$	
20% × 3,500	700	(Income statement)
Accumulated depreciation as per the trial balance	700	
Accumulated depreciation	1,400	(Statement of financial position)

We can now prepare the financial statements.

Step 3: Preparing the financial statements

- **Hint.** Tick each item in the trial balance and/workings as it is entered.
- **Hint.** Enter the reference number of the 'workings' where relevant.

Income statement of Yusuf for the period ended 30 November 20X3

	$	$	$
Sales			125,658
Less: returns			(6,341)
Net sales			119,317
Opening inventory		5,000	
Purchases	64,726		
Carriage inwards	908		
	65,634		
Less: returns	(1,902)		
Net purchases		63,732	
		68,732	
Less: closing inventory (W1)		(5,700)	
Cost of goods sold			(63,032)
Gross profit			56,285
Bank deposit interest (W2)			400
Discount received			3,765
			60,450

Bank charges (W3)	60	
Carriage outwards	272	
Vehicle expenses	1,349	
Electricity	1,803	
Wages and salaries	11,550	
Rent and local business tax (W4)	5,733	
Irrecoverable debts and allowance (W5)	1,408	
Stationery and postages	2,081	
Discount allowed	5,652	
Depreciation		
Office equipment (W6)	1,000	
Vehicles (W6)	700	
Finance cost	600	
		(32,208)
Net profit		28,242

Statement of financial position of Yusuf as at 30 November 20X3

Assets	Cost ($)	Acc. Depreciation ($)	Carrying amount ($)
Non-current assets			
Office equipment	10,000	(2,550)	7,450
Vehicles	3,500	(1,400)	2,100
	13,500	(3,950)	9,550
Current assets			
Inventory			5,700
Receivables		11,257	
Less: irrecoverable debts		(1,207)	
Less: allowance for receivables		(201)	
			9,849

Prepayments	3,067	
Accrued interest receivable	400	
Bank deposit	10,000	
Bank	4,797	
		33,813
		43,363
Capital and liabilities		
Capital at the start of the year		4,300
Add: net profit		28,242
		32,542
Less: drawings		(15,000)
		17,542
Non-current liabilities		
Loan		16,000
Current liabilities		
Payables	7,983	
Accruals (W3)	60	
Sales tax payable	1,325	
Employee income tax payable	453	
		9,821
		43,363

Illustration 1

JW Ltd had, among others, the following balances in the books at 30 June 20X9

	Debit ($)	*Credit* ($)
Motor vehicles at cost	200	
Motor vehicles acc. depreciation at 1 July 20X8		70
Fixtures at cost	60	
Fixtures acc. depreciation at 1July 20X8		20
Office equipment at cost	125	
Office equipment – acc. depreciation at 1 July 20X8		45
Trade receivables	580	
Allowance for receivables at 1July 20X8		10
Insurance	90	
Sales commission	40	

The following adjustments have not yet been made in the books:

(i) Motor vehicles are depreciated over 4 years on the straight-line basis. On 31 March 20X9, a motor vehicle that had cost $20,000 on 1 July 20X6 was disposed of for $8,000. It is the company's policy to charge a full year's depreciation in the year of purchase, and hence none in the year of disposal. No entries have been made for the disposal.

(ii) Fixtures are depreciated on the straight-line basis over 10 years, on an actual time basis (i.e. from the date of acquisition). On 1 October 20X8, fixtures were purchased for $40,000, which have not been entered in the books.

(iii) Office equipment is depreciated at 20 per cent per annum on the reducing-balance basis.

(iv) On 30 June 20X9, it was decided to write off an irrecoverable debt of $80,000 and to make an allowance for receivables of 3 per cent of the remaining receivables.

(v) The insurance figure above covers the period 1 July 20X8 to 30 September 20X9.

(vi) Sales representatives are paid commission, which amounts to 5 per cent of the previous month's sales. The commission is due for payment on the 15th of the following month. During June 20X9, sales amounted to $120,000.

Required:

(a) Prepare ledger accounts for all the above items, showing clearly all calculations, transfers to the income statement for the year ending 30 June 20X9, and balance to be carried down at 30 June 20X9.

(b) Show the 'expenses' section of the income statement for the year ending 30 June 20X9, to include all the items above.

(c) Show the extracts from the non-current assets, current assets and current liabilities sections of the statement of financial position at 30 June 20X9, which includes balances for the above items.

(d) Explain briefly why depreciation is charged in the income statement, but does not affect cash balances.

Solution

This solution does not utilise a 'depreciation expense' account or a 'irrecoverable debts expense' account. Although many businesses do maintain such accounts, it is often considered unnecessary and time-consuming to produce them in the computer-based assessment. Instead of transferring the depreciation to such an expense account, the amount is transferred directly to the income statement.

(a)

Motor vehicles at cost

		$			$
1 Jul X8	Balance b/d	200	31 Mar X9	Disposals a/c	20
			30 Jun	X9 Balance c/d	180
		200			200

Motor Vehicles – accumulated depreciation

		$			$
31 Mar X9	Disposals (W1)	10	1 Jul 98	Balance b/d	70
30 Jun X9	Balance c/d	105	30 Jun X9	Income statement (W2)	45
		115			115

Disposal of non-current assets

		$			$
31 Mar X9	Motor vehicles at cost	20	31 Mar X9	Motor vehicle accumulated depreciation	10
				Cash	8
				Loss on disposal (IS)	2
		20			20

Fixtures at cost

		$			$
1 Jul X8	Balance b/d	60	30 Jun X9	Balance c/d	100
1 Sep X8	Purchase (bank)	40			
		100			100

Fixtures – accumulated depreciation

		$			$
30 Jun X9	Balance c/d	29	1 Jul X8	Balance b/d	20
			30 Jun X9	Income statement (W3)	9
		29			29

Office equipment at cost

		$			$
1 Jul X8	Balance b/d	125	30 Jun X9	Balance c/d	
		125			125

Office equipment – accumulated depreciation

		$			$
30 Jun X9	Balance c/d	61	1 Jul X8	Balance b/d	45
			30 Jun X9	Income statement (W4)	16
		61			61

Irrecoverable debts written off

		$			$
30 Jun X9	Receivables	80	30 Jun X9	Income statement	80
		80			80

Trade receivables

		$			$
30 Jun X9	Balance c/d	580	30 Jun X9	Irrrecoverable debts (IS)	80
				Balance c/d	500
		580			580

Allowance for receivables

		$			$
30 Jun X9	Balance c/d	15	1 Jul X8	Balance b/d	10
				Income statement (W5)	5
		15			15

Insurance

		$			$
1 Jul X8	Bank	90	30 Jun X9	Prepaid c/d (W6)	18
				Income statement	72
		90			90

Sales commission payable

		$			$
30 Jun X9	Bank (during year)	40	30 Jun X9	Income statement	46
	Accrued c/d (W7)	6			
		46			46

Workings

(W1) **Motor Vehicles – depreciation on disposed vehicle**

	$000
Cost on 1 July 20X6	20
Depreciation y/e 30 June 20X7: 20 ÷ 4	5
Depreciation y/e 30 June 20X8: 20 ÷ 4	5
Total depreciation to be removed	10

(W2) **Motor vehicles – depreciation**

Motor vehicles – cost at 30 June 20X9	180
Depreciation = 180 ÷ 4 years =	45

Note: The depreciation rate could also be expressed as 25% on cost.

(W3) **Fixtures – depreciation on existing items**

	$000	$000
Cost at 1 July 20X8	60	
Depreciation = 60 ÷ 10		6
Depreciation on new items:		
Cost at 1 September 20X8	40	
Depreciation = 40 ÷ 10 × 9/12		3
Total for the year		9

(W4) **Office equipment – depreciation**

	$000
Cost b/d	125
Depreciation b/d	45
Carrying amount b/d	80

(W5) **Allowance for receivables**

	$000
Receivables (prior to irrecoverable debts)	580
Irrecoverable debts written off	(80)
Revised receivables	500
Allowance for receivables 3% × 500 =	15
Less: existing allowance for receivables	(10)
	5

(W6) **Insurance Prepaid**

	$000
Insurance paid for 15 months	90
Prepaid = 3/15 × 90	(18)
Income statement charge	72

(W7) **Sales commission accrued**

	$000
Sales commission paid	40
Accrued = 5% × 120	6
Income statement charge	46

(b) Income statement for the year ended 30 June 20X9 (extract)

Expenses	$000
Depreciation	
Motor vehicles	45
Fixtures	9
Office equipment	16
Loss on disposal of non-current assets	2
Irrecoverable debts written off	80
Allowance for receivables	5
Insurance	72
Sales commission	46

(c) Statement of financial position at 30 June 20X9 (extract)

	Cost ($000)	Acc. Dep'n ($000)	Carrying amount ($000)
Non-current assets			
Motor vehicles	180	(105)	75
Fixtures	100	(29)	71
Office equipment	125	(61)	64
	405	(195)	210
Current assets			
Receivables		500	
Less: allowance for receivables		(15)	
			485
Prepaid insurance			18
Current liabilities			
Accrued commission			6

(d) Depreciation is a means of spreading the cost of non-current assets (less any expected sale proceeds) over their expected useful life, so as to charge the income statement with a portion of their cost to reflect the usage of assets in earning revenue.

If depreciation were not charged then the profits would be overstated. There is a danger that these profits would be paid out as dividends (or as drawings in the case of a sole trader), thereby depleting the cash balances and the capital employed in the business. When the asset was disposed of, the whole of the decrease in value since purchase would appear as a charge in that period's income statement, thereby distorting the profits.

Cash is paid out when a non-current asset is paid for, not when depreciated. Cash comes in when the asset is disposed of. Accounting for depreciation does not involve any movement of cash and does not provide a means of replacing non-current assets at the end of their lives, unless cash is set aside as a separate transaction.

4 Chapter summary

This chapter has shown how:

- a transaction can be traced from a ledger account to a trial balance, and from there to the financial statements – income statement or statement of financial position;
- financial statements are prepared from a trial balance and a list of adjustments, which need to be made to finalise the financial statements.

The whole of this chapter should be regarded as a **'must know'** topic if you are to be successful in passing the examination. Although you will not have to prepare a complete set of financial statements with adjustments from the trial balance, any element could be examined at this level. Preparation of financial statements from a trial balance with adjustments will be an assumed knowledge topic for further studies in financial accounting.

This chapter has brought together much of what has been learnt in previous chapters. It is a good point to consolidate your studies before moving on to the remaining chapters in this learning system.

Test your understanding questions.

Test your understanding 1

The following is an extract from the trial balance of ABC Ltd at 31 December 20X4:

	Debit ($)	Credit ($)
Sales		73,716
Returns inwards/outwards	5,863	3,492
Cash discounts allowed/received	871	1,267

The figure to be shown in the trading account for net sales is:

A $66,586

B $66,982

C $67,853

D $70,224

Test your understanding 2

A company's working capital was $43,200. Subsequently, the following transactions occurred:

- payables were paid; 3,000 by cheque;
- an irrecoverable debt of $250 was written off;
- inventory valued at $100 were sold for $230 on credit.

Working capital is now:

$................

Test your understanding 3

Working capital will reduce by $500 if:

A goods costing $3,000 are sold for $3,500 on credit

B goods costing $3,000 are sold for $3,500 cash

C non-current assets costing $500 are purchased on credit

D non-current assets with a carrying amount of $750 are sold for $250 cash

Test your understanding 4

A business has opening inventory of $12,000 and closing inventory of $18,000. Purchase returns were $5,000. The cost of goods sold was $111,000. Purchases were:

$...............

Test your understanding 5

At the beginning of the year, the balance on the allowance for receivables account was $6,000, representing 4 per cent of receivables. At the end of the year, receivables amounted to $150,000, but it was decided that the allowance should be increased to 5 per cent of receivables. Which of the following is correct?

Account entry	Income statement	Net receivables on statement of financial position	Allowance for receivables account
A	$1,500 credit	$142,500	$7,500 credit
B	$1,500 debit	$148,500	$1,500 debit
C	$1,500 debit	$142,500	$7,500 credit
D	$7,500 debit	$142,500	$13,500 credit

Test your understanding 6

The following is an extract from the trial balance of a business for its most recent year:

	Debit ($)	Credit ($)
Heat and light	22,000	
Rent and local business tax	27,000	
Non-current assets	80,000	
Acc. depreciation on non-current assets		20,000

Gross profit has already been calculated as being $85,000.

Depreciation is to be calculated at 25 per cent on the reducing balance. At the end of the year, heat and light to be accrued is $4,000, and rent and local business tax to be prepaid is $2,500.

The correct net profit is:

$...............

Test your understanding 7

GBA is a sole trader, supplying building materials to local builders. He prepares his financial statements to 30 June each year. At 30 June 20X5, his trial balance was as follows:

	Debit ($)	Credit ($)
Capital at July 20X4		55,550
Purchases & Sales	325,500	625,000
Returns inwards & outwards	2,300	1,700
Discounts allowed & received	1,500	2,500
Inventory of building materials at 1 July 20X4	98,200	
Packing materials purchased	12,900	
Distribution costs	18,700	
Rent and insurance	6,100	
Telephone	4,200	
Car expenses	4,400	
Wages	47,900	
Allowance for receivables at 1 July 20X4		1,000
Heat and light	1,850	
Delivery vehicles cost	112,500	
Delivery vehicles acc. depreciation at July 20X4		35,000
Equipment cost	15,000	
Equipment acc. depreciation at July 20X4		5,000
Receivables and payables	95,000	82,000
Loan		4,400
Finance cost	800	
Bank deposit account	15,000	
Bank current account	26,500	
Drawings	23,800	
	812,150	812,150

The following additional information at 30 June 20X5 is available:

(1) Closing inventory:

	$
Building materials	75,300

(2) Prepayments:

	$
Rent and insurance	450

(3) Accrued expenses:

	$
Heat and light	400
Telephone	500

(4) Receivables have been analysed as follows:

	$
Current month	60,000
30 to 60 days	20,000
60 to 90 days	12,000
Over 90 days	3,000

Allowance to be made for receivables as follows:

30 to 60 days	1%
60 to 90 days	2.5%
Over 90 days	5%(after writing off $600)

(5) At 1 July 20X4, GBA decided to bring one of his family cars, valued at $8,000, into the business. No entries have been made in the business books for its introduction.

(6) Depreciation is to be provided as follows:
- 20 per cent on cost for delivery vehicles;
- at 25 per cent on the reducing balance for the car;
- at 25 per cent on the reducing balance for equipment.

Required:

(a) Insert the missing items into the income statement for the year ended 30 June 20X5, set out below.

Income statement of GBA for the year ended 30 June 20X5

	$	$	$
Sales			625,000
Less: Returns inwards			......
			......
Cost of sales			
Opening inventory		98,200	
Purchases	325,500		
Less: Returns outwards	......		
		......	
		......	
Less: Closing inventory		......	
			......
Gross profit			......
Add:			
Discounts received			......
Decrease in allowance for receivables			
			......

Less:		
Discounts allowed	......	
Packing materials consumed	......	
Distribution costs	18,700	
Rent and insurance	......	
Telephone	......	
Car expenses	4,400	
Wages	......	
Heat and light	......	
Sundry expenses	......	
Finance cost	......	
Irrecoverable debts written off in year	......	
Depreciation of delivery vehicles	......	
Depreciation of cars	......	
Depreciation of equipment	......	
		......
Profit		......

(b) Insert the missing figures into the statement of financial position set out below.

Statement of financial position of GBA as at 30 June 20X5

Assets	Cost ($)	Acc. Depn. ($)	Carrying Amount ($)
Non-current assets			
Delivery vehicles	112,500	......	......
Cars	......	......	......
Office equipment	15,000	......	......
	......	......	......

Current assets			
Inventory		......	
Receivables	......		
Less: allowance	......		
		......	
Prepayments		......	
Accrued revenue		......	
Bank deposit account		15,000	
Bank current account		26,500	
			......
			......
Capital and liabilities			
Capital at 1 July 20X4			55,550
Add: capital introduced			......
Add: profit for the year			......
Less: drawings			......
Current liabilities			
Payables		......	
Accruals		......	
Loan		......	
			......
			......

(c) With regard to the transactions in the business of GBA, which of the following transactions affect:

- profit
- cash at bank

	Affects profit	Affects Cash at bank
Payments to suppliers		
Depreciation		
Sales invoiced to customers		
Drawings in cash		
Irrecoverable debts written off		

Test your understanding 8

PLJ has been in business for some years and has kept her drawings slightly below the level of profits each year. She has never made a loss, and therefore feels that her business is growing steadily. You act as her accountant, and she has passed you the following list of balances at 30 April 20X7.

	$000
Capital at 1 May 20X6	228
Drawings	14
Plant at cost	83
Plant – acc. Depreciation at May 20X6	13
Office equipment at cost	31
Office equipment – acc. depreciation at May 20X6	8
Receivables	198
Payables	52
Sales	813
Purchases	516
Returns inwards	47
Discount allowed	4
Allowance for receivables at 1 May 20X6	23
Administration costs	64
Salaries	44
Loan to a friend, repayable in 6 months	25
Bank overdraft	50
Irrecoverable debts written off	77

(i) You ascertain that inventory at 1 May 20X6 was $84,000 and inventory at 30 April 20X7 was $74,000.

(ii) On 1 November 20X6, she brought her personal computer, valued at $2,000, from home into the office; no entries have been made for this.

Required:

(a) Insert the missing items into the trial balance at 30 April 20X7, set out below, after adjusting for the computer that PLJ has brought from home, but prior to making any other adjustments.

Trial balance of PLJ as at 30 April 20X7

	Debit $000		Credit $000
Capital at 1.5.X6	......	or	......
Capital introduced	......	or	......
Drawings	......	or	......
Plant at cost	......	or	......
Plant – acc. depreciation at 1.5.X6	......	or	......
Office equipment at cost	......	or	......
Office equipment – acc. depreciation at 1.5.X6	......	or	......
Receivables	......	or	......
Payables	......	or	......
Sales	......	or	......
Purchases	......	or	......
Returns inwards	......	or	......
Discount allowed	......	or	......
Allowance for receivables at 1.5.X6	......	or	......
Administration costs	......	or	......
Salaries	......	or	......
Loan to friend, repayable in 6 months	......	or	......
Bank	......	or	......
Irrecoverable debts written off	......	or	......
Inventory at 1.5.X6	......	or	......
	......	or	......

(b) You are also given the following information at 30 April 20X7:

(i) Depreciation on plant is charged at 10 per cent per annum on cost. Depreciation on office equipment is charged at 20 per cent per annum on the carrying amount at the year end.

(ii) Administration costs include insurance prepaid of $3,000.

(iii) Salaries accrued amount to $2,000.

(iv) It is agreed that the allowance for receivables figure is to remain at $23,000.

Insert the missing figures into the income statement set out below.

	$000	$000
Sales		813
Less: returns inwards		......
		......
Less: cost of goods sold		
Opening inventory	......	
Purchases	516	
	......	
Less: Closing inventory	......	
Cost of sales		......
Gross profit		......
Less: expenses		
Discount allowed	......	
Administration costs	......	
Salaries	......	
Irrecoverable debts written off	77	
Depreciation of plant	......	
Depreciation of office equipment	......	
		......
Net profit		......

(c) Insert the missing figures into the statement of financial position set out below.

Assets	Cost ($000)	Acc. Depreciation ($000)	Carrying amount ($000)
Non-current assets			
Plant	83	......	......
Office equipment	......	......	......
	......	......	......
Current assets			
Inventory		......	
Receivables	198		
Less: allowance	......		
		......	
Loan		......	
Prepayment		......	
			......
			......
Capital and liabilities			
Capital			......
Net profit			......
Less: drawings			(14.0)
			......
Current liabilities			
Payables		52	
Accruals		......	
Bank overdraft		......	
			......
			......

Test your understanding answers

Test your understanding 1

C

Net sales is calculated as follows:

	$
Sales	73,716
Less: returns inwards	(5,863)
Net sales	67,853

Discounts are those arising from prompt payment (i.e. cash discounts) and do not appear in the trading account section of the income statement, but are brought into the income statement after the calculation of gross profit.

Test your understanding 2

Working capital is not affected by movements between current assets and current liabilities, so the payment of payables by cheque would result in a lower bank balance and lower payables, but would have no effect on working capital. The writing off of an irrecoverable debt of $250 would reduce receivables, and hence working capital. The sale of inventory would increase receivables by $230, but only decrease inventory by $100, so working capital would be increased by $130. The net effect of these items on working capital would be to decrease working capital by $120, so the final result would be $43,200 – $120 = $43,080.

Test your understanding 3

C

A and B both involved the exchange of an asset (inventory) with another asset of $500 more. This would result in an increase in working capital of $500. D would result in an increase in working capital of $250. Only C will result in a decrease in working capital, as a non-current asset is acquired by increasing payables.

Test your understanding 4

Reconstruction of cost of goods sold to establish the purchases figure:

	$	$
Opening inventory		12,000
Add: purchases*	122,000	
Less: returns	(5,000)	
		117,000
Less: Closing inventory		(18,000)
Cost of goods sold		111,000

* Found by difference

Test your understanding 5

C

The final allowance must be 5 per cent of receivables of $150,000, that is, $7,500. This will provide the balance for the allowance account, to be deducted from the receivables figure. Therefore, receivables are $142,500. Thus, only answers A or C can be considered. The change in the allowance from $6,000 to $7,500 is an additional charge to the income statement, thus C is the correct answer.

Test your understanding 6

The income statement would be:

	$	$
Gross profit as calculated		85,000
Less: expenses		
Heat and light (22,000 + 4,000)	26,000	
Rent and local business tax (27,000 - 2,500)	24,500	
Depreciation (25% × 60,000)	15,000	
		(65,500)
Net Profit		19,500

Test your understanding 7

- You will find it helpful to set out workings for most of the adjustments. They will help you to derive the correct figures to enter into the boxes provided.
- Remember there is already a balance on the allowance for receivables account.
- Make sure you deal correctly with returns and discounts.

(a) **Income statement of GBA for year ended 30 June 20X5**

	$	$	$
Sales			625,000
Less: Returns inwards			(2,300)
			622,700
Cost of sales			
Opening inventory		98,200	
Purchases	325,500		
Less: Returns outwards	(1,700)		
		323,800	
		422,000	
Less: Closing inventory		(75,300)	
			(346,700)
Gross profit			276,000
Add:			
Discounts received			2,500
Decrease in allowance for receivables ($1,000 – $620) *			380
			278,880

Less:		
Discounts allowed	1,500	
Packing materials consumed	12,900	
Distribution costs	18,700	
Rent and insurance ($6,100 – $450)	5,650	
Telephone ($4,200 + $500)	4,700	
Car expenses	4,400	
Wages	47,900	
Heat and light ($1,850 + $400)	2,250	
Finance cost	800	
Irrecoverable debts written off in year	600	
Depreciation of delivery vehicles ($112,500 × 20%)	22,500	
Depreciation of cars ($8,000 × 25%)	2,000	
Depreciation of equipment ($15,000 – 5,000) × 25%	2,500	
		(126,400)
Profit		152,480

* Allowance for the year = (1% × 20,000) + (2.5% × 12,000) + (5% × (3,000 – irrecoverable debt of 600)) = $620. The allowance at the beginning of the year was $1,000. Therefore, we must decrease the allowance by $380, hence release income into the income statement.

(b) **Statement of financial position of GBA as at 30 June 20X5**

Assets	Cost ($)	Acc. Depn. ($)	Carrying Amount ($)
Non-current assets			
Delivery vehicles	112,500	(57,500)	55,000
Cars	8,000	(2,000)	6,000
Office equipment	15,000	(7,500)	7,500
	135,500	67,000	68,500
Current assets			
Inventory		75,300	
Receivables ($95,000 – $600)	94,400		
Less: allowance	(620)		
		93,780	
Prepayments		450	
Bank deposit account		15,000	
Bank current account		26,500	
			211,030
			279,530
Capital and liabilities			
Capital at 1 July 20X4			55,550
Add: capital introduced (car)			8,000
Add: profit for the year			152,480
Less: drawings			(23,800)
			192,230

Current liabilities		
Payables	82,000	
Accruals ($400 + $500)	900	
Loan	4,400	
		87,300
		279,530

(c) With regard to the transactions in the business of GBA, which of the following transactions affect:

– profit

– cash at bank

	Affects profit	**Affects Cash at bank**
Payments to suppliers		✓
Depreciation	✓	
Sales invoiced to customers	✓	
Drawings in cash		✓
Irrecoverable debts written off	✓	

Test your understanding 8

- Take care to choose the correct side for the items in the trial balance, in particular returns, discounts and allowance for receivables.
- Remember to add in the computer that the proprietor has introduced, and to depreciate it.
- Notice that there is no change in the allowance for receivables, so there is no charge to the income statement, but remember to deduct the balance from receivables on the statement of financial position.

(a) **Trial balance of PLJ as at 30 April 20X7**

	Debit $000	Credit $000
Capital at 1.5.X6		228
Capital introduced		2
Drawings	14	
Plant at cost	83	
Plant – acc. depreciation at 1.5.X6		13
Office equipment at cost (31 + 2)	33	
Office equipment – acc. depreciation at 1.5.X6		8
Receivables	198	
Payables		52
Sales		813
Purchases	516	
Returns inwards	47	
Discount allowed	4	
Allowance for receivables at 1.5.X6		23
Administration costs	64	
Salaries	44	
Loan to friend, repayable in 6 months	25	
Bank overdraft		50
Irrecoverable debts written off	77	
Inventory at 1.5.X6	84	
	1,189	1,189

(b) Income statement of PLJ for the year ended 30 April 19X7

	$000	$000
Sales		813
Less: returns inwards		(47)
		766
Less: cost of goods sold		
Opening inventory	84	
Purchases	516	
	600	
Less: Closing inventory	(74)	
Cost of sales		(526)
Gross profit		240
Less: expenses		
Discount allowed	4	
Administration costs (64 – 3)	61	
Salaries (44 + 2)	46	
Irrecoverable debts written off	77	
Depreciation of plant (83 × 10%)	8.3	
Depreciation of office equipment ((31 + 2) – 8) × 20%	5	
		(201.3)
Net profit		38.7

(c) **Statement of financial position of PLJ as at 30 April 20X7**

Assets	**Cost** ($000)	**Accum. Depreciation** ($000)	**Carrying amount** ($000)
Non-current assets			
Plant	83	(21.3)	61.7
Office equipment	33	(13.0)	20.0
	116	(34.3)	81.7
Current assets			
Inventory		74	
Receivables	198		
Less: allowance	(23)		
		175	
Loan		25	
Prepayment		3	
			277
			358.7
Capital and liabilities			
Capital (258 + 2)			230.0
Net profit			38.7
Less: drawings			(14.0)
			254.7
Current liabilities			
Payables		52	
Accruals		2	
Bank overdraft		50	
			104
			358.7

chapter

13

Organising the Bookkeeping System

Chapter learning objectives

When you have completed this chapter, you should be able to:

- explain the purpose of accounting records and their role in the accounting system;
- understand the divisions of the ledger;
- prepare daybooks for sales, purchases and returns;
- prepare accounts for sales and purchases, including personal accounts;
- prepare cash and bank accounts,
- prepare petty cash statements under an imprest system;
- prepare journal entries.

1 Introduction

So far, the bookkeeping exercises you have seen and tried for yourself have involved only a small number of transactions, and you have therefore been able to keep all your ledger accounts in one place (even on one page!), with no difficulty in locating a particular ledger account or transaction if you wanted to check it again. Furthermore, producing a trial balance from a small number of ledger accounts is fairly quick, and any errors can easily be located by tracing through the entries again.

In this chapter we look at ways of organising the bookkeeping system for organisations with a larger number of transactions, where the ledger accounts may be too numerous to keep in one place, and where the number of transactions is too great for one person to handle. We also look at some of the supporting books and systems that help to maintain accuracy, security and control over the accounting records.

2 Organising the ledger accounts

In larger organisations, a single ledger may not be sufficient to hold all the ledger accounts because:

- there may be too many transactions for one person to maintain,
- and it might become difficult to trace individual accounts.

it is common for the ledger accounts to be divided into sections, known as 'divisions of the ledger'. Double entry is still maintained as before, but ledger accounts of the same type are grouped together. A common division of the ledger is as follows:

- all receivable accounts kept in the **sales ledger** (also known as the **receivables ledger**);
- all payable accounts kept in the **purchase ledger** (also known as the **payables ledger** or **bought ledger**);
- all bank and cash accounts kept in a **cash book** with perhaps a separate **petty cash book** as well;
- all others accounts kept in the **nominal ledger** (also known as the **general ledger**).

Do note that the sales and purchase ledgers are for personal accounts. They **do not** contain the sales and purchases accounts – these are found in the nominal ledger.

Advantages of dividing the ledger

The advantages of dividing the ledger are the following:

- individual ledger accounts can be located more easily;
- the workload can be shared among several members of the staff;
- by having one person entering one 'half' of a transaction (e.g. crediting the sales account), and another person entering the other 'half' of the transaction (e.g. debiting the receivables account), it is possible to reduce the chance of errors and fraud;
- staff who maintain one of the divisions, for example the sales ledger, can become experts in that area;
- additional controls can be built into the bookkeeping system to check accuracy.

We shall look at this last advantage in more detail in chapter 14.

3 Supporting books and records

With a larger number of transactions, more errors are likely to occur, and with the ledger now divided into sections, with different people maintaining them, it is possible that there may be delays in keeping the accounts up to date, or that transactions may be omitted.

It is possible to maintain other books, records, lists and so on, that, although not part of the ledger, help in recording and controlling the transactions in the ledger. These books are known collectively as **books of prime entry** ('prime' means 'first') – and the transactions are 'captured' here first, before being entered in the ledger accounts.

Most businesses of any size maintain records of their transactions in the following types of books of prime entry:

- **daybooks** (because they are intended to be written up on a daily basis);
- **cash books;**
- **journals** (another word for 'diary' which also means 'a daily record');

4 Sales, purchases and returns daybooks

The source document for sales and purchases is known as an invoice; for returns, the source document is a credit note. A typical invoice (or credit note) will contain the following details:

- invoice (credit note) number and date;
- name and address of the supplier;
- name and address of the customer;
- quantity and description of the goods supplied;
- the price per unit for the goods, with details of any trade discount given;
- the total price charged for the goods, excluding sales tax;
- the amount of sales tax;
- the total payable, before any cash discounts;
- the amount and terms of cash discount available;
- the due date for payment.

Source documents

Every transaction should be evidenced by a document showing the details of the transaction. These are known as 'source documents'. There are different kinds for different types of transaction. Some originate outside the organisation (such as invoices received from suppliers), some originate inside the organisation but are sent to outsiders (such as invoices sent to customers), and others originate inside and remain inside the organisation (such as details of accruals at the end of the period).

Recording transactions in the daybooks

The four types of transaction identified earlier in this chapter are each recorded in their own specialist daybook.

Each of the books can be thought of as a listing device. They each contain columns to record the facts of the transaction. At regular intervals, they are totalled as part of the summarising process.

Such a daybook will have the following headings:

Date	Ref	Personal details	Goods value ($)	Sales tax ($)	Total invoice/ credit note value ($)

The personal details would be the name of the supplier or customer as appropriate.

Example 13.A

ABC Ltd had the following transactions during the first week of July 20X2:

1 Jul	Bought goods on credit from JB cost $1000
	Sold goods on credit to JSA & Co. for $800
2 Jul	Sold goods on credit to PB Ltd for $80
	Returned goods to JB because they were faulty $80
3 Jul	Bought goods on credit from AL Ltd cost $600
4 Jul	JSA & Co. returned unwanted goods $200
5 Jul	Returned goods to AL Ltd $120
6 Jul	Sold goods on credit to CAL for $400
7 Jul	CAL returned goods as unsuitable $120
	Sold goods on credit to BC for $240

All items are subject to sales tax at 20 per cent.

Prepare the daybooks to record these transactions.

Solution

Purchases daybook

Date	Doc. no	Personal details	Goods value ($)	Sales tax ($)	Total invoice value ($)
1 Jul	001	JB	1,000	200	1,200
3 Jul	002	AL Ltd	600	120	720
			1,600	320	1,920

Sales daybook

Date	Doc. no	Personal details	Goods value ($)	Sales tax ($)	Total invoice value ($)
1 Jul	101	JSA & Co.	800	160	960
2 Jul	102	PB Ltd	80	16	96
6 Jul	103	CAL	400	80	480
7 Jul	104	BC	240	48	288
			1,520	304	1,824

Returns inwards daybook

Date	Doc. no	Personal details	Goods value ($)	Sales tax ($)	Credit note value ($)
4 Jul	901	JSA & Co.	200	40	240
7 Jul	902	CAL	120	24	144
			320	64	384

Returns outwards daybook

Date	Doc. no	Personal details	Goods value ($)	Sales tax ($)	Credit note value ($)
2 Jul	9001	JB	80	16	96
5 Jul	9002	AL Ltd	120	24	144
			200	40	240

Remember that if there was trade discount given on any of the above transactions, it would be deducted prior to calculating the sales tax, and the net amount would be recorded in the 'goods value' column.

Making the ledger entries

The daybooks can be totalled and the totals entered in the nominal ledger accounts periodically.

Using the above example 13.A the double entry would be as follows:

Purchase daybook		$
Debit	Purchases account	1,600
Debit	Sales tax account	320
Credit	Payables account	1,920

Sales daybook		$
Debit	Receivables account	1,824
Credit	Sales tax account	304
Credit	Sales account	1,520

Returns in daybook		$
Debit	Returns inwards account	320
Debit	Sales tax account	64
Credit	Receivables account	384

Returns out daybook		$
Debit	Payables account	240
Credit	Sales tax account	40
Credit	Returns outwards account	200

It is important to note the double entry is made in the nominal ledger, however we must still record the entries in the purchase and sales ledger to enable us to identify the amount owed to or due from the business.

Cross-referencing the entries

To enable the source of the ledger entries to be traced, a system of cross-referencing can be used. Each page in the daybooks is given a reference – for example, sales daybook page 23 (abbreviated to SD23) – and each page in the ledger accounts is given a reference, for example, SLC3 might indicate the sales ledger, Section C, p. 3, where CAL's (a customer) ledger account can be found. Extra columns can be added to the daybooks and ledger accounts to show these cross-references. These columns are called 'folio columns'. Thus the ledger entries for all of the above items can be shown as follows:

Sales Ledger

BC (B22)

		$	$
4 Jul	104	288	

CAL (C14)

		$			$
6 Jul	103	480	7 Jul	902	144

JSA & Co. (J4)

		$			$
1 Jul	101	960	4 Jul	901	240

PB Ltd (P35)

		$			$
2 Jul	102	96			

Purchase Ledger

AL Ltd (A42)

		$			$
5 Jul	9002	144	3 Jul	002	720

JB (J7)

		$			$
2 Jul	9001	96	1 Jul	001	1,200

Nominal Ledger

Purchases (01)

		$			$
7 Jul	PDB97	1,600			

Sales (02)

		$			$
			7 Jul	SDB118	1,520

Returns inwards (03)

		$			$
7 Jul	RIDB28	320			

Returns outwards (04)

		$	7 Jul	RODB28	200

Sales tax (99)

		$			$
7 Jul	PDB97	320	7 Jul	SDB118	304
	RIDB28	64		RODB25	40

The double entry is now complete.

Test your understanding 1

Enter the following transactions for the month of March in the appropriate daybooks and ledgers of PQR, an office equipment retailer. Assume sales tax at 20 per cent.

March

1	Sold four typewriters on credit to Office Services, list price $80 each, allowing 10% trade discount
4	Bought six calculators on credit from Abdul & Co. at $12 each net
12	Sold duplicating machine on credit to J. Hoy for $350
16	Sold four calculators on credit to Chow, list price $20 each, allowing 10% trade discount
17	Office Services returned one damaged typewriter
20	Bought six typewriters on credit from Ace Co., list price $40 each. Allowed 15% trade discount
25	Sold two duplicating machines on credit to Mills & Co., list price $350, allowing 10% trade discount

Extending the use of daybooks

The examples above assumed that only sales of the organisation's products, and purchases of its goods for sale or raw materials, were entered in the daybooks. This used to be the case when most of an organisation's transactions were in goods for sale. Nowadays, organisations have a wide range of expenses and services too, and the daybooks can be extended to cater for these also. As an example, consider a purchase daybook that is used to record all the organisation's purchases on credit as follows:

Date	Doc. no	Details	Purchases ($)	Stationery ($)	Heat and light ($)	Motor expenses ($)	Sales tax ($)	Total ($)
1 Jan	001	ABC Ltd	1,000				175	1,175
2 Jan	002	XYZ		400			70	470
3 Jan	003	PQ Ltd	2,000				350	2,350
4 Jan	004	GL Motors					21	141
	005	ABC Ltd	4,000				700	4,700
5 Jan	006	XYZ		200			35	235
	007	Genlec			600		105	705
6 Jan	008	RS Motors				240	42	282
7 Jan	009	Goodgas			400		70	470
		Totals	7,000	600	1000	360	1,568	10,528

The credit entries to the payables accounts would be made immediately, but the nominal ledger entries to purchases, stationery, heat and light, motor expenses and sales tax would be made in total at the end of the period.

5 The cash books

Again, the term 'cash book' dates back to the days when organisations dealt only in actual cash transactions. Nowadays businesses rarely deal in cash, and so the term 'cash book' refers to any book that records monies received and paid.

Further detail

It was stated earlier that the cash books have a dual purpose, both as books of prime entry and as part of the ledger. As part of the ledger, they are used to maintain the bank and cash ledger accounts, but because of the importance of keeping bank and cash records up to date they are the first place of entry for **all** bank and cash transactions.

The banking system

Today's banking system is highly automated, with large numbers of transactions being conducted electronically. However, many organisations still use cheques to make payments, and paying-in slips to make deposits to their accounts. Some common methods of transacting business through a bank account are as follows:

- **By cheque** - The **drawer** makes out a cheque to the person being paid (the **payee**). The cheque is entered in the drawer's ledger accounts at once, and sent to the payee. The payee pays it into his own bank account some days later, using a paying-in slip to record its details and that of other cheques paid in at the same time. The bank clearing system passes it to the drawer's bank for approval and payment, with the result that it is taken out of the drawer's bank account. This is known as **presenting a cheque** for payment. Until the cheque is accepted by the drawer's bank, it is considered to be **uncleared** and the bank has the right to return it as **dishonoured** if there is something amiss with it, or there are insufficient funds in the drawer's account. The time delay between making out a cheque and it being cleared depends on various factors, such as postal delays, administrative delays, holiday periods and so on. Each cheque has a reference number by which it can be identified.
- **By bankers automated clearing system (BACS)** - This avoids the use of the postal system and the writing of numerous cheques by creating a transfer between the bank accounts of different organisations. It is a faster means of payment and it is also more cost-effective when there are regular payments to the same people. The account holder produces a list of the payments to be made at any particular time. There are also specialised types of automated payments suitable for the immediate transfer of funds both within the country and outside the country.
- **By direct debit or standing order** - These work in a similar manner to each other, and are suitable for regular payments to a particular person. The bank makes the transfer automatically.
- **By bank-initiated transactions** - The transactions such as the charging of fees for maintaining the account (bank charges), interest paid on overdrawn balances, interest received, charges for dealing with dishonoured cheques and so on.

An organisation may both make and receive payments by any of these methods.

The cash book

At its simplest, the cash book is no more than an ordinary ledger account, used to record the movements in the bank account. Some organisations use it to record cash movements as well as bank movements, by using two 'money' columns on each side as follows:

Date	Details	Ref.	Bank ($)	Cash ($)	Date	Details	Ref.	Bank ($)	Cash ($)
1 Jan	Balance b/d		400	50	3 Jan	ABC Ltd	00123	100	
4 Jan	XYZ Ltd	101	200		5 Jan	Wages			20
8 Jan	Cash sales			120	5 Jan	Office equipment	00124	300	
10 Jan	PQR Ltd	102	150		8 Jan	Advertising	00125	125	
	RST Ltd	102	170		12 Jan	Wages			30
14 Jan	Cash banked	103	50		14 Jan	Cash banked			50
					14 Jan	Balance c/d		445	70
			970	170				970	170
15 Jan	Balance b/d		445	70					

Discount columns

The cash book can also be used to indicate cash discount that has been given or received. We looked at the recording of cash discount in chapter 5. We saw how, when cash discount is received or given, the amount is credited/debited to discounts received/discounts allowed account. Cash discount often involves a large number of small-value transactions, so it is possible that the nominal ledger (which contains the discount accounts), would soon fill up with the detail of a large number of small-value transactions. By adding an extra column to each side of the cash book, the discount can be identified at the point of payment (which is when it becomes known), and the total of those columns used to make the entries in the discount accounts.

Example 13.B

Zadie Traders Ltd had a favourable balance of $216 in its business bank account as at the start of business on 2 May 20X8. The following is a list of bank transactions for the week ending 7 May 20X8:

2 May Paid an insurance premium of $130 by cheque

3 May Paid an invoice for $110 from Goodies Ltd in full after deducting 10% for prompt settlement

4 May Received a cheque for $314 from Freda Dexter, a credit customer. Ms Dexter was settling an invoice for $320 and had been entitled to $6 discount

6 May Paid employees their week's wages of $182 by cheque

Record these transactions in the cash book of Zadie Traders Ltd below.

Solution

Date	Details	Bank ($)	Disc. all'd ($)	Total ($)	Date	Details	Bank ($)	Disc. rec'd ($)	Total ($)
1 May	Balance b/d	216			2 May	Insurance	130		130
4 May	Dexter	314	6	320	3 May	Goodies	99	11	110
					6 May	Wages	182		182
						Balance c/d	119		
		530	6	320			530	11	422
7 May	Balance b/d	119							

The cash book shows the balance on the bank account and can also be used to make entries to the other accounts, i.e. debit payables with $110 and credit discount received with $11 (net effect agrees with the bank entry of a credit for $9).

A much better layout would be to record the entries in a cash receipts book and a cash payments book and to analyse each entry ready for the double entry process:

Cash receipts book:

Date	Details	Bank $	Receivables $	Discount allow. $
4 May	Dexter	314	314	6

The cash book can be used to record the double entry:

		$
Debit	Bank account	314
Debit	Discounts allowed	6
Credit	Receivables (gross amount 314 + 6)	320

Cash payments book:

Date	Details	Bank $	Insurance $	Wages $	Payables $	Discount rec. $
2 May	Insurance	130	130			
3 May	Goodies	99			99	11
6 May	Wages	182		182		
		411	130	182	99	11

The cash book can be used to record the double entry:

		$
Debit	Insurance	130
Debit	Wages	182
Debit	Payables (gross amount 99 + 11)	110
Credit	Discounts received	11
Credit	Bank account	411

As well as entering the amount of each payment and receipt in the total columns, the amount would also be entered in one or other of the analysis columns. This means that when the book is totalled, at regular intervals, it will be immediately apparent how much cash has been received from receivables, how much paid to payables, how much paid in wages and so on. The totals can be used to make ledger entries, but can also be used in the control process covered in chapter 14.

Test your understanding 2

N Ramrod keeps cash and bank records. At the close of business on 29 May 20X1 he reached the bottom of a page and carried forward the following:

	Discount ($)	Cash ($)	Bank ($)	
Total b/f	27.40	114.10	214.30	Debit side
Total b/f	40.10	74.50	210.00	Credit side

The following sums were received on 30 May 20X1:

Cheque from J Cuthbertson for $120 in settlement of an account for $125

Cash from N Green $40

Cheque from Xu for $75 in settlement of an account for $76.50

The following payments were made on 30 May 20X1:

Cheque to Morris Brown for $140.40

Cheque to local council in payment of local business tax for the half-year $150.40

N Ramrod cashed a cheque for private drawings of $50 and took an additional $50 from the office cash for the same purpose.

You are required to:

Write up N Ramrod's cash and bank records and balance them at close of business on 30 May 20X1.

Authorising bank payments

All payments out of the bank account should be authorised by a senior member of staff. Two signatories may be required for amounts of more than a certain, fixed figure.
All items to be paid should be evidenced by source documents, for example, invoices, that have been approved for payment.

The petty cash book

The petty cash book is similar in many ways to the cash books described earlier in this chapter except that it is intended to be used for small payments made in cash.

It usually operates on an **imprest** system whereby an agreed balance of cash is held by an individual nominated as the petty cashier. This person can often be a junior member of staff due to the fact that he or she is responsible only for small sums of money that are tightly controlled. Small payments of cash and reimbursements of expenses to employees are then made via the petty cash system and at the end of each week (or other agreed period) the amount paid out of petty cash is reimbursed from the main cash book to restore the imprest (balance) to its agreed level. The amount to be reimbursed is evidenced by **petty cash vouchers** raised by the petty cashier, and signed by the person receiving the cash, as evidence of receipt. The cash itself can be counted and compared to the balance in the petty cash book.

Further detail

The petty cash book would not normally receive income other than from the main cashier, although such a possibility does exist, and so its design concentrates on the analysis of expenditure by using a columnar approach as illustrated by the example below. At the end of each accounting period the columns are totalled. The balance on the petty cash account is carried forward to the next accounting period.

Controls over petty cash

The following controls and security over petty cash should be found in a business:

- The petty cash must be kept in a petty cash box.
- The petty cash box must be secured in a safe.
- The person responsible for petty cash must be reliable and know what he/she is doing.
- All petty cash must be supported by invoices.
- Petty cash vouchers must be signed by the claimant and the person responsible for running the petty cash.
- Regular spot checks must be carried out to ensure that the petty cash is accurate.

Example 13.C

Beechfield Ltd make use of a petty cash book as part of their bookkeeping system. The following is a summary of the petty cash transactions for the month of November 20X9.

		$
1 Nov	Opening petty cash book float received from cashier	350
2 Nov	Cleaning materials	5
3 Nov	Postage stamps	10
6 Nov	Envelopes	12
8 Nov	Taxi fare	32
10 Nov	Petrol for company car	17
14 Nov	Typing paper	25
15 Nov	Cleaning materials	4
16 Nov	Bus fare	2
20 Nov	Visitors' lunches	56
21 Nov	Mops and brushes for cleaning	41
23 Nov	Postage stamps	35
27 Nov	Envelopes	12
29 Nov	Visitors' lunches	30
30 Nov	Photocopying paper	40

You are required to draw up a petty cash book for the month using analysis columns for stationery, cleaning, entertainment, travelling and postages. Show clearly the receipt of the amount necessary to restore the float and the balance brought forward for the start of the following month.

Solution

Debit ($)	Date	Details	Total ($)	Stat'y ($)	Cleaning ($)	Ent'ment ($)	Travel ($)	Post ($)
350	1 Nov	Cashier						
	2 Nov	Materials	5		5			
	3 Nov	Stamps	10					10
	6 Nov	Envelopes	12	12				
	8 Nov	Taxi	32				32	
	10 Nov	Petrol	17				17	
	14 Nov	Paper	25	25				
	15 Nov	Materials	4		4			
	16 Nov	Bus fare	2				2	
	20 Nov	Lunches	56			56		
	21 Nov	Mops, etc.	41		41			
	23 Nov	Stamps	35					35
	27 Nov	Envelopes	12	12				
	29 Nov	Lunches	30			30		
	30 Nov	Paper	40	40				
321	30 Nov	Cashier						
	30 Nov	Balance c/d	350					
671			671	89	50	86	51	45

The totals of the various expense columns are then debited to those accounts in the nominal ledger.

The amount reimbursed is equal to the amount paid from the petty cash, i.e. $321. This will be taken from the bank account into petty cash.

The accounting entries will be to **debit the analysed expense accounts and credit bank**.

Test your understanding 3

Explain briefly the operation of the imprest system of controlling petty cash.

Test your understanding 4

The petty cash imprest is restored to $100 at the end of each week. The following amounts are paid out of petty cash during week 23:

Stationery	$14.10, including sales tax at 20%
Travelling costs	$25.50
Office refreshments	$12.90
Sundry payables	$24.00 plus sales tax at 20%

The amount required to restore the imprest to $100 is:

$............

6 The journal

In a bookkeeping system involving the use of books of prime entry, it is inevitable that there will be transactions that do not correspond with the main books of prime entry used, that is, the daybooks and cash books. In order to complete the system, another book is needed in which to capture sundry items prior to entering them in the ledger. This book is called 'the journal' and is used for a wide variety of transactions, such as:

- the purchase and sale of non-current assets on credit;
- depreciation;
- the write-off of irrecoverable debts;
- allowances for receivables;
- accruals and prepayments;
- transfers between accounts, such as the transfers to income statement at year end;
- the correction of errors;
- opening entries when a new business is formed;
- entries when another business in acquired;

The correction of errors will be considered in the next chapter.

The journal is used to record any transaction that does not fit into any of the other books of prime entry, that is, transactions that are not sales or purchases on credit, and transactions not involving cash.

The journal has debit and credit columns. However, these are not part of the double-entry system. They are merely a memorandum of what is going to be recorded in the ledger accounts for a particular transaction or adjustment. It is also common for journal entries to be authorised by a senior accountant. In the narrative to a journal entry it is possible to add more information about the transaction, and to cross reference to other documentation.

It is common for a computer-based assessment question to ask for the journal entries for a transaction.

This is sometimes used as an alternative to asking for the ledger entries. You must, therefore, know how to layout a journal and record the debits and credits of a transaction.

The layout of the journal

The basic layout is as follows:

Date	Account name/details	Debit ($)	Credit ($)	Explanation

Using the journal for transactions

Example 13.D

The following transactions are to be entered in the journal:

1 May Purchased plant on credit from J Smith for $1,000 plus sales tax at 20 per cent.

3 May Wrote off the following irrecoverable debts.

P Taylor	$500
M Morris	$300
Y Bhatti	$100

4 May Sold office machinery for $800 to A Bell on credit. The machinery had cost $1,000 and had been depreciated by $400.

Solution

Date	Account name/details	Debit ($)	Credit ($)	Explanation
1 May	Plant	1,000		Purchase of plant on credit, see invoice No. X123
	Sales tax	200		
	J Smith		1,200	
3 May	Irrecoverable debt expenses	900		Irrecoverable debts – see irrecoverable debt file reference May 003
	Taylor		500	
	Morris		300	
	Bhatti		100	
4 May	Office machinery at cost		1,000	Office machinery sold on credit, see invoice No. Y345
	Office machinery accum. depreciation	400		
	A Bell	800		
	Profit on disposal		200	

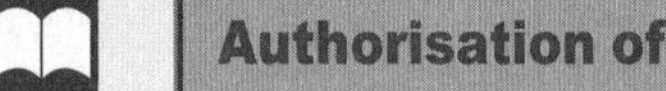

Authorisation of journal entries

Because journal entries involving adjustments and transfer have no source documents to support them, it is vital that all such entries are authorised by a senior member of staff. This can be done by signing the journal entries, or by referencing them to other forms of authorisation, for example, letters, minutes and so on.

7 Chapter summary

This chapter introduced you to a variety of books, records and documents that can assist in the recording of financial transactions, especially applicable to larger organisations.

These include:

- daybooks (books of prime entry);
- the use of the journal;
- divisions of the ledger;
- cash books.

Much of the chapter is concerned with the physical maintenance of these books and records, but you should also appreciate how they fit into the overall system of control of the bookkeeping system.

Test your understanding questions.

Test your understanding 5

An organisation's cash book has an opening balance in the bank column of $485 credit. The following transactions then took place:

- cash sales $1,450, including sales tax of $150;
- receipts from customers of $2,400;
- payments to payables of $1,800 less 5 per cent cash discount;
- dishonoured cheques from customers amounting to $250.

The resulting balance in the bank column of the cash book should be:

$...........

Test your understanding 6

An organisation restores its petty cash balance to $500 at the end of each month. During January, the total column in the petty cash book was recorded as being $420, and hence the imprest was restored by this amount. The analysis columns, which had been posted to the nominal ledger, totalled only $400. This error would result in:

A no imbalance in the trial balance

B the trial balance being $20 higher on the debit side

C the trial balance being $20 higher on the credit side

D the petty cash balance being $20 lower than it should be

Test your understanding 7

A book of prime entry is one in which:

A the rules of double-entry bookkeeping do not apply

B ledger accounts are maintained

C transactions are entered prior to being recorded in the ledger accounts

D the personal accounts with customers and suppliers

Test your understanding answers

Test your understanding 1

Sales daybook

Date	Doc. no	Personal details	Goods value ($)	Sales tax ($)	Total invoice value($)
1 Mar	001	Office Services	288.0	57.60	345.60
12 Mar	002	J. Hoy	350.0	70.00	420.00
16 Mar	003	Chow	72.00	14.40	86.40
25 Mar	004	Mills & Co	630.00	126.00	756.00
			1340.00	268.00	1,608.00

Purchases daybook

Date	Doc. no	Personal details	Goods value ($)	Sales tax ($)	Total invoice value ($)
4 Mar	101	Abdul & Co	72.00	14.40	86.40
20 Mar	102	Ace Co	204.00	40.80	244.80
			276.00	55.20	331.20

Sales returns daybook

Date	Doc. no	Personal details	Goods value ($)	Sales tax ($)	Credit note value ($)
17 Mar	999	Office Services	72.00	14.40	86.40
			72.00	14.40	86.40

Sales Ledger

Office Services

		$			$
1 Mar	001	345.60	17 Mar	999	86.40

J. Hoy

		$			$
12 Mar	002	420.00			

Chow

		$			$
16 Mar	003	86.40			

Mills & Co

		$			$
25 Mar	004	756.00			

Purchase Ledger

Abdul & Co

		$			$
			4 Mar	101	86.40

Ace Co

		$			$
			20 Mar	102	244.80

Nominal Ledger

Sales

		$			$
			31 Mar	Sales daybook	1,340.00

Purchases

		$			$
31 Mar	Purchases daybook	276.00			

Sales returns

		$			$
31 Mar	Sales returns daybook	72.00			

Sales tax

		$			$
31 Mar	Purchases daybook	55.20	31 Mar	Sales daybook	268.00
	Sales returns daybook	14.40			

Test your understanding 2

Date	Details ($)	Disc. all'd ($)	Cash ($)	Bank ($)	Date	Details	Disc. all'd ($)	Cash ($)	Bank ($)
29 May	Balance b/d	27.40	114.10	214.30	29 May	Balance b/d	40.10	74.50	210.00
30 May	J Cuthbertson	5.00		120.00	30 May	Morris Brown			140.40
	N Green		40.00			Rates			150.40
	Xu	1.50		75.00		Drawings		50.00	50.00
	Balance c/d			141.50		Balance c/d		29.60	
		33.90	154.10	550.80			40.10	154.10	550.80

Test your understanding 3

The imprest system of controlling petty cash is based on a set 'float' of cash that the petty cashier commences with. This amount is used to pay for small items during the coming week or month, for which a petty cash voucher should be prepared. At the end of the period (or when the cash runs out), the vouchers can be totalled and the amount spent is reimbursed to the petty cashier so as to commence the next period with the same 'float'.

Test your understanding 4

	$
Stationery	14.10
Travel	25.50
Refreshments	12.90
Sundry payables ($24 × 1.20)	28.80
	81.30

Test your understanding 5

The calculation is as follows:

	$
Opening overdraft	(485)
Add: receipts, inc. sales tax	(3,850)
	3,365
Less: payments after discount	(1,710)
	1,655
Less: dishonoured cheques	(250)
	1,405

Test your understanding 6

C

The petty cash book will have been credited with $420 to restore the imprest, whereas the expense accounts will have been debited with only $400. Therefore, the credit side of the trial balance will be $20 higher than the debit side.

Test your understanding 7

C

A is incorrect as the journal is one of the books of prime entry in which double-entry rules do apply. B is incorrect – ledger accounts are not maintained in books of prime entry. D is incorrect as personal accounts are ledger accounts that are maintained outside the main ledgers.

chapter

14

Controlling the Bookkeeping System

Chapter learning objectives

When you have completed this chapter, you should be able to:

- explain the need for financial controls;
- explain the methods of preventing errors;
- explain the types of fraud;
- prepare a bank reconciliation;
- prepare control accounts;
- prepare a reconciliation of control accounts to individual ledger accounts;
- prepare suspense accounts and corrections of errors;
- explain the importance of computers in accounting.

1 Introduction

No bookkeeping system can be guaranteed to be entirely free of errors. Human beings are fallible, and even automated and computerised systems are less than perfect. For example, a computer cannot possibly know that a supplier has sent you an invoice that never arrived.

In this chapter we look at a number of ways in which the bookkeeping system can be checked for accuracy, and ways in which errors and omissions can be rectified.

Specific topics which are covered include:

- bank reconciliations
- control accounts
- suspense accounts.

2 The need for financial controls

Financial controls are needed to:

- Provide **a check on the accuracy** of entries made in the ledgers. It is very easy to make a mistake posting entries, i.e. errors of omission, duplication, principle, etc. The control accounts check the accuracy of the postings made in both the personal accounts (sales and purchase ledger) and the nominal ledger. The bank reconciliation checks the accuracy of the banks records and the cashbook produced by the business and may highlight income or charges that have been missed by the business, e.g. bank charges.
- **Segregate duties** - by having people doing different duties we reduce the chance of fraud, e.g. one person does not produce all entries for a whole transaction from start to finish. The sales ledger would be prepared by one person and then the nominal ledger by another. This prevents someone creating a "made up" sale and receivables account to enable them to make a payment in order to get money out of the business unethically!

3 Preventing errors

There are a number of ways in which errors can be prevented, or at least limited in their number and effect. Many of these also prevent deliberate fraud.

Authorisation procedures

Transactions should be authorised at an appropriate level. For example,

- the purchase of major non-current assets should be justified/agreed by senior management and recorded in the minutes of meetings;
- cheques for large amounts should require two signatures;
- new receivable and payable accounts should be authorised by a senior person;
- all purchase orders should be authorised by a responsible officer;
- all payments made should be approved. In particular,
  - payments to suppliers should be checked against goods received, invoices and credit notes;
  - refunds to customers should be authorised;
  - payrolls should be checked and authorised prior to making payment.

Documentation

Documentation should be used to give evidence of transactions, and should be properly filed and referenced. This helps to provide an 'audit trail' of transactions through the system. As an example, consider the ordering of goods for resale, and the documentation involved.

- **Raising of the order**. On official order forms, properly authorised, after obtaining several quotations.
- **Receipt of goods**. Checked on arrival, checked with order, shortages and breakages recorded.
- **Receipt of invoice**. Checked with order and receipt of goods; prices, discounts and calculations checked.
- **Payment of invoice**. Only after all credit notes have been received, and checked with purchase ledger account prior to payment.

Organisation of staff

Staff should be properly recruited, trained and supervised. No one person should have complete control over any section of the bookkeeping system. Duties should be shared out between different members of staff. This is known as **segregation of duties**.

This can be illustrated by considering the procedures arising from selling goods on credit. In summary the tasks involved are:

- issuing sales invoices;
- issuing credit notes;
- credit control;
- banking receipts from customers.

If one person were to be solely responsible for all (or even more than one) of these tasks, it would be easy for money to be diverted and the corresponding paperwork destroyed or falsified. Staff should also rotate their duties from time to time.

Safeguarding assets

Assets should be properly maintained, insured, utilised, valued and recorded.

Detecting errors

Some errors may come to light purely by chance, and some are never found at all. For example, if you receive a cheque from a customer who has no outstanding balance on his account, it is possible that an invoice has been omitted from the books. If you never receive the cheque, the error might never come to light.

It would be extremely unwise to trust to chance, and therefore there are several checks that can be incorporated to help detect errors.

Spot checks

These are particularly useful in detecting fraud. For example, spot checks on petty cash balances may uncover 'teeming and lading' activities, whereby an employee borrows money from the petty cash on a regular basis, but puts it back when the imprest is being checked, only to remove it again afterwards.

Spot checks are also commonly carried out on bank balances, ledger accounts and inventories.

Comparison with external evidence

External evidence is among the most useful in determining the reliability of records. Examples include:

- confirmation of balances with receivables and payables;
- confirmation of bank balances with the bank.

Reconciliations

A reconciliation is a comparison of records to identify differences and to effect agreement. There are several types of reconciliation that can be carried out.

- Producing a trial balance. If the debit and credit totals do not agree, it is obvious that an error has been made.
- Reconciling the accounts of the organisation with records received from other organisations. Two common reconciliations of this type are:
  - bank reconciliations, where the bank account maintained by the organisation is reconciled with the statement issued by the bank;
  - supplier reconciliations, where the ledger account maintained by the organisation is reconciled with a statement of the ledger account in the supplier's books.

Both of these types of reconciliation are considered in more detail later in this chapter.

- Reconciling groups of ledger accounts with a control account. Control accounts are considered in more detail later in this chapter.

Carrying out an audit

An audit is a check on the accounting records and financial statements of the organisation. It does not entail a complete check on every bookkeeping entry, but rather examines the systems and procedures in place that should contribute to the reliability of the accounting records. The role of audit is discussed in more detail in chapter 15.

Types of fraud

Fraud can be defined as "intentional deceit, trickery or breach of confidence perpetrated for profit or to gain some unfair or dishonest advantage." The legal definition does vary between different legal authorities but fraud is usually considered to be a crime, punishable in criminal courts. Offences can lead to punishments such as fines, compensation and even prison.

Fraud includes the acts of bribery, coercion, blackmail and extortion. However, the acts most relevant to the accounting function of a business include asset misappropriation (theft or misuse of company assets) and manipulation of the financial statements. Often, theft of assets also includes manipulation of the accounts as the fraudster may attempt to cover their fraud by altering accounting records.

Acts such as theft of cash or inventory and unauthorised use of company funds by management are the more obvious examples of fraud. Fraudulent manipulation of the financial statements is more difficult to identify. For example; directors are allowed to alter the accounting policies they apply to financial statements (e.g. historic cost or revaluation methods). They should select the policy that is most relevant to the company and, if they change a policy, they should clearly indicate the financial impact of this change by restating the prior year's financial statements and describing the affect of the change in a note to the accounts. If, however, they change policy, with the intention of deceiving the shareholders of the company, this would constitute a fraud.

Perhaps the most famous example of financial statements fraud was committed by the directors of a company called Enron. In this case the directors used many accounting mechanisms to inflate the profits and the share price of the business and to hide debts so that they did not appear in the financial statements. When Enron's share price hit its peak ($90 in August 2000) the executive directors began to sell their shares, knowing that the company was massively loss making and that the share price would soon fall. This is also known as insider dealing.

Following the uncovering of accounting irregularities both Enron (at the time the second biggest company in the world) and its auditor, Arthur Andersen (one of the big 5 global accountancy firms), collapsed. Many of the directors of Enron were charged with criminal offences, including the Chief Executive Officer, Jeffrey Skilling, who was sentenced to nearly 25 years in jail.

4 Bank reconciliation statements

Bank reconciliations are an essential 'must know' topic.

The purpose of a bank reconciliation statement is to check the accuracy of an organisation's bank account record by comparing it with the record of the account held by the bank. In Chapter 13 we saw that there is often a timing delay between the transaction occurring (and therefore being recorded in the cash book) and it being processed by the bank. It is this timing difference that is usually the cause of any difference between the balances. However, there are some transactions of which the organisation will not be aware until they receive their bank statement. These include bank charges, commissions and dishonoured cheques (where the drawer's bank has refused to honour the cheque drawn upon it), and may also include direct debits and standing orders if the account holder has not been separately notified of their being paid.

In order to ensure that both the bank's and the organisation's records are correct, a comparison is made of the two sets of records and a reconciliation statement produced.

Note debits and credits are reversed on the bank statement because it is being recorded from the banks point of view.

Differences between the bank statement and the cash book

When attempting to reconcile the bank statement with the cash book, there are three differences between cash book and bank statement:

- unrecorded items
- timing differences
- errors

Further detail

Unrecorded items

These are items included in the bank statement but not in the cash book. This could be due to the fact the business has forgotten to include them or they were not aware of them until the bank statement arrived. These could be:

- bank charges
- direct debits
- standing orders
- interest
- dishonoured cheques

These must now be recorded in the cash book.

Timing differences

These items have been recorded in the cash book, but due to the bank clearing process have not been recorded in the bank statement:

- outstanding/unpresented cheques – cheques sent to suppliers but not yet cleared by the bank
- outstanding/uncleared lodgements – cheques received by the business by not yet cleared by the bank

The bank statement needs to be adjusted for these:

	$
Balance as per bank statement	X
Less: unpresented cheques	(X)
Plus: unpresented lodgements	X
Balance as per revised cash book	X

Errors

These can be found in either the cash book or the bank statement and must be adjusted appropriately.

The steps taken to undertake a bank reconciliation are:

Step 1 – Tick off all items in **both** the cash book and the bank statement.

Step 2 – Update the cash book for unticked items in the bank statement.

Step 3 – Prepare the bank reconciliation with the unticked items in the cash book.

Example 14.A

The following extract from the cash book of ABX Limited for the month of June shows the company's bank transactions:

	$		$
Balance b/d	9,167	Purchase ledger	1,392
Sales ledger	4,023	Employees' income tax	2,613
Cash sales	2,194	Sales tax payable	981
Sales ledger	7,249	Cheques cashed	3,290
		Balance c/d	14,357
	22,633		22,633

The company's bank statement for the same period is as follows:

	Debit ($)	Credit ($)	Balance ($)
Opening balance			7,645
Lodgement 000212		2,491	10,136
Cheque 000148	969		9,167
Insurance D/D	2,413		6,754
Lodgement 000213		4,023	10,777
Cheque 000149	1,392		9,385
Cheque 000150	2,613		6,772
Cheque 000152	3,290		3,482
Lodgement 000214		2,194	5,676
Bank charges	563		5,113

You are required to reconcile the balances shown in the cash book and the bank statement.

Solution

Step 1 – compare the entries shown in the cash book with those on the bank statement and match them. This is shown below where letters have been used to match the items together.

	$		$
Balance b/d	9,167	Purchase ledger (c)	1,392
Sales ledger (a)	4,023	Employees' income tax (d)	2,613
Cash sales (b)	2,194	Sales tax payable	981
Sales ledger	7,249	Cheques cashed (e)	3,290
		Balance c/d	14,357
	22,633		22,633

	Debit ($)	Credit ($)	Balance ($)
Opening balance			7,645
Lodgement 000212		2,491	10,136
Cheque 000148	969		9,167
Insurance D/D	2,413		6,754
Lodgement 000213		4,023 (a)	10,777
Cheque 000149	1,392 (c)		9,385
Cheque 000150	2,613 (d)		6,772
Cheque 000152	3,290 (e)		3,482
Lodgement 000214		2,194 (b)	5,676
Bank charges	563		5,113

When the matching is complete there will usually be items on the bank statement that are not shown in the cash book, and items entered in the cash book that are not shown on the bank statement.

Some of these may relate to the previous period – in this example the opening balances were not the same. There is a lodgement (reference 000212) and a cheque (number 000148) that are not in the cash book of the period. A simple calculation shows that these items represent the difference between the opening balances. These are, therefore, timing differences that do not affect the bank reconciliation at 30 June.

Step 2 – There are some items on the bank statement that have not been entered in the cash book. These are the direct debit for insurance and the bank charges. The cash book balance needs to be amended for these:

	$	$
Balance as shown in cash book		14,357
Less:		
Insurance	2,413	
Bank charges	563	
		(2,976)
Amended cash book balance		11,381

Step 3 – The remaining difference between the amended cash book balance and the bank statement balance is caused by timing differences on those items not matched above:

	$
Balance as per bank statement	5,113
Add: uncleared lodgement	7,249
	12,362
Less: unpresented cheque	(981)
Balance as per cash book	11,381

You should note that this statement commenced with the balance as per the bank statement and reconciled it to the balance shown in the cash book.

Remember the **revised** cash book figure is always the bank figure used in the statement of financial position.

e.g

Illustration 1

From the following information, prepare a statement that shows any necessary corrections to the cash book balance and a statement that reconciles the bank statement balance with the corrected cash book balance.

	$
Balance as per cash book	1,245
Unpresented cheques	890
Bank charges not entered in cash book	100
Receipts not yet credited by bank	465
Dishonoured cheque not entered in cash book	170
Balance as per bank statement	1,400

Solution

	$
Original cash book balances	1,245
Less: amounts not yet entered	
Bank charges	(100)
Dishonoured cheque	(170)
Corrected cash book balance	975
Balance per bank statement	1,400
Add: outstanding lodgements	465
Less: unpresented cheques	(890)
Balance as per corrected cash book	975

Test your understanding 1

Cash book (bank columns only)

		$			$
1 Jan	Balance	600	18 Jan	D Anderson	145
13Jan	Umberto	224	28 Jan	R Patrick	72
13 Jan	L Bond	186	30 Jan	Parveen	109

Bank statement

		Debit ($)	*Credit* ($)	*Balance* ($)
1 Jan	Balance			635
3 Jan	H Turner	35		600
13 Jan	Umberto		224	824
23 Jan	D Anderson	145		679
31 Jan	Standing order	30		649

Using the information given above:

(a) prepare a corrected cash book;

(b) draw up a bank reconciliation statement.

Reconciliation of suppliers' statements

Many suppliers send monthly statements to their customers, showing the position of that customers, account in their own records, and this provides an ideal opportunity to check the accuracy of the organisation's records with those of another. A reconciliation of payable balances to supplier statements is no different from carrying out a bank reconciliation, as shown below.

Example 14.B

Included in the payables ledger of J Cross, a shopkeeper, is the following account that disclosed that the amount owing to one of his suppliers at 31 May 20X4 was $472.13.

Payables ledger

20X4		$	20X4		$
18 May	Purchase returns	36.67	1 May	Balance b/d	862.07
27 May	Purchase returns	18.15	16 May	Purchases	439.85
27 May	Adjustment (overcharge)	5.80	25 May	Purchases	464.45
31 May	Discount received	24.94	25 May	Adjustment (undercharge)	13.48
31 May	Bank	1,222.16			
31 May	Balance c/d	472.13			
		1,779.85			1,779.85

J Cross in account with Nala Merchandising Company – Statement of account

20X4		*Debit* ($)	*Credit* ($)	*Balance* ($)
1 May	BCE			1,538.70 Dr
3 May	DISC		13.40	1,525.30 Dr
	CHQ		634.11	891.19 Dr
5 May	ALLCE		29.12	862.07 Dr
7 May	GDS	256.72		1,118.79 Dr
10 May	GDS	108.33		1,227.12 Dr
11 May	GDS	74.80		1,301.92 Dr
14 May	ADJ	13.48		1,315.40 Dr
18 May	GDS	162.55		1,477.95 Dr
23 May	GDS	301.90		1,779.85 Dr
25 May	ALLCE		36.67	1,743.18 Dr
28 May	GDS	134.07		1,877.25 Dr
29 May	GDS	251.12		2,128.37 Dr
30 May	GDS	204.80		2,333.17 Dr
31 May	GDS	91.36		2,424.53 Dr
31 May	BCE			2,424.53 Dr

Abbreviations: BCE – balance; CHQ – cheque; GDS – goods; ALLCE – allowance; DISC – discount; ADJ – adjustment.

You are required to prepare a statement reconciling the closing balance on the supplier's account in the payables ledger with the closing balance shown on the statement of account submitted by the supplier.

Solution

As we saw with bank reconciliation statements the technique is to match the items first and then construct a reconciliation statement.

Payables ledger

20X4		$	20X4		$
18 May	Purchase returns (a)	36.67	1 May	Balance b/d	862.07
27 May	Purchase returns (r)	18.15	16 May	Purchases (b)	439.85
27 May	Adjustment (overcharge) (t)	5.80	25 May	Purchases (c)	464.45
31 May	Discount received (s)	24.94	25 May	Adjustment (undercharge)	13.48
31 May	Bank (s)	1,222.16			
31 May	Balance c/d	472.13			
		1,779.85			1,779.85

J Cross in account with Nala Merchandising Company – Statement of Account

20X4		Debit ($)	Credit ($)	Balance ($)
1 May	BCE			1,538.70 Dr
3 May	DISC		13.40(p)	1,525.30 Dr
	CHQ		634.11(p)	891.19 Dr
5 May	ALLCE		29.12(p)	862.07 Dr
7 May	GDS	256.72(b)		118.79 Dr
10 May	GDS	108.33(b)		1,227.12 Dr
11 May	GDS	74.80(b)		1,301.92 Dr
14 May	ADJ	13.48(d)		1,315.40 Dr
18 May	GDS	162.55(c)		1,477.95 Dr
23 May	GDS	301.90(c)		1,779.85 Dr
25 May	ALLCE		36.67(a)	1,743.18 Dr
28 May	GDS	134.07(q)		1,877.25 Dr
29 May	GDS	251.12(q)		2,128.37 Dr
30 May	GDS	204.80(q)		2,333.17 Dr
31 May	GDS	91.36(q)		2,424.53 Dr
31 May	BCE			2,424.53 Dr

The items marked 'p' reconcile the opening balances.

Reconciliation statement

	$	$
Balance as per payables ledger		472.13
Add:		
Goods despatched by supplier not entered in ledger (q)	681.35	
Returns not yet recognised by supplier (r)	18.15	
Payments/discounts not yet recognised by supplier (s)	1,247.10	
Adjustment not yet recognised by supplier (t)	5.80	
		1,952.40
Balance as per supplier's statement		2,424.53

5 Control accounts

Control accounts are an essential 'must know' topic.

- Control accounts are nominal ledger accounts that summarise a large number of transactions. As such they are part of the double entry system.
- They are used to prove the accuracy of the ledger accounting system.
- They are mainly used with regard to receivables - **sales ledger control account** and payables - **purchase ledger control account**.

When a company transfers the daily total of the sales daybook into the nominal ledger the double entry is:

Dr	Sales ledger control account (receivables)	X
Cr	Sales	X

When they transfer the total of the purchase daybook the double entry is:

Dr	Purchases	X
Cr	Purchase ledger control account (payables)	X

At the same time most businesses will maintain what is referred to as a **'memorandum**.' This is a separate list of individual receivable and payable amounts due from each customer and to each supplier, respectively. This simple 'list of balances' is used as a record so that companies know how much each customer is due to pay and how much they are due to pay each supplier. This assists with credit control and cash flow management. A key control operated by a business is to compare the total balance on the control account at the end of the accounting period with the total of all the separate memorandum balances. In theory they should be identical. This is referred to as a control account reconciliation.

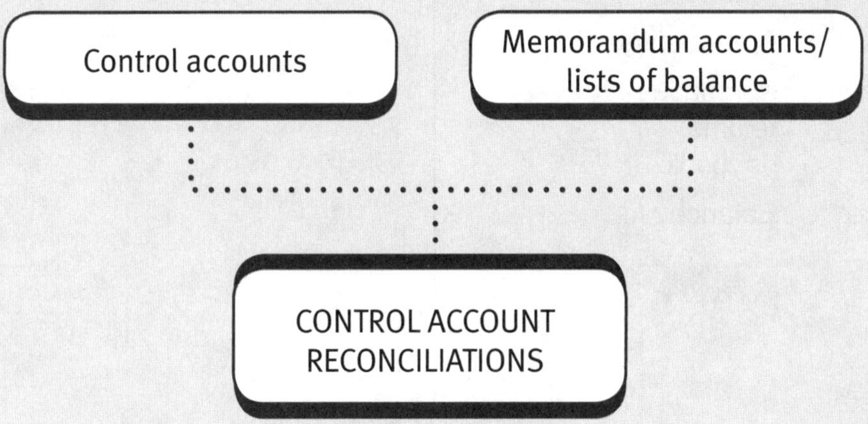

The sales ledger control account (receivables) may include any of the following entries:

Sales ledger control account

20X1		$	20X1		$
1 Jan	Balance b/d	X	31 Jan	Sales returns daybook	X
31 Jan	Sales daybook	X	31 Jan	Cash book Received	X
	Dishonoured cheque	X		Discount allowed	X
				Irrecoverable debt	X
				Contra entry	X
			31 Jan	Balance c/d	X
		X			X
1 Feb	Balance b/d	X			

The purchase ledger control account (payables) may include any of the following entries:

Purchase ledger control account

20X1		$	20X1		$
1 Jan	Cash book Received	X	1 Jan	Balance b/d	X
31 Jan	Discount received	X	31 Jan	Purchase daybook	X
	Contra entry	X			
	Purchase returns daybook	X			
31 Jan	Balance c/d	X			
		X			X
			1 Feb	Balance b/d	X

Example 14.C

An organisation has four receivables, with the following balances at 1 January 20X1:

	$
Khan	437
P Binns	1,046
J Harris	93
Bloggs	294
Total	1,870

The sales daybook for January is as follows:

Sales daybook

Date	Customer	Goods ($)	Sales tax ($)	Total ($)
20X1				
10 Jan	J Harris	200	35	235
17 Jan	P Binns	400	70	470
23 Jan	Khan	600	105	705
		1,200	210	1,410

The sales returns daybook for January is as follows:

Sales returns daybook

Date	**Customer**	**Goods ($)**	**Sales tax ($)**	**Total ($)**
20X1				
12 Jan	J Harris	80	14	94
23 Jan	P Binns	120	21	141
		200	35	235

The cash book (debit side) for the same day includes the following entries:

Received from receivables

Date	Details	($)	Discount ($)
20X1			
14 Jan	C Bloggs	125	5
16 Jan	P Binns	570	30
		695	35

You are required to write up the personal accounts in the sales ledger and the control account, and to reconcile the control account to the total of the sales ledger balances.

Solution

Sales ledger accounts (personal accounts) - memorandum accounts

Khan

20X1		$	20X1		$
1 Jan	Balance b/d	437			
23 Jan	Invoice	705	31 Jan	Balance c/d	1,142
		1,142			1,142
1 Feb	Balance b/d	1,142			

P Binns

20X1		$	20X1		$
1 Jan	Balance b/d	1,046	16 Jan	Cash	570
17 Jan	Invoice	470	16 Jan	Discount	30
			23 Jan	Sales returns	141
			31 Jan	Balance c/d	775
		1,516			1,516
1 Feb	Balance b/d	775			

J Harris

20X1		$	20X1		$
1 Jan	Balance b/d	93	12 Jan	Sales returns	94
10 Jan	Invoice	235	31 Jan	Balance c/d	234
		328			328
1 Feb	Balance b/d	234			

C Bloggs

20X1		$	20X1		$
1 Jan	Balance b/d	294	14 Jan	Cash	125
				Discount	5
			31 Jan	Balance c/d	164
		294			294
1 Feb	Balance b/d	164			

A list of receivables' balances extracted at 31 January 20X1 is as follows:

	$
Khan	1,142
P Binns	775
J Harris	234
C Bloggs	164
Total	2,315

The sales ledger control account can be compiled from the total of the entries made to the individual receivables accounts, using the totals in the various books of prime entry, as follows:

Sales ledger control account

20X1		$	20X1		$
1 Jan	Balance b/d	1,870	31 Jan	Sales returns daybook	235
31 Jan	Sales daybook	1,410	31 Jan	Cash book Received	695
				Discount allowed	35
			31 Jan	Balance c/d	2,315
		3,280			3,280
1 Feb	Balance b/d	2,315			

If all has gone well, the individual postings to the **sales ledger should exactly equal the total postings made to the nominal ledger**. It follows that if we add up the balances on all the personal accounts in the sales ledger we should reach a total that exactly equals the balance on the receivables control account in the nominal ledger. The same applies in the case of the purchase ledger. By performing this exercise at regular intervals we are, in effect, checking that postings to the ledgers are accurate. The exercise is sometimes seen as performing a 'trial balance' on the ledgers.

The status of the control account

The status of a control account is not an easy concept to grasp. Particular care should be made in ensuring that you understand this issue as it is the basis of many computer-based assessment questions.

So far we have considered that the double entry is completed by entering each transaction in the receivables personal accounts in the sales ledger, and entering the totals of sales, returns, sales tax, cash received and discounts allowed in the nominal ledger. Now that we have introduced a control account, it might appear that we are duplicating the entries in the sales ledger. Obviously, this cannot happen, as the ledger accounts will be out of balance. We cannot have **both** the receivables accounts and the control account as part of the double-entry system. Therefore, one or other of these must be treated as being outside the double-entry system. The records that are outside the double-entry system are known as **memorandum accounts**.

In computerised systems, it is common for the sales ledger to be a separate component of the bookkeeping system, and for the control account to exist in the nominal ledger. But it is also acceptable to regard the control account as a memorandum account.

Illustration 2

Briefly explain the meaning of each of the entries in the following receivables account:

P Richmond

		$			$
1 Jan	Balance b/d	465	13 Jan	Cheque	450
6 Jan	Sales	240		Discount	15
8 Jan	Sales	360	17 Jan	Returns	40
			31 Jan	Balance c/d	560
		1,065			1,065
1 Feb	Balance b/d	560			

Solution

- 1 January: balance. P Richmond owes this amount at 1 January.
- 6/8 January: sales. P Richmond has been sold these amounts on credit.
- 13 January: cheque and discount. P Richmond has paid $450 by cheque to clear a debt of $465, having been allowed a cash discount of $15. It is likely that this was in payment of the opening balance on 1 January.
- 17 January: P Richmond has returned goods and been allocated a credit of $40 to be offset against the amount owing.
- 31 January: balance $560. P Richmond owes this amount at 31 January.

Example 14.D

You have been asked to prepare control accounts in order to produce end-of-year figures for receivables and payables for inclusion in the draft final accounts of Korrinna Company for the year ended 30 November 20X8.

You obtain the following totals for the financial year from the books of original entry:

Cash book

	$
Discounts allowed	6,805
Cash and cheques from customers	287,601
Discounts received	3,415
Cash and cheques paid to suppliers	233,078
Customer's cheque dishonoured	251

The following totals have been extracted from the daybooks for the year:

	$
Purchases daybook	247,084
Sales daybook	306,580
Returns inwards daybook	6,508
Returns outwards daybook	4,720

According to the audited financial statements for the previous year, receivables and payables as at the close of business on 30 November 20X7 were $44,040 and $63,289, respectively.

You are required to draw up the relevant control accounts for the year ending 30 November 20X8, entering the closing balances for receivables and payables.

Solution

Sales ledger control account

	$		$
Balance b/d	44,040	Discounts allowed	6,805
Sales	306,580	Cash and cheques	287,601
Cheque dishonoured	251	Returns inwards	6,508
		Balance c/d	49,957
	350,871		350,871

Purchase ledger control account

	$		$
Discounts received	3,415	Balance b/d	63,289
Cash and cheques	233,078	Purchases	247,084
Returns outwards	4,720		
Balance c/d	69,160		
	310,373		310,373

The entries in the control accounts reflect respectively the effect of the transactions on the value of Korrinna Company's receivables (sales ledger control account) and payables (purchase ledger control account).

In the sales ledger control account the debit entries are those transactions that cause the asset of receivables to increase, whereas decreases are recorded on the credit side of the control account.

In the purchase ledger control account the debit entries are those transactions that cause the liability of payables to decrease, whereas increases are recorded on the credit side of the control account.

Debit	**Credit**
Increases in assets	Decreases in assets
Decreases in liabilities	Increases in liabilities

Note that the transactions are entered individually in the personal accounts of the customers and also entered in total in the control account.

You should also note that every entry in the personal accounts should also be included in the control account and vice versa – if the control account balance agrees with the total of the individual account balances it is highly likely that the double entry has been posted correctly. Note, however, that if a transaction is posted to the wrong personal account this will not be found by the reconciliation of the control account balance.

Illustration 3

Ascertain the value of credit sales from the following information:

	$
Opening receivables	23,750
Closing receivables	22,400
Cash sales	14,000
Receipts from receivables	215,000
Discounts allowed	4,500
Irrecoverable debts written off	2,250
Dishonoured cheques	2,500

Solution

Sales ledger control account

	$		$
Opening receivables	23,750	Receipts	215,000
Sales	?	Discounts	4,500
Dishonoured cheques	2,500	Irrecoverable debts w/off	2,250
		Closing receivables	22,400
	244,150		244,150

The sales figure is the balancing figure required, that is $244,150 – $23,750 – $2,500 = $217,900.

Contra entries

When a business is both a supplier and a customer of your business it is common for an agreement to be made to set off the sums receivable and payable, and for a single cheque to be sent between the parties to settle the net balance. The entry to record the setting off of the balances is known as a contra entry.

Example 14.E

The following accounts are taken from the accounting records of Z Ltd:

Sales ledger

AP Ltd

	$		$
Balance b/d	1,815		

Purchase ledger

AP Ltd

	$		$
		Balance b/d	792

Solution

The balance of $792 in the purchase ledger is set off against the sales ledger balance using a contra entry:

Sales ledger

AP Ltd

	$		$
Balance b/d	1,815	Purchase ledger (contra)	792

Purchase ledger

AP Ltd

	$		$
Sales ledger contra	792	Balance b/d	792

AP Ltd would send a cheque to Z Ltd for $1,023 to clear its sales ledger balance.

The same entries must be made in the control accounts, that is debit the purchase ledger control account with $792, and credit the sales ledger control account with $792. Note that it is always the smaller of the two balances that is transferred, but the entries of 'debit purchase ledger' and 'credit sales ledger' always occur.

The contra would also be entered in the journal (as its book of prime entry), but remember that the journal is not part of the double-entry system.

Credit balances in the sales ledger; debit balances in the purchase ledger

Normally, sales ledger accounts have debit balances, and purchase ledger accounts have credit balances. But it can happen that the reverse occurs. For example, a receivable may have paid his invoice, and then returns some goods that are faulty. The entries on the return would be to debit returns inwards and credit the receivable – which means that he acquires a credit balance. The same might occur with a supplier, whereby you have paid his invoice and later return goods. Strictly speaking, receivables with credit balances are payables, and vice versa, but it is not normal to move them from one ledger to the other.

Thus it is possible to have credit balances in the sales ledger and debit balances in the purchase ledger. Very often, these balances are wiped out when the customer orders more goods, or we order goods from the supplier. But sometimes it happens that there are no further orders, and a refund is required. With receivables, the entries are debit the receivable and credit bank, and with payables the entries are credit the payable and debit bank.

Test your understanding 2

Compile a sales ledger control account from the following information:

	$
Opening balances	Debit 14,500, credit 125
Sales on credit	27,500
Sales return	850
Irrecoverable debts written off	500
Cash sales	420
Cheques received from receivables	19,800
Cash discount allowed	480
Dishonoured cheques	750
Contras to the purchases ledger	340
Refunds to credit customers	125

The control account and allowance for receivables

An allowance for receivables is made when it is felt that a proportion of receivables may not honour their debts in full, but the identity of the individual receivables is not known. Refer back to Chapter 5 to refresh your memory on the bookkeeping treatment of these provisions.

The important point to remember is that **no entries are made in the receivables ledger accounts** for allowances for receivables, and therefore no entry is made in the sales ledger control account either.

Advantages of control accounts

- They check the accuracy of the ledger accounts that they control.
- They enable 'segregation of duties' by allocating the job of maintaining the sales/ purchase ledger to one person, and the job of maintaining the control account to another person, thereby reducing the risk of fraud.
- They enable the trial balance to be prepared more speedily, as the receivables and payables total can be extracted from the control accounts rather than waiting for the individual accounts to be balanced and totalled.
- They enable speedier identification of reasons why the trial balance may not balance – if the control account disagrees with its ledger balances, it prompts investigation into the entries in that area

Reconciling control accounts and ledger accounts

The control account must be checked against the total of balances in the relevant ledger, on a regular basis, and any difference between the two must be investigated. Assuming that the control account has been prepared using totals from the books of prime entry, it is usual to 'work backwards' through the tasks that have been carried out, before checking individual entries. The sequence for a sales ledger control account could be as follows:

(i) Rework the balance on the control account; check that irrecoverable debts have been entered, contras have been properly recorded, and that the account does not contain the allowance for receivables.

(ii) Check that all totals have been correctly transferred from the books of prime entry to the control account (look especially for discounts allowed, which may have been omitted).

(iii) Recalculate the list of receivable balances (look especially for credit balances listed as debits, check contras and bad debts written off).

(iv) Recalculate the columns in the books of prime entry (look at the sequence of invoice numbers to see if one is missing; look also in the cash book for refunds made to receivables).
If the balances are still incorrect, it will be necessary to start looking at entries in detail:

- cross-check the net, sales tax and totals for each invoice/credit note in the daybooks;
- cross-check the net, discount and total for each receipt in the cash book;
- cross-check the calculation of the balances on the individual receivable accounts;

– cross-check the entry of each invoice, credit note, receipt and so on in the receivable accounts.

In computerised systems there is much less chance of arithmetical error, but omissions and mispostings can still occur.

Once the errors have been identified, corrections must be made to the sales ledger accounts, the control account or both.

Example 14.F

Cathy maintains a sales ledger control account. At 31 March 20X1, the balance on the control account was calculated as being $128,545, while the total of individual balances extracted from the sales ledger was $128,106. An examination of the books and records revealed the following:

(i) The total of $29,450 for sales in the sales daybook had been posted as $29,540.

(ii) The credit balance of $128 on a receivable account had been listed as a debit balance.

(iii) An irrecoverable debt of $240 had been correctly written off in the receivable account, but no entry had been made in the control account.

(iv) Discounts allowed totalling $185 had been entered on the wrong side of the control account.

(v) A credit balance of $95 in the purchase ledger had been set off against the same person's balance in the sales ledger, but no entries had been made in the control account.

(vi) The total on the debit side of a receivable account had been overcast by $100.

You are required to reconcile the two totals.

Solution

Each adjustment is likely to affect either the control account or the individual balances; it is also possible that an error affects both.

Adjustments to receivables balance	$
Total per original list	128,106
(ii) credit balance listed as debit (2 x $128)	(256)
(vi) debit side overcast	(100)
Revised total	127,750

Adjustments to control account (probably easiest to show this as a ledger account):

	$		$
Balance b/d	128,545	(i) error in sales daybook	90
		(iii) irrecoverable debts written off	240
		(iv) discounts allowed (2 x $185)	370
		(v) contra	95
		Revised balance	127,750
	128,545		128,545

6 Suspense account and correction of errors

The nature of a suspense account is not an easy concept to grasp. Particular care should be made in ensuring that you understand this issue as it is the basis of many computer-based assessment questions. To record transactions is difficult enough; to put right a transaction which has already been recorded incorrectly is more difficult. This ability to correct errors is a good test of bookkeeping competence and thus is a common computer-based assessment question.

We have already seen that since every transaction has debit and credit entries of equal value, then when the accounts are balanced and a trial balance extracted the sum of the debit and credit balances are equal. However, this is to assume that all of the transactions are correctly posted to the ledger accounts and that the ledger account balances are correctly calculated. If the trial balance does not balance, then an error or errors have been made.

There are many different reasons why a trial balance may not balance:

(a) incorrect additions in individual ledger accounts;

(b) only one side of the transaction has been posted;

(c) different values have been entered to the debit and credit sides of the respective ledger accounts.

When the trial balance does not balance, every effort should be made to find the errors and correct them, but occasionally they cannot be found quickly and in these circumstances a **suspense account** is opened and used to record the difference until the errors can be found. The use of the suspense account allows financial statements to be prepared subject to the correction of the errors. The prudent approach is to treat the suspense account balance as an expense (rather than an asset) if it is a debit balance and as a liability (rather than as revenue) if it is a credit balance. When the errors are found they should be corrected and an explanation given.

The corrections are made through the journal in the first instance, and then in the ledger accounts. If the error is one that has affected the agreement of the trial balance, then the suspense account will be involved in the correction of the error.

Example 14.G

On 31 December 20X1 a trial balance was extracted from the ledgers of Marconi and the total of the debit side was found to be $77 less than the total of the credit side. A suspense account was opened to record the difference. Later, the following errors were discovered:

(1) A cheque for $150 paid to Bond had been correctly entered in the cash book but not in Bond's account or the control account.

(2) The purchases account had been undercast by $20.

(3) A cheque received for $93 from Smith had been correctly entered in the cash book but had not been entered in Smith's account or the control account.

Solution

The journal entry and resulting entries in the suspense account are as follows:

Journal	**Dr**	**Cr**
	$	$
Bond	150	
Suspense		150
(Being correction of an error whereby only one entry was posted)		
Purchases	20	
Suspense		20
(Being correction of an error of addition in the purchases account)		
Suspense	93	
Smith		93
(Being correction of an error whereby only one entry was posted)		

Suspense

	$		$
From trial balance	77	Bond	150
Smith	93	Purchases	20
	170		170

It is important to consider whether any corrections to errors will affect profit. Only movements on expense and income account will have an effect. Debit entries in the journal will reduce profit and credit entries in the journal will increase profit.

Test your understanding 3

The following trial balance was extracted from the books of Jane Smith on 31 March 20X1:

	Dr	*Cr*
	$	$
Premises	50,000	
Motor vans	7,400	
Sundry receivables	1,680	
Sundry payables		2,385
Purchases	160,260	
Sales		200,490
Wages	12,000	
Drawings	1,600	
Capital		30,000
	232,940	232,875

As the trial balance totals did not agree, the difference was posted to a suspense account. The following errors were discovered:

(1) The purchase of a motor van had been entered in the motor van account as $3,860 instead of $3,680.

(2) The total of the purchases book $32,543 had been posted to the purchases account as $32,453.

(3) The proprietress had withdrawn $140 for private use during March that had been debited to the wages account.

(4) A cash discount of $25 allowed by Diane Jones, a payable, had not been entered in Diane Jones's account.

You are required to take the above information into account and show:

(a) journal entries to correct the errors;

(b) the suspense account written up and balanced.

7 Computers in accounting

The use of computers to maintain bookkeeping records and produce financial statements is now widespread, even in small organisations. The use of computers is not specifically part of your syllabus, but no accounting textbook would be complete without mentioning some of the features and problems that such systems possess.

It is important, however, that you recognise that computers must perform the same bookkeeping tasks that have been described manually in this book. The double-entry system must still be maintained, and adequate controls must be in place to ensure its accuracy. In computer-based assessment questions, you will normally be required to answer questions on the assumption that the system is a manual one, so if you work in an organisation that has a sophisticated computerised accounting system, try to relate the principles of bookkeeping described here to those that take place in the computerised system.

Using computers provides a range of benefits such as:

- speed of input and processing of data;
- speed and flexibility of producing information;
- ability to manage large numbers of accounts and transactions;
- improved accuracy;
- automatic update of all related accounts in a transaction, with a single entry;
- less storage space required;
- additional checks on the input of data, for example, dates (31 November is not allowed), limits (no person can work more than 100 hours in a week), ranges (hourly wage rates are between $7.60 and $12.50) and so on.

However, the biggest single drawback of computerised systems is that the user cannot physically see what is happening to the bookkeeping system and errors and omissions cannot be readily identified.

Of course, many computerised accounting systems are 'self-balancing', in that a single transaction is input, and is used to update the ledger accounts, the daybooks, the control accounts, perhaps even the inventory records, and it is all too easy to assume that everything has been done correctly. Unfortunately, this is not always the case.

Aspects of computerised accounting systems

There are many different types of computerised system. Some lend themselves to large organisations, others to smaller organisations. Typical configurations are:

(i) a mainframe computer that has a very large capacity, supported by a minicomputer (slightly smaller) and perhaps several personal computers for individual users. Such a system might involve the users in entering data into the system, and accessing the results directly.

(ii) Networked computers, where the files are held centrally, but updated and accessed from remote locations by users.

(iii) Stand-alone computers, where files are held on individual computers, updated by those users.

All of these configurations have security implications. For example, some may allow individual users to update the ledger accounts. It is important that there is sufficient segregation of duties in this situation. Others may only allow access to the balances, but not the facility to amend those balances.

In all cases, the ledger accounts will have to balance and a trial balance will be produced. This may be part of the 'month-end routine', which typically produces totals of the transactions during, and balances at the end of, the month. The month-end routine would provide lists and totals of invoices issued and received, payments made, expenses incurred, as well as end-of-month balances of receivables, payables, inventories, bank and cash, and expenses. The computer system will also be capable of making adjustments to the accounts for accruals, prepayments, allowance for receivables and so on. These will normally be input via a journal entry, as in a manual system.

Accounting coding systems

By now you will realise that a busy organisation will have a large number of ledger accounts and subsidiary records within and outside the accounting system. Using the titles of accounts to locate and cross-reference transactions could be difficult in such situations. Imagine the tax authorities maintaining all the records of taxpayers according to their names. There will be hundreds of thousands of taxpayers with the surnames Smith, or Khan or Jones – and thousands called John Smith or Helen Jones. Each needs a unique code to identify them from the others. The same applies to accounting systems. The ledger accounts require unique codes, as do inventory items, employees on the payroll and so on.

We could simply number them 1, 2, 3 and so on, but that would not be particularly helpful in locating an individual item. Some kind of coding system is needed. This is particularly important in computerised systems, which use codes to transfer data throughout the system.

Organisations could perhaps start with the five main categories of ledger accounts, for example

- Assets Code 1
- Liabilities Code 2
- Capital Code 3
- Expenses Code 4
- Revenues Code 5

and then further subdivide them into more minor categories, for example:

- Non-current assets Code 12
- Current assets Code 13

Non-current assets could be further divided into types, for example, plant (1), motor vehicles (2), office equipment (3) and so on.

Codes could be included to identify the location of such items within the organisation, e.g. sales department, purchasing department, wages department, factory locations. This would enable depreciation to be charged to the department that utilises the item.

The following structure illustrates how a coding system may be used for a nominal ledger in a large organisation.

A six-digit code is used: the first digit represents the functional analysis; digits 2 and 3 represent the cost centre (i.e. the department); and digits 4–6 represent the type of expense involved.

Function	**Cost centre (within production)**	**Nominal ledger expense analysis**
1 Production	10 Machining	100 Raw material X
2 Sales	11 Assembly	101 Raw material Y
3 Administration	12 Finishing	201 Skilled-labour wages
		202 Unskilled-labour wages
		203 Salaries
		301 Rent
		601 Postage
		602 Stationery

An example code could be 110202, which represents unskilled-labour wage cost incurred in the machining cost centre of the production function.

It is generally accepted that codes should be:

(a) **Unique**. In order to avoid ambiguity, each item must have only one possible code.

(b) **Useful**. There is no point in using a code if there is to be no benefit from its use. The code will have to be learned by the users of the system so that it may be both applied and understood.

(c) **Compact**. It is generally accepted that the shorter the code the easier it is to learn and therefore the likelihood of mistakes and confusion is reduced. Thus, a code should be as short and compact as possible.

(d) **Meaningful**. If the code can be made meaningful by the characters of the code being connected in some way to the item that the code represents, the code will be more easily remembered and understood.

(e) **Self-checking**. The biggest problem with the use of codes is that users of the codes remember them incorrectly. To ensure that the information to be provided by the system is of value, each of the codes used must be validated. If a numeric code is used it can be designed in such a way as to be self-checking – this will help in identifying coding mistakes and avoid the production of incorrect information.

(f) **Expandable**. When designing a coding system it is important to consider the requirements of the organisation in the future. The design of accounting systems often involves a large amount of time and this is then followed by a period when the users are learning the system. If the code is not expandable, then it is likely that the system will have to be changed sooner rather than later. This will be costly in design time and will cause difficulties because the users of the system will have to learn the new system.

(g) **Standard size**. If codes are of varying size, then different users may write the same code differently. For example, if a part of a coding system comprises up to four characters, then the three-digit code AB1 could be written in a number of ways, with spaces and dashes in different places. Using AB01 would prevent this.

8 Chapter summary

This chapter has outlined a variety of controls and checks that can be incorporated into or alongside the bookkeeping system to:

- help prevent errors and fraud;
- detect errors if they do occur;
- correct errors, often via the journal, once they have been discovered.

These controls and checks include:

- bank reconciliations,
- control accounts,
- suspense accounts.

The chapter concluded with an explanation of:

- computers in accounting,
- coding systems.

Test your understanding questions

Test your understanding 4

The cash book shows a bank balance of $5,675 overdrawn at 31 August 20X5. It is subsequently discovered that a standing order for $125 has been entered twice, and that a dishonoured cheque for $450 has been debited in the cash book instead of credited. The correct bank balance should:

$...............

Test your understanding 5

A supplier sends you a statement showing a balance outstanding of $14,350. Your own records show a balance outstanding of $14,500. The reason for this difference could be that:

A the supplier sent an invoice for $150 that you have not yet received

B the supplier has allowed you $150 cash discount that you had omitted to enter in your ledgers

C you have paid the supplier $150 that he has not yet accounted for

D you have returned goods worth $150 that the supplier has not yet accounted for

Test your understanding 6

A suspense account shows a credit balance of $130.
This could be due to:

A omitting a sale of $130 from the sales ledger

B recording a purchase of $130 twice in the purchases account

C failing to write off an irrecoverable debt of $130

D recording an electricity bill paid of $65 by debiting the bank account and crediting the electricity account

Test your understanding 7

You are given the following information:

	$
Receivables at 1 January 20X3	10,000
Receivables at 31 December 20X3	9,000
Total receipts during 20X3	
(including cash sales of $5,000)	85,000

Sales on credit during 20X3 amount to:

$...............

Test your understanding 8

Your cash book at 31 December 20X3 shows a bank balance of $565 overdrawn. On comparing this with your bank statement at the same date, you discover that

- a cheque for $57 drawn by you on 29 December 20X3 has not yet been presented for payment;
- a cheque for $92 from a customer, which was paid into the bank on 24 December 20X3, has been dishonoured on 31 December 20X3.

The correct bank balance to be shown in the statement of financial position at 31 December 20X3 is:

$...............

Test your understanding 9

After calculating your company's profit for 20X3, you discover that

- a non-current asset costing $50,000 has been included in the purchases account;
- stationery costing $10,000 has been included as closing inventories of raw materials, instead of as inventories of stationery.

These two errors have had the effect of:

A understating gross profit by $40,000 and understating net profit by $50,000

B understating both gross profit and net profit by $40,000

C understating gross profit by $60,000 and understating net profit by $50,000

D overstating both gross profit and net profit by $60,000

Test your understanding 10

Your firm's cash book at 30 April 20X8 shows a balance at the bank of $2,490. Comparison with the bank statement at the same date reveals the following differences:

	$
Unpresented cheques	840
Bank charges not in cash book	50
Receipts not yet credited by the bank	470
Dishonoured cheque not in cash book	140

The correct bank balance at 30 April 20X8 is:

$...............

Test your understanding 11

The following information relates to a bank reconciliation.

(i) The bank balance in the cash book before taking the items below into account was $8,970 overdrawn.

(ii) Bank charges of $550 on the bank statement have not been entered in the cash book.

(iii) The bank has credited the account in error with $425, which belongs to another customer.

(iv) Cheque payments totalling $3,275 have been entered in the cash book but have not been presented for payment.

(v) Cheques totalling $5,380 have been correctly entered on the debit side of the cash book but have not been paid in at the bank.

What was the balance as shown by the bank statement before taking the items above into account?

$...............

Test your understanding 12

Which of the following is not the purpose of a sales ledger control account?

A A sales ledger control account provides a check on the arithmetic accuracy of the personal ledger

B A sales ledger control account helps to locate errors in the trial balance

C A sales ledger control account ensures that there are no errors in the personal ledger

D Control accounts deter fraud

Test your understanding 13

When reconciling the payables ledger control account with the list of payable ledger balances of M, the following errors were found:

the purchase daybook had been overstated by $500;

the personal ledger of a supplier had been understated by $400.

What adjustment must be made to correct these errors?

	Control account	List of payable balances
A	Cr $500	Decrease by $400
B	Dr $500	Increase by $400
C	Dr $400	Increase by $500
D	Cr $400	Decrease by $500

Test your understanding 14

Z's bank statement shows a balance of $825 overdrawn. The bank statement includes bank charges of $50, which have not been entered in the cash book. There are unpresented cheques totalling $475 and deposits not yet credited of $600. The bank statement incorrectly shows a direct debit payment of $160, which belongs to another customer.

The figure for the bank balance in the statement of financial position should be: $.......... overdrawn

Test your understanding 15

The assistant accountant of BC Ltd has prepared a sales ledger control account at 30 September 20X5 for you to reconcile with the list of sales ledger balances at that date. The control account balances are:

Debit balances	$226,415
Credit	$1,250

The list of balances extracted from the sales ledger totals $225,890. You discover the following:

(i) The credit balances have been included on the list of receivables as debit balances.

(ii) A sales invoice for $6,400 plus sales tax at 17.5 per cent has been recorded in the sales daybook as $4,600 plus sales tax at 17.5 per cent. It has been entered correctly in the sales ledger.

(iii) Cash discounts allowed amounted to $840 and cash discounts received amounted to $560; the only entry in the control account for discounts is a debit for cash discounts received.

(iv) A dishonoured cheque for $450 from a customer has been recorded correctly in the control account, but no entry has been made in the receivable's personal account.

(v) A contra entry between the sales and purchase ledgers of $750 has been omitted from the control account.

(vi) The control account contains receipts from cash sales of $860 but does not contain the invoices to which these receipts refer; no entries have been made in the sales ledger for these invoices or receipts.

(vii) No entries have been made in the control account for irrecoverable debts written off ($2,150) and allowance for receivables ($2,400). Ignore sales tax for item (vii)

Required:

Complete the table below to show the entries needed in the sales ledger control account to correct the present balance; consider each of the seven items mentioned if no entry is required in the control account, write N/E' in the 'Description' column and ignore the other columns.

	Description (max. 4 words each)	**Debit/Credit?**	**Amount $**
(i)			
(ii)			
(iii)			
(iv)			
(v)			
(vi)			
(vii)			

(b) Complete the missing figures given below to calculate the revised sales ledger control account balance:

	$
Original balance	225,165
Add: debit entries required	
Less: credit entries required	
Revised balance	

(c) **Two** of the seven items noted above required adjustment to the list of sales ledger balances. Insert the missing entries into the statement given below:

	$
Original sales ledger balances	225,890

Items requiring adjustment

Item no.	Description (max. two words each)	Adjustment $
	Total adjustment	
	Corrected total	

(d) State four facilities that a computerised sales ledger system might offer to BC Ltd (max. 3 words each).

(i)	
(ii)	
(iii)	
(iv)	

Test your understanding 16

After calculating net profit for the year ended 31 March 20X8, WL has the following trial balance:

	Debit ($)	Credit ($)
Land and buildings – cost	10,000	
Land and buildings – acc. depreciation at 31 March 20X8		2,000
Plant – cost	12,000	
Plant – acc. depreciation at 31 March 20X8		3,000
Inventory	2,500	
Receivables	1,500	
Bank	8,250	
Payables		1,700
Rent prepaid	400	
Wages accrued		300
Capital account		19,400
Profit for the year ended 31 March 20X8		9,750
	34,650	36,150

A suspense account was opened for the difference in the trial balance. Immediately after production of the above, the following errors were discovered:

(i) A payable account had been debited with a $300 sales invoice (which had been correctly recorded in the sales account).

(ii) The heat and light account had been credited with gas paid $150.

(iii) G Gordon had been credited with a cheque received from G Goldman for $800. Both are receivables.

(iv) The insurance account contained a credit entry for insurance prepaid of $500, but the balance had not been carried down and hence had been omitted from the above trial balance.

(v) Purchase returns had been overcast by $700.

Required:

(a) Complete the table below to indicate the journal entries necessary to correct each of the above errors.

Item	Name of account	Debit amount ($)	Credit amount ($)
(i)			
(ii)			
(iii)			
(iv)			
(v)			

(b) Insert the missing items into the suspense account given below, in respect of any errors that you have identified in (a), and total the account:

Suspense account

	$	Description	Item no.	$
Balance as per trial balance				

(c) Name the type of error that has occurred in each of items (i) and (iii) above (max. five words each).

(i)	
(iii)	

(d) Insert the missing items into the boxes below to show the recalculated net profit for the year to 31 March 20X8:

		$
First draft profit		9,750
Adjustment re: heat and light		
Adjustment re: purchase returns		
Revised net profit		

(e) Insert the missing figures into the statement of financial position of WL at 31 March 20X8, given below:

	Cost	Acc. Depn.	Carrying Amount
Assets	$	$	$
Non-current assets			
Land and buildings	10,000	(2,000)	
Plant	12,000	(3,000)	
	22,000	(5,000)	
Current assets			
Inventory			
Receivables			
Prepayments			
Bank			

Capital and liabilities

Capital

Add: Profit for the year

Current liabilities

Payables

Accrual

Test your understanding answers

Test your understanding 1

Cash book

		$			$
1 Jan	Balance b/d	600	18 Jan	D Anderson	145
13 Jan	Umberto	224	28 Jan	R Patrick	72
31 Jan	L Bond	186	30 Jan	Parveen	109
			31 Jan	Standing order	30
			31 Jan	Balance c/d	654
		1,010			1,010
1 Feb	Balance b/d	654			

Bank reconciliation statement at 31 January

	$
Balance as per bank statement	649
Add: receipts not lodged	186
Less: unpresented cheques (109 + 72)	(181)
Balance as per cash book	654

Test your understanding 2

Sales ledger control account

	$		$
Opening balances	14,500	Opening balances	125
Sales on credit	27,500	Sales returns	850
Dishonoured cheques	750	Irrecoverable debts w/off	500
Refunds	125	Cheques received	19,800
		Cash discount allowed	480
		Contras to purchase ledger	340
		Closing balances	20,780
	42,875		42,875

Test your understanding 3

Journal entries		**Dr ($)**	**Cr ($)**
Item 1	Suspense account	180	
	Motor vans		180
Item 2	Purchases	90	
	Suspense account		90
Item 3	Drawings	140	
	Wages		140
Item 4	Diane Jones (trade payable)	25	
	Suspense account		25

Suspense account

	$		$
Motor van	180	Balance b/d	65
		Purchases	90
		Sundry payables	25
	180		180

Test your understanding 4

The correct bank balance can be found as follows:

	$	
Cash book balance	5,675	overdrawn (credit)
Correct standing order error	125	debit
Reverse error of dishonoured cheque	450	credit
Enter dishonoured cheque correctly	450	credit
Correct balance	6,450	overdrawn

Test your understanding 5

B

The supplier's records show a smaller amount owing than your own records. This could not be due to an invoice not received as this would further increase the amount owing according to your records. If you have paid the supplier, this would further reduce the balance in his records. If you have returned goods, this would also reduce the balance in his records. If you are to account for cash discount in your records, this would reduce the balance in your records to agree to the supplier's.

Test your understanding 6

B

A credit balance on the suspense account indicates that the debit total of the trial balance was higher than the credit total. An error that could cause this would involve either too great a value having been debited, too little a value having been credited, or a combination of these where an item has been recorded as a debit when it ought to have been a credit.

(a) would result in too little having been debited to the customer's account.

(b) would result in an additional debit entry, therefore this is the correct answer.

(c) would not cause any imbalance in the trial balance as both the debit and credit entries will have been omitted.

(d) would not cause any imbalance in the trial balance as both a debit and a credit entry have been made even though.

(e) they were the wrong way round.

Test your understanding 7

Sales can be found by constructing a mini sales control account:

	$		$
Receivables at 1.1.X3	10,000	Receipts, less cash sales	80,000
Sales	?	Receivables at 31.12.X3	9,000
	89,000		89,000

Sales = $79,000 (balancing item)

Test your understanding 8

The cash book balance needs adjusting for the dishonoured cheque, and the bank balance needs adjusting for the unpresented cheque. The correct balance for the statement of financial position is therefore:

$565 overdrawn + dishonoured cheque $92 = $657 overdrawn

Test your understanding 9

A

Including a non-current asset in the purchases account has overstated purchases, and hence has overstated cost of goods sold; this has the effect of understating gross profit. Including stationery inventories with closing inventories of raw materials has the effect of increasing closing inventories of raw materials, which then understates the cost of goods sold, and hence overstates gross profit. So, gross profit has been understated by $50,000 and overstated by $10,000 – a net understatement of $40,000.

Inventory of stationery should reduce the total of stationery expenses in the income statement. Omitting to consider the closing inventories will have overstated the expenses. An overstatement of gross profit and an overstatement of expenses by the same amount (because of the stationery error) will have no effect on net profit. Therefore, the only effect on net profit will be the understatement due to the non-current asset error.

The result, therefore, is that gross profit has been understated by $40,000 and the net profit understated by $50,000.

Test your understanding 10

	$
Original cash book figure	2,490
Adjustment re: charges	(50)
Adjustment re: dishonoured cheque	(140)
	2300

Test your understanding 11

Cash book	**$**	**Bank statement**	**$**
Balance	(8,970)	Balance	(11,200)
Bank charges	(550)	Credit in error	(425)
		Unpresented cheques	(3,275)
		Outstanding deposits	5,380
	(9,520)		(9,520)

Test your understanding 12

C

Test your understanding 13

B

Test your understanding 14

	$
Bank statement – overdrawn	(825)
Unpresented cheques	(475)
Deposits outstanding	600
Direct debit error	160
Bank balance – overdrawn	(540)

Test your understanding 15

- Remember to include the sales tax element in the incorrect sales invoice.
- Allowance for receivables never appears in the control account, nor is it adjusted for in the individual's account.

(a)

	Description	Debit/Credit?	Amount $
(i)	N/E		
(ii)	Error in daybook	Debit	2,115
(iii)	Discount allowed	Credit	560
	Discount received	Credit	840
(iv)	N/E		
(v)	Contra	Credit	750
(vi)	Cash sales	Debit	860
(vii)	Irrecoverable debts written off	Credit	2,150

(b)

	$
Original balance	225,165
Add: debit entries required	2,975
Less: credit entries required	(4,300)
Revised balance	223,840

(c)

	Description (max. two words each)	Adjustment $	
	Sales ledger balances	225,890	
(i)	Credit balances	(2,500)	(This is a reversal)
(iv)	Dishonoured cheque	450	
		223,840	

(d)

(i) Speed.
(ii) Accuracy
(iii) Control accounts.
(iv) Aged receivable analysis.

Test your understanding 16

- Part (a) is straightforward, but take care to identify those corrections that involve the suspense account.
- To assist with Part (d), examine the journal entries; identify those that affect profit (i.e. revenue or expense accounts); if they are being debited, this will reduce profit; if they are being credited this will increase profit.

(a) Journal entries

		Debit $	Credit $
(i)	Receivable	300	
	Payable		300
(ii)	Heat and light	300	
	Suspense account		300
(iii)	G Gordon	800	
	G Goldman		800
(iv)	Insurance prepaid	500	
	Suspense account		500
(v)	Purchase returns	700	
	Suspense account		700

(b)

Suspense account

	$		$
Balance as per trial balance	1,500	Heat and light (ii)	300
		Insurance (iv)	500
		Purchase return (v)	700
	1,500		1,500

(c) (i) Error of principle
(iii) Error of commission

	$
First draft profit	9,750
Adjustment re: heat and light	(300)
Adjustment re: purchase returns	(700)
Revised net profit	8,750

(e) Statement of financial position of WL as at 31 March 20X8

	Cost	Acc. Depn.	Carrying Amount
Assets	$	$	$
Non-current assets			
Land and buildings	10,000	(2,000)	8,000
Plant	12,000	(3,000)	9,000
	22,000	(5,000)	17,000
Current assets			
Inventory		2,500	
Receivables (1,500 + 300)		1,800	
Prepayments (400 + 500)		900	
Bank		8,250	
			13,450
			30,450

Capital and liabilities		
Capital		19,400
Add: Profit for the year		8,750
		28,150
Current liabilities		
Payables (1,700 + 300)	2,000	
Accrual	300	
		2,300
		30,450

chapter

15

The Regulatory Framework of Accounting

Chapter learning objectives

When you have completed this chapter, you should be able to:

- identify why we have a framework and how it is implemented;
- explain the influence of legislation on published accounting information for organisations;
- explain the role of accounting standards in preparing financial statements;
- explain approaches to creating accounting standards.
- identify the different accounting conventions;
- identify the requirements for external audit and the basic processes undertaken;
- explain the meaning of fair presentation;
- distinguish between external and internal audit;
- explain the purpose and basic procedures of internal audit.

1 Introduction

The objective of accounting is to present financial information to users, as we saw in chapter 1. **Users need to be able to rely on the information provided in those financial statements to enable them to make appropriate decisions.**

You have perhaps realised by now that there are often several alternative ways of valuing items entered in the bookkeeping system, and different methods of determining how much of an item should be shown in the income statement and how much in the statement of financial position. You will probably also realise that some of these depend entirely on judgement and opinion. All of these 'estimates' affect the profit and the position shown by the statement of financial position.

Accountants need some guidance in the way in which they prepare the financial statements. This chapter looks at some of the ways in which accountants take decisions on methods of accounting and valuation for certain items. This chapter also looks at the role of auditors, who check that the rules on accounting have been followed.

2 Why do we need regulation?

Regulation is needed because:

- it ensures the financial statements can be relied upon by a variety of users to make decisions and
- it promotes consistency to help users interpret the financial statements.

Different countries will be subject to variety of economic, social and political factors. As a result, the way in which published accounts are regulated will vary from country to country.

3 Elements of regulation

A regulatory framework may consist of any of the following elements:

- local law;
- local accounting standards;
- international accounting standards;
- conceptual framework;
- requirements of international bodies, i.e. EU.

The IASB Framework for the Preparation and Presentation of Financial Statements (the 'Framework')

Accounting is a social science not a natural science, like physics and chemistry. Whereas physics and chemistry have natural laws, accounting has to develop its own 'laws', which are the conventions listed above. It is important that the IFRSs produced by the IASB are consistent with the conventions and that the accounting standards are consistent with each other. In order to help ensure that this occurs the IASC produced a document which provides a framework within which all standards are set. This document underpins all accounting standards and provides the platform from which all future standards will be developed. This document is the 'Framework', which we have already mentioned in chapter 1, and which has implicitly been the basis for many of the discussions in the preceding chapters. The Framework deals with the fundamental issues in financial reporting and a brief list of its contents is given below.

- The objective of financial statements – to provide useful information, such as statement of financial position and income statement to users.
- Underlying assumptions and qualitative characteristics – these are the conventions discussed earlier, for example accruals, going concern, materiality, prudence and recognition.
- The elements of financial statements – these are the five main components of an income statement and statement of financial position – revenue, expenses, assets, capital and liabilities.
- The measurement of profit and capital maintenance – different methods of measuring profit, for example CPP and CCA, and the concept of capital maintenance, using different methods of asset valuation, for example value in use and replacement cost.

Company law

Most countries have legislation applying to companies and this is generally known as 'company law'. The amount of detail in company law will vary between countries but in general they cover broad issues rather than detailed aspects of accounting. Company law often states which companies are required to have their financial statements audited by a registered auditor.

Financial accounting information is vital to shareholders when making investment decisions. This is reflected in the successful operation of world stock markets, where every day billions of dollars are traded in acquiring and selling shares in companies. Each stock market contains the largest companies in that economy and the values of those companies are reflected in their share prices.

Given the significance of this mechanism to the health of national economies most countries have legislation to identify the form and content of the financial statements. This ensures that users of the information (primarily the stock market) have good quality, relevant information to enable them to continue making their investment decisions.

For example; the Companies Act 2006 is the primary source of company law in the UK. It provides comprehensive guidance with regard to matters such as: corporate governance; company formation; communications to shareholders; auditor liability; preparation and submission of financial statements; and company administration (such as the need for a company secretary and a company constitution). All companies formed in the UK must abide by this legislation.

There are presently no European-wide company laws as such. However a number of minimum standards exist for member states of the European Union. Perhaps the most significant EU directive was the adoption of IFRS as the basis for preparing financial statements for all listed business in the EU since 2005.

The accountancy profession

Many countries have their own professional accountancy qualification. In the USA, for example, they are known as Certified Public Accountants (CPA). Some countries do not have their own professional accountancy qualification in which case trainee accountants take the qualification of another country. This will also apply if students in a country believe that the accountancy qualification in another country is more prestigious than their own domestic qualification. Thus some professional accountancy bodies which were originally just domestic have become international qualifications. Two examples in the UK are:

- The Chartered Institute of Management Accountants (CIMA),
- The Association of Chartered Certified Accountants (ACCA).

These bodies insist on their members being properly qualified, not only by passing examinations but also by obtaining appropriate practical experience, updating their skills and knowledge on a regular basis, and maintaining certain professional standards based on an ethical code.

International accounting standards

The Fundamentals of Financial Accounting syllabus states that no knowledge of any specific accounting treatment contained in the international financial reporting standards (IFRSs) is necessary. This Learning System has not, therefore, made mention of these IFRSs, but nevertheless this text is based on IFRSs. The influence of IFRSs on the text has three main affects:

(1) **Terminology.** This text uses the words, phrases, definitions and so on found in IFRSs.

(2) **Presentation.** The presentation of the financial statements and particularly the statement of financial position and statement of cash flows follow the IFRS formats. The syllabus states that the formats in IAS 1 Presentation of Financial Statements (Revised) and IAS 7 Statement of Cash Flows are to be followed when preparing these financial statements.

(3) **Technical.** The technical requirements of the IFRS have been followed.

4 International Financial Reporting Standards (IFRS)

Due to the increasingly global nature of investment and business operation there has been a move towards the 'internationalisation' of financial reporting. This 'harmonisation' was considered necessary to provide consistent and comparable information to an increasingly global audience.

If companies use different methods of accounting then before any decisions can be made about different entities the accounts would have to be re-written so that the accounting concepts and principles applied are the same; only then relevant comparisons be made.

These IFRSs are very important and a brief description of how they are issued is given below.

There are four separate but related bodies which control the setting of IFRSs. They are organised as in the figure below.

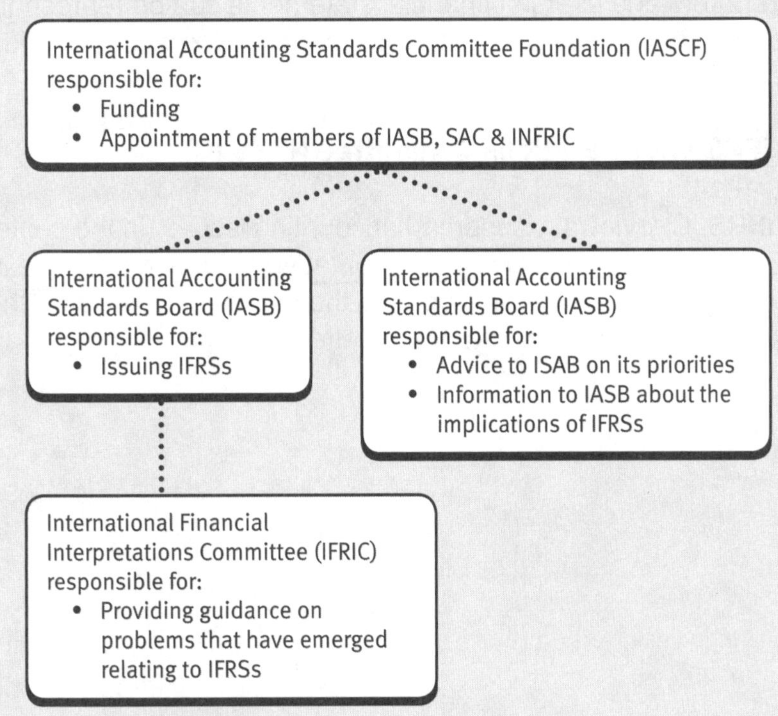

International Financial Reporting Standards (IFRS) Foundation

The IFRS Foundation (formerly known as the International Accounting Standards Committee Foundation (IASC)) is the supervisory body for the IASB and is responsible for governance issues and ensuring each member body is properly funded.

The principal objectives of the IFRS Foundation are to:

- develop a set of high quality, understandable, enforceable and globally accepted financial reporting standards;
- promote the use and rigorous application of those standards;
  to take account of the financial reporting needs of emerging economies and small and medium sized entities;
- bring about the convergence of national and international financial reporting standards.

International Accounting Standards Board (IASB)

The IASB is the independent standard setting body of the IFRS foundation. Its members are responsible for the development and publication of IFRSs and interpretations developed by the IFRS IC. Upon its creation the IASB also adopted all existing International Accounting Standards.

All of the most important national standard setters are represented on the IASB and their views are taken into account so that a consensus can be reached. All national standard setters can issue IASB discussion papers and exposure drafts for comment in their own countries, so that the views of all preparers and users of financial statements can be represented. Each major national standard setter 'leads' certain international standard setting projects.

The IFRS Interpretations Committee (IFRS IC)

The IFRS IC reviews widespread accounting issues (in the context of IFRS) on a timely basis and provides authoritative guidance on these issues (IFRICs). Their meetings are open to the public and, similar to the IASB, they work closely with national standard setters.

The IFRS Advisory Council (IFRS AC)

The IFRS AC is the formal advisory body to the IASB and the IFRS Foundation. It is comprised of a wide range of members who are affected by the IASB's work. Their objectives include:

- advising the IASB on agenda decisions and priorities in the their work;
- informing the IASB of the views of the Council with regard to major standard-setting projects, and
- giving other advice to the IASB or to the Trustees.

Further detail

Members of these bodies are drawn from preparers of financial statements (accountants), and users of financial statements (banks, analysts, stock exchange, government, etc.), all from different parts of the world.

The IASB sets IFRSs; a previous body, known as the International Accounting Standards Committee (IASC) set International Accounting Standards (IAS). When the IASB came into existence it adopted all of the IAS issued by the IASC. Thus we have in existence two sets of standards – IFRS and IAS, with the IAS being the older standards. In general, when reference is made to IFRS, it includes the IASs.

Many countries which previously set their own accounting standards still have their own standard-setting boards, for example the Financial Accounting Standards Board (FASB) in the USA, and the Accounting Standards Board (ASB) in the UK. However, these national boards are working with the IASB and are trying to reach convergence between their own national standards and the international standards.

Countries in the European Union (EU) – for example Germany, France, Italy and the UK – are generally required to use IFRSs when preparing the financial statements of companies listed (quoted) on a stock exchange. Once an IFRS has been developed by the IASB it is scrutinised by the EU to see whether it should be adopted for use by member states. It takes advice from two committees before adopting an IFRS – the Accounting Regulatory Committee and the European Financial Reporting Advisory Group (EFRAG). So far all IFRSs have been adopted, apart from certain sections of one particular standard.

Accountants are obliged to follow accounting standards and the enforcement of IFRSs is left to each individual country. In the UK, for example, the enforcement agencies are the Financial Services Authority (FSA) and the Financial Reporting Review Panel (FRRP).

Development of an IFRS

The procedure for the development of an IFRS is as follows:

- The IASB identifies a subject and appoints an advisory committee to advise on the issues.
- The IASB publishes an exposure draft for public comment, being a draft version of the intended standard.
- Following the consideration of comments received on the draft, the IASB publishes the final text of the IFRS.
- At any stage the IASB may issue a discussion paper to encourage comment.
- The publication of an IFRS, exposure draft or IFRIC interpretation requires the votes of at least eight of the 15 IASB members.

5 Accounting concepts

There is no agreed list of accounting concepts. Authors differ in the relative importance they attribute to each of the possible concepts that can be identified but there is a fair degree of consensus that the conventions discussed below are of particular importance.

The concepts can be related to each other, and they can also be related to the qualitative characteristics discussed in chapter 1. However, at this stage they are presented as stand-alone individual concepts.

The main ones are as follows:

The business entity concept

This principle means that the financial accounting information presented in the financial statements relates only to the activities of the business and not to those of the owner. From an accounting perspective the business is treated as being separate from its owners.

The accruals and matching concept

This means that transactions are recorded when revenues are earned and when expenses are incurred. This pays no regard to the timing of the cash payment or receipt.

For example; if a business enters into a contractual arrangement to sell goods to another entity the sale is recorded when the contractual duty has been satisfied; that is likely to be when the goods have been supplied and accepted by the customer. The payment may not be received for another month but in accounting terms the sale has taken place and should be recognised in the financial statements.

Further detail

There are two concepts combined here, but they interrelate. They arise from the need to identify transactions within particular accounting periods.

The accruals concept states that expenditure incurred in a particular accounting period should be accounted for in that period, irrespective of whether or not it has been invoiced or paid for. For example, if a business has engaged lawyers to do some legal work, the accrual may be made for that legal work even though the lawyers may not have yet submitted their invoice. Similarly, revenue that has been earned in that period should be accounted for in that period, irrespective of the date of invoice or the receipt of monies from the transaction. For example, if a business has some money in a deposit account at a bank, an accrual may be made for the interest due to be received even though the interest has not yet appeared on the bank statement. The convention applies equally to all transactions, whether involving revenue, expenses, assets or liabilities. If the transaction has occurred during the period, then it should be accounted for.

The matching concept is similar, but goes one step further, in that it attempts to match the revenue earned in a period with the expenses consumed in earning that revenue. It may happen that expenditure has been incurred in a period, but it has not been used to generate revenue during that same period. An example of this is goods purchased that remain unused at the end of the period. They have not been used to generate revenue in the period of purchase, so they are not included as part of the cost of goods sold in that period; on the assumption that they will be used to generate revenue in the future. They are carried forward and matched with the sales of the future. Thus the trading account has 'cost of goods sold' rather than 'purchases' as the expense item, and closing inventories are carried forward to be matched with the sales revenue of the next period.

The going concern concept

The going concern concept assumes that the business will continue in operation for the foreseeable future, which is taken to be at least one year. In previous chapters you have implicitly implemented this concept; for example, in calculating depreciation, you have assumed that there will be future years against which the cost of the non-current asset can be allocated. When calculating accruals and prepayments, you have assumed that there will be a next year.

This concept has particular importance for valuing assets in the statement of financial position. For example, if a business was not a going concern, then we would have to value non-current assets at their estimated selling price which might be more or less than historic cost. Similarly, we might have to reduce the value of inventories, if we anticipated that we would be forced to sell all the inventory in a very short period of time and would have to reduce the price to achieve this.

Other concepts

The money measurement concept

This limits the recognition of accounting events to those that can be expressed in money terms. This concept thus excludes the recording of many other economic factors that are being debated under the title of social responsibility accounting. For example, no value is attributed to key employees within the organisation. Monetary measurements are used because if all the items covered by an accounting statement are stated as an amount of money, then the cost of the items can be seen and their aggregate cost determined. There is thus a unity of meaning that makes financial statements readily understood and provide a common denominator for financial analysis.

The objectivity concept

Financial statements should not be influenced by the personal bias of the person preparing them. Thus, figures used in financial statements should be objective. Ideally, this should mean that any two accountants would produce the same figure, for example, for profit. In practice, there is always some judgement when preparing financial statements but when exercising that judgement the accountant should be neutral and not trying to produce, for example, a larger, or smaller, profit to benefit his/her own purposes. Financial statements which are objective should be reliable.

The dual aspect concept

This concept is the basis of double-entry bookkeeping and it means that every transaction entered into has a double effect on the position of the entity as recorded in the ledger accounts at the time of that transaction.

The realisation concept

This concept states that we recognise sales revenue as having been earned at the time when goods or services have been supplied, i.e. when the contractual obligation has been satisfied. In basic terms, sales are realised when the right to receive revenue has been earned by the reporting entity.

If income has been earned but not yet received we should also recognise a matching asset as well as the sales revenue. The asset represents the right to receive benefit (usually cash), from the customer.

Take particular care with goods sold on a 'sale-or-return' basis – the goods are not strictly 'sold' until they have been accepted by the buyer or the deadline for return has passed. Strictly speaking the sale of these goods should only be recognised by a company when they are virtually certain that the goods will not be returned and the sale transaction is therefore complete.

The periodicity concept

It can be argued that the only correct measurement of an organisation's profitability is that which is made at the end of the organisation's life. However, there is a need to assess the financial position (i.e. statement of financial position) and performance (i.e. income statement) of an organisation during its life by producing periodic financial statements.

This concept enables comparisons to be made between one period and the other.

The historical cost concept

The historical cost of an asset is the original amount paid for an asset when it was acquired. An advantage of this convention is that the historical cost is objective. We saw in Chapter 10 that non-current assets are stated at historical cost, less accumulated depreciation. If some other value was used, for example the amount the asset could be sold for, this would be subjective and as a result the financial statements may be less reliable for users.

The materiality concept

Accounting statements are prepared for the benefit of various user groups. It is essential that the information provided is both significant and easily understood. The materiality concept ensures that the information provided is clear by omitting items that are not significant to the user in understanding the overall financial position of the organisation. Thus the materiality concept should make the financial statements relevant to users. The distinction between what is significant and what is not varies depending on the size of the organisation, and is a matter for judgement. Determining at what point an item becomes material depends partly on value, partly on the nature of the item concerned and partly on its effect on the results that will be reported.

As a general rule, items with a relatively small (5 per cent of net profit) monetary value are not significant. The concept can be applied to the classification of items as 'revenue expenditure' rather than 'capital expenditure'. For example, the purchase of light bulbs is strictly capital expenditure as the bulbs will be used over several years (and therefore they should be depreciated over their estimated useful life). However, their value is very small and therefore it is justifiable to treat them as revenue expenditure and included in the income statement in the period in which they were bought. Another example is the treatment of inventory of stationery at the end of a period – the matching convention dictates that the cost of unused inventory should be carried forward as an asset, but most organisations would find this cumbersome, and the effect on profit minimal, and therefore many would choose to make no adjustment for such inventory, unless their value is material.

Materiality can also be applied to 'aggregation'. Individually material items should be disclosed separately in the financial statements, but immaterial items may be aggregated together. For example, sales of goods would be aggregated, whereas the disposal of a material building would be separately disclosed.

The stable monetary unit concept

Financial statements are prepared in monetary terms, using the dollar, yen and so on. It is assumed that the monetary value of a currency is stable from one period to the next; however, this is not the case as most economies experience inflation. No adjustment is made to financial statements to allow for inflation or deflation. This means that when comparing the profit of one year with the next, this is not a true comparison as part of any increase may be attributable to inflation.

The consistency concept

The consistency concept is that the accounting treatment of like items should be consistently applied from one accounting period to the next. The usefulness of financial accounting lies to a considerable extent in the conclusions that may be drawn from the comparison of the financial statements of one year with those of a preceding year, or of one company with another. Much of the information thus derived would be useless if the choice of accounting methods were not applied consistently year by year. An example of an area where consistency is important is the method of valuing inventories.

The prudence concept

When preparing financial statements there may be some uncertainty about some transactions. The prudence concept requires that caution should be applied when exercising judgement about these uncertainties. The concept of prudence ensures that a business should not lay claim to any profits before they have been earned with reasonable certainty. Also, it should anticipate losses that it expects to incur in future periods by immediately writing them off to the income statement. Whenever a subjective judgement must be included in the financial statements, the figure that gives the lower profit should be chosen. This prevents profits being overstated. Similarly, assets should not be overstated for statement of financial position purposes, but liabilities are generally recognised even where their likelihood is only probable, provided that their value can be estimated with sufficient reliability.

Further detail

Accounting policies and estimation techniques

Accounting policies are the principles, conventions, rules etc. applied by a company when calculating the assets and liabilities, revenue and expenses, which will appear in the statement of financial position and income statement. Management should use those policies which it believes will be most useful to those who rely on the financial statements. These users will include, for example, shareholders and lenders, as discussed in chapter 1. Management can assess which policies will be most useful by considering the characteristics of useful information, as discussed in chapter 1, including, for example, relevance and reliability.

The implementation of accounting policies requires certain items to be estimated. We have seen that the preparation of financial statements relies on judgement and that not all figures can be called 'accurate'. Accountants have developed a number of techniques to arrive at figures which have to be estimated. For example, we have seen that companies calculate an allowance for receivables, but this is only an estimate as to which trade receivables will not pay. This allowance may be calculated as a percentage of total receivables or as an allowance for specific customers. Either way, both of these are techniques to estimate bad debts. Another example is depreciation, where the straight-line method and the reducing-balance method are two techniques used to estimate the consumption of a non-current asset in a specific period.

The historical cost concept and its alternatives

Traditionally, financial statements have been prepared using the historical cost concept – and, to a large extent, still are. This is a system of accounting in which all values are based on the historical costs incurred.

This means that all of the assets, liabilities, expenses and revenue are recorded using the costs and prices ruling at the time of the transaction as the basis of any accounting entries. This method is objective as each value can be supported by the amount paid to the third party at the time of the transaction.

However, it is accepted that this concept has many shortcomings, and over the years many attempts have been made by accountants to develop alternative valuation methods. The main difficulty with the concept is that in times of changing price levels, it has the effect of overstating profits and understating asset values.

Consider the purchase of two parcels of land: one was purchased 3 years ago for $5,000 and the second parcel, identical in terms of size and function, is purchased in the current year for $9,000.

If you told an external user that you have two parcels of land; one valued at $5,000 and one at $9,000 they would assume that the second parcel was either larger or more valuable to the business. This, however, is not the case; they are identical. They were just purchased in different economic circumstances.

So here the historical cost concept has painted a misleading picture of the assets of a business.

Consider a second example: you purchase a parcel of land today for $10,000. You do absolutely nothing to it, leaving it to grow wild. Alternatively you could have purchased 100,000 units of your company's core raw material.

Two years later you sell that land, completely untended, for $12,000. With that $12,000 you could now purchase 100,000 units of your company's core raw material, which has also inflated in value.

In your accounts you record a $2,000 profit. However, ask yourself: has your company actually received any increased benefit from owning this land? No: your purchasing power is the same as it was two years ago. So have you really made a profit and is it misleading to the users of your accounts to suggest as such?

Why is this a problem? Well consider a further example:

you set up a business and you acquire 10,000 widgets from a supplier for $10 each, which costs $100,000 in total. You sell them for $10.50 each, earning revenue of $105,000.

You have just made a profit of $5,000; you can pat yourself on the back for some business well done. Or can you?

In the interim period the purchase cost of your widgets has increased to $11. So how many replacements can you now purchase for your business with your $105,000? Only 9,545: your business has just shrunk because you have not earned enough revenue to replace your inventories. You should have priced your product at $11.50 so that you could have replaced all 10,000 and kept some profit for yourself.

It can be seen that the use of the historical cost concept thereby overstates profits and understates statement of financial position asset values. This reduces the usefulness of financial statements produced using this concept.

The theory of capital maintenance

As seen in the example above; in inflationary times, the profit may only be sufficient to replace inventory, assets and pay for expenses, if the same level of activity is to be maintained. In that case, it is not really a 'profit' at all, as we think of profits as being an improvement. Indeed, the profit may not even be sufficient to maintain that level of activity, and – even worse – if some or all of the profits are paid out to the owners of the business, the level of activity may have to be reduced. In this case, the organisation has failed to maintain sufficient capital to support the level of activity.

Capital maintenance is therefore important as it implies profit is only earned if the value of the organisation's net assets or operating capacity has increased during the accounting period.

Two methods have been used as the basis of solving this problem: **current purchasing power accounting and current cost accounting.** Neither of these are examinable for this paper.

The role of the auditor

As we have seen, financial statements are prepared to provide information to a variety of different user groups. If the statements are to be useful they must be reliable and reasonably accurate. Accounting systems must therefore be designed to ensure that sufficient accuracy exists. In accounting terms we refer to financial statements as giving a fair presentation, or as being true and fair. It is the role of the auditor to ascertain that the financial statements are properly prepared in accordance with company law and accounting standards.

It is not, however, the responsibility of the auditor to actually prepare the financial statements – this is the responsibility of management (the directors in a limited company). In some cases, the auditors are engaged to prepare the financial statements, but this is in addition to their audit duties, and is still the responsibility of management.

Some organisations are required by law to have their financial statements audited by an independent, qualified accountant. Others choose to have their financial statements audited on a voluntary basis, as the existence of an audit report may be beneficial to them.

Fair presentation or true and fair

Fair presentation or 'true and fair' means that financial statements prepared for external publication should fairly reflect the financial position of the organisation. They should be free of material misstatements arising from negligence or deliberate manipulation. It may not be economically viable to test every single transaction, or to ensure 100 per cent accuracy, but fair presentation assumes that the financial statements do not contain any significant errors that would affect the actions of those reading them. This is based on the materiality convention discussed below. It is the duty of the registered auditor to test the financial statements for material misstatement and to report on whether they are presented fairly.

The materiality convention and the auditor

The purpose of an audit is to allow the auditor to form an opinion and to report accordingly on whether or not the financial statements fairly present the position and performance of a company.

To achieve this the auditor tests the transactions, accounting balances and disclosures reported in the financial statements. They cannot test everything so they select samples for testing based upon their assessment of where the greatest risk of material misstatement lies.

Following testing the auditor considers the results and conclusions of the tests, evaluating in particular any identified misstatements.

If the auditor concludes that the financial statements are free from material misstatement they issue an unmodified audit report, usually stating the opinion that the financial statements are fairly presented (or true and fair).

If they conclude that the financial statements are materially misstated or, for whatever reason, they are not able to satisfactorily conclude, they issue a modified form of opinion.

On the whole auditors perform two broad forms of test. The first is known as **controls testing**, which involves assessing the reliability of accounting systems, procedures and controls. If these appear to be working satisfactorily, the auditors can place a degree of reliance on them that means that they do not need to test those areas in detail. If there are areas of doubt, areas of high risk or items of a material nature, the auditors may choose to carry out more detailed testing designed to detect material misstatement, known as **substantive testing.**

The role of the internal auditor

Many larger organisations have their own internal audit department. The work of an internal audit department is varied and depends largely on the requirements of management. However, the following investigations are common to internal auditors:

- risk assessment;
- testing of control systems;
- designing control systems;
- assessing compliance with relevant laws and regulations; and assessing the accuracy of accounting records and internal financial reports, such as management accounts.
- advising on accounting systems;
- carrying out tests on the accounting records and internal management reports.

Further detail

The value-for-money audit

The audit of an organisation does not have to be strictly confined to the legal requirements. Audits can be carried out on a number of other areas, such as the efficiency of management, the design and implementation of computerised systems, and so on. One type of audit is the value-for-money audit, where a business (or even a division or department) is scrutinised in terms of its economy, efficiency and effectiveness.

Economy is a measure of the cost of the resources used within the operation. Efficiency is a measure of the resources consumed in comparison to the outputs produced by an operation. Effectiveness is a measure of the achievement of operational goals and targets.

The role of management

In a sole trade business or a partnership the owners of the business are answerable only to themselves. They own the business and they are responsible for the day-to-day operation of it.

In a limited company this is not necessarily the case. With the exception of owner managed companies, it is likely that shareholders do not have any involvement in the day-to-day operation in the business. They provide the capital and they recruit directors to manage the business on their behalf.

In return the directors will receive remuneration in the form of salary and bonuses. The profit generated by the company, however, is the property of the shareholders.

It is the responsibility of the directors/management to ensure that the assets of the organisation are safeguarded. This might involve ensuring that:

- all assets are recorded correctly, exist, and are properly maintained and insured;
- procedures are in place to prevent misappropriation or misuse of assets;
- the accounting system is efficient and effective;
- no expenditure is undertaken, or liability incurred, without proper procedures for its authorisation and control;
- the financial statements are prepared in accordance with current legislation and accounting standards.

The term often given to these responsibilities is 'the stewardship function'. Management acts as stewards on behalf of shareholders, members and other beneficiaries, and may be answerable if they fail in this duty. That is not to say that it is their responsibility to make as much profit as possible, or even that they are to blame if losses are made, but they must take appropriate steps to minimise the risks, within the confines of the business world.

Internal audit versus External audit

Issue:	**External audit**	**Internal audit**
Qualifications and eligibility	Must be a member of appropriate professional body i.e. ICAEW, ACCA (NOT CIMA), cannot be an employee or officer.	No legal requirements re qualifications.
	Ethical and professional requirements from profession re integrity, objectivity etc.	No formal requirement re these issues, but would expect to apply best practice.
Responsibility	Specified by law – CA 2006 in UK – what they must report upon e.g. whether financial statements show true and fair view.	As determined by the company – usually much broader than external audit. May include reporting on economy, efficiency and effectiveness of operations i.e. value for money.
Appointment	By members at AGM.	By company – as employee.
Term of office	Annually – from one AGM to the next.	As per contract of employment – usually continuing basis.
Removal	Can resign or be removed by members at AGM.	Can resign or be sacked like any other employee.

Reporting	Addressed to members (i.e. shareholders) and reports on specified issues.	Reports addressed to senior management – ideally Audit Committee if listed company.
	Reports normally standard format per best practice.	Reports customised depending upon the nature and extent of work done.
Publicity of reports	Available with financial statements and filed at Companies House.	Usually remain confidential within the company.

6 Chapter summary

In this chapter we have looked at:

- the regulatory framework, which includes company law and accounting standards;
- the main accounting conventions underlying the preparation of financial statements;
- an outline of the purpose of internal and external audit;
- the stewardship role of management.

Test your understanding questions

Test your understanding 1

If, at the end of the financial year, a company makes a charge against the profits for stationery consumed but not yet invoiced, this adjustment is in accordance with the concept of:

A materiality

B accruals

C consistency

D objectivity

Test your understanding 2

The historical cost concept:

A fails to take account of changing price levels over time

B records only past transactions

C values all assets at their cost to the business, without any adjustment for depreciation

D has been replaced in accounting records by a system of current cost accounting

Test your understanding 3

If the owner of a business takes goods from inventory for his or her own personal use, the accounting concept to be considered is:

A prudence

B capitalisation

C money measurement

D separate entity

Test your understanding 4

Sales revenue should be recognised when goods and services have been supplied; costs are incurred when goods and services have been received.
The accounting concept that governs the above is:

A consistency

B materiality

C realisation

D dual aspect

Test your understanding 5

The capital maintenance concept implies that

A the capital of a business should be kept intact by not paying out dividends

B a business should invest its profits in the purchase of capital assets

C non-current assets should be properly maintained

D profit is earned only if the value of an organisation's net assets or its operating capability has increased during the accounting period

Test your understanding 6

In times of rising prices, the historical cost concept:

A understates asset values and profits

B understates asset values and overstates profits

C overstates asset values and profits

D overstates asset values and understates profits

Test your understanding 7

Which one of the following is not a necessary part of the stewardship function?

A To maximise profits

B To safeguard assets

C To ensure adequate controls exist to prevent or detect fraud

D To prepare the financial statements

Test your understanding 8

Who issues International Financial Reporting Standards:

A The International Auditing and Assurance Standards Board (IAASB)

B The Stock Exchange

C The International Accounting Standards Board (IASB)

D The government

Test your understanding 9

Which of the following is **not** an accounting concept?

A Prudence

B Consistency

C Depreciation

D Accruals

Test your understanding 10

Which of the following statements is correct?

A External auditors report to the directors

B External auditors are appointed by the directors

C External auditors are required to give a report to shareholders

D External auditors correct errors in financial statements

Test your understanding 11

The concept of capital maintenance is important for:

A the sources of finance

B the measurement of profit

C the relationship of debt to equity

D the purchase of non-current assets

Test your understanding 12

The fundamental objective of an external audit of a limited company is to:

A give advice to shareholders

B detect fraud and errors

C measure the performance and financial position of a company

D provide an opinion on the financial statements

Test your understanding 13

Which one of the following statements most closely expresses the meaning of fair presentation?

A There is only one 'fair presentation' view of a company's financial statements

B Fair presentation means there are no errors in the financial statements

C Fair presentation means the financial statements are accurate

D Fair presentation is largely determined by compliance with IFRSs

Test your understanding answers

Test your understanding 1

B

The accruals convention implies that the profits must be charged with expenses consumed, irrespective of whether or not an invoice has been received.

Test your understanding 2

A

Transactions are normally included at their original cost to the business, but that does not preclude reductions in these figures for depreciation and other adjustments, therefore C is incorrect. The accounting professions have attempted to introduce systems of current cost accounting in the past, but these have not been successful.

Test your understanding 3

D

The separate entity concept states that the transactions of the business and those of the owner should be kept separate. Therefore, any money, goods or services taken out of the business by the owner should be treated as private transactions.

Test your understanding 4

C

Test your understanding 5

D

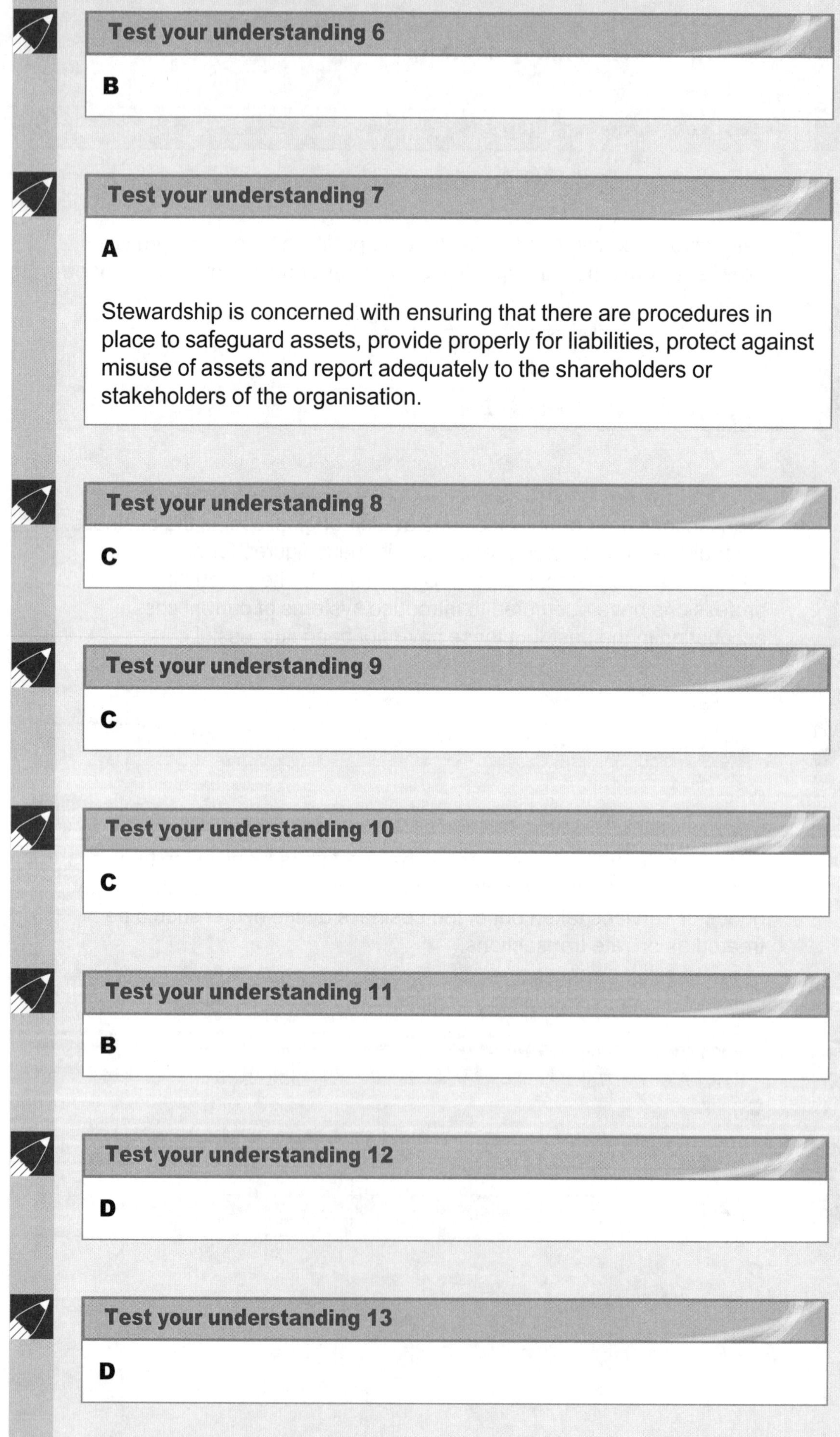

Test your understanding 6

B

Test your understanding 7

A

Stewardship is concerned with ensuring that there are procedures in place to safeguard assets, provide properly for liabilities, protect against misuse of assets and report adequately to the shareholders or stakeholders of the organisation.

Test your understanding 8

C

Test your understanding 9

C

Test your understanding 10

C

Test your understanding 11

B

Test your understanding 12

D

Test your understanding 13

D

chapter

16

Incomplete Records

Chapter learning objectives

When you have completed this chapter, you should be able to:

- calculate missing figures for a variety of situations, e.g. sales, purchases, expenses, opening capital;
- prepare accounts from incomplete records.

1 Introduction

So far, we have been looking at the preparation of financial statements from a ledger, with the results summarised in the trial balance. But not every business uses the full system of daybooks, ledger accounts and so on. Particularly in small businesses, there may not be management time or the financial expertise available. Even in larger businesses, it occasionally happens that accounting records are lost, damaged or destroyed. For all these reasons it may sometimes be necessary to prepare an income statement and statement of financial position from more limited information than we have been given in previous chapters.

All the contents of this chapter should be considered important for the examination, as it provides a good test of your knowledge of bookkeeping, which is essential to pass the computer-based assessment. The ability to prepare financial statements from incomplete records may be regarded as more difficult than from complete records, which you have studied in the previous chapters.

2 Calculating 'missing figures'

There are a number of different ways which we can use to calculate missing figures and balances, such as:

- Accounting equation method;
- Balancing figure approach;
- Profit ratios – mark up and margin.

3 Accounting equation method

If an organisation does not keep its records in double-entry form, with the production of a trial balance, the preparation of the income statement and statement of financial position may require some figures to be ascertained from other records and information. For example, a common situation is where the owner of a business has not kept records of his drawings from the business, but there are other figures available that would enable the drawings figure to be determined.

The accounting equation is usefully employed in this situation:

Assets = Liabilities + Capital

From this the value of capital can be calculated at any time. A change in the value of capital can be caused by only three things:

(1) an introduction/withdrawal of capital;

(2) net profit or loss for the period;

(3) drawings.

Thus, if the opening and closing values of capital are known then, provided that the value of profit and of capital introductions/withdrawals are known, the value of drawings can be calculated.

In an organisation that does not keep full ledger accounts, there may be several figures that need to be determined with the aid of other figures that can be verified. There are several techniques to identify these missing figures.

4 Balancing figure approach

The balancing figure approach, using ledger accounts, is commonly used in the following way:

Ledger account	**Missing figure**
Receivables	Credit sales, Money received from receivables
Payables	Credit purchases, Money paid to payables
Cash at hand	Drawings, Money stolen
Cash at bank	Cash sales, Cash stolen

Sales figures

It is common in organisations that do not keep full bookkeeping records to find that some figures regarding sales are unavailable. It might be that opening receivables lists have been mislaid, or cash sales have not been recorded, or discounts given to customers might have been overlooked.

Drawing up the equivalent of a sales ledger control account will enable the missing figure to be determined. Of course, it will not be a 'proper' sales ledger control account, because there is unlikely to be a sales ledger, but the technique is the same.

The idea is to insert in the ledger accounts all known information, and then to derive the missing information as a balancing figure.

To take sales as an example:

- we probably know our opening figure for receivables – it is the figure that appeared in last year's statement of financial position;
- we probably know our closing receivables – they are the people who owe us money now;
- bank statements should indicate the amount received from customers in the form of cheques and other types of receipts (though we may have to look back through all the statements for the period in order to derive this information);
- we may have records of cash sales (e.g. till rolls) that will indicate the amounts received from cash customers;
- by entering all these known amounts into the sales total account we can derive a sales figure for the period as a balancing figure.

Note that, although we normally exclude cash sales from the sales ledger control account, it is permissible to include them in the 'sales total account' in order to get a complete total of sales, whether for cash or on credit.

This can be simplified using the following ledger account:

Sales ledger control account

20XI		$	20XI		$
1 Jan	Balance b/d	X	In year	Bank - cash from customers	X
In year	**Sales (balancing figure)**	**X**	In year	Cash discounts allowed	X
			In year	Irrecoverable debt written off	X
			31 Dec	Balance c/d	X
		X			X

Test your understanding 1

Jaswinder knows that his receivables at 1 January 20X1 were $27,000, and during the year he received $140,000 in cheques from customers, after allowing $2,000 in cash discounts for prompt payment. He wrote off an irrecoverable debt of $5,000 during the year, and his closing receivables at 31 December 20X1 amount to $24,500.

Required:

Calculate the value of his sales for the year.

Purchases figures

These are calculated in the same way as sales figures.

This can be simplified using the following ledger account:

Purchase ledger control account

20XI		$	20XI		$
In year	Bank - cash paid to suppliers	X	1 Jan	Balance b/d	X
In year	Cash discounts received	X	In year	**Purchases (balancing figure)**	**X**
31 Dec	Balance c/d	X			
		X			X

Expenses figures

As with purchases, a ledger account is drawn up that is entered up with the known figures, and the missing figure is deduced as the figure required to make the account balance.

Expense account

20XI		$	20XI		$
1 Jan	Prepayment b/d	X	1 Jan	Accrual b/d	X
In year	Bank	X	In year	Prepayment	X
In year	Accrual	X	In year	**IS (balancing figure)**	**X**
		X			X

Test your understanding 2

Jaswinder paid an electricity bill during the year of $550. On 1 January, he knew that $120 was owing for electricity consumed in the previous year, and on 31 December he knew that $140 had been consumed in the current year, but not yet billed.

Required:

Calculate the charge to the income statement for the year.

Cash and bank summaries

It is common for incomplete records questions to commence with a summary of the cash and bank transactions. Such a summary is called a **receipts and payments account.** Very often, there is a missing figure in these – commonly the figure for owner's drawings. Preparing such a summary (which is in effect just a copy of the cash book) enables the missing figure to be determined.

This can be simplified using the following ledger accounts:

Cash at bank

20XI		$	20XI		$
1 Jan	Balance b/d	X	In year	Cash paid to suppliers PLCA	X
In year	Cash received from customers SLCA	X	In year	Expenses	X
In year	Bankings from cash at hand	X	In year	Money stolen (balancing item)	
In year	Sundry income	X	In year	Drawings	X
			31 Dec	Balance c/d	X
		X			X

Cash at hand

20XI		$	20XI		$
1 Jan	Balance b/d	X	In year	Cash purchases	X
In year	Cash sales	X	In year	Cash expenses	X
In year	Bankings from cash at hand	X	In year	Money stolen (balancing item)	X
In year	Sundry income	X	In year	Money banked	X
			In year	Drawings	
			31 Dec	Balance c/d	X
		X			X

5 Gross profit mark-up and margin

Gross profit **mark-up means the profit is based on the cost of sales**, e.g. mark-up of 25% means 25% has been added to the cost of sales to find the selling price. In a 25% mark-up situation the following cost structure would apply:

	$	%
Sales	750	125
Cost of sales	600	100
Gross profit	150	25

This means that if we are given the cost of $600 in the question and the mark-up of 25% we can calculate the selling price of $750 by adding 25% to the cost of $600. We can also calculate the cost if we given the selling price by dividing the selling price by 125 and multiplying it by 100.

In a mark-up situation the cost will **always** represent 100% and the selling price will **always** represent 100 plus the mark-up%.

Gross profit **margin means the profit is based on the selling price**, e.g. margin of 25% means 25% of the selling price is profit. In a 25% margin situation the following cost structure would apply:

	$	%
Sales	800	100
Cost of sales	600	75
Gross profit	200	25

This means that if we are given the selling price of $800 in the question and the margin of 25% we can calculate the cost of $600 by taking 25% from the selling price of $800. We can also calculate the selling price if we given the cost by dividing the cost by 75 and multiplying it by 100.

In a margin situation the selling price will **always** represent 100% and the cost will **always** represent 100 less the margin%.

Test your understanding 3

Margin 25%
Sales $150,000
Opening inventory $10,000
Closing inventory $20,000
Purchases ?

You are required to complete a trading account from the above information.

A comprehensive illustration

Since commencing business several years ago as a cloth dealer, Shareef has relied on annual receipts and payments accounts for assessing progress. These accounts have been prepared from his business bank account through which all business receipts and payments are passed.
Shareef's receipts and payments account for the year ended 31 March year 10 is as follows:

Receipts and payments account

	$		$
Opening balance	1,680	Drawings	6,300
Sales receipts	42,310	Purchases payments	37,700
Proceeds of sale of grandfather clock	870	Motor van expenses	2,900
Loan from John Scott	5,000	Local business tax	570
Closing balance	1,510	Wages – John Jones	3,200
		Workshop rent	700
	51,370		51,370

Additional information

(a) The grandfather clock sold during the year ended 31 March year 10 was a legacy received by Shareef from the estate of his late father.

(b) The loan from John Scott was received on 1 January year 10. Interest is payable on the loan at the rate of 10 per cent per annum.

(c) In May year 10, Shareef received from his suppliers a special commission of 5 per cent of the cost of purchases during the year ended 31 March year 10.

(d) On 1 October year 9, Shareef engaged John Jones as a salesman. In addition to his wages, Jones receives a bonus of 2 per cent of the business's sales during the period of his employment; the bonus is payable on 1 April and 1 October in respect of the immediately preceding 6-month period.
Note: It can be assumed that sales have been at a uniform level throughout the year ended 31 March year 10.

(e) In addition to the items mentioned above, the assets and liabilities of Shareef were as follows:

	Year 9	Year 10
At 31 March	**($)**	**($)**
Motor van at cost	4,000	4,000
Inventories at cost	5,000	8,000
Trade receivables	4,600	12,290
Motor vehicle expenses prepaid	–	100
Workshop rent accrued due	–	200
Trade payables	2,900	2,200

(f) It can be assumed that the opening and closing balances in the above receipts and payments account require no adjustment for the purposes of Shareef's financial statements.

(g) As from 1 April year 9, it has been decided to calculate the depreciation on the motor van annually at the rate of 20 per cent of the cost. (It is assumed that the motor van will have no residual value.)

You are required to produce the income statement for the year ended 31 March year 10 and a statement of financial position at that date of Shareef.

Solution

The value of sales and purchases can be found by using total accounts:

Sales ledger control

	$		$
Balance b/d	4,600	Sales receipts	42,310
Sales	50,000	Balance c/d	12,290
	54,600		54,600

Purchases ledger control

	$		$
Purchases payments	37,700	Balance b/d	2,900
Balance c/d	2,200	Purchases	37,000
	39,900		39,900

It is then a fairly simple matter to complete the income statement.

Income statement of Shareef for the year ended 31 March year 10

	$	$
Sales		50,000
Opening inventory	5,000	
Purchases	37,000	
	42,000	
Closing inventory	(8,000)	
		(34,000)
Gross profit		16,000
Motor van expenses (2,900 – 100)	2,800	
Workshop rent (700 + 200)	900	
Local business tax	570	
Wages – John Jones (3,200 + (2% × 50,000 × 6/12))	3,700	
Loan interest (10% × 5,000 × 3/12)	125	
Depreciation (4,000 × 20%)	800	
	8,895	
Commission receivable (37,000 × 5%)	(1,850)	
		(7,045)
Net profit		8,955

The opening capital value can be calculated by applying the accounting equation to the values of assets and liabilities at 31 March year 9.

Assets	$
Motor van	4,000
Inventory	5,000
Trade receivables	4,600
Bank	1,680
	15,280
Liabilities	
Payables	2,900
Capital at 31 March year 9	12,380
	15,280

Statement of financial position of Shareef as at 31 March year 10

Assets	**Cost** $	**Acc. Depreciation** ($)	**Carrying Amount** ($)
Non-current assets			
Motor van	4,000	(800)	3,200
Current assets			
Inventory		8,000	
Receivables		12,290	
Prepayments		100	
Commission receivable		1,850	
			22,240
			25,440

Capital and liabilities

Capital at the start of the year 10		12,380
Capital introduced		870
Net profit		8,955
		22,205
Less: drawings		(6,300)
Capital at the end of the year 10		15,905
Non-current liability		
Loan from John Scott		5,000
Current liabilities		
Trade payables	2,200	
Accrued rent	200	
Wage bonus	500	
Loan interest accrual	125	
Bank overdraft	1,510	
		4,535
		25,440

The approach taken in this solution is typical of what is needed.

- Head up a sheet of paper for the income statement and another for the statement of financial position.
- Work line by line through the standard income statement format – sales, opening inventories, purchases and so on – entering the details given in the question. Workings may be needed for some of the figures, particularly sales and purchases. If so, do them on a separate sheet of paper and cross-reference as appropriate.
- Work through the statement of financial position in the same way, if necessary calculating as a working the opening balance of capital brought forward.

6 Chapter summary

In this chapter we have looked at the main techniques involved in preparing financial statements:

- from incomplete records.

Apart from the use of some new terminology in the financial statements of non-profit-making organisations, this chapter builds on the knowledge and skills of previous chapters, in particular:

- the preparation of control accounts;
- the distinction between capital and revenue transactions;
- adjustments for accruals and prepayments;
- the accounting equation:

Test your understanding questions

Test your understanding 4

Angela is in business but does not keep full accounting records. For the year ended 31 December 20X5 she is able to provide you with the following information:

	At 1 January ($)	At 31 December ($)
Inventory	2,950	3,271
Receivables	325	501
Payables for purchases	736	1,014
Accrued wages payable	74	83

You are able to prepare the following summary of her cash and bank transactions for the year:

Cash	$	Bank	$
Opening balance	49	Opening balance	920
Receipts		Receipts	
Shop takings	5,360	Cheques from customers	1,733
Cheques cashed	260	Shop takings paid in	3,995
	5,669		6,648
Payments		Payments	
Purchases	(340)	Purchases	(2,950)
Wages	(102)	Wages	(371)
Other expenses	(226)	Other expenses	(770)
Drawings	(820)	Purchase of van	(1,250)
Paid into bank	(3,995)	Cash withdrawn	(260)
Closing balance	186	Closing balance	1,047

Angela believes that one customer owing $27 will definitely not pay. On the basis of past experience, she believes that about 4 per cent of the remaining receivables may not pay. The van is to be depreciated at the rate of 20 per cent per annum, straight line, and assuming no residual value.

You are required to prepare Angela's income statement and statement of financial position for 20X5.

Test your understanding 5

Potter has always kept his account in proper double-entry form, but they were all destroyed following a fire at his offices on 31 December 20X5. His accountants had the following statement of financial position as at 31 December 20X4:

	$	$
Assets		
Non-current assets (carrying amount)		
Land and buildings		80,000
Motor vehicles		8,000
Fixtures		7,500
		95,500
Current assets		
Inventory	18,800	
Receivables	16,200	
Bank	9,600	
		44,600
		140,100
Capital and liabilities		
Capital		97,200
Non-current liabilities		
10% loan		30,000
Current liabilities		
Trade payables	11,000	
Accrued expenses:		
Loan interest	1,500	
Local business tax	400	
		12,900
		140,100

You obtain the following additional information:

(i) Cheques received from receivables during the year were $78,900; sales amounted to $80,500 and cash discount was allowed to some receivables.

(ii) Purchases during the year were $45,250 and payables at 31 December 20X5 were $9,550.

(iii) Payments made by cheque during the year included wages $9,600, motor expenses $2,250, general expenses $2,550, loan interest $3,000, drawings $4,000 and local business tax for the 18 months to 31 March 20X6 $2,400.

(iv) A bill of $500 for motor expenses was awaited at 31 December 20X5.

(v) At 31 December 20X5, inventory was $16,000 and receivables $17,300.

(vi) Depreciation is to be charged on the carrying amount at 25 per cent on motor vehicles and at 20 per cent on fixtures.

Required:

Prepare the income statement and statement of financial position for 20X5.

Test your understanding answers

Test your understanding 1

This can be done by drawing up a sales ledger control account, and inserting the known figures. The unknown figure for sales can then be determined as the figure required to balance the account.

Sales ledger control account

20XI		$	20XI		$
1 Jan	Balance b/d	27,000	In year	Bank	140,000
In year	**Sales (balancing figure)**	**144,500**	In year	Cash discounts allowed	2,000
			In year	Irrecoverable debt written off	5,000
			31 Dec	Balance c/d	24,500
		171,500			171,500

The missing sales figure is $144,500.

Test your understanding 2

The ledger account for electricity would appear as follows:

Electricity

20XI		$	20XI		$
In year	Bank	550	1 Jan	Balance b/d	120
31 Dec	Balance c/d	140	31 Dec	**Income statement (balancing figure)**	**570**
		690			690

The missing income statement figure is $570.

Test your understanding 3

	$	$	%
Sales		150,000	100
Cost of sales			
Opening inventory	10,000		
Purchases **(balancing figure)**	122,500		
Closing inventory	(20,000)		
		112,500	75
Gross profit		37,500	25

This question is based on margin which means the profit is based on sales. In cost structure terms this means the sales are 100% and profit 25%, hence cost of sales must represent 75%. When we have calculated the total amount for cost of sales as 75% of $15,000 we can work out the purchases as the balancing amount.

Test your understanding 4

Begin with the income statement, using total accounts to calculate sales and purchases.

Income statement of Angela for the year ended 31 December 20X5

	$	$
Sales (W1)		7,269
Opening inventory	2,950	
Purchases (W2)	(3,568)	
	6,518	
Less: closing inventory	(3,271)	
Cost of goods sold		(3,247)
Gross profit		4,022
Wages (W3)	482	
Other expenses (226 + 770)	996	
Irrecoverable debts	27	
Change in allowance for receivables (501 – 27) × 4%	19	
Depreciation (20% × 1,250)	250	
		(1,774)
Net profit for the year		2,248

Statement of financial position of Angela as at 31 December 20X5

Assets	Cost ($)	Acc. Depreciation ($)	Carrying Amount ($)
Non-current assets			
Van	1,250	(250)	1,000
Current assets			
Inventory		3,271	
Receivables less allowance (474 – 19)		455	
Bank		1,047	
Cash		186	
			4,959
			5,959
Capital and Liabilities			
Balance at 1 January 20X5 (W4)			3,434
Net profit for the year		2,248	
Less: drawings		(820)	
Retained profit for the year			1,428
			4,862
Current liabilities			
Payables		1,014	
Accrued wages		83	
			1,097
			5,959

Workings

(W1) **Sales**

Receivables account

	$		$
Balance b/d	325	Bank	1,733
Credit sales (balancing figure)	**1,909**	Irrecoverable debt	27
		Balance c/d (501 – 27)	474
	2,234		2,234

Sales total account

	$		$
Income statement	**7,269**	Cash – shop takings	5,360
		Credit sales (sales account balance)	1,909
	7,269		7,269

(W2) **Purchases**

Payables account

	$		$
Bank	2,950	Balance b/d	736
Balance c/d	1,014	**Credit purchases (balancing figure above)**	**3,228**
	3,964		3,964

Purchases total account

	$		$
Cash	340	**Income statement**	**3,568**
Credit purchases (balancing figure above)	3,228		
	3,568		3,568

(W3) **Wages**

Wages account

	$		$
Cash	102	Balance b/d	74
Bank	371	**Income statement**	**482**
Balance c/d	83		
	556		556

(W4) **Capital opening balance**

Capital as at 1 January 20X5

	$
Inventory	2,950
Receivables	325
Bank	920
Cash	49
	4,244
Less: liabilities (736 + 74)	(810)
	3,434

Test your understanding 5

- This is a straightforward incomplete records question, involving the calculation of several missing figures. The preparation of a 'workings' section, clearly labelled, is essential in providing these figures.
- This question also requires you to prepare a bank summary to determine the end-of-year bank balance.

Workings

(W1)

	$
Purchases	45,250
Opening payables	11,000
	56,250
Closing payables	(9,550)
Paid to payables	**46,700**

(W2)

Sales	80,500
Opening receivables	16,200
	96,700
Cheques received	(78,900)
	17,800
Closing receivables	(17,300)
Cash discount allowed	**500**

(W3) **Local business tax**

Paid	2,400
Accrued at start	(400)
	2,000
Prepaid at end (2,400 × 3/18)	(400)
Charge to the income statement	1,600

(W4)

		$
Bank summary		
Opening balance		9,600
Receipts		
Receivables		78,900
		88,500
Payments		
Payables (W1)	46,700	
Wages	9,600	
Motor expenses	2,250	
General expenses	2,550	
Loan interest	3,000	
Drawings	4,000	
Local business tax	2,400	
		(70,500)
Closing bank balance		18,000

(W5)

Depreciation

	$
Motor vehicles (25% × $8,000)	2,000
Fixtures (20% × $7,500)	1,500
	3,500

Income statement of Potter for the year ended 31 December 20X5

	$	$
Sales		80,500
Less: cost of sales		
Opening inventory	18,800	
Purchases	45,250	
	64,050	
Less: closing inventory	(16,000)	
		(48,050)
Gross profit		32,450
Less: expenses		
Discounts allowed (W2)	500	
Wages and salaries	9,600	
Local business tax (W3)	1,600	
Motor expenses (2,250 + 500)	2,750	
General expenses	2,550	
Loan interest	3,000	
Depreciation (W5)	3,500	
		(23,500)
Net profit for the year		8,950

Statement of financial position of Potter as at 31 December 20X5

Assets		*Carrying Amount* ($)
Non-current assets		
Land and buildings		80,000
Motor vehicles (8,000 – 2,000)		6,000
Fixtures (7,500 – 1,500)		6,000
		92,000
Current assets		
Inventory	16,000	
Receivables	17,300	
Prepayments (W3)	400	
Bank (W4)	18,000	
		51,700
		143,700
Capital and liabilities		
Capital at 1 January		97,200
Profit for the year		8,950
		106,150
Less: drawings		(4,000)
		102,150
Non-current liabilities		
Loan		30,000
Current liabilities		
Payables	9,550	
Accrued expenses		
Motor expenses	500	
Loan interest	1,500	
		11,550
		143,700

chapter

17

Income and Expenditure Statements

Chapter learning objectives

When you have completed this chapter, you should be able to:

- account for annual and life memberships;
- prepare a subscriptions account;
- prepare a bar trading account;
- prepare income and expenditure accounts.

1 Introduction

So far, we have been looking at the preparation of financial statements for profit making organisations.

In this chapter we will look at the records kept by non-profit-making bodies, such as clubs and societies.

2 Financial statements of non-profit-making bodies

In this section we look at the financial statements of organisations such as clubs and societies, which are not primarily set up for the purpose of trading and making a profit (although they may engage in some trading activities, for example, running a bar for the use of members and visitors).

3 Accounting terminology for non-profit-making bodies

In chapter 1, we learned that some organisations exist, not with the main intention of making profits in the long term, but with the objective of providing facilities to their members or others who may benefit from their activities. These organisations are often clubs and societies. They may have trading activities, and they will often engage in profitable activities that increase the net assets of the organisation. However, this increase in net assets is not attributed directly to the members, but is used to expand and improve the organisation, or to provide benefits for those whom the organisation exists to support.

Local government is another example of a non-profit-making organisation, but the financial statements of local government are outside the scope of your syllabus.

The financial statements prepared for these organisations are similar to those prepared for other trading organisations described earlier in this text, and they utilise the same accounting concepts and principles, but some of the terminology used is different. It is usual for the following to be prepared for these organisations.

Receipts and payments account. This is a summary of the organisation's cash and bank transactions for a period. It is common for these organisations to operate a single-entry accounting system and thus the receipts and payments account is the starting point for the preparation of other accounting statements.

Income and expenditure statement (or account). This is similar to the income statement of a trading organisation. It shows the income and expenditure of a particular period and follows the same accounting principles as described for trading organisations earlier in this text. However, the following differences should be noted:

- The word **'income'** is used rather than revenue.
- The terms profit and loss, the difference between the income and expenditure of the period is referred to as **surplus or deficit**.

Why don't we call it a profit?

The reason for this is that the organisation does not, in principle, exist in order to make a profit. Sometimes, however, the organisation has sections within itself or holds specific events with the deliberate intent of making profits that are used to subsidise the costs of the organisation's other activities: for example, it may have a bar selling drinks at a profit, or might hold a dinner dance for which tickets are sold. In these circumstances a separate 'trading account' is prepared for each such activity. The profit or loss arising is transferred to the income and expenditure account.

Statement of financial position

The statement of financial position of a non-trading organisation is similar to that of a sole trader, showing assets and liabilities at the statement of financial position date. However, the organisation does not have an owner. The equivalent of the owner's capital is referred to as the **accumulated fund**.

4 Accounting for membership fees and subscriptions

Another significant difference between these organisations and the trading organisation is that their income is mainly derived from their members in membership fees. Different organisations have different membership schemes but the most common are as follows.

Annual membership fees

This type of scheme requires members to pay a fee annually in order to retain membership. In accounting terms, this normally coincides with the date for preparing the annual financial statements, but care must be taken to adjust appropriately for **subscriptions in advance (a liability) and for subscriptions in arrears (an asset).** If a member has outstanding subscriptions it is unlikely that legal action will be taken to recover them (because of the legal costs involved and the difficulty of proving the debt), so it is common for them to be written off as an irrecoverable debt. However, each organisation will have its own policy.

Therefore, you will be required to prepare a subscriptions account in order to calculate the correct amount of income in the income and expenditure statement for the year.

The subscriptions account would appear as follows:

Subscriptions receivable

20X8		$	20X8		$
1 Jan	In arrears b/d	X	1 Jan	In advance b/d	X
				Bank - amount received	X
31 Dec	In advance c/d	X	31 Dec	In arrears c/d	X
	Income and expenditure	X			
		X			X
20X9			20X9		
1 Jan	In arrears b/d	X	1 Jan	In advance b/d	X

Test your understanding 1

A club receives subscriptions during 20X8 of $17,400. At the start of 20X8, $100 was owing for fees in respect of 20X7, and $300 had been paid during the previous year in respect of 20X8 fees. At the end of 20X8, $150 was still owing for 20X8 fees, and $250 had been paid in advance for 20X9.

Required:

Prepare the subscriptions account.

Entrance fees

These are fees payable in addition to the annual subscription when a person first joins the organisation as a member (they may also be referred to as joining fees). For accounting purposes they are normally considered to relate to the number of years and credit is taken for them gradually in the income and expenditure statement. The time period used is a matter for the organisation to decide but, for example, if a period of 5 years were used and the entrance fee paid were $50, then $10 would be treated as revenue in each of the 5 year's; income and expenditure statements following the admission to membership.

The accounting treatment would be to create a liability in the statement of financial position on receipt of the $50 and then to transfer $10 from this account each year. This is shown below:

Entrance fees

	$		$
Income and expenditure	10	Bank	50

Life membership fees

As its name suggests, this means that a member only makes one payment and for this receives membership for life. In accounting terms, this is treated similarly to the entrance fees described above: a statement of financial position liability is created on receipt of the fee, and a proportion of it is transferred to the income and expenditure statement over a period of time in accordance with the policy of the organisation.

A club received the following life membership fees in each of its first 2 years:

	$
Year 1	1,500
Year 2	800

The club's policy is to take credit for life membership fees in equal amounts over 10 years. The entries in the ledger accounts would appear as follows:

Life membership

20X1		$	20X1		$
31 Dec	Income and expenditure	150	1 Jan	Bank	1,500
	Balance c/d	1,350			
		1,500			1,500
20X2			20X2		
31 Dec	Income and expenditure	230	1 Jan	Balance b/d	1,350
	Balance c/d	1,920		Bank	800
		2,150			2,150

The amount transferred to income and expenditure in year 2 is made up of:

	$
10% of year 1 fees = 10% × $1,500	150
10% of year 2 fees = 10% × $800	80
	230

5 The financial statements of non-trading organisations

Step 1: You may need to prepare a bar trading account if the club has a bar. The profit or loss from the bar activities will then be transferred to the main income and expenditure statement for the club.

Bar trading account of Bentley Sports Club for the year ended 31 March 20X1

	$	$
Bar takings		X
Opening inventory	X	
Purchases	X	
Closing inventory	(X)	
		(X)
Gross profit		X
Less: bar expenses, e.g. wages		(X)
Net profit		X

Step 2: Now prepare the income and expenditure statement.

Income and expenditure statement of Bentley Sports Club for the year ended 31 March 20X1

	$	$
Income		
Ordinary subscriptions	X	
Life subscriptions	X	
Sundry income, e.g. raffle tickets, dances, interest	X	
Bar profit (from step 1 above)	X	
		X
Expenditure		
Painting of clubhouse	X	
Maintenance of grounds	X	
Insurances	X	
General expenses	X	
Wages	X	
Rent	X	
Depreciation	X	
		X
Surplus for the year		X

Step 3: Prepare the statement of financial position.

Statement of financial position of Bentley Sports Club as at 31 March 20X1

Assets	Cost ($)	Accumulated Depreciation ($)	Carrying Amount ($)
Non-current assets			
Furniture and fittings	X	(X)	X
Current assets			
Bar inventory		X	
Subscriptions in arrears		X	
Bank		X	
Cash in hand		X	
			X
			X
Accumulated Fund and Liabilities			
Accumulated fund b/f			X
Surplus for the year			X
			X
Life membership fund			X
			X
Current liabilities			
Bar purchase payables		X	
Subscriptions in advance		X	X
			X

Illustration 1

The following receipts and payments account for the year ended 31 March year 11 for the Green Bank Sports Club has been prepared by the treasurer, Waseem.

Receipts and payments account

Receipts	$	Payments	$
Balances b/d		Painting of clubhouse	580
1 April year 10		Maintenance of grounds	1,310
Cash in hand	196	Bar steward's salary	5,800
Bank current account	5,250	Insurances	240
Members' subscriptions:		General expenses	1,100
Ordinary	1,575	Bank investment account	1,500
Life	800	Secretary's wages	200
Annual dinner ticket sales	560	Annual dinner expenses	610
Bar takings	21,790	New furniture and fittings	1,870
		Bar purchases	13,100
		Rent of clubhouse	520
		Balances c/d	
		31 March year 11	
		Bank current account	3,102
		Cash in hand	239
	30,171		30,171

The following additional information has been given:

(i) Ordinary membership subscriptions received in advance at 31 March year 10 were $200. The subscriptions received during the year ended 31 March year 11 included $150 in advance for the following year.

(ii) A life membership scheme was introduced on 1 April year 9. Under the scheme, life membership subscriptions are $100 and are apportioned to revenue over a 10-year period. Life membership subscriptions totalling $1,100 were received during the first year of the scheme.

(iii) The club's bank investment account balance at 31 March year 10 was $2,676. During the year ended 31 March year 11 interest of $278 was credited to the account.

(iv) All the furniture and fittings in the club's financial statements at 31 March year 10 were bought in January year 8 at a total cost of $8,000. It is the club's policy to calculate depreciation annually on non-current assets at 10 per cent of the cost of such assets held at the relevant year end. The furniture and fittings are not expected to have any residual value. Accumulated depreciation b/fwd totalled $2,400.

(v) Other assets and liabilities of the club were:

	Year 10	Year 11
At 31 March	**$**	**$**
Bar inventory	1,860	2,110
Insurances prepaid	70	40
Rent accrued due	130	140
Bar purchases payables	370	460

You are required:

(a) to draw up the bar trading and income statement for the year ended 31 March year 11;

(b) to draw up the club's income and expenditure statement for the year ended 31 March year 11 and a statement of financial position at that date;

(c) to outline the advantages and disadvantages of receipts and payments accounts for organisations such as the Green Bank Sports Club.

Solution

(a) Bar trading account of Green Bank Sports Club for the year ended 31 March year 11

	$	$
Bar takings		21,790
Opening inventory	1,860	
Purchases (460 + 13,100 – 370)	13,190	
	15,050	
Closing inventory	(2,110)	
		(12,940)
Gross profit		8,850
Bar steward's salary		(5,800)
Net profit		3,050

(b) Income and expenditure statement of Green Bank Sports Club for the year ended 31 March year 11

	$	$
Income		
Ordinary subscriptions (1,575 – 150 + 200)	1,625	
Life subscriptions (1,100/10 + 800/10)	190	
Bank interest	278	
Bar profit	3,050	
		5,143
Expenditure		
Painting of clubhouse	580	
Maintenance of grounds	1,310	
Insurances (240 – 40 + 70)	270	
General expenses	1,100	
Secretary's wages	200	
Loss on annual dinner (560 – 610)	50	
Rent of clubhouse (520 + 140 – 130)	530	
Depreciation of furniture and fittings (9,870 × 10%)	987	
		5,027
Surplus for the year		116

Statement of financial position of Green Bank Sports Club as at 31 March year 11

Assets	Cost ($)	Accumulated Depreciation ($)	Carrying Amount ($)
Non-current assets			
Furniture and fittings	9,870	(3,387)	6,483
Current assets			
Bar inventory		2,110	
Insurance prepaid		40	
Bank investment (2,676 + 1,500 + 278)		4,454	
Bank current account		3,102	
Cash in hand		239	
			9,945
			16,428
Accumulated Fund and Liabilities			
Accumulated fund b/f (W1)			13,962
Surplus for the year			116
			14,078
Life membership fund (W2)			1,600
			15,678
Current liabilities			
Bar purchase payables		460	
Subscriptions in advance		150	
Rent accrual		140	
			750
			16,428

(W1) **Assets – liabilities = capital**

Assets = 196 (cash) + 5,250 (bank) + 1,860 (inventory) + 70 (prepayments) + 2,676 (investment) + 8,000 (fixtures and fittings) – 2,400 (accumulated depreciation) =15,652

Liabilities = 130 (accurals) + 370 (payables) + 200 (prepaid income) + 990 (lifetime membership) = 1,690

Captial = 15,652 – 1,690 = 13,962

Lifetime membership = 1,100 – 110 = 990 (see workings 2 below)

(W2) **Lifetime membership**

Life membership

20X0		$	20X0		$
31 Dec	Income and expenditure (1,100/10)	110	1 Jan	Bank	1,100
	Balance c/d	990			
		1,100			1,100
20X1			20X1		
31 Dec	Income and expenditure (1,100/10) + (800/10)	190	1 Jan	Balance b/d	990
	Balance c/d	1,600		Bank	800
		1,790			1,790

(c) The receipts and payments account provides a summary of the cash and bank transactions that have occurred during year 11.

Advantages

- It can easily be reconciled to bank statements and balances of cash in hand.
- It is easy to understand.

Disadvantages

- It does not recognise revenue and expenses as they arise, only as monies are received and paid. As such it does not conform to the accruals or matching conventions.
- It does not show the assets/liabilities of the club, and does not differentiate between capital and revenue expenditure.

Test your understanding 2

The Teesdon Tennis Club had the following assets and liabilities on 1 January 20X1:

	$
Land and buildings	45,000
Equipment	7,000
Cash in bank	1,360
Subscriptions in arrear	190
Subscriptions in advance for 20X1	70
Rent paid in advance	60

During the year ended 31 December 20X1 the club had the following receipts:

	$
Subscriptions for the year 20X1	9,000
Subscriptions from previous years	190
Subscriptions in advance for 20X2	70
Hire of courts	750
Loans from club members	5,000

and made the following payments:

	$
General expenses	5,400
Rent (for 12 months 1 April 20X1-31 March 20X2)	360
New furniture (cost $5,000 balance payable 20X2)	2,500
Repaid loan in part	1,500

You are required:

(a) to calculate the accumulated fund on 1 January 20X1;

(b) to prepare the subscriptions account;

(c) to prepare:

(i) the receipts and payments account;

(ii) the income and expenditure statement for the year ended 31 December 20X1 and a statement of financial position on that date.

6 Chapter summary

In this chapter we have looked at the main techniques involved in preparing financial statements:

- for non-profit-making organisations.

Apart from the use of some new terminology in the financial statements of non-profit-making organisations are prepared in a similar way to profit making organisations.

Test your understanding questions

Test your understanding 3

In a not-for-profit organisation, the accumulated fund is:

A non-current liabilities plus current liabilities plus current assets

B non-current assets less current liabilities less non-current liabilities

C the balance on the general reserves account

D non-current assets plus net current assets less non-current liabilities

Test your understanding 4

An income and expenditure statement (or account) is:

A a summary of the cash and bank transactions for a period

B another name for a receipts and payments account

C similar to an income statement in reflecting revenue earned and expenses incurred during an period

D a statement of financial position as prepared for a non-profit-making organisation

Test your understanding 5

A club received subscriptions during 20X5 totalling $12,500. Of these, $800 related to 20X4 and $400 related to 20X6. There were subscriptions in arrears at the end of 20X5 of $250. The subscriptions to be included in the income and expenditure statement for 20X5 amount to:

$..................

Test your understanding 6

Life membership fees payable to a club are usually dealt with by:

A crediting the total received to a life membership fees account and transferring a proportion each year to the income and expenditure statement

B crediting the total received to the income and expenditure statement in the year in which these fees are received

C debiting the total received to a life membership fees account and transferring a proportion each year to the income and expenditure statement

D debiting the total received to the income and expenditure statement in the year in which these fees are received

Test your understanding 7

A club's membership fees account shows a debit balance of $150 and a credit balance of $90 at 1 June 20X7. During the year ending 31 May 20X8, subscriptions received amounted to $4,750. Subscriptions overdue from the year ended 31 May 20X7, of $40, are to be written off. On 31 May 20X8, subscriptions paid in advance amount to $75.
The amount to be transferred to the income and expenditure statement for the year ending 31 May 20X8 is:

$.................

Test your understanding 8

The subscriptions receivable account of a club commenced the year with subscriptions in arrears of $50 and subscriptions in advance of $75. During the year, $12,450 was received in subscriptions, including all of the arrears and $120 for next year's subscriptions. The amount to be taken to the income and expenditure statement for the year is:

$.................

Test your understanding 9

The following is the receipts and payments account of the Long Lane Social Club for the year ended 31 December 20X5:

Receipts	**$**	**Payments**	**$**
Balance at 1 January	2,300	Bar licence fees	2,000
Bar takings	139,050	Cleaner's wages	4,340
Sales of refreshments	5,400	Refreshments purchased	2,890
Sales of dance tickets	1,880	Secretary's expenses	3,690
Sale of equipment	2,400	General expenses	2,090
Subscriptions	4,120	Payables for bar supplies	93,030
		Invested in bank deposit a/c	16,000
		Barperson's wages	9,500
		New equipment	8,000
		Rent	3,620
		Dance expenses	2,700
		Balance at 31 December	7,290
	155,150		155,150

Other assets and liabilities at 1 January and 31 December were as follows:

	1 Jan	**31 Dec**
	$	**$**
Premises at cost	105,000	105,000
Equipment at cost	5,400	?
Payables for bar supplies	2,270	1,960
Subscriptions in advance	480	350
Subscriptions in arrears	–	280
Inventory of bar supplies	9,500	8,350
Rent prepaid	1,000	1,100

You are also told that

(i) All the equipment owned at the start of the year was sold and replaced during the year. Depreciation of 10 per cent per annum is to be provided on the new equipment. It is assumed that the equipment will have no residual value.

(ii) The bank had credited $1,000 interest to the bank deposit account at 31 December 20X5.

Required:

(a) Prepare a bar trading account for the year ended 31 December 20X5.

(b) Prepare an income and expenditure account for the year to 31 December 20X5.

(c) Prepare an income statement and statement of financial position.

Test your understanding 10

The HB tennis club was formed on 1 April 20X0 and has the following receipts and payments account for the 6 months ended 30 September 20X0:

Receipts	**$**	**Payments**	**$**
Subscriptions	12,600	Purchase of equipment	4,080
Tournament fees	465	Groundsperson's wages	4,520
Bank deposit interest	43	Rent	636
Sale of club ties	373	Heating and lighting	674
Life membership fees	4,200	Postage and stationery	41
		Court maintenance	1,000
		Tournament prizes	132
		Purchase of club ties	450
		Balance c/d	6,148
	17,681		17,681

Notes:

(1) The annual subscription fee is $300. On 30 September, there were five members who had not paid their subscriptions, but this money was received on 4 October 20X0.

(2) The equipment is expected to be used by the club for 5 years, after which time it will need to be replaced. Its estimated scrap value at that time is $50.

(3) During the 6 months, the club purchased 100 ties printed with its own design. Forty of these ties remained unsold at 30 September 20X0.

(4) The club has paid rent in advance on 30 September 20X0 of $68.

(5) The club treasurer estimates that the following amounts should be accrued for expenses:

	$
Grounds person's wages	40
Postage and stationery	12
Heating and lighting	53

(6) The life membership fees received relate to payments made by four families. The scheme allows families to pay $1,050, which entitles them to membership for life without further payment. It has been agreed that such receipts would be credited to income and expenditure in equal instalments over 10 years.

Required:

(a) Calculate the following items to be included in the income and expenditure statement for the period, using the boxes provided.

(i) Subscriptions

	$
Subscriptions received for the year	
Subscriptions accrued for the year	
Total subscriptions for the year	
Subscriptions for the 6 months	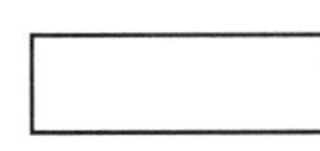

(ii) Profit from the sale of club ties

	$	$
Sales of ties		
Purchases of ties		
Less: closing inventory		
Profit		

(iii) Life membership fees

	$
Amounts received	
Annual equivalent	
Amount to include in I & E	

(iv) Depreciation of equipment

	$
Cost	
Annual depreciation	
Amount to include in I & E	

(b) Insert the missing items into the income and expenditure statement given below.

Income and expenditure statement of HB Tennis Club for the 6 months ended 30 September 20X0

	$	±	$	$
Income				
Subscriptions				☐
Income from tournaments	☐	☐	=	☐
Interest received on bank deposit				43
Profit from sale of club ties				☐
Life membership				☐
				☐
Expenditure				
Groundsperson's wages	☐	☐	= ☐	
Rent	☐	☐	= ☐	
Heat and light	☐	☐	= ☐	
Postage and stationery	☐	☐	= ☐	
Court maintenance			1,000	
Depreciation of equipment			☐	
				☐
Excess of income over expenditure				☐

Test your understanding 11

The Questing Theatre Club is an amateur dramatic club that rents premises in which it has established a theatre and bar for the use of its members. The club's treasurer has produced the following summary of the club's receipts and payments during the year ended 31 May 20X2:

Receipts and payments account for the year ended 31 May 20X2

Receipts	**$**	**Payments**	**$**
Cash and bank balances b/d	1,120	Secretarial expenses	550
Members' subscriptions	4,460	Rent of premises	1,990
Donations	500	Production expenses	18,800
Bar takings	25,900	Bar suppliers	14,700
Ticket sales	17,320	Bar expenses	4,180
Grants and subsidies	13,800	Fees of guest artists	900
		Stationery, printing & publicity	1,100
		Purchase of theatre equipment	15,100
		Other expenses	4,820
		Cash and bank balances c/d	960
	63,100		63,100

The treasurer has also been able to supply the following information:

	1 June 20X1	**31 May 20X2**
	$	**$**
Subscriptions in arrears	350	460
Subscriptions in advance	160	60
Owing to bar suppliers	1,300	1,650
Bar inventory	2,670	2,330
Production expenses owing	2,490	1,540
Stationery, printing and publicity prepaid	400	300
Valuation of bar equipment	14,500	11,500
Valuation of theatre equipment	35,000	46,000

The club's chairman is keen that the report given to members should show the profit or loss made by the bar and the surplus or deficit made on theatre productions. Only those items that can be directly allocated to the bar or the theatre productions are to be included.

Required:

(a) Prepare the club's subscriptions account.

(b) Prepare the bar trading account.

(c) Prepare the productions trading account.

(d) Prepare the Questing Theatre Club's income and expenditure statement for the year ended 31 May 20X2.

Test your understanding answers

Test your understanding 1

The subscriptions account would appear as follows:

Subscriptions receivable

20X8		$	20X8		$
1 Jan	In arrears	100	1 Jan	In advance	300
				Received	17,400
31 Dec	In advance	250	31 Dec	In arrears	150
	Income and expenditure	17,500			
		17,850			17,850
20X9			20X9		
1 Jan	In arrears	150	1 Jan	In advance	250

Test your understanding 2

Solution

(a) Accumulated fund on 1 January 20X1

$45,000 (land and buildings) + $7,000 (equipment) + $1,360 (bank) + $190 (accrued income) – $70 (prepaid income) + $60 (prepaid expenses) = $53,540

(b)

Subscriptions

20X1	$	20X1	$
Balance b/d	190	Balance b/d	70
Income and expenditure a/c	9,070	Bank	9,260
Balance c/d	70		
	9,330		9,330
		20X2	
		Balance b/d	70

(c) (i) Receipts and payments account for the year ended 31.12.20X1

20X1	$	20X1	$
Balance b/d	1,360	General expenses	5,400
Subscriptions (9,000 + 190 + 70)	9,260	Rent	360
Hire of courts	750	Furniture	2,500
Loan from club members	5,000	Loan repayment	1,500
		Balance c/d	6,610
	16,370		16,370

(ii) Income and expenditure statement for the year ended 31.12.20X1

	$	$
Subscriptions (part b)	9,070	
Hire of courts	750	
		9,820
General expenses	5,400	
Rent (360 × 9/12) + 60	330	
		(5,730)
Surplus of income over expenditure		4,090

Statement of financial position as at 31.12.20X1

Assets	$	$
Non-current assets (carrying amount)		
Land and buildings		45,000
Equipment (7,000 + 5,000)		12,000
		57,000
Current assets		
Rent paid in advance	90	
Cash at bank	6,610	
		6,700
		63,700
Accumulated fund and liabilities		
Accumulated fund balance b/f		53,540
Surplus for the year		4,090
		57,630
Non-current liability		
Loans from club members (5,000 – 1,500)		3,500
Current liabilities		
Subscriptions paid in advance	70	
Payables for furniture	2,500	
		2,570
		63,700

Test your understanding 3

D

Accumulated fund is equivalent to capital, so answer D is correct.

Test your understanding 4

C

An income and expenditure statement (or account) is commonly prepared by a not-for-profit organisation as an alternative to an income statement. A summary of cash and bank transactions, and a receipts and payments account, are one and the same thing: they both include capital transactions, for example, payments for non-current assets, and neither takes account of accrued and prepaid income or expenses. Thus answers A and B are incorrect. A statement of financial position is a statement of assets, liabilities and capital or accumulated fund.

Test your understanding 5

The calculation is:

	$
Subscriptions received in 20X5	12,500
Less: relating to 20X4	(800)
Less: relating to 20X6	(400)
	11,300
Add: subscriptions in arrears	250
	11,550

Test your understanding 6

A

Life membership fee represents income in advance and this is credited to a life membership fees account. A proportion of income is transferred to the income and expenditure statement over the assumed life of the membership.

Test your understanding 7

Subscriptions account

		$			$
1/6/X7	Balance b/d	150	1/6/X7	Balance b/d	90
31/5/X8	Balance c/d	75		Bank	4,750
31/5/X8	I & E*	4,655		Irrecoverable debts	40
		4,880			4,880

*Balancing figure

Test your understanding 8

	$
Received in year	12,450
Arrears at the beginning	(50)
In advance at the beginning	75
In advance at the end	(120)
Total to income and expenditure	12,355

Test your understanding 9

- Prepare workings for missing figures.
- Take care with subscriptions in advance and in arrears.
- An income and expenditure statement is drawn up using the same principles as an income statement. Revenue is earned during the period, irrespective of its receiptor non-receipt, and expenditure includes expenses incurred during the period, irrespective of payment.

Workings

(W1) **Purchases**

	$
Paid to payables	93,030
Plus: closing payables	1,960
Less: opening payables	(2,270)
	92,720

(W2) **Equipment**

Carrying amount at 1January	5,400
Proceeds of sale	(2,400)
Loss on disposal	3,000

(W3) **Subscriptions**

Received during the year	4,120
In advance at the start of the year	480
In arrears at the end of the year	280
	4,880
Less: in advance at the end of the year	(350)
Income and expenditure statement	4,530

(a) Bar trading account of Lane Social Club for the year ended 31 December 20X5

	$	$
Sales		139,050
Less: cost of sales		
Opening inventory	9,500	
Purchases (W1)	92,720	
	102,220	
Less: closing inventory	(8,350)	
		(93,870)
Gross profit		45,180
Less: expenses		
Barperson's wages	9,500	
Bar licence fees	2,000	
		(11,500)
Net profit		33,680

(b) Income and expenditure statement of Long Lane Social Club for the year ended 31 December 20X5

	$	$	$
Income			
Bar profit		33,680	
Profit on refreshments			
Sales	5,400		
Purchases	(2,890)		
		2,510	
Subscriptions (W3)		4,530	
Interest receivable		1,000	
			41,720
Expenditure			
Loss on dance: ticket sales	1,880		
Expenses	2,700		
		820	
Cleaner's wages		4,340	
Secretary's expenses		3,690	
General expenses		2,090	
Rent (3,620 + 1,000 – 1,100)		3,520	
Loss on sale of equipment (W2)		3,000	
Depreciation (8,000 × 10%)		800	
			(18,260)
Surplus for the year			23,460

(c) Statement of financial position of Long Lane Social Club as at 31 December 20X5

Assets	Cost ($)	Accum. dep'n ($)	Carrying amount ($)
Non-current assets			
Premises	105,000	——	105,000
Equipment	8,000	(800)	7,200
	113,000	(800)	112,200
Current assets			
Bar inventory		8,350	
Subscriptions in arrears		280	
Rent prepaid		1,100	
Bank deposit (16,000 + 1,000)		17,000	
Bank		7,290	
			34,020
			146,220
Accumulated fund and liabilities			
Accumulated fund			
Balance at 1 January 20X5 (see note i)			120,450
Surplus for the year			23,460
			143,910
Current liabilities			
Payables		1,960	
Subscriptions in advance		350	
			2,310
			146,220

Note:

(i) The opening accumulated fund can be taken as the balancing figure, as the question does not specifically ask for a separate calculation of this. However, if you wish to check the accuracy of the figure, then an opening statement of affairs can be produced.

Statement of affairs of Long Lane Social Club as at 1 January 20X5

	$	$
Assets		
Premises		105,000
Equipment		5,400
Bar inventory		9,500
Rent prepaid		1,000
Bank		2,300
		123,200
Payables	2,270	
Subscriptions in advance	480	
		(2,750)
Accumulated fund on 1 January 20X5		120,450

Test your understanding 10

- Identify the capital and revenue receipts/payments.
- Adjust the receipts and payments for the effects the notes produce.
- Prepare the financial statements in good format.

(a) (i) **Subscriptions**

	$
Subscriptions received for the year	12,600
Subscriptions accrued for the year (5 × 300)	1,500
Total subscriptions for the year	14,100
Subscriptions for the 6 months	7,050

(ii) **Profit from the sale of club ties**

	$	$
Sales of ties		373
Purchases of ties (100 × 45)	450	
Less: closing inventory (40 × 45)	(180)	
		(270)
Profit		103

(iii) **Life membership fees**

	$
Amounts received	4,200
Annual equivalent	420
Amount to include in I & E	210

(iv) **Depreciation of equipment**

	$
Cost	4,080
Annual depreciation (4,080 – 50)/5	806
Amount to include in I & E	403

(b) **Income and expenditure statement of HB Tennis Club for the 6 months ended 30 September 20X0**

	$	$
Income		
Subscriptions		7,050
Income from tournaments (465 – 132)		333
Interest received on bank deposit		43
Profit from sale of club ties		103
Life membership (4 × $1,050/10 × 6/12)		210
		7,739
Expenditure		
Groundsperson's wages (4,520 + 40)	4,560	
Rent (636 – 68)	568	
Heat and light (674 + 53)	727	
Postage and stationery (41 + 12)	53	
Court maintenance	1,000	
Depreciation of equipment	403	
		(7,311)
Excess of income over expenditure		428

Test your understanding 11

- The bar trading account requires a calculation of bar purchases.
- A separate 'surplus on theatre productions' calculation is required.
- The theatre productions deficit includes depreciation of the theatre equipment (but not the cost of the equipment, as this is a capital item). The value of the theatre equipment has gone up during the year owing to the new purchases, but has then fallen to take account of depreciation.
- The income and expenditure statement follows the normal accounting rules involved in the preparation of income statements, that is, it should include the income earned and the expenses consumed during the period, with relevant adjustments for accruals and prepayments.
- Grants and subsidies are to be treated as revenue receipts on the assumption that they were received in respect of revenue expenditure.

(a) **Subscriptions**

	$		$
Subscriptions in arrears b/d	350	Subscriptions in advance b/d	160
Subscriptions in advance c/d	60	Receipts	4,460
Income and expenditure	4,670	Subscriptions in arrears c/d	460
	5,080		5,080

(b) (i) **Bar purchases**

	$		$
Payments to suppliers	14,700	Owing at 1.6.X1	1,300
Owing at 31.5.X2	1,650	Purchases	15,050
	16,350		16,350

(ii) **Bar trading account for the year ended 31 May 20X2**

	$	$
Sales		
Less: cost of goods sold		25,900
Inventory at the start of the year	2,670	
Purchases	15,050	
	17,720	
Inventory at the end of the year	(2,330)	
		(15,390)
Gross Profit		10,510
Less:		
Bar expenses	4,180	
Depreciation (14,500 - 11,500)	3,000	
		(7,180)
Bar profit		3,330

(c) (i) **Productions expenses**

	$		$
Payments	18,800	Owing at 1.6.X1	2,490
Owing at 31.5.X2	1,540	Purchases	17,850
	20,340		20,340

(ii) **Depreciation of theatre equipment**

	$		$
Value at 1.6.X1	35,000	Value at 31.5.X2	46,000
Purchases	15,100	Depreciation	4,100
	50,100		50,100

(iii) **Productions trading account for the year ended 31 May 20X2**

	$	$
Ticket sales		17,320
Less: cost of productions		
Productions expenses	17,850	
Fees of guest artists	900	
Depreciation of theatre equipment	4,100	
		(22,850)
Deficit on productions		(5,530)

(d) (i) **Stationery, publicity and printing**

	$		$
Prepaid at 31.5.X1	400	Prepaid at 31.5.X2	300
Payments	1,100	Income and expenditure	1,200
	1,500		1,500

(ii) **Income and expenditure statement Questing Theatre Club for the year ended 31 May 20X2**

	$	$
Income		
Member subscriptions		4,670
Donations		500
Surplus on bar		3,330
Grants and subsidies*		13,800
		22,300
Expenditure		
Deficit on productions	5,530	
Secretarial expenses	550	
Rent of premises	1,990	
Stationery, printing and publicity	1,200	
Other expenses	4,820	
		(14,090)
Surplus		8,210

*Grants and subsidies have been treated as revenue receipts.

chapter

18

The Manufacturing Account

Chapter learning objectives

When you have completed this chapter, you should be able to:

- identify why manufacturing accounts are needed;
- identify different types of inventories;
- explain and calculate direct costs, indirect costs, prime costs, factory cost of production and factory cost of goods completed;
- prepare manufacturing accounts.

1 Introduction

In our examples so far we have been dealing with businesses that purchase goods for onward sale to customers – in other words, with retail and wholesale businesses. We now turn our attention to manufacturing businesses.

In most respects the financial statements of a manufacturing business show no differences from what we have already learned. Its statement of financial position will be identical, though it is worth noting that the asset of inventories in a manufacturing company may be made up of four separate items:

- **bought-in goods** – those bought in as finished goods and to be sold to customers,
- **finished goods** – those already manufactured and ready for sale to customers,
- **work in progress** – i.e. partly completed goods, and
- **raw materials** – purchased from suppliers and not yet used in production.

The income statement will be almost identical. The one exception is that instead of the cost of finished goods purchased in the year, the trading account will show the cost of finished goods manufactured in the year.

It is this final item that leads to the one major difference in the financial statements of a manufacturing business.

Establishing the cost of finished goods manufactured in the year is not such a simple process as finding the total of finished goods purchased by a retailer. Indeed, it requires a whole new account – **the manufacturing account** – to arrive at this cost.

The manufacturing account, in an identical way to the trading account, is a sub-section of the income statement. The name 'manufacturing account' does not appear within the income statement but it is nevertheless a very important part of the income statement.

2 Why is a manufacturing account needed?

Manufacturers may sell their finished product directly to the public, or may sell it to a wholesaler/retailer or to another trading organisation. The income statement is used to bring together the revenue and expenditure of trading and operating the business, and this still applies to a manufacturing business. However, the calculation of the cost of goods sold by a retail or wholesale organisation is fairly straightforward, that is, opening inventories, plus purchases, less closing inventories. Calculating the costs of goods manufactured is often more complex than this, as the firm will incur not only the cost of materials but also labour costs and other expenses incurred in manufacturing. The manufacturing account is used to bring together the costs of manufacturing during the period.

Inventories in manufacturing organisations

The manufacturing process will involve three stages:

Stage 1 The acquisition of raw materials.

Stage 2 The modification or processing of those materials, with the addition of labour and other expenses.

Stage 3 The production of finished goods.

However, some raw materials purchased during a period will still be unmodified at the end of the period, while some will only be partly modified. In addition, there will be some finished goods produced during the period that remain unsold. The organisation might also buy in ready-made items for sale. Therefore, at the beginning and end of a period, there could be four types of inventories on the statement of financial position:

- bought-in goods;
- finished goods;
- work in progress;
- raw materials.

It is important to remember that the trading account must still be used to show the sales revenue earned and the cost of goods sold, not the cost of goods manufactured. The trading account will therefore bring together opening inventories of finished goods, cost of completed goods manufactured during the period, less closing inventories of finished goods. The manufacturing account will contain all of the manufacturing costs, with adjustments for opening and closing inventories of raw materials and work in progress.

It is also important to appreciate that the manufacturing account is used solely to bring together expenses – it does not include any revenue from sales.

3 Costs to include in the manufacturing account

We have already mentioned that the cost of raw materials will be contained within the manufacturing account. The calculation of raw materials consumed in the manufacturing process is exactly the same as the calculations you have previously used in the trading account of retail and wholesale organisations, that is:

- opening Inventory of raw materials;
- plus purchases of raw materials (including carriage inwards and less returns);
- less closing Inventory of raw materials.

However, other manufacturing costs must also be considered.
The following terms are considered key to understanding the manufacturing account.

Other direct costs

A direct cost is one that can be identified with units of production; very often it is a cost that varies according to the level of production. You will learn more about this cost behaviour in your studies of Fundamentals of Management Accounting. Obviously, raw materials are direct costs in that they directly vary with the level of production.

Examples of other direct costs are:

- **Direct labour (also known as production labour).** The wages and associated costs of those producing the goods;
- **Direct expenses.** Other costs that can be identified with units of production. These are more difficult to establish, as most expenses are more general in nature, but examples of direct expenses might be equipment hire for a special production run, power costs for a particular machine, and royalties payable on the production of certain products. You will not encounter direct expenses very often, however, and such expenses are likely to be highlighted if they are to be regarded as such.

Prime cost

The prime cost is the total of direct costs, that is, direct materials consumed, direct labour and direct expenses (if any). It should be clearly shown as a subtotal in the manufacturing account.

Indirect costs

These include all the other costs of manufacturing that are not part of prime cost. They are also referred to as manufacturing overheads, production overheads or factory overheads. Examples include:

- factory rent;
- factory heating, lighting and insurance;
- wages and salaries paid to factory supervisors and maintenance engineers (also known as indirect factory labour);
- depreciation of non-current assets used in manufacturing.

Note that only costs associated with manufacturing are included. Do not include costs associated with selling, distribution of goods sold or general administrative costs.

Factory cost of production

Factory cost of production is the total of prime cost and indirect costs consumed in the factory, and is another important subtotal to be shown in the manufacturing account.

Work in progress

The factory cost of production is the total of new costs introduced to the factory. However, there may already be some work in progress in the factory system at the start of the period. Some of this will be completed during the period, but there will probably still be some unfinished, and some new work in progress at the end of the period. We need to adjust the factory cost of production to add in the opening work in progress and deduct the closing work in progress. This is shown in the final section of the manufacturing account.

Factory cost of goods completed

This is the end result of the manufacturing account, and its balance is incorporated into the trading account.

4 Layout of manufacturing and trading accounts

As stated earlier, the trading account is the place to show the sales revenue earned and the cost of goods sold. In manufacturing organisations, however, the calculation of cost of goods sold will not include purchases and inventories of raw materials, but will instead include the factory cost of goods completed and opening and closing inventories of finished goods. The part of the income statement in the box is the manufacturing account; in effect the 'factory cost of goods completed' is a substitute for the 'purchases' which we have previously found in the trading account of a retailer.

Income statement (extract) for the year ended 31 December 20X1

	$	$	$	$
Sales				645,000
Less: cost of goods sold				
Opening Inventory of finished goods			55,000	
Opening Inventory of raw materials		12,000		
Purchases of raw materials		235,000		
		247,000		
Closing Inventory of raw materials		(14,000)		
Raw materials consumed		233,000		
Direct manufacturing wages		153,000		
Direct factory expenses		15,000		
Prime cost		**401,000**		
Production overhead:				
Factory supervisors' wages	30,000			
Heating and lighting	16,000			
Factory rent	12,000			
		58,000		
Factory costs incurred		**459,000**		
Opening work in progress	26,000			
Closing work in progress	(21,000)			
		5,000		

Factory cost of goods completed	**464,000**	
	519,000	
Less: closing Inventory of finished goods	(35,000)	
Cost of goods sold		(484,000)
Gross profit		161,000

5 Income statement for manufacturing organisations

These are exactly as for other organisations. The income statement will implicitly have two sub-sections – the manufacturing account and the trading account, and will contain sundry revenues and all other expenses incurred in running the business.

6 Statements of financial position for manufacturing organisations of inventories to be shown

These are also prepared as for other organisations, except that there is likely to be three or four types of inventory:

- bought-in goods for resale;
- finished goods;
- work in progress;
- raw materials.

The accounting system

The accounting system for manufacturing organisations

Ledger accounts will be prepared in the same way as for other organisations, except that there will be additional ledger accounts for items connected with manufacturing, such as direct factory labour, indirect factory labour, and Inventory of work in progress and finished goods. Some items of expense, however, may not be separately established or invoiced. For example, premises insurance might consist of a single invoice covering all the buildings. In such cases, it is necessary to apportion the expenses between manufacturing and other elements (often described as 'factory' and 'office'). In computer-based assessment questions, you will be told what proportions to apply.

The manufacturing account, just as the trading account, and income statement as a whole, is part of the double-entry bookkeeping system. Hence it is called the manufacturing 'account' and is a ledger account which can be debited and credited. The items that appear in it will all have an equivalent opposite entry in either the nominal ledger or the trading account. For example, expenses such as direct factory labour will be debited to the direct factory labour ledger account during the year, and then, at the end of the year, the balance will be transferred to the manufacturing account (debit manufacturing account; credit direct factory labour).

The balance on the manufacturing account is transferred to the trading account at the end of the year (debit trading account; credit manufacturing account).

The key to questions in this area is to adopt a methodical approach. Remember that your aim in the manufacturing account is to arrive at the total cost of manufacturing the finished goods in the year. This can be regarded as comprising of three elements:

- the costs directly attributable to the goods produced, such as the raw materials they contain, and the wages of personnel directly involved in manufacturing;
- the indirect factory costs, sometimes called factory overheads. These might include the costs of heating and lighting the factory, the rent on factory premises and the wages of factory supervisors;
- an adjustment for opening and closing work in progress, similar to the treatment of opening and closing Inventory of finished goods in a trading account.

Illustration 1

G Club is a manufacturer of spare parts and the following balances were some of those appearing in his books at 31 December year 4.

	$
Capital	56,932
Inventory at 1 January year 4	
Raw materials	11,000
Work in progress	16,000
Finished goods	20,090
Inventory at 31 December year 4	
Raw materials	17,000
Work in progress	18,000
Finished goods	18,040
Wages	
Direct manufacturing	203,080
Factory supervisors	13,325
General office	10,200
Warehouse	19,300
Direct factory power	95,000
Heating and lighting	9,000
Purchase of raw materials	256,000
Carriage outwards	986
Plant and machinery	80,000
Premises	120,000
Returns inwards	420
Office equipment	15,000
Rent	6,000
Administrative expenses	1,800
Receivables	14,000
Payables	12,000
Cash in hand	3,662
Sales	800,290
Bank overdraft	25,641

For the year ended 31 December year 4, you are required to prepare:

(a) the income statement of G Club;

(b) the statement of financial position of G Club.

The costs of heating and lighting, and rent are to be apportioned as follows: factory 1/2, warehouse 1/3, offices 1/6.

Solution

(a) **Income statement of G Club for the year ended 31 December year 4**

	$	$	$	$
Sales				800,290
Less: returns inwards				(420)
				799,870
Opening inventory of finished goods			20,090	
Opening inventory of raw materials		11,000		
Purchases of raw materials		256,000		
		267,000		
Closing inventory of raw materials		(17,000)		
Raw materials consumed		250,000		
Direct manufacturing wages		203,080		
Direct factory power		95,000		
Prime cost		548,080		
Production overhead				
Factory supervisors' wages	13,325			
Heating and lighting (9,000 × 1/2)	4,500			
Rent (6,000 × 1/2)	3,000			
		20,825		
Factory costs incurred		568,905		
Opening work in progress	16,000			
Closing work in progress	(18,000)			
		(2,000)		
Factory cost of goods completed			566,905	
			586,995	
Closing inventory of finished goods			(18,040)	

Cost of sales			(568,955)
Gross profit			230,915
Warehouse costs			
Wages	19,300		
Heating and lighting (9,000 × 1/3)	3,000		
Rent (6000 × 1/6)	2,000		
		24,300	
Office costs			
Wages	10,200		
Heating and lighting (9,000 × 1/6)	1,500		
Rent (6,000 × 1/6)	1,000		
Administration expenses	1,800		
		14,500	
Selling and distribution costs			
Carriage outwards		986	
			(39,786)
Net profit for the year			191,129

(b) **Statement of financial position of G Club as at 31 December year 4**

Assets	$	$	$
Non-current assets			
Premises			120,000
Plant and machinery			80,000
Office equipment			15,000
			215,000
Current assets			
Inventory			
Raw materials	17,000		
Work in progress	18,000		
Finished goods	18,040		
		53,040	
Receivables		14,000	
Cash in hand		3,662	
			70,702

		285,702
Capital and liabilities		
Capital		56,932
Add: net profit		191,129
		248,061
Current liabilities		
Payables	12,000	
Bank overdraft	25,641	
		37,641
		285,702

Test your understanding 1

What are the component parts of prime cost?

7 Chapter summary

In this chapter we have looked at the production of an income statement, incorporating manufacturing and trading accounts, and a statement of financial position for a manufacturing organisation. You should be able to identify the items that are to be included in the manufacturing account, in particular:

- the calculation of prime cost;
- factory cost of production;
- factory cost of goods completed;
- the adjustment for work in progress at the beginning and end of the period.

You should appreciate that the only difference in the trading account from that of a non-manufacturing organisation is the substitution of **'factory cost of goods completed' for 'purchases'**.

Although you will not be required to produce a complete manufacturing account in your exam it is still important to understand how these are produced with regards to your future studies. Your exam may require you to prepare any part of the manufacturing account.

Manufacturing accounts are quite straightforward if you take care with your workings, and adopt a methodical approach. Make sure that you clearly label workings, and cross-reference them to the financial statements: this is much clearer than attempting to squash them on to the face of the financial statements themselves, as some of them may involve several elements to their calculation. A suggested approach is as follows:

- **Step 1** Read the question completely before starting. Note particularly if a statement of financial position is required or not.
- **Step 2** Label the trial balance with the destination of the various items. If a statement of financial position is not required, you will not need all of the items on the statement of financial position (e.g. bank balances, receivables, payables).
- **Step 3** Set out a page of workings before you start. Work through the notes to the financial statements, in the order given, and make the necessary adjustments:
  (a) adjust the trial balance figures for any accruals and prepayments, then split between manufacturing and the rest of the income statement;
  (b) calculate depreciation and split between manufacturing and the rest of the income statement;

(c) calculate any other adjustments, for example, bad debts and allowance for receivables;

(d) adjust for any other items, such as goods on sale or return, errors and corrections.

- **Step 4**

  (a) Enter the sales, less any returns inwards in the trading account;

  (b) Enter opening inventories of finished goods in the trading account.;

  (c) Commence your manufacturing account and enter all relevant figures, using your workings where necessary:

  – raw materials opening inventory, plus purchases, less closing inventory (remember to adjust for returns outwards and carriage inwards);

  – other direct costs, for example, wages, direct power, to give prime cost;

  – indirect factory costs (production overheads);

  – adjust for work in progress (add opening inventory, deduct closing inventory);

  – the final result is the factory cost of goods completed.

- **Step 5** Complete the trading account:

  (a) less closing inventory of finished goods;

  (b) this gives cost of goods sold;

  (c) the difference between sales and cost of goods sold is gross profit.

- **Step 6** Prepare the remainder of the income statement, using your workings where necessary.

- **Step 7** Prepare the statement of financial position (if required), remembering that you are likely to have several types of closing inventory to show.

Test your understanding questions

Test your understanding 2

The following information relates to a company at its year end:

	$
Inventory at beginning of year	
Raw materials	10,000
Work in progress	2,000
Finished goods	34,000
Inventory at end of year	
Raw materials	11,000
Work in progress	4,000
Finished goods	30,000
Purchases of raw materials	50,000
Direct wages	40,000
Royalties on goods sold	3,000
Production overheads	60,000
Distribution costs	55,000
Administration expenses	70,000
Sales	300,000

The cost of goods manufactured during the year is:

$................

Test your understanding 3

If work in progress decreases during the period, then:

A prime cost will decrease

B prime cost will increase

C the factory cost of goods completed will decrease

D the factory cost of goods completed will increase

Test your understanding 4

An increase in the figure for work in progress will:

A increase the prime cost

B decrease the prime cost

C increase the factory cost of goods completed

D decrease the factory cost of goods completed

Test your understanding 5

Your firm has the following manufacturing figures:

	$
Prime cost	56,000
Factory overheads	4,500
Opening work in progress	6,200
Factory cost of goods completed	57,000

Closing work in progress is:

$..............

Test your understanding 6

The prime cost of goods manufactured is the total of:

A all factory costs before adjusting for work in progress

B all factory costs of goods completed

C all materials and labour

D direct factory costs

Test your understanding 7

The following information relates to M Ltd:

At 30 September	**20X1**	**20X0**
	$	$
Inventory of raw materials	75,000	45,000
Work in progress inventory	60,000	70,000
Inventory of finished goods	100,000	90,000
For the year ended 30th September 20X1		
Purchases of raw materials	150,000	
Manufacturing wages	50,000	
Factory overheads	40,000	

The prime cost of production in the manufacturing account for the year ended 30 September 20X1 is:

$..............

Test your understanding 8

M makes agricultural machinery, for sale to major suppliers in the industry. The following figures are extracted from his trial balance at the end of the most recent year.

	$000
Sales	2,200
Purchases of parts	650
Carriage inwards	40
Carriage outwards	100
Returns inwards	80
Returns outwards	60
Manufacturing labour	200
Factory supervisory labour	75
Office salaries	108
Other costs	
Heating and lighting	165
Rent and insurance	122
Factory machinery at cost	1,000
Accumulated depreciation of factory machinery	400
Delivery vehicles at cost	300
Accumulated depreciation of vehicles	100
Office machinery at cost	120
Accumulated depreciation of office machinery	80
Opening inventory:	
Raw materials	175
Work in progress	425
Finished goods	115

At the end of the year, the following information is also available:

(a)

	$000
Closing inventory	
Raw materials	147
Work in progress	392
Finished goods	138

(b)

	$000
Heat and light accrued	15
Rent prepaid	22

(c) Seventy-five per cent of heat, light, rent and insurance is considered to be applicable to the manufacturing processes.

(d) Depreciation is to be calculated as follows:

- factory machinery, 10 per cent, straight line;
- delivery vehicles, 20 per cent, reducing balance;
- office machinery, 25 per cent, reducing balance.

(e) Delivery vehicles are used entirely for the delivery of finished goods.

(f) Office machinery is used 25 per cent for the operation of factory information systems.

Required:

Prepare the manufacturing account and income statement.

Test your understanding answers

Test your understanding 1

The component parts of prime cost are direct materials, direct labour and direct expenses (overheads).

Test your understanding 2

Cost of goods manufactured is found as follows:

	$
Opening inventory of raw materials	10,000
Purchases of raw materials	50,000
Less: closing inventory of raw materials	(11,000)
	49,000
Direct wages	40,000
Prime cost	89,000
Production overheads	60,000
	149,000
Less: increase in work in progress (2,000 – 4,000)	(2,000)
Cost of goods manufactured	147,000

Test your understanding 3

D

A decrease in work in progress means fewer goods are partly complete, thus the value of completed goods will be higher. A and B are incorrect as work in progress has no effect on prime cost.

Test your understanding 4

D

A and B are incorrect as work in progress has no effect on prime cost. An increase in work in progress means that more production is in a partly finished state and therefore less has been completed, therefore C is incorrect. .

Test your understanding 5

	$
Prime cost	56,000
Factory overheads	4,500
Opening WIP	6,200
Closing WIP (ß)	(9,700)
Factory cost of goods completed	57,000

The closing WIP must be the balancing item to agree to the factory cost completed of $57,000.

Test your understanding 6

D

Test your understanding 7

The answer is: $170,000

Prime cost means the total of direct costs, that is direct materials consumed, direct labour and direct expenses.

	$
Opening inventory of raw materials	45,000
Purchase of raw materials	150,000
Closing inventory of raw materials	(75,000)
Raw materials consumed in production	120,000
Manufacturing wages	50,000
Prime cost	170,000

Test your understanding 8

- Categorise items before you start the income statement.
- Remember to make adjustments for accruals and prepayments, and the calculation of depreciation, before splitting items between manufacturing account, trading account and the remainder of the income statement.
- Some items in the question might not be required for your answer.

Income statement of M for the year ended . . .

	$000	$000	$000	$000
Sales				2,200
Less: returns inwards				(80)
				2,120
Opening inventory of finished goods			115	
Opening inventory of raw materials		175		
Purchases	650			
Carriage inwards	40			
	690			
Less: returns outwards	(60)			
		630		
		805		
Less: closing inventory of raw materials		(147)		
Direct materials		658		
Direct labour		200		
Prime cost		858		

Factory indirect overheads				
Supervisory labour	75			
Heat and light (75% × (165 + 15))	135			
Rent and insurance (75% × (122 – 22))	75			
Depreciation				
Factory machinery (10% × $1,000)	100			
		385		
Factory cost of production		1,243		
Opening work in progress	425			
Less: closing work in progress	(392)			
		33		
Factory cost of goods completed			1,276	
			1,391	
Less: closing inventory of finished goods			(138)	
Cost of sales				(1,253)
Gross profit				867
Expenses				
Carriage outwards			100	
Office salaries			108	
Heat and light (25% × (165 + 15))			45	
Rent and insurance (25% × (122 – 22))			25	
Depreciation				
Delivery vehicles (20% × (300 – 100))			40	
Office machinery (25% × (120 – 80))			10	
				(328)
Net profit				539

chapter

19

The Financial Statements of Limited Companies

Chapter learning objectives

When you have completed this chapter, you should be able to:

- prepare financial statements from trial balance for a limited company;
- prepare a statement of changes in equity;
- identify the different sources of finance for a limited company;
- incorporate taxation into limited company financial statements;
- calculate dividends for ordinary and preference shares;
- prepare accounts for the issue of shares.

1 Introduction

Many businesses are constituted in the form of limited companies. The nature of limited companies was mentioned very briefly in chapter 1 and you should refer back to refresh your memory. In this chapter we look at some of the features of limited companies that have an impact on the content and presentation of their financial statements.

We also look at one further accounting statement that companies are required to include in their financial statements – the statement of changes in equity.

2 Limited companies

- A company is a separate legal entity that may sue and be sued.
- It may have many owners who may or may not be directly involved in the day-to-day running of the business.
- Each of these owners is known as a shareholder or member of the company. They become shareholders by buying shares in the company when the company is formed. Shares are discussed in more detail later on in the chapter but basically you pay an amount to own part of the company.
- The liability of the members to the company is limited. This means that if a company's assets are insufficient to pay its liabilities the shareholders cannot be required to pay more than the amount paid, or agreed to be paid for their shares, and thus their personal assets are protected. This contrasts with the position of sole traders. In law, the business of a sole trader and the individual owning the business are the same person. Thus the business obligations must be met by its owner even if this means selling private assets or leads to the individual being declared bankrupt.

The financial statements of a company are normally filed annually at a public bureau, in a form prescribed by company law and international financial reporting standards (IFRSs) (this is not within your syllabus and is not included in this Learning System). However, the internal financial statements of companies are within your syllabus and use the same principles as have already been learned to prepare the financial statements of sole traders.

Company structure

As trading organisations grow in size, the limited financial resources of their owners often restrict the organisation's ability to grow any further. In order to avoid this difficulty many larger organisations use a company structure.

3 IAS 1 Presentation of Financial Statements

The required formats for published company financial statements are provided by IAS1. This requires the following components to be presented:

- a statement of comprehensive income, which may include a manufacturing account (if appropriate, depending on the organisation's activities dealt with in chapter 18) and a trading account;
- a statement of changes in equity;
- a statement of financial position;
- a statement of cash flows.

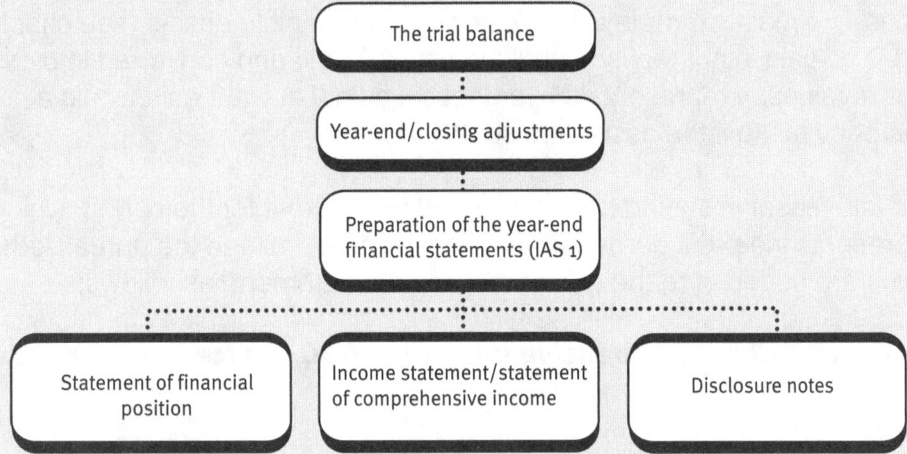

The statement of comprehensive income comprises an income statement, which you will already be familiar with from the previous chapters. It has an additional section which is discussed in more detail later in the chapter.

The only statements different from those of a sole trader are the statement of changes in equity and the statement of cash flows. The statement of changes in equity shows the increase or decrease in equity in a company, where the equity is the name for 'capital' in a limited company. **Thus in a limited company the accounting equation is assets = equity + liabilities.**

In a sole trader's statement of financial position we show the change in capital as:

	$
Capital brought forward at the beginning of the year	X
Add: capital introduced (if any)	X
Add: profit for the year	X
Less: drawings for the year	(X)
Capital at the end of the year	X

This is effectively the same as the statement of changes in equity in a company, except that in company financial statements the statement of changes in equity is shown as a separate financial statement and only the final totals are entered in the statement of financial position. Also, in company financial statements any capital introduced would be 'share' capital, and the money taken out by the owners is called 'dividends', not drawings. The statement of changes in equity is discussed in more detail later in the chapter.

The statement of comprehensive income

This is simply an extension of the income statement. The reason for this is that some gains the business makes during the year are not realised gains.The main example is the revaluation of tangible assets (see chapter 11). The gain is not realised until the asset is sold and converted into cash. The revaluation represents a hypothetical gain (i.e. what gain would a company make if the asset was sold).

For this reason it should not be included in net profit for the period, which represents the profit earned from realised sales. Instead the unrealised gains are added onto the end of the income statement, as follows:

Statement of comprehensive income of ABC Ltd for the year ended 20X8

	$000
Revenue	1000
Cost of sales – (e.g. expenses relating to production such as purchases, inventory, etc.)	(640)
Gross profit	360
Administrative expenses – (e.g. expenses such as admin wages, etc.)	(90)
Distribution costs – (e.g. expenses such as delivery costs, delivery/warehouse wages, etc.)	(10)
Operating profit	260
Investment income (e.g. dividends and interest received)	5
Finance cost (e.g. interest paid)	(20)
Profit before tax	245
Tax expense	(80)
Profit for the period	165
Other comprehensive income:	
Gain/loss on property revaluation	25
Total comprehensive income for the year	190

Taxation in company financial statements

We can see from the above example of the statement of comprehensive income an additional item appears in the financial statements of companies is that of taxation. In a sole trader's business, this is a personal charge, and so does not appear in the financial statements. But in the case of a limited company, a company is a separate legal entity and as such is liable to pay tax on its profits and so it does appear in the financial statements. At the end of each year an estimate is made by the company of the amount of its taxation liability and an accrual is made in its accounts.

The ledger entries to record the taxation charge are:

Debit	Taxation expense account	X
Credit	Taxation liability account	X

When the liability is finally agreed with the tax authorities there may be a difference compared with the estimate: the difference is compensated for when preparing the estimate for the following year's tax liability.

For example, if in year one we estimate the liability to be $100,000 but we only have to pay $95,000 we have over-provided for the tax. Therefore, in year two we must tax credit for the $5,000 over-provision in the statement of comprehensive income.

To summarise:

The statement of financial position liability = the current year's tax estimate (what we currently expect to pay)
The statement of comprehensive **income tax expense = the current year's tax estimate + under-provision from the previous year or - over-provision for the previous year.**

In this Learning System, the tax on company profits is referred to by the generic name 'income tax' though in different countries it may have another name, for example corporation tax in the UK.

Test your understanding 1

Revels estimated last year's tax charge to be $230,000. As it happened, their tax advisor settled with the tax authorities at $222,000. The difference arose because the financial statements were submitted some time before the tax computation. Therefore the directors had to make a prudent estimate of the potential tax liability to put in the accounts.

This year, Revels estimate their tax bill to be $265,000, but they are a little confused as to how this should be reflected in the financial statements. Which of the following is correct for the end of the current year?

	Statement of financial position liability	**Statement of comprehensive income tax expense**
A	$257,000	$265,000
B	$273,000	$265,000
C	$265,000	$257,000
D	$265,000	$273,000

Directors of limited companies

Limited companies are owned by the shareholders, but it is not common, especially in larger companies, for the shareholders to be involved in the day-to-day running of the company. Instead, the shareholders appoint directors to carry out those duties. Directors are merely employees of the company, and their duties are remunerated by salaries, fees, commission and so on, all of which are regarded in the same way as wages paid to any other employee, and appear in the statement of comprehensive income as an expense. Of course, in some companies, directors also own shares, but the two roles (as director and shareholder) are separate, and are recorded separately.

Sources of finance for a limited company

The statement of financial position of a company is similar to that of a sole trader, but there are usually a number of different sources of finance. This could be in the form of:

- debt, e.g. loans, redeemable preference shares.
- equity, e.g.ordinary shares, irredeemable preference shares.

Further detail - sources of finance

Debt

The main type of debt finance you are likely to come across is a debenture or loan note.

Debentures/loan notes

The written acknowledgement of a debt by a company and normally containing details as to payment of interest and the terms of repayment of the principal sum.

A debenture may be secured on some or all of the assets of the company. This means that if the company fails to repay the loan, or cannot keep up with the interest payments, the debenture holders can seize the assets on which their loan is secured and sell them to recover their money.

In accounting terms, a debenture is the same as a loan; it may be a current or non-current liability depending on the date of repayment of the principal. The interest payments are compulsory, irrespective of the level of profits, and are a normal expense, accounted for on an accruals basis (i.e. the full amount of interest arising during the accounting period must be charged in the statement of comprehensive income, regardless of the date of payment of that interest).

Equity

Share capital

The owners' investment is in the form of shares. The most common forms of share are ordinary shares and preference shares.

Ordinary shares

Shares that entitle the holders to the remaining divisible profits at the discretion of the directors (and, in a liquidation, the assets) after prior interests – for example, payables have been paid. Shareholders will receive this is the form of a dividend.

Preference Shares

Shares carrying a fixed rate of dividend, the holders of which, subject to the conditions of issue, have a prior claim to any company profits available for distribution. Preference shareholders may also have a prior claim to the repayment of capital in the event of a winding up.

When presenting a company statement of financial position, each of these types of share capital should be shown as a separate source of finance.

When a company is formed, the legal documents state the authorised share capital of the company. This is analysed into a number of shares, each having a nominal value. The authorised share capital is the amount of capital that may be issued without obtaining permission from the company's shareholders. The nominal value is also known as the par value.

Issues of shares by a company may be at nominal value or at a higher price. If they are issued at the higher price, the difference between this and the nominal value is known as the share premium.

When shares are issued, there are a number of stages before the share certificates are issued to their owners. Often, part of the issue price is payable on application for the shares, with further payments being requested later.

Redeemable or irredeemable preference shares

Redeemable means the company agrees to buy back the shares from the shareholder at a certain date in the future, hence a type of loan and treated as debt, i.e. current or non-current liability.

Irredeemable shares are treated as normal equity.

Share terminology

Each share has a nominal or par value, often $1, 50c or 25c. This is an arbitrary value assigned to a share, which is often perceived as the share's minimum value. This value remains fixed, whereas the market value of the share (the value at which the share is actively traded) fluctuates over time. This value is often used as a means of calculating dividends to shareholders (paid as a percentage of the nominal value).

Shares are sold, in the first instance, by a company at an issue price. This is at least equal to the nominal value of the share, but often exceeds it. Once shares have been sold to the public the shareholders may then sell their shares privately. The value at which the shares are trading on the open market is referred to as the market value.

The market value of a share fluctuates according to the success and perceived expectations of a company. If a company is listed on the stock exchange, the value is determined by reference to recent transactions between buyers and sellers of shares. This value does not feature in the financial statements.

Other terminology to be aware of:

- **Issued share capital** is the share capital that has actually been issued to shareholders. The number of issued shares is used in the calculation of dividends.
- **Called-up** share capital is the amount of the nominal value paid by the shareholder plus any further amounts that they have agreed to pay in the future.
- **Paid up** share capital is the amount of the nominal value which has been paid at the current date.

4 Accounting for share issues

If a company were to issue shares the double entry to record this raising of finance would be:

Debit	Bank account (issue price × no. shares)	X
Credit	Share capital account (nominal value × no. shares)	X
Credit	Share premium account (ß (i.e. the difference between the issue price and the nominal value × no. of shares sold).	X

Both the share capital and share premium accounts are shown on the statement of financial position within the 'Equity' section.

Test your understanding 2

Alberto issues 200,000 25c shares at a price of $1.75 each.

Required:

Show this transaction using ledger accounts.

Sometimes shares may not be paid for in full upon issue. Therefore, we must use an application and allotment account in addition to the share capital and premium account.

Illustration 1

Z Ltd plans to issue 100,000 ordinary shares of $1 nominal value at an issue price of $1.50 each. $0.75 per share is payable on application, $0.25 per share on confirmation that the shares have been issued and the balance of $0.50 per share on first call by Z Ltd in 3 months' time. This is for the share premium.

Required:

Prepare the bookkeeping entries to record the share issue.

Solution

The double entry to record the receipt of the application monies is as follows:

	Debit ($)	Credit ($)
Bank	75,000	
Application a/c (Being cash received from applicants.)		75,000
Allotment a/c	25,000	
Application a/c	75,000	
Share capital		100,000

(Being the creation of share capital from successful applications and the recording of amounts due on allotment.) When the allotment monies are received the entry is:

	Debit ($)	Credit ($)
Bank	25,000	
Allotment a/c		25,000

In 3 months' time, Z Ltd will request the final payment of $0.50 per share. This is known as a call for payment. In this example, this represents the share premium. The double entry would be:

	Debit ($)	Credit ($)
Bank	50,000	
Share premium		50,000

When the statement of financial position is drawn up, the 'Equity' section will show:

	$
Ordinary shares of $1 each	100,000
Share premium	50,000

Dividends

The amount paid to the company's shareholders as a return for investing in the company is known as a dividend.

- Dividends are often paid in two instalments: one during the year is known as an **interim dividend**; the other, which is usually paid after the end of the financial year, is known as a **final dividend.**
- The total amount of the dividends is shown in the statement of changes in equity.

Particular attention has to be given to the final dividend at the end of the year. The normal procedure is for directors to **propose** a final dividend; this is then voted upon as a resolution at the annual general meeting which takes place after the year end. If the proposal is approved, then the directors **declare** that a dividend will be paid. The key point here is, at what time should we recognise the final dividend in company financial statements? The answer is, **only when the dividend has been declared.**

This means that in most circumstances the dividends which are paid in a year are the final dividends of the previous year and the interim dividend of the current year.

Illustration 2

A company has a year end of 31 March. In the year ended 31 March 20X2 no interim dividend was paid, but on the 29 March 20X2 the shareholders approved and declared the payment of a proposed dividend of $15,000. The dividend was paid on 15 April 20X2.

Required:

What entries would appear in the financial statements for the year ended 31 March 20X2 in relation to dividends?

Solution

Statement of changes in equity (shown as a reduction to profit)	$15,000
Statement of financial position – current liabilities – dividend accrual	$15,000

The dividends were proposed **and** declared before the end of the year, hence an accrual is made in the financial statements.

The accounting entries will be to debit the dividends account and credit the accruals account.

Illustration 3

A company has a year end of 31 December. On the 1 July 20X7, the directors declare an interim dividend of $10,000. On the 31 December 20X7, the directors propose a final dividend of $12,000. On the 1 March 20X8 at the annual general meeting the proposed final dividend for 20X7 is approved, and the directors declare that the dividend will be paid. On the 1 July 20X8, the directors declare an interim dividend of $11,000. On the 31 December 20X8, the directors propose a final dividend of $13,000. On the 1 March 20X9 at the annual general meeting the proposed final dividend for 20X8 is approved, and the directors declare that the dividend will be paid.

Required:

What will be the dividends appearing in the statement of changes in equity in the year ended 20X8?

Solution

Final dividend for 20X7	$12,000
Interim dividend for 20X8	$11,000
	$23,000

The $23,000 will appear in the trial balance for the year ended 31 December 20X8. The double entry will be debit 'dividends', credit 'bank'.

The dividend of $23,000 does **NOT** appear of the income statement as an expense but as a distribution of profit in the statement of changes in equity. This statement can be seen later on in the chapter in full.

Note the dividends proposed were not approved until after the end of the year, hence not included in the current year's dividends.

Further detail - dividends

Directors do not have to pay the dividends in two instalments – interim and final – and in some companies there may only be one dividend payment at the end of the year. In this case, the dividend that will normally appear in the statement of changes in equity will be the dividend which was proposed in the previous year but declared and paid in the current year. For example, the financial statements for 20X4 will include the proposed dividend of 20X3.

It should be noted that the directors do not have to propose any dividends – the payment of dividends is entirely at their discretion. If the shareholders were not happy with this situation, they would try and remove these directors and replace them with directors who were prepared to propose a dividend.

There may be some occasions where the directors declare a final dividend before the end of the year, but do not pay the dividend until after the year end. This may occur where a meeting of the shareholders has been held before the year end to approve a proposed dividend. In this situation, the accruals convention will be applied, and the declared dividend will appear in the statement of changes in equity, and there will also be a 'dividend liability' in the current liabilities in the statement of financial position.

Dividends on ordinary shares

Ordinary shareholders are also known as equity shareholders. Their shares do not qualify for any special benefits, although they are often entitled to vote at general meetings. An ordinary shareholder is not entitled to any particular dividend payment, although if the directors decide to declare a dividend it can be as small or as large as they see fit. The ordinary shareholders are regarded as the 'main' shareholders in a company. The profits that are retained in the company belong to them, and would be repaid to them in the event that the company ceases to exist.

Do take care, when computing dividends, to read the question carefully. If the question states that the ordinary dividend is to be 10¢ per share, you need to calculate how many shares are in issue. For example, if the share capital in the statement of financial position is described as 'Ordinary shares of 50¢' and they are stated at $500,000, then there are 1 million ordinary shares ($500,000/0.50). The dividend in this example would be 1 million × 10¢ = $100,000.

Dividends on preference shares

Preference shareholders are so known because they received preferential treatment in the payment of dividends, and in the repayment of capital in the event that the company ceases to exist. A preference share carries a fixed rate of dividend. The important point to remember is that if the ordinary shareholders are to receive a dividend, then the preference shareholders must receive theirs first.

There are many different types of preference shares and you will study these in more detail in later studies. For the purposes of this Learning System, it is assumed that all preference shares are 'irredeemable', which means that the preference shares have no fixed repayment date. In any questions containing preference shares, the dividends will have been paid and there will be no need to make any further adjustment.

Test your understanding 3

A company has $100,000 of ordinary shares at a par value of 10¢ each and 100,000 5 per cent preference shares at a par value of 50¢ each. The directors decided to declare a dividend of 5¢ per ordinary share.

The total amount to be paid out in dividends amounts to: $..............

5 Reserves

- There are two types of reserves: **capital reserves and revenue reserves.**
- The difference between these is that capital reserves may not be distributed as dividends.
- Examples of capital reserves are share premium (see above) and revaluation reserves – created when a company revalues its assets (often land and buildings). Since the increase in value is based on a professional valuation and has not been realised by a sale, the increase in value (or profit) cannot be distributed to shareholders. For example, if a company had property in the statement of financial position at $200,000 and it was revalued to $275,000, the property would be increased to $275,000 in the statement of financial position and a revaluation reserve would be created for $75,000. Further detail can be seen on revaluation reserves in chapter 11.

- Revenue reserves are the accumulated and undistributed profits of a company. The most common is the balance remaining on the statement of changes in equity at the end of each year. This appears as a reserve called 'retained earnings' in the statement of financial position. However, the directors may decide to set aside a portion of the remaining profits into a separate reserve account, for either general or specific purposes. A specific reserve is used to identify the accumulation of profits for a specific future purpose. Despite the fact that several revenue reserve accounts may exist, they are all available to be used for the payment of dividends if required.

It is important to realise that the existence of reserves does not indicate a fund of cash. The creation of a reserve may well be simply a bookkeeping transaction, debiting retained profits reserve and crediting a general reserve.

6 Statement of comprehensive income

We introduced the statement of comprehensive income very briefly earlier in the chapter. We now return to this subject to discuss it in more detail. In previous chapters we have referred to the income statement when discussing the revenue and expenses in sole proprietors. In limited companies this is referred to as the statement of comprehensive income. The statement of comprehensive income has two sections – the 'income statement' section and the 'other comprehensive income' section. The income statement section is similar to that of sole proprietors, except for differences in terminology and taxation noted earlier in the chapter. The 'income statement' section includes all items from 'Sales' to 'Profit for the period'.

The section for 'other comprehensive income' can contain several items and you will learn about these later in your studies at more advanced levels. With regard to the assessment for Fundamentals of Financial Accounting, there is **only one item you need to know**, and that is the revaluation of property. If a company revalues a property, then the **amount of the gain is included in 'other comprehensive income'**.

This gain is added to the profit for the period to give 'total comprehensive income for the period'. An illustration of this is given below.

Statement of comprehensive income of ABC Ltd for the Year Ended 30 June 20X8

	$000
Revenue	1000
Cost of sales	(640)
Gross profit	360
Operating expenses (e.g. rent, power, telephone, etc.)	(100)
Operating profit	260
Investment income	5
Finance cost	(20)
Profit before tax	245
Income tax	(80)
Profit for the period	165
Other comprehensive income	
Gain on property revaluation	25
Total comprehensive income for the period	190

Although the first section has been referred to above as the 'income statement' section, this title does not appear in the statement. A company may choose to present its statement of comprehensive income as two separate statements. In this case the two statements are called the 'income statement ' and the 'statement of comprehensive income'. The title 'income statement' does appear, and the statement of comprehensive income begins with the profit for the period.

The two statements would be presented as follows:

Statement one:

Statement of comprehensive income of ABC Ltd for the Year Ended 30 June 20X8

Income Statement

	$000
Revenue	1000
Cost of sales	(640)
Gross profit	360
Operating expenses (e.g. rent, power, telephone, etc.)	(100)
Operating profit	260
Investment income	5
Finance cost	(20)
Profit before tax	245
Income tax	(80)
Profit for the period	165

Statement two:

Statement of comprehensive income

Profit for the period	165
Other comprehensive income	
Gain on property revaluation	25
Total comprehensive income for the period	190

As can be seen above, there is little difference in practice between the two presentations. In this Learning System, it will normally be assumed that a single statement is prepared and this will be referred to as the 'statement of comprehensive income'. There will only rarely be an 'other comprehensive income' section, as this only applies when there is a revaluation of property.

The total comprehensive income for the year will be shown in the statement of changes in equity, analysed between profit for the period and the net gain on property revaluation. For purposes of the assessment, if the examiner refers to:

- an income statement, then just an income statement is required

- a statement of comprehensive income, then either:
  - a statement with two sections is required, as in the first illustration above
  - or, two statements are required, as in the second illustration above

In general, the examiner will make clear from the amount of information given and the nature of the question the exact format required to answer the question.

- 'other comprehensive income', then just this section of a comprehensive income statement is required.

Statement of changes in equity

We introduced the statement of changes in equity very briefly earlier in the chapter and now that we have discussed share capital, reserves and dividends in more detail, we can return to the statement of changes in equity. As the name implies, the statement shows the change in equity from the beginning of the year to the end of the year. Equity is the shareholders' capital in the company and comprises shares and reserves. These may be increased by, for example:

- Share issues
- Total comprehensive income.

These may be decreased by, for example:

- Dividends.

There may be a transfer between reserves; this will not increase or decrease the reserves in total but will change the individual balances.

A full example of a statement of changes in equity is given opposite.

Statement of changes in equity of Hi Tech Ltd for the year ended 31 December 20X8

	Ordinary Shares	Share Premium	Revaluation Reserve	Retained Earnings	Total
	$000	$000	$000	$000	$000
Balance 1.1.X8	1,000	500	400	400	2,300
Profit for the year				600	600
Dividends				(200)	(200)
Shares issued	600	150			750
Revaluation property			80		80
Balance 31.12.X8	1,600	650	480	800	3,530

Statement of financial position of Hi Tech Ltd as at 31 December 20X8

Equity	$000
Ordinary shares	1,600
Share premium	650
Revaluation reserve	480
Retained earnings	800
	3,530

These points are brought together in the following example.

Example 19.A

The trial balance of ABC Ltd at 30 September 20X1 is set out below:

	Debit $000	Credit $000
Premises at cost	800	
Plant and equipment at cost	460	
Motor vehicles at cost	124	
Accumulated depreciation at 1.10.20X0:		
Premises		160
Plant and equipment		210
Motor vehicles		63
Inventory at 1.10.20X0		
Raw materials	41	
Work in progress	27	
Finished goods	76	
Sales of finished goods		2,702
Purchase of raw materials	837	
Carriage inwards	24	
Direct wages	658	
Heat, light and power	379	
Salaries	96	
Advertising	45	
Telephone, postage and stationery	23	
Trade receivables and payables	256	113
Employee income tax payable		57
Balance at bank	363	
Ordinary shares of $1 each		650
5% preference shares of $1 each		100
Share premium		250
Retained earnings		432
10% debentures (repayable year 20X9)		200
Bank deposit account	496	
Bank interest received		19
Ordinary dividend paid	31	
Preference dividend paid	5	
Rent	215	
	4,956	4,956

Notes:

(1) The closing inventory at 30 September 20X1 valued at cost were as follows:

	$
Raw materials	37,000
Work in progress	18,000
Finished goods	39,000

(2) An analysis of the raw materials consumed during the year shows that $73,000 related to the use of indirect materials.

(3) The following amounts had been prepaid on 30 September 20X1:

	$
Rent	25,000
Telephone	2,000

(4) The following amounts should be accrued for expenses at 30 September 20X1:

	$
Direct wages	57,000
Salaries	14,000
Heat, light and power	61,000

(5) An analysis of the salaries cost for the year is:

	$
Production	49,000
Selling and distribution	30,000
Administration	31,000

(6) An allowance for receivables is to be created equal to 5 per cent of closing receivables after writing off an irrecoverable debt of $16,000. These expenses are to be treated as selling and distribution items.

(7) During the year, a motor vehicle was sold for $13,000 when it had a carrying amount of $14,000. Its original cost was $24,000. The only entry made in respect of this transaction was to credit sales of finished goods and debit bank with the proceeds.

(8) Depreciation is to be calculated on all non-current assets held on 30 September 20X1, at the following rates:

Premises	5% p.a. on cost
Plant and equipment	20% p.a. reducing balance
Motor vehicles	20% p.a. on cost

It is assumed that none of the non-current assets has any expected residual value. The depreciation charge for the year is to be apportioned as follows:

	Production	*Selling*	*Admin.*
Premises	80%	10%	10%
Plant and equipment	70%	10%	20%
Motor vehicles	20%	60%	20%

(9) Other expenses are to be apportioned as follows:

	Production	*Selling*	*Admin.*
Heat, light and power	80%	10%	10%
Telephone, postage and stationery	10%	60%	30%
Rent	70%	10%	20%

(10) Income tax of $39,000 on the profit for the year is to be accrued.

(11) The premises were revalued to $850,000 at the end of the year.

You are required:

(a) to prepare the statement of comprehensive income, incorporating the manufacturing and trading accounts for the year ended 30 September 20X1;

(b) to prepare the statement of changes in equity for the year ended 30 September 20X1;

(c) to prepare the company's statement of financial position at 30 September 20X1..

Solution

(a) **Statement of comprehensive income of ABC Ltd for the year ended 30 September 20X1**

	$000	$000	$000
Sales (2,702 – 13)			2,689
Opening inventory of finished goods		76	
Opening inventory of raw materials	41		
Purchases of raw materials	837		
Carriage inwards	24		
	902		
Closing inventory of raw materials	(37)		
	865		
Indirect materials consumed	(73)		
Direct materials consumed	792		
Direct wages (658 + 57)	715		
Prime cost	1,507		
Production overhead			
Indirect materials consumed	73		
Heat, light and power ((379 + 61) × 80%)	352		
Telephone, postage, stationery ((23 – 2) × 10%)	2.1		
Salaries	49		
Rent ((215 – 25) × 70%)	133		
Depreciation			
Premises ((5% × 800) × 80%)	32		
Plant ((20% x (460 – 210) × 70%)	35		
Motor vehicle ((20% × 100) × 20%)*	4		
Loss on disposal of vehicle ((14 – 13) × 20%)	0.2		
Factory cost incurred	2,187.3		
Opening work in progress	27		
Closing work in progress	(18)		

Factory cost of goods completed	2,196.3	
	2,272.3	
Closing inventory of finished goods	(39)	
		(2,233.3)
Gross profit		455.7

	$000	$000
Gross profit		455.7
Selling and distribution		
Heat, light and power ((379 + 61) × 10%)	44	
Telephone, postage and stationery ((23 – 2) × 60%)	12.6	
Advertising	45	
Salaries	30	
Rent ((215 – 25) × 10%)	19	
Depreciation		
Premises ((5% x 800) × 10%)	4	
Plant ((20% × (460 – 210) × 10%)	5	
Motor vehicle ((20% x 100) × 60%)	12	
Loss on disposal of vehicle (1 × 60%)	0.6	
Irrecoverable debt written off	16	
Change in allowance for receivables ((256 – 16) × 5%)	12	
		(200.2)
Administration		
Heat, light and power ((379 + 61) × 10%)	44	
Telephone, postage and stationery ((23 – 2) × 30%)	6.3	
Salaries	31	
Rent ((215 – 25) × 20%)	38	

Depreciation		
Premises ((5% x 800) × 10%)	4	
Plant ((20% × (460 – 210) × 20%)	10	
Motor vehicle ((20% x 100) × 20%)	4	
Loss on disposal of vehicle ((14 – 13) × 20%)	0.2	
		[137.5]
Operating profit		118.0
Investment income	19	
Finance cost (10% × $200)	(20)	
		(1)
Profit before taxation		117
Income tax		(39)
Profit for the period		78
Other comprehensive income		
Gain on property revaluation		250
Total comprehensive income		328

(b) **Statement of changes in equity of ABC Ltd for the year ended 30 September 20X1**

	Ord Shares	Pref Shares	Share Premium	Reservation Reserve	Retained Earnings	Total
	$	$	$	$	$	$
Balance at 1 October 20X0	650	100	250		432	1,432
Comprehensive income for the period				250	78	328
Dividends – ordinary					(31)	(31)
Dividends – preference					(5)	(5)
Balance at 30 September 20X1	650	100	250	250	474	1,724

(c) **Statement of financial position of ABC Ltd as at 30 September 20X1**

Assets	Cost ($000)	Acc. Depn ($000)	Carrying Amount ($000)
Non-current assets			
Premises	850	–	850
Plant and equipment	460	(260)	200
Motor vehicles	100	(73)	27
	1,410	(333)	1,077
Current assets			
Inventory			
Raw materials	37		
Work in progress	18		
Finished goods	39	94	
Receivables (256 – 16)	240		
Less: allowance	(12)		
		228	
Prepayments (25 + 2)		27	
Bank deposits		496	
Balance at bank		363	
			1,208
			2,285
Equity and liabilities			
Ordinary shares of $1 each			650
Preference shares of $1 each			100
Share premium			250
Revaluation reserve			250
Retained earnings			474
			1,724

Non-current liabilities		
10% debentures		200
Current liabilities		
Trade payables	113	
Employee income tax payable	57	
Accruals (57 + 14 + 61)	132	
Debenture interest	20	
Income tax	39	
		361
		2,285

Note:

- On the assumption that the debentures have been in issue throughout the year, it is necessary to provide for a full year's interest, and to show a liability for that interest on the statement of financial position.
- The revaluation of the premises occurs at the end of the year. This means the current year's depreciation is still calculated on the original amount of $800 = $800 @ 5% = $40. At the revaluation date the accumulated depreciation of $200 ($160 b/fwd plus the $40 for the year), will be transferred to the revaluation reserve. This means the revaluation reserve will show an amount of $50 (increase in from cost of $800 to $850) and the accumulated depreciation of $200. The total of $250 in the revaluation reserve represents the change in carrying value of $600 ($800 cost - accumulated depreciation of $200) to the revalued amount of $850. This revaluation is also shown as "other comprehensive income".

7 Chapter summary

In this chapter we have looked at:

- the preparation of financial statements for limited companies;
- the preparation of a statement of changes in equity;
- the treatment of certain transactions in the financial statements of companies:
  - taxation,
  - other comprehensive income,
  - the revaluation of property,
  - dividends,
  - debentures,
  - reserves.
- the bookkeeping entries to record the issue of shares;
- the different types of finance such as ordinary share issues, debentures, loan stock, redeemable and non-redeemable preference shares.

Test your understanding questions

Test your understanding 4

Revenue reserves are:

A accumulated and undistributed profits of a company

B amounts that cannot be distributed as dividends

C amounts set aside out of profits to replace revenue items

D amounts set aside out of profits for a specific purpose

Test your understanding 5

The correct ledger entries needed to record the issue of 200,000 $1 shares at a premium of 30¢, and paid for by cheque, in full, would be:

Test your understanding 6

A company has authorised share capital of one million ordinary shares of $1 each, of which 800,000 have been issued at a premium of 50¢ each, raising capital of $1,200,000. The directors are considering allocating $120,000 for dividend payments this year. This amounts to a dividend of: .... cents per share

Test your understanding 7

A company has authorised capital of 50,000 5 per cent preference shares of $2 each and 500,000 ordinary shares with a nominal value of 20¢ each. All of the preference shares have been issued, and 400,000 ordinary shares have been issued at a premium of 30¢ each. Interim dividends of 5¢ per ordinary share plus half the preference dividend have been paid during the current year. A final dividend of 15¢ per ordinary share is declared and half the preference dividend. The total of dividends payable for the year is:

$...............

Test your understanding 8

Which one of the following would you expect to find in the statement of changes in equity in a limited company for the current year?

A Ordinary dividend proposed during the current year, but paid in the following year

B Ordinary dividend declared during the current year, but paid in the following year

C Directors' fees

D Auditors' fees

Test your understanding 9

The revaluation of a property is shown:

A Property in the statement of financial position, other comprehensive income and revaluation reserves

B Property in the statement of financial position and the statement of changes in equity

C Property in the statement of financial position, income statement and revaluation reserves

D None, as companies are not allowed to revalue property

Test your understanding 10

An income statement includes the following line items:

A Sales to gross profit

B Sales to operating profit

C Sales to profit before tax

D Sales to profit for the period

The next set of questions are harder questions to prepare you for your studies at the next level of financial accounting - paper F1. These questions are far harder than you would expect to be examined at paper C02 but are good questions to bridge the gap between the two papers. Therefore, use these questions as revision questions of C02 in preparation for your studies in F1.

Test your understanding 11

The accountant of Fiddles plc has begun preparing financial statements, but the work is not yet complete. At this stage, the items included in the trial balance are as follows:

	$000
Land	100
Buildings	120
Plant and machinery	170
Accumulated depreciation of plant and machinery	120
$1 Share capital	100
Retained earnings	200
Receivables	200
Payables	110
Inventory	190
Operating profit	80
Debentures (16%)	180
Allowance for receivables	3
Bank balance (asset)	12
Suspense (debit balance)	1

Notes (i)–(vii) are to be taken into account.

(i) The sales ledger control account figure, which is used in the trial balance, does not agree with the total of the sales ledger balances. A contra of $5,000 has been entered correctly in the individual ledger accounts but has been entered on the wrong side of both control accounts.
A batch total of sales of $12,345 has been entered in the double-entry system as $13,345, although individual ledger account entries for these sales were correct.
The balance of $4,000 on sales returns account has inadvertently been omitted from the trial balance, though correctly entered in the ledger records.

(ii) A standing order of receipt from a regular customer for $2,000, and bank charges of $1,000, have been completely omitted from the records.

(iii) A receivable for $1,000 is to be written off. The allowance for receivables balance is to be adjusted to 1 per cent of receivables.

(iv) The opening inventory figure had been overstated by $1,000 and the closing inventory figure understated by $2,000.

(v) Any remaining balance on suspense account should be treated as purchases if a debit balance and as sales if a credit balance.

(vi) The debentures were issued 3 months before the year end. No entries have been made as regards interest.

(vii) A dividend of 10 per cent of share capital was declared before the year end, but not paid until after the year end.

Required:

(a) Prepare the journal entries to cover items in notes (i)–(v) above.

(b) Calculate the revised profit and then prepare the statement of financial position for the year.

Test your understanding 12

ABC Ltd prepares its financial statements to 31 October each year. Its trial balance at 31 October 20X3 was as follows:

	Debit $000	Credit $000
Premises – cost	600	
Manufacturing plant – cost	350	
Office equipment – cost	125	
Accumulated depreciation at 1 November 20X2		
Premises		195
Manufacturing plant		140
Office equipment		35
Inventory at 1 November 20X2		
Raw materials	27	
Work in progress	18	
Finished goods	255	
Sales of finished goods		2,350
Purchases of raw materials	826	
Returns inwards and outwards	38	18
Direct wages	575	
Heat, light and power	242	
Salaries	122	
Printing, postage and stationery	32	
Rent and insurances	114	

Loan interest paid	12	
Loan		250
Trade receivables and payables	287	75
Allowance for receivables		11
Sales tax account		26
Dividend paid	10	
Ordinary shares of $1 each		500
Share premium account		100
Retained earnings		442
Bank balance	509	
	4,142	4,142

The following additional information at 31 October 20X3 is available:

(i) Closing inventory

Raw materials	$24,000
Work in progress	$19,000
Finished goods	$147,000

(ii) Prepayments

Rent	$17,000
Insurance	$4,000

(iii) Accruals

Direct wages	$15,000
Salaries	$8,000

(iv) Salaries are to be apportioned as follows

Manufacturing	20%
Administration	80%

(v) Irrecoverable debts to be written off amount to $47,000, including sales tax at 17.5 per cent. The company maintains a separate irrecoverable debts account. The debts have all been outstanding for more than 6 months.
Note: In the case of irrecoverable debts that have been outstanding for more than 6 months, the sales tax (which will already have been accounted for on the sale of the goods) can be reclaimed from the tax authorities.

(vi) The allowance for receivables is to be amended to 2.5 per cent of receivables, after adjusting for irrecoverable debts written off.

(vii) Depreciation of non-current assets is to be provided as follows:

Premises	2 per cent on cost
Plant	10 per cent on cost
Office equipment	20 per cent on reducing balance

Twenty-five per cent of premises depreciation is to be apportioned to the manufacturing account. Note: It is to be assumed that there is no expected residual value.

(viii) The loan was taken out on 1 November 20X2, and the capital is to be repaid as follows:

1 January 20X4	$100,000
1 January 20X5	$100,000
1 January 20X6	$50,000

Interest is to be charged on the outstanding capital at 20 per cent per annum.

(ix) Other expenses are to be apportioned as follows:

Heat, light and power	1/2 manufacturing
	1/2 selling and administration
Rent and insurance	1/3 manufacturing
	2/3 administration

(x) One line of finished goods inventory, currently recorded at $8,000, has a net realisable value of $3,000.

(xi) A final dividend of 10¢ per share is to be proposed.

(xii) An accrual for income tax of $35,000 is to be made on the profits of the year.

Required:

(a) Prepare the manufacturing account for the year ended 31 October 20X3.

(b) Prepare the statement of comprehensive income for the year ended 31 October 20X3.

(c) Prepare the statement of changes in equity for the year ended 31 October 20X3.

(d) Prepare the statement of financial position at 31 October 20X3.

Test your understanding 13

FPC Ltd is a manufacturing company that sells its goods to wholesalers. Its trial balance at 31 March 20X6 was as follows:

	Debit $	Credit $
Issued share capital, $1 ordinary shares		750,000
10% debentures, repayable 2X15		200,000
Retained earnings at 1 April 20X5		98,000
Premises – at cost	900,000	
Premises – accumulated depreciation at 1 April 20X5		360,000
Plant – at cost	150,000	
Plant – accumulated depreciation at 1 April 20X5		75,000
Sales		2,960,000
Raw materials purchased	1,500,000	
Carriage outwards	10,000	
Carriage inwards	15,000	
Returns outwards		22,000
Returns inwards	14,000	
Receivables	220,000	
Payables		300,000
Bank balance	500,000	
Inventory at 1 April 20X5		
Raw materials	60,000	
Work in progress	30,000	
Finished goods	70,000	
Direct labour	600,000	
Discounts allowed	4,000	
Discounts received		2,500
Rent	120,000	
Insurance	100,000	
Factory supervisors' salaries	150,000	
Office wages and salaries	175,000	
Sales officers' commission	113,500	
Administration expenses	45,000	
Sales tax account		8,500
Allowance for receivables at 1 April 20X5		7,000
Irrecoverable debts written off	6,500	
	4,783,000	4,783,000

The following additional information at 31 March 20X6 is available:

(i) Closing inventory:

	$
Raw materials	80,000
Work in progress	42,500
Finished goods	100,000

(ii) Rent prepaid amounts to $10,000.

(iii) Insurance prepaid amounts to $20,000.

(iv) Twenty per cent of rent and insurance is to be regarded as factory cost.

(v) Direct labour accrued amounts to $17,500.

(vi) Included in the above trial balance are finished goods sold on a sale or return basis, which must be accepted or rejected by 15 April 20X6. Their selling price is $35,000 and their cost price is $27,000. Sales tax is not applicable on these goods.

(vii) The premises are to be depreciated at 2 per cent per annum, straight line. The plant is to be depreciated at 10 per cent per annum, straight line. Twenty-five per cent of premises depreciation is to be regarded as factory cost. Seventy-five per cent of plant depreciation is to be regarded as factory cost.

(viii) The allowance for receivables is to be amended to 5 per cent of receivables.

(ix) Sales officers' commission for the year is to be 5 per cent of net sales.

(x) Administration expenses include stationery, which has been recorded at its total invoice value of $9,400, including sales tax at 17.5 per cent. The sales tax is reclaimable.

(xi) The debentures were issued on 1 October 20X5. Interest is due on 1 April and 1 October annually in arrears.

(xii) Corporation tax of $22,000 is to be accrued for the year.

(xiii) A dividend of 3c per share is proposed.

Required:

(a) Prepare the statement of comprehensive income for the year ended 31 March 20X6.

(b) Prepare the statement of changes in equity retained earnings column for the year ended 31 March 20X6.

(c) For each of the following items that appear in the financial statements of FPC Ltd, state an accounting concept which affects its treatment:

(i) inventory of raw materials.

(ii) goods on sale or return.

(iii) allowance for receivables.

Test your understanding answers

Test your understanding 1

C

The statement of financial position liability should always be this year's estimate, i.e. $265,000.

The statement of comprehensive income represents this year's estimate less the over-provision for the previous year, i.e. $230,000 - $222,000 = $8,000 over-provision.

Test your understanding 2

Cash

	$		$
Share capital/premium (200,000 × $1.75)	350,000		

Share Capital

	$		$
		Cash (200,000 × 25c)	50,000

Share Premium

	$		$
		Cash (350,000 - 50,000)	300,000

Test your understanding 3

The share capital consists of:

	$
Preference shares, 100,000 at 50¢	50,000
Ordinary shares, 1,000,000 at 10¢	100,000

Thus the preference dividend amounts to 5 per cent of $50,000, that is $2,500, and the ordinary dividend amounts to 5¢ × 1 million shares = $50,000, giving a **total dividend of $52,500**.

Test your understanding 4

A

Revenue reserves can be distributed as dividends, so B is incorrect. Revenue reserves are not set aside to replace revenue items; they could be set aside for a specific purpose but this is only one use of revenue reserves.

Test your understanding 5

	Debit	**Credit**
Share premium		60,000
Share capital		200,000
Bank	260,000	

Test your understanding 6

Dividends are declared only on issued shares, and are based on the nominal value.

If the company has $800,000 share capital with a nominal value of $1 each = 800,000 shares

The total dividend of $120,000/800,000 = 15¢ per share.

Test your understanding 7

The total dividend payable is $85,000

Ordinary dividend = 400,000 shares × (0.05 interim and 0.15 final) = $80,000
Preference dividend = 50,000 shares × $2 = $100,000 × 5% = $5,000

Note: ordinary dividends are payable **per share** and preference dividends are payable **on value**.

Test your understanding 8

B

Dividends proposed are shown in the statement of changes in equity when they are declared. The dividend should be approved at the annual general meeting and subsequently paid. Directors' and auditors' fees are normal business expenses and appear in the statement of comprehensive income.

Test your understanding 9

A

Property in the statement of financial position, comprehensive income and revaluation reserves. The property is revalued, the gain is shown in 'other' comprehensive income and the gain is added to revaluation reserves in the statement of financial position.

Test your understanding 10

D

Sales to profit for the period.

Test your understanding 11

- This is quite a complex question involving the correction of errors and adjustments to the figures contained in the ledger accounts, prior to the preparation of financial statements.
- The correction of the control account is particularly important as it is part of the trial balance.
- The adjustments to opening and closing inventory also requires careful consideration: the error in opening inventory means that the retained earnings balance brought forward is overstated and the operating profit for the period is understated; the error in closing inventory means that the operating profit figure in the list of balances is understated and the inventory figure is understated.
- The debenture interest should be calculated as one-quarter of the annual figure, as they have been issued for only 3 months.

(a) **Journal**

	Debit ($)	Credit ($)
(i) Payables (2 x 5,000)	10,000	
Receivables		10,000
Operating profit (sales) (13,345 – 12,345)	1,000	
Receivables		1,000
Operating profit (sales returns)	4,000	
Suspense account		4,000
(ii) Bank ($2,000 – $1,000)	1,000	
Operating profit (bank charges)	1,000	
Receivables		2,000
(iii) Operating profit (bad debts w/off)	1,000	
Receivables		1,000
Allowance for receivables (Note 1)	1,140	
Operating profit (reduction in allowance)		1,140
(iv) Inventory	2,000	
Operating profit (closing inventory)		2,000
Retained earnings b/fwd	1,000	
Operating profit		1,000
(v) Suspense (balance) (Note 2)	3,000	
Operating profit (sales)		3,000

Notes:

(1) The allowance for receivables is to become 1 per cent of $186,000 = $1,860 (a reduction of $1,140 from the original $3,000). New receivables balance = $200 – 1 – 10 – 2 – 1 = $186.

(2) The balance of the suspense account was $1,000 debit (found by adding up the balances given in the question); transaction (i) above credited the suspense account with $4,000, therefore the final balance was $3,000 credit – and as per the instruction in note (v), this is to be added to the sales account.

(b) **Revised operating profit**

		$
Original operating profit		80,000
(i)	Sales	(1,000)
	Sales returns	(4,000)
(ii)	Bank charges	(1,000)
(iii)	Irrecoverable debt	(1,000)
	Allowance for receivables	1,140
(iv)	Opening inventory	1,000
	Closing inventory	2,000
(v)	Sales	3,000
(vi)	Debenture interest (180,000 × 16% × 3/12)	(7,200)
Revised operating profit		72,940

Statement of changes in equity of Fiddles plc (Retained earnings only)

	$
Balance at start of period (200,000 – 1,000)	200,000
Prior period adjustment - note iv	(1,000)
Profit for the period	72,940
Dividend (100,000 × 10%)	(10,000)
Balance at end of period	261,940

Statement of financial position of Fiddles plc

Assets	$	$	$
Non-current assets			
Land			100,000
Buildings			120,000
Plant and machinery			
Cost		170,000	
Accumulated depreciation		120,000	
			50,000
			270,000
Current assets			
Inventory (190 + 2)		192,000	
Receivables	186,000		
Less: allowance	1,860		
		184,140	
Bank (12 + 1)		13,000	
			389,140
			659,140
Equity and liabilities			
Share capital			100,000
Retained earnings			261,940
			361,940
Non-current liabilities			
Debentures			180,000
Current liabilities			
Payables (110 – 10)		100,000	
Debenture interest		7,200	
Dividends declared		10,000	
			117,200
			659,140

Test your understanding 12

- Commence this question by preparing a workings section, adjusting for the various points given to you in the notes, with adjustments and apportionments clearly labelled.
- It might also help to label the figures in the trial balance according to their destination, that is, manufacturing account, statement of comprehensive income, statement of changes in equity, statement of financial position – and a note of items to be apportioned between different accounts.

(a) **Manufacturing account of ABC Ltd for the year ended 31 October 20X3**

	$000	$000	$000
Opening inventory of raw materials		27	
Purchases of raw materials	826		
Less: returns	(18)		
		808	
		835	
Less: closing inventory of raw materials		(24)	
Direct materials			811
Direct labour (575 +15)			590
Prime cost			1,401
Indirect factory costs			
Heat, light and power (50% × $242)		121	
Salaries (20% × (122 + 8))		26	
Rent and insurance (1/3 ×(114 – 21))		31	
Depreciation of plant (10% × $350)		35	
Depreciation of premises (25% × (2% × 600))		3	
			216
Total factory cost			1,617
Change in work in progress			
Opening inventory		18	
Less: closing inventory		(19)	
			(1)
Factory cost of goods transferred			1,616

(b) Trading and statement of comprehensive income of ABC Ltd for the year ended 31 October 20X3

	$000	$000
Sales		2,350
Less: returns		(38)
		2,312
Less: cost of goods sold		
Opening inventory of finished goods	255	
Factory cost of goods transferred	1,616	
	1,871	
Less: closing inventory of finished goods (147 - 5)	(142)	
(Inventories written down (8 – 3))		
		(1,729)
Gross profit		583
Less: expenses		
Heat, light and power (242 × 50%)	121	
Salaries ((122 + 8) × 80%)	104	
Printing, post and stationery	32	
Rent and insurance ((114 – 21) × 2/3)	62	
Change in allowance for receivables (2.5% × 240) – 11	(5)	
Irrecoverable debts written off (47 – 7)	40	
Depreciation		
Premises (75% x (2% × 600))	9	
Office equipment (20% × (350 – 140))	18	
		(381)
Operating profit		202
Finance cost (250 × 20%)		(50)
Profit before tax		152
Income tax		(35)
Profit for the period		117
Other comprehensive income		–
Total comprehensive income		117

(c) **Statement of changes in equity of ABC Ltd for the year ended 31 October 20X3**

	Share Capital	Share Premium	Retained Earnings	$000
Balance at start of period	500	100	442	1,042
Total comprehensive income			117	117
Dividends paid			(10)	(10)
Balance at end of period	500	100	549	1,149

(d) **Statement of Financial position of ABC Ltd as at 31 October 20X3**

	Cost ($000)	Acc. Dep'n ($000)	Carrying amount ($000)
Assets			
Non-current assets			
Premises	600	(207)	393
Plant	350	(175)	175
Office equipment	125	(53)	72
	1,075	(435)	640
Current assets			
Inventory			
Raw materials	24		
Work in progress	19		
Finished goods	142		
		185	
Receivables (287 – 47)	240		
Less: allowance	(6)		
		234	
Prepayments (17 + 4)		21	
Bank balance		509	
			949
			1,589

Equity and liabilities

Ordinary share capital		500
Share premium account		100
Retained earnings		549
		1,149
Non-current liability		
Loan repayable (250 – 100)		150
Current liabilities		
Trade payables	75	
Accruals (15 + 8 + 50 – 12)	61	
Sales tax liability (26 – 7)	19	
Income Tax	35	
Loan repayable in 12 months	100	
		290
		1,589

Note that the dividend is ignored because it is only proposed.

Test your understanding 13

- This question involves a manufacturer, with all the usual adjustments and apportionments required.
- Prepare a workings section, with adjustments and apportionments clearly labelled.

(a) **Statement of comprehensive income of FPC Ltd for year ended 31 March 20X6**

	$	$	$	$
Sales				2,925,000
Less: returns				(14,000)
Net sales				2,911,000
Opening inventory of finished goods			70,000	
Opening inventory of raw material		60,000		
Purchases	1,500,000			
Carriage inwards	15,000			
	1,515,000			
Less: returns outwards	(22,000)			
Net purchases		1,493,000		
		1,553,000		
Less: closing inventory of raw material		(80,000)		
Direct material		1,473,000		
Direct labour		617,500		
Prime cost		2,090,500		
Factory indirect expenses				
Rent and rates	22,000			
Insurance	16,000			
Factory supervisors' salaries	150,000			
Depreciation – premises	4,500			
Depreciation – plant	11,250			
		203,750		
		2,294,250		

Opening work in progress	30,000		
Less: closing work in progress	(42,500)		
		(12,500)	
Factory cost of goods completed		2,281,750	
		2,351,750	
Less: closing inventory of finished goods (100,000 + 27,000)		(127,000)	
Cost of goods sold			(2,224,750)
Gross profit			686,250
Discount received			2,500
			688,750
		$	$
Less: expenses			
Carriage outwards		10,000	
Discount allowed		4,000	
Rent		88,000	
Insurance		64,000	
Office wages and salaries		175,000	
Sales officers' commission		145,550	
Administration expenses		43,600	
Allowance for receivables		2,250	
Irrecoverable debts written off		6,500	
Depreciation – premises		13,500	
Depreciation – plant and machinery		3,750	
			(556,150)
Operating profit			132,600
Debenture interest paid			(10,000)
Profit before tax			122,600
Income tax			(22,000)
Profit for the period			100,600

Workings

Rent	as per trial balance $120,000, less prepaid $10,000 = $110,000 20% factory = $22,000; 80% administration = $88,000
Insurance	as per trial balance $100,000, less prepaid $20,000 = $80,000 20% factory = $16,000; 80% administration = $64,000
Direct labour	as per trial balance $600,000, add accrued $17,500 = $617,500
Sales	as per trial balance $2,960,000, less sale or return $35,000 = $2,925,000
Receivables	as per trial balance $220,000, less sale or return $35,000 = $185,000
Depreciation	Plant: 10% of $150,000 = $15,000 75% factory 5 $11,250; 25% administration = $3,750 premises: 2% of $900,000 = $18,000 25% factory = $4,500; 75% administration = $13,500
Allowance for receivables	5% of $185,000 = $9,250, less previous balance $7,000 = $2,250
Sales officers' commission	5% of $2,911,000 = $145,550, less already paid $113,500 = $32,050 accrued
Administration expenses	as per trial balance $45,000, less incorrect sales tax $1,400 = $43,600

(b) **Statement of changes in equity of FPC Ltd for year ended 31 March 20X6 - Retained earnings**

	$000
Balance at start of period	98,000
Profit for the period	100,600
Balance at end of period	198,600

Note: The dividend is ignored because it is proposed.

(c) (i) consistency concept
(ii) matching concept
(iii) prudence concept

chapter

20

The Statement of Cash Flows

Chapter learning objectives

When you have completed this chapter, you should be able to:

- prepare a statement of cash flows.

1 Introduction

In this chapter we will look briefly at a further accounting statement that companies are required to include in their financial statements – the statement of cash flows.

In this section we shall illustrate the preparation of a statement of cash flows, which is often prepared for limited companies but may also be prepared for other types of organisation. It should be noted that a 'cash flow statement' has been renamed 'statement of cash flows' in accordance with IAS 1 (Revised) Presentation of Financial Statements.

2 What is a statement of cash flows?

- A statement of cash flows recognises the **importance of liquidity** to a business by reporting the effect of the transactions of the business during the period on the bank, cash and similar liquid assets.
- At its simplest, it is a summary of receipts and payments during the period, but this method of presentation does not answer a common question asked by the readers of financial statements: 'Why does the profit made during the period not equate to an increase in cash and bank balances?' What is needed, therefore, is a statement that commences with the profit made during the period, and shows how that profit, and other transactions during the same period, have affected the flow of cash into and out of the company.

The syllabus states that the presentation for a statement of cash flows should be based on IAS 7 Statement of Cash Flows and that requirement is followed in this Learning System.

Why does the profit earned not equal the change in bank and cash balances?

There are three main reasons why this does not occur:

(1) Profit is calculated on an accruals basis, which means that revenue is taken when it is earned, not when it is received, and expenses are deducted on the same basis to match with that revenue. Bank and cash balances change when monies are received and paid out. Thus the bank balance will be different from profit due to items such as the inventory balance, unpaid receivables and payables, accruals and prepayments, both at the start and at the end of the period. For example, an increase in inventory means more cash has flowed out; an increase in receivables means less cash has flowed in; an increase in payables means less cash has flowed out.

(2) The calculation of profit includes some items that do not affect cash at all or affect it differently. For example, profit is after deducting depreciation, which involves no movement in cash. The profit or loss on disposal of a non-current asset will be taken into the profit calculation, but it is the **proceeds of sale** that affect cash. In addition, there may be other accrued items in the statement of comprehensive income, for example taxation. Similarly, the change in allowance for receivables is a non-cash item. These do not affect cash at the same time as the accrual is made, for example, taxation may be paid after the year end, thus the amount of tax paid out during a period will be the bill for the previous year, not that for the current year.

(3) Bank and cash balances are affected by some items that do not affect profit, such as the purchase of non-current assets (only depreciation affects profit), the raising of additional capital or the repayment of loans.

The benefits of cash flow statements

A statement of cash flows is needed as a consequence of the differences between profits and cash, as explained earlier. It helps to assess:

- liquidity and solvency – an adequate cash position is essential in the short term both to ensure the survival of the business and to enable debts and dividends to be paid.
- financial adaptability – will the company be able to take effective action to alter its cash flows in response to any unexpected events?
- future cash flows – an adequate cash position in the longer term is essential to enable asset replacement, repayment of debt and fund further expansion.

The bottom line is: cash flow means survival. A company may be profitable but, if it does not have an adequate cash position, it may not be able to pay its debts, purchase goods for resale, pay its staff etc.

The cash flow statement also highlights where cash is being generated, i.e. either from operating, financing or investing activities. A business must be self sufficient in the long term; in other words it must generate operating cash inflows or it will be reliant on the sale of assets or further finance to keep it afloat.

Cash flows are also objective; they are matters of fact, whereas the calculation of profit is subjective and easy to manipulate.

3 Presentation

IAS 7 Statement of cash flows requires companies to prepare a statement of cash flows as part of their annual financial statements. The cash flow must be presented using standard headings. Note: there are two methods of reconciling cash from operating activities, which will be discussed later in this chapter.

Statement of cash flows for ABC Ltd for the year ended 31 December 20X8

		$
Cash flows from operating activities		
Cash generated from operations		X
Interest paid		(X)
Taxation paid		(X)
Net cash from operating activities		X
Cash flows from investing activities		
Purchase of non-current assets	(X)	
Proceeds from the sale of non-current assets	X	
Interest received	X	
Dividends received	X	
Net cash from investing activities		X
Cash flows from financing activities		
Issue of shares	X	
Loan repaid	(X)	
Loan issued	X	
Dividends paid	(X)	
Net cash from financing activities		X
Net increase in cash and cash equivalents		X
Cash and cash equivalents b/fwd		X
Cash and cash equivalents c/fwd		X

Key points

- Operating activities are the principal revenue-producing activities of the business. This section of the statement begins with cash generated from operations. This figure can be calculated using either the direct or indirect method.

- Investing activities are cash spent on non-current assets, proceeds of sale of non-current
assets and income from investments.
- Financing activities include the proceeds of issue of shares, dividends paid to them and long-term borrowings made or repaid.
- Net increase or decrease in cash and cash equivalents is the overall increase (or decrease) in cash and cash equivalents during the year. This can be calculated by comparing the level of cash and cash equivalents on the statement of financial position for the current and previous years.
- Cash means cash in hand and bank account balances, including overdrafts.
- Cash equivalents means current asset investments (short-term, highly liquid investments, e.g. a 30 day bond).

4 Cash generated from operations

The starting point for a statement of cash flows is the cash flow from operations. 'Operations' are the normal, everyday activity of the company that earn it profit, and that result in cash flow.

There are two methods of calculating cash from operations – the direct (outside of the C02 syllabus)or indirect method.

Indirect method

This method reconciles between profit before tax (as reported in the income statement) and cash generated from operations as follows:

The result will be as follows:

	$	$
Operating profit		X
Depreciation charge for the period	X	
(Profit) or Loss on disposal of non-current assets	(X)/X	
Finance cost	X	
Investment income	(X)	
(Increase)/decreases in inventory levels	(X)/X	
(Increase)/decreases in receivables	(X)/X	
Increase/(decrease) in payables	X/(X)	
		X
Cash generated from operations		X

Illustration 1

A company had the following items on its statements of financial position at the end of year 1 and year 2:

	Year 1 $	Year 2 $
Inventory	35,000	25,000
Receivables	24,000	28,000
Payables	31,000	33,000

In addition, the statement of comprehensive income for year 2 included the following items:

	$	$
Gross profit		90,000
Less:		
General expenses	17,000	
Depreciation on plant	10,000	
Loss on disposal of plant	4,000	
		(31,000)
Operating profit		59,000
Add: Investment income		13,000
Less: Finance cost		(3,000)
Profit before tax		69,000
Income tax		(12,000)
Profit for the year		57,000

What is the cash generated from operations for year 2?

Solution

	$
Operating profit	59,000
Depreciation	10,000
Loss on disposal of non-current assets	4,000
Decrease in inventory (35,000 – 25,000)	10,000
Increase in payables (31,000 – 33,000)	2,000
Increase in receivables (24,000 – 28,000)	(4,000)
Cash generated from operations	81,000

5 Cash flows from operating activities

We now need to calculate the cash from operating activities by deducting the following items from cash generated from operations:

(a) interest paid;

(b) tax paid;

Note that in both cases, **it is the sum actually paid during the period that is included**. In the case of tax, this will often be last year's tax liability.

Calculation of interest/income taxes paid

The cash flow should be calculated by reference to:

- the charge to profits for the item (shown in the income statement); and
- any opening or closing payable balance shown on the statement of financial position.

A ledger account working may be useful:

Tax/Interest liability

	$		$
Cash **(balancing figure)**	X	Balance b/d	X
Balance c/d	X	Income statement charge	X
	X		X

6 Cash flows from investing activities

This section of the statement of cash flows shows the purchase of non-current assets and the proceeds on their disposal. Whilst in practice all the relevant information would be known, in the computer-based assessment it is quite common for a question to give you only part of the information, and you have to calculate the missing information. An example of this is shown below relating to the purchase/sale of a non-current asset.

These amounts are often the trickiest to calculate within a statement of cash flows. It is therefore recommended that a ledger account workings are used.

The following ledger accounts will be required for each class of assets (see chapters 10 and 11):

- cost account
- accumulated depreciation account
- disposals account (where relevant).

Data provided in the source financial statements should then be entered into these ledger accounts and the required cash flows found – often as balancing figures.

NB. If there is evidence of a revaluation, remember to include the uplift in value on the debit side of the asset cost account as this is a non-cash movement.

The interest and dividends received is straight forward and you can find these figures in the statement of comprehensive income.

7 Cash flows from financing activities

This section of the statement of cash flows shows the proceeds from issuing shares. A computer-based assessment question will often not tell you that shares have been issued; you have to work this out by looking to see if the ordinary or preference share capital has increased, together with the movement on share premium Similarly, you will have to look at any debentures or loans to see if they have increased, in which there will be a cash flow in, or if they have decreased, in which case there will be a cash flow out.

The payment of dividends will be found in the statement of changes in equity. This figure will normally be the cash paid to shareholders in the year. However, you should check to see if there is an accrual for dividends under current liabilities in the statement of financial position.

If there is, this means that the directors have declared a dividend before the year end, but paid it after the year end. If this is the case, then you will have to work out what cash was actually paid to the shareholders for dividends. This is similar to the treatment of taxation and an example is given below.

Illustration 2

Continuing from illustration 1, suppose that the dividends in the statement of changes in equity was $30,000 and that other items on the statements of financial position were as follows:

	Year 1	Year 2
Non-current assets*	$	$
Plant at cost	100,000	120,000
Acc. depreciation	(20,000)	(22,000)
	80,000	98,000
Current assets		
Bank and cash	63,000	101,000
Share capital	100,000	120,000
Non-current liabilities		
Debenture	30,000	21,000
Current liabilities		
Taxation	16,000	12,000

*Plant which had cost $15,000 and had a carrying amount of $7, 000 was sold during the year.

Dividends paid in the year were $20,000.

Complete the statement of cash flows.

Solution

Notice that the plant at cost has increased by $20,000 although we know that an asset with a cost of $15,000 has been sold. This means that an asset must have been purchased for $35,000. Similarly, notice that the depreciation given in the statement of comprehensive income was $10,000 – and yet the accumulated depreciation in the statement of financial position has increased by only $2,000. This is because the accumulated depreciation on the asset sold must have been $8,000.

There must have been an asset sold during the year, and its cost and depreciation will have been taken out of the ledger accounts. Refer back to chapters 10 and 11 to revise the ledger accounts for disposals of non-current assets. If the plant had a carrying amount of $7,000 and it was sold at a loss of $4,000, then the proceeds must have been $3,000. Thus we have been able to work out the missing information of how much was received when the plant was sold. We can reconstruct the relevant non-current-asset accounts as follows:

Plant at cost

	$		$
Opening balance b/d	100,000	Disposal	15,000
Purchases **(balancing figure)**	35,000	Closing balance c/d	120,000
	135,000		135,000

Plant disposals

	$		$
Plant at cost	15,000	Plant depreciation	8,000
		Loss on disposal	4,000
		Proceeds of sale **(balancing figure)**	3,000
	15,000		15,000

Tax liability

	$		$
Cash **(balancing figure)**	16,000	Balance b/d	16,000
Balance c/d	12,000	Income statement	12,000
	28,000		28,000

We can now prepare the statement of cash flows for the year ended year 2 as follows:

	$	$
Cash flow from operating activities		
Cash generated from operations (from illustration 1 above)		81,000
Finance cost (from illustration 1 above)		(3,000)
Tax paid		(16,000)
Net cash from operating activities		62,000
Cash flows from investing activities		
Proceeds of sale of non-current assets	3,000	
Payments to acquire non-current assets	(35,000)	
Investment income (from illustration 1 above)	13,000	
Net cash used in investing activities		(19,000)
Cash flows from financing activities		
Equity dividends paid	(16,000)	
Proceeds from issue of shares (120 – 100)	20,000	
Repayment of debentures (30 – 21)	(9,000)	
Net cash used in financing activities		(5,000)
Net increase in cash and cash equivalents		38,000
Cash and cash equivalents at the beginning of the period		63,000
Cash and cash equivalents at the end of the period		101,000

Test your understanding 1

From the following information, construct a statement of cash flows:

	$
Operating profit for the year, after charging depreciation of $22,300	215,500
Purchase of non-current assets during the year	80,000
Repayment of non-current loan	45,000
Issue of shares at nominal value	100,000
Changes in working capital during the year	
Increase in inventory	22,500
Decrease in receivables	18,000
Decrease in payables	14,500
Taxation paid	25,000
Dividends paid	5,000

Statement of cash flows for sole traders

The preparation of a statement of cash flows is not restricted to limited companies. Indeed, the statement is a useful source of information for any kind of organisation.

For sole traders, dividends would be replaced by cash drawings, and share capital issued would be replaced by cash introduced by the owner. Taxation would not appear at all, being a private transaction. Otherwise, the preparation of the statement of cash flows would follow the same principles as for limited companies.

8 Chapter summary

In this chapter we have looked at:

- the preparation of a statement of cash flow ;
- why profit does not equal cash flow.

Test your understanding questions

Test your understanding 2

A business has made a profit of $8,000 but its bank balance has fallen by $5,000. This could be due to:

A depreciation of $3,000 and an increase in inventories of $10,000

B depreciation of $6,000 and the repayment of a loan of $7,000

C depreciation of $12,000 and the purchase of new non-current assets for $25,000

D the disposal of a non-current asset for $13,000 less than its carrying amount

Test your understanding 3

Extracts from the financial statements of CFS Ltd are set out below.

Statement of comprehensive income CFS Ltd for the year ended 31 December 20X8

	$000	$000
Turnover		300
Cost of sales		(150)
Gross profit		150
Profit on sale of non-current asset		75
		225
Expenses	15	
Depreciation	30	
		(45)
Net profit		180

	Balances as at 31 December	
	20X7	**20X8**
	$000	$000
Inventory, receivables, current liabilities (net)	40	50

What figure would appear in the statement of cash flows of CFS Ltd for the year ended 31 December 20X8 in respect of cash generated from operations?

$...............

Test your understanding 4

The movement on the plant and machinery account for X Ltd is shown below:

	$
Cost b/d	10,000
Additions	2,000
Disposals	(3,000)
Cost c/d	9,000
Acc. Depreciation b/d	2,000
Charge for the year	1,000
Disposals	(1,500)
Acc. Depreciation c/d	1,500
Carrying amount b/d	8,000
Carrying amount c/d	7,500

The profit on the sale of the machine was $500. What figures would appear in the statement of cash flows of X Ltd under the heading of investing activities?

A Movement on plant account $500 and profit on disposal of $500

B Movement on plant account $500 and proceeds on sale of plant $2,000

C Purchase of plant $2,000 and profit on disposal of $500

D Purchase of plant $2,000 and proceeds on sale of plant $2,000

Test your understanding 5

Avtar Ltd had the following statement of financial position at 31 March 20X1 and 20X2:

Assets	**20X1 $000**	**20X2 $000**
Non-current assets at cost	1,000	1,300
Accumulated depreciation	(400)	(600)
	600	700
Current assets		
Inventory	800	1,400
Receivables	2,700	3,100
Bank	200	–
	4,300	5,200
Equity and liabilities		
Share capital	1,000	1,300
Share premium	500	700
Retained earnings	1,200	1,240
	2,700	3,240
Current liabilities		
Payables	1,300	1,580
Declared ordinary dividend	300	260
Bank overdraft	–	120
	4,300	5,200

During the year to 31 March 20X2, non-current assets costing $50,000 were sold for $40,000 cash. Accumulated depreciation on these to 31 March 20X1 was $20,000.

Required:

(a) Insert the missing figures into the ledger accounts below in order to calculate the additions to non-current assets, the profit or loss on sale of non-current assets, and the depreciation charge in the income statement for the year to 31 March 20X2.

Non-current assets at cost

	$000		$000
Balance b/d		Disposals a/c	
Additions		Balance c/d	
	___		___
	___		___

Non-current asset – accumulated depreciation

	$000		$000
Disposals a/c		Balance b/d	
Balance c/d		Charge for the year	
	___		___
	___		___

Non-current assets – disposals

	$000		$000
Non-current assets at cost		Non-current assets acc. depn.	
Profit on sale of non-current assets		Disposal proceeds	
	___		___
	___		___

(b) Prepare the statement of cash flows given below for the year ending 31 March 20X2.

Test your understanding 6

The draft financial statements for B Ltd are set out below.

Income statement of B Ltd for the year ended 30 September 20X7

	$000
Turnover	600
Cost of sales	(410)
Gross profit	190
Profit on sale of non-current asset	10
	200
Operating expenses	(70)
Depreciation	(30)
Operating profit	100
Interest	(15)
Profit for the period	85

Note: Dividends of $50,000 were declared before the year end and paid after the year end.

Statement of financial position of B Ltd as at 30 September 20X6 and 20X7

	20X7 $000	20X7 $000	20X6 $000	20X6 $000
Assets				
Non-current assets (see note)		450		520
Current assets				
Inventory	65		50	
Receivables	80		30	
Bank and cash	30		15	
		175		95
		625		615

Equity and liabilities				
Share capital		400		400
Retained earnings		95		60
		495		460
Non-current liability				
Loan		20		100
Current liabilities				
Payables	60		20	
Dividends	50		35	
		110		55
		625		615

Note: B Ltd purchased non-current assets for $40,000 during the year ended 30 September 20X7.

Required:

Prepare the statement of cash flow.

Test your understanding answers

Test your understanding 1

Statement of cash flows

	$	$
Cash flows from operating activities		
Operating profit		
Add:	215,500	
Depreciation	22,300	
Decrease in receivables	18,000	
Less:	(22,500)	
Increase in inventory	(14,500)	
Decrease in payables		
Cash generated from operations		218,800
Taxation paid		(25,000)
		193,800
Cash flows from investing activities		
Purchase of non-current assets		(80,000)
Cash flows from financing activities		
Issue of shares	100,000	
Loan repaid	(45,000)	
Dividends paid	(5,000)	
		50,000
Net increase in cash		163,800

Test your understanding 2

C

	$
Profit	8,000
Add: depreciation	12,000
Net cash inflow	20,000
Purchase of non-current assets	(25,000)
Decrease	(5,000)

Test your understanding 3

	$000
Net profit	180
Add: depreciation	30
Less: profit on sale of non-current asset	(75)
Less: change in working capital	(10)
	125

Test your understanding 4

D

Test your understanding 5

(a)

Non-current assets at cost

	$000		$000
Balance b/d	1,000	Disposals a/c	50
Additions (balancing figure)	350	Balance c/d	1,300
	1,350		1,350

Non-current asset – accumulated depreciation

	$000		$000
Disposals a/c	20	Balance b/d	400
Balance c/d	600	Charge for the year (balancing figure)	220
	620		620

Non-current assets – disposals

	$000		$000
Non-current assets at cost	50	Non-current assets acc. depn.	20
Profit on sale of non-current assets	10	Disposal proceeds	40
	60		60

(b) **Statement of cash flows for the year ended 31 March 20X2**

	$000	$000
Cash flow from operating activities		
Increase in retained earnings (1,240 – 1,200)	40	
Add: dividends declared	260	
Add: depreciation	220	
Less: profit on sale of non-current assets	(10)	
	510	
Less: increase in inventory (1,400 – 800)	(600)	
Less: increase in receivables (3,100 – 2,700)	(400)	
Add: increase in payables (1,580 – 1,300)	280	
		(210)
Cash flow from investing activities		
Proceeds of sale of non-current assets	40	
Non-current assets purchased	(350)	
		(310)
Cash flow from financing activities		
Dividends paid (last year's)	(300)	
Shares issued (1,300 + 700) – (1,000 + 500)	500	
		200
Decrease in bank balance		(320)
Bank at beginning of period		200
Bank at end of period		(120)

Test your understanding 6

Cash-flow statement of B Ltd for the year ended 30 September 20X7

	$000	$000
Cash flow from operating activities		
Cash generated from operations – see workings		95
Interest		(15)
		80
Cash flows from investing activities		
Sale of non-current assets – see workings	90	
Purchase of non-current asset	(40)	
		50
Cash flows from financing activities		
Dividends paid (last year's)	(35)	
Repayment of loan (100 – 20)	(80)	
		(115)
Net increase in bank and cash		15
Opening bank and cash		15
Closing bank and cash		30

Workings

	$
Operating activities	
Operating profit	100
Adjustment for non-cash flow items	
Profit sale of non-current asset	(10)
Depreciation	30
	120

Adjustment for working capital	
Increase in inventory (65 – 50)	(15)
Increase in receivables (80 – 30)	(50)
Increase in payables (60 – 20)	40
	95
Sale of non-current assets	
Carrying amount (520 + 40 – 30 – 450)	80
Profit on sale	10
Proceeds on sale	90

chapter

21

The Interpretation of Financial Statements

Chapter learning objectives

When you have completed this chapter, you should be able to:

- understand the importance of interpretation of financial statements;
- calculate profitability ratios;
- calculate liquidity ratios;
- calculate efficiency ratios;
- calculate gearing ratios;
- calculate investment ratios;
- explain and discuss the results of your calculations;
- suggest possible reasons for good/poor results or differences to previous years, other companies or expectations.

1 Introduction

You have now reached one of the most important areas of study in this subject – the use and interpretation of accounting information. You now know how to prepare financial statements for various organisations, from a variety of different sources of data, but now we return to the content of chapter 1 and the questions it posed:

- What is accounting;
- who uses financial statements and for what purpose,
- and what makes financial statements useful?

The mechanics of the preparation of financial statements form only the start of the accounting process, the end result of which is to provide users with information to enable them to make decisions. The mere presentation of a set of financial statements does not necessarily achieve that objective, and this chapter looks at ways of making that information more meaningful.

Understanding the whole of this chapter should be regarded as essential for examination success.

2 What is meant by 'interpretation of financial statements'?

Financial statements provide a great deal of information. However, **one difficulty with these statements is that they show only absolute figures** for a particular period, and at the end of that period. **To enable users to make informed decisions, the statements on their own do not always provide sufficient information, even though they have been prepared in accordance with international financial reporting standards.**

Further detail

Suppose that Company A has a trading account that shows sales revenue of $100,000 and the profit for the year is $5,000. What does this tell you? It tells you that the sales revenue is $100,000 and the profit is $5,000. Is this good or bad? Is this to be expected? Is this comparable with other organisations? Can a user of the financial statements make decisions on the basis of this information?

The answer is no. That information on its own is not of use. Let us consider two other companies as well. Company B has sales revenue of $200,000 and profit for the year of $6,000. Company C has sales revenue of $300,000 and profit for the year of $4,500. Which of the three organisations is best? That depends on what the user is looking for.

If the user is looking for the organisation with the highest revenue, that is Company C. If (s)he is looking for the organisation with the highest profit, that is Company B. Which organisation is most successful, in terms of its profit? You might think it is Company B, with its higher profit. But Company B achieved that profit from sales of $200,000, whereas Company A had only half that level of sales yet achieved a profit of only $1,000 less than Company B.

We are now embarking on an important area of accounting, that of comparison. We are starting to compare profit with sales revenue, and we are comparing one firm with another. That is the key technique of the interpretation of financial statements – comparison of one with another.

Company	Sales revenue	Profit
A	$100,000	$5,000
B	$200,000	$6,000
C	$300,000	$4,500

There are comparisons we can make here. Although Company B had the highest profit, it was only 3 per cent of its sales revenue. That is found by the following formula:

$$\frac{\text{Profit}}{\text{Sales}} \times 100 = \%$$

Company A achieved a profit of 5 per cent of sales, and Company C achieved a profit of only 1.5 per cent. So Company C looks poor.

But that is taking only 1 year as information. It would be useful to look at last year's results and see if any of the companies have improved their profits.

It might also be useful to compare the profit with other figures, apart from sales. Suppose that the capital employed in Company A is $50,000. A profit of $5,000 is a 10 per cent return on that capital. Suppose that Company C's capital employed is only $30,000. Its return on that capital is 15 per cent – so an investor might prefer to choose Company C, while a lender might prefer Company B.

The point is that different users are looking for different information, which a set of financial statements on its own does not necessarily provide. Comparing figures with other figures is a useful additional tool in providing information to support decision-making. **These tools are known as the techniques of ratio analysis.**

3 Calculating ratios

A ratio is simply a comparison of one figure with another.

If we have a company making a profit of $5,000 on sales revenue of $100,000 we could calculate a ratio to compare the percentage of profit with sales revenue for each year.

This would result in us dividing the profit by the sales revenue as follows:

$$\frac{5,000}{100,000} \times 100 = 5\%$$

This ratio means for every $1of sales revenue we make, 5% of it would result in profit.

Ratios use simple calculations based upon the interactions in sets of data. For example; changes in costs of sale are directly linked to changes in sales activity. Changes in sales activity also have an effect upon wages and salaries, receivables, inventory levels etc. Ratios allow us to see those interactions in a simple, concise format.

Ratios are of limited use on their own, thus, the following points should serve as a useful checklist if you need to analyse data and comment on it:

- What does the ratio literally mean?
- What does a change in the ratio mean?
- What is the norm?
- What are the limitations of the ratio?

Using the ratios

Calculating the ratios is only one step in the analysis process. Once that is done, the results must be compared with other results. Comparison is commonly made between:

- previous accounting periods;
- other companies (perhaps in the same type of business);
- budgets and expectations;
- government statistics;
- other ratios.

4 Types of ratios

Ratios can be classified into various groupings, according to the type of information they convey. The main groupings are as follows:

- profitability (performance) ratios;
- liquidity (solvency) ratios;
- efficiency (use of assets) ratios;
- capital structure (gearing) ratios;
- security (investors) ratios.

The last group, security ratios, is not part of your syllabus for this subject. The above list is not exhaustive – a ratio can be compiled from any data if it can be usefully interpreted.

The following income statement and statement of financial position will be used to illustrate the calculation and interpretation of accounting ratios.

Income statement for the year ended 31 December year 8

	$	$
Sales		23,636
Opening inventory	1,225	
Purchases	8,999	
	10,224	
Closing inventory	(1,425)	
Cost of sales		(8,799)
Gross profit		14,837
Expenses		(5,737)
Operating profit		9,100
Interest payable on bank loan		(450)
Profit before tax		8,650
Income tax		(1,000)
Profit for the period		7,650

Statement of financial position as at 31 December year 8

Assets	$	$
Non-current assets		14,135
Current assets		
Inventory	1,425	
Receivables	542	
Bank	7,037	
Cash in hand	697	
		9,701
		23,836
Equity and liabilities		
Equity		18,250
Non-current liability		
Bank loan		4,500
Current liability		
Payables		1,086
		23,836

5 Profitability ratios

These are also known as **performance ratios**. They compare profit at different levels with other figures, and are often presented as percentages.

Gross profit margin

On a unit basis the gross profit represents the difference between the unit sales price and the direct cost per unit. The margin works this out on an average basis across all sales for the year.

This ratio (also known as the gross profit to sales revenue ratio) is calculated by:

$$\frac{\text{Gross profit}}{\text{Sales revenue}} \times 100\% = \frac{14,837}{23,636} \times 100 = 62.8\%$$

It shows us that for every $1 in sales revenue 62.8% of it will be gross profit, i.e. approximately 63¢.

What does this mean?

It is normally expressed as a percentage, but do try to understand the meaning of the percentage. The calculation shows that for every $1 of sales revenue, 62.8 ¢ were available to support the remaining expenses, the possible payment of dividends and the retention of profits for the future. While its value is useful for comparing the results of similar businesses, the trend of gross profit margins over time is a more appropriate use of the ratio.

Suppose the ratio in the previous year had been 64.3 per cent. How can we interpret the decline over the year?
There are several possibilities:

- sales revenue declined;
- sales revenue remained the same, but costs have increased;
- sales revenue increased, but costs increased by a greater proportion;
- it was necessary to keep sales prices steady, despite rising costs, in order to retain market share;
- suppliers increased their prices, or perhaps the firm lost the advantage of trade discounts;
- the sales mix changed: if several different products are being sold they will not all be equally profitable. It is possible that in the current year we sold a higher proportion of the less profitable products.

You can perhaps see that the above changes can be classified as either volume changes or price changes.

The gross profit margin could be a measure of the effectiveness of the sales team, pricing policies, purchasing methods and (in a manufacturing organisation) the production processes.

The decline will not be as a result of holding inventory, as this is adjusted for in the cost of sales calculation.

Gross profit mark-up

This ratio is an alternative measure of profitability. It is calculated by:

$$\frac{\text{Gross profit}}{\text{Cost of sales}} \times 100\% = \frac{14{,}837}{8{,}799} \times 100 = 168.6\%$$

It shows us that the selling price of the goods was equal to the cost of those goods, plus 168.6 per cent of the cost. In other words, for every $1 we spent on the cost of goods, we added $1.69 (approximately) to arrive at a selling price of $2.69.

Operating profit margin

This ratio (also known as the net profit margin) is calculated by:

$$\frac{\text{Operating profit}}{\text{Sales revenue}} \times 100\% = \frac{9{,}100}{23{,}636} \times 100 = 38.5\%$$

It shows us that for every $1 in sales revenue 38.5% of it will be net profit, i.e. approximately 39¢.

The operating margin is an expansion of the gross margin and includes all of the items that come after gross profit but before finance charges and taxation, such as selling and distribution costs and administration costs.

If the gross margin is a measure of how profitably a company can produce and sell its products and services, the operating margin also measures how effectively the business manages/administers that process.

What does this mean?

The value of this ratio lies in its comparison over time and with other organisations and the industry average. In this example the operating profit percentage was 38.5 ¢. In itself, this has no meaning – only by comparing it as stated is it possible to derive any benefit from the calculation. To interpret this percentage fully would involve an examination of its components. Given that operating profit is equal to gross profit less expenses, a change in this percentage could arise either from a change in gross profit or from a change in one or more of the expenses deducted from gross profit. Further analysis would be needed.

By the time you have reached operating (net) profit, there are many more factors to consider. If you are provided with a breakdown of expenses you can use this for further line-by-line comparisons. Bear in mind that:

- some costs are fixed or semi-fixed (e.g. property costs) and therefore not expected to change in line with revenue;
- other costs are variable (e.g. packing and distribution, and commission).

Test your understanding 1

Given a selling price of $350 and a gross profit mark-up of 40 per cent, the cost price would be: $...............

Test your understanding 2

A business operates on a gross profit margin of 33 1/3 per cent. Gross profit on a sale was $800, and expenses were $680. The operating profit margin is: .... per cent.

Return on capital ratios

People who invest their money in a business are interested in the return the business is earning on that capital. Expressing this return in the form of a ratio enables comparison with other possible investment opportunities.

This ratio is a key measure of return. It measures the amount of earnings generated per $1 of capital, and is usually stated as a percentage. The ratio can be calculated in several different ways, according to the information required of it, and depending on what is meant by the two terms 'capital employed' and 'return'. In this Learning System, two methods of calculating the return on capital are discussed – the return on total capital employed (ROCE) and the return on equity (ROE).

- **Capital employed** can consist of total capital employed (equity + non-current liabilities) or just equity. In using total capital employed we include long-term loans as well as equity, and this is used when calculating ROCE. When calculating ROE, just the equity is used. You should remember that equity is share capital plus all of the reserves. Furthermore, it is more correct to use the average of capital employed during the year, as the profit has been earned throughout the year. The capital at the start of the year will have been different, having been affected by share issues, loan issues or repayments, and the addition of profit for the year. However, in many computer-based assessments, the question may just require you to use the capital at the end of the year.
- **Return** is another way of describing profit. The profit figure to be taken will depend on which figure is taken for capital employed. If capital employed is taken as being total capital employed, then it is the operating profit figure that is required to be used as the 'return', as this is the profit available to finance the total investment in the business. If the capital employed is equity, then the return is the 'profit for the period', which is the last line in the income statement. In other words, it is the profit for the year, after interest and after tax.

The **ROCE** is:

$$\frac{\text{Operating profit}}{\text{Average capital employed}} \times 100\%$$

This expresses the profit that is available to all providers of long-term capital, as a percentage of that capital. Using the figures from the financial statements above, the calculation is:

$$\frac{9{,}100}{18{,}925} \times 100 = 48\%$$

Average total capital employed is arrived at by taking the average of:

	$
Closing total capital employed (18,250 + 4,500)	22,750
Opening total capital employed (22,750 – 7,650 retained profit)	15,100
	37,850 ÷ 2 = $18,925

In simple terms ROCE measures how much operating profit is generated for every $1 capital invested in the business. In this example 48c generated for every $1invested.

Don't forget capital employed means equity + non-current liabilities.

Further detail

Note that the profit figure used when calculating opening capital is 'retained' profit. This would normally be the profit after the payment of dividends and would be found in the statement of changes in equity. However, in this example there are no dividends paid and therefore the figure is taken from the income statement.

Overdrafts less cash balances, that is net overdrafts, are normally excluded from capital employed. This assumes that overdrafts are temporary and are not considered to be a source of permanent finance for the business.

The **ROE** is:

$$\frac{\text{Profit for the period}}{\text{Average equity}} \times 100\%$$

This expresses the profit that is available only to shareholders, as a percentage of their funds. The calculation is also known as return on net assets, as equity = assets – liabilities (which is a re-arrangement of the accounting equation).

Using the figures in the financial statements above, the calculation is:

$$\frac{7,650}{14,425} \times 100 = 53\%$$

Average equity is arrived at by taking the average of:

	$	
Closing equity	18,250	
Opening equity (18,250 – 7,650 profit)	10,600	
	28,850	÷2 = $14,425

In simple terms ROE measures how much of the final profit is generated for the shareholders for every $1 capital invested by them. In this example 53c generated for every $1invested.

Further detail

If it is not possible to calculate the average capital employed, then use the closing capital figure, but bear in mind that it may not be representative of the capital employed throughout the year.

Net asset turnover

The net asset turnover is:

$$\frac{\text{Sales revenue}}{\text{Capital employed (net assets)}} = \text{times p.a.}$$

It measures management's efficiency in generating revenue from the net assets at its disposal. This is similar to ROCE but in this case we measure the amount of sales revenue generated for every $1 capital invested in the business. Generally speaking, the higher the ratio the more efficient the business is.

Using the figures in the financial statements above, the calculation is:

$$\frac{23{,}636}{18{,}925} = 1.25 \text{ times}$$

Average total capital employed is arrived at by taking the average of:

	$	
Closing total capital employed (18,250 + 4,500)	22,750	
Opening total capital employed (22,750 – 7,650 retained profit)	15,100	
	37,850	÷ 2 = $18,925

This means for every $1 invested in the business $1.25 of sales revenue has been generated.

Relationship between ratios

ROCE can be subdivided into operating profit margin and asset turnover.

$$\text{Operating margin} \times \text{Asset turnover} = \text{ROCE}$$

$$\frac{\text{Operating profit}}{\text{Sales revenue}} \times \frac{\text{Sales revenue}}{\text{Capital employed}} = \frac{\text{Operating profit}}{\text{Capital employed}}$$

We can show this using the above examples in the chapter:

$$\frac{9{,}100}{23{,}636} \times \frac{23{,}636}{18{,}925} = \frac{9{,}100}{18{,}925}$$

$$= 38.5\% \qquad = 1.25 \qquad = 48\%$$

6 Liquidity ratios

These are also known as **solvency ratios**, as they refer to the ability of the business to pay its payables in the short term.

There are two main liquidity ratios.

The current ratio

This is also known as the working capital ratio, as it is based on working capital or net current assets. It is a measure of the liquidity of a business that compares its current assets with those payables due to be paid within 1 year of the statement of financial position date (otherwise known as current liabilities). It is calculated as:

$$\frac{\text{Current assets}}{\text{Current liabilities}} = \frac{9{,}701}{1{,}086} = 8.9 : 1$$

This means for every $1 owed by the business it has $8.90 in assets to pay the debt.

Notice how the ratio is expressed, as a comparison of assets with liabilities. The ratio can also be stated as:

Current assets : current liabilities

What does it mean?

The importance of this ratio is the information it gives about the liquidity of a business. Current liabilities all have to be settled in cash within a reasonably short space of time. Does the company have sufficient liquid resources to do this? Clearly, its cash and bank balances are liquid; receivables should convert into cash quite soon; and inventories will presumably soon be sold, again eventually generating cash. The calculation tells us that the company has $8.90 in current assets with which to pay every $1 of its current liabilities.

A high ratio, such as the one in our example, means that current assets are easily sufficient to cover current liabilities. A ratio of below one – meaning that current liabilities exceed current assets – could imply danger of insolvency. It used to be thought that a ratio of 2:1 was ideal, but this depends on the type of business and its reliance on credit transactions.

Although a high ratio gives comfort to payables, it may mean that the company is holding more in current assets than it requires in the short term. This is wasteful, as current assets rarely earn income – inventories need to be sold in order to produce profits, receivables will not pay more than the amount outstanding, and bank balances may earn only very small amounts of interest. Indeed, a company with a high level of inventories might indicate difficulty in selling them, while a high level of receivables might indicate poor credit control.

Current ratio

The current ratio measures the adequacy of current assets to meet the company's short-term liabilities. It reflects whether the company is in a position to meet its liabilities as they fall due.

Traditionally, a current ratio of 2:1 or higher was regarded as appropriate for most businesses to maintain creditworthiness. However, more recently a figure of 1.5:1 is regarded as the norm.

The current ratio should, however, be looked at in the light of what is normal for the business. For example, supermarkets tend to have low current ratios because:

- there are few trade receivables;
- there is a high level of trade payables;
- there is usually very tight cash control, to fund investment in developing new sites and improving sites.

It is also worth considering:

- availability of further finance, e.g. is the overdraft at the limit? – very often this information is highly relevant but is not disclosed in the accounts;
- seasonal nature of the business – one way of doing this is to compare the interest charges in the income statement with the overdraft and other loans in the statement of financial position; if the interest rate appears abnormally high, this is probably because the company has had higher levels of borrowings during the year;
- long-term liabilities, when they fall due and how will they be financed;
- nature of the inventory – where inventories are slow moving, the quick ratio probably provides a better indicator of short-term liquidity.

The quick ratio

This is also known as the *acid test ratio* and is calculated by:

$$\frac{\text{Current assets excluding inventories}}{\text{Current liabilities}} = \frac{8,276}{1,086} = 7.6 : 1$$

or it can be expressed as: **Current assets excluding inventories : current liabilities**

The quick ratio is also known as the acid test ratio because by eliminating inventory from current assets it provides the acid test of whether the company has sufficient liquid resources (receivables and cash) to settle its liabilities.

What does it mean?

This is similar to the current ratio, but takes the more prudent view that inventories may take some time to convert into cash, and therefore the true liquidity position is measured by the relationship of receivables and cash only to current liabilities. The calculation tells us that the company has $7.60 in 'quick' assets with which to pay each $1 in its current liabilities. Again, a very high ratio is very comforting, but may be wasteful as mentioned above. Generally, a ratio of 1:1 is considered 'ideal' but many retail companies with very regular cash sales have very low quick ratios, due to their lack of receivables.

A low ratio might need further investigation before conclusions can be drawn, for example, if the current liabilities figure includes payables not due for payment until well into the next accounting period (e.g. income tax), the figure may be distorted.

Test your understanding 3

A company has the following current assets and liabilities at 31 October 20X8:

	$000
Current assets	
Inventory	970
Receivables	380
Bank	40
	1,390
Current liabilities	
Payables	420

When measured against accepted 'norms', the company can be said to have:

A a high current ratio and an ideal acid test ratio

B an ideal current ratio and a low acid test ratio

C a high current ratio and a low acid test ratio

D ideal current and acid test ratios

7 Efficiency ratios

These are also referred to as **use of assets ratios**. They measure the efficiency of the management of assets, both non-current and current.

Sales: non-current assets (non-current asset turnover)

This is the sales revenue generated per $1 of non-current assets.

$$\frac{\text{Sales revenue}}{\text{Non-current assets}} = \frac{23{,}636}{14{,}135} = \$1.67$$

This tells us that for every $1 invested in non-current assets, sales revenue of $1.672 was earned. This figure is meaningless on its own – it is commonly compared with previous years' results, as comparison between firms is less useful.

Inventory days

Inventory may be analysed by calculating the ratio of inventory to cost of sales, and then multiplying by the number of days in a year to give inventory days.

The calculation is:

$$\frac{\text{Inventory}}{\text{Cost of sales}} \times 365 = \text{inventory days}$$

$$\frac{1,425}{8,799} \times 365 = 59 \text{ days}$$

This figure gives the number of days that on average an item is in inventory before it is sold; this may alternatively be expressed as the number of days a firm could continue trading if the supply of goods ceased.

This could also be calculated using average inventory. This is calculated by taking the opening and closing inventory for the period and dividing by 2, i.e. $1,225 + $1,425 = $2,650/2 = $1,325.

This would result in:

$$\frac{1,325}{8,799} \times 365 = 55 \text{ days}$$

What does it mean?

This tells us that in the past year, this was the average inventory days. By using the inventory at the end of the year, this tells us what the inventory days will be in the future, assuming cost of sales remains the same.

The number of inventory days is relevant to the context of the business; in a manufacturing company, it will approximate to the production cycle and in a cream cake shop to 1 day!

If inventory days are relatively high, this may indicate that inventory is too high and there is additional finance tied up in inventory which could perhaps be used more effectively elsewhere. If cash is paid out when the inventories are purchased, but the cash does not come back in until the inventory is sold to a customer, then this temporary negative cash flow will have to be financed by the company. Moreover, if the inventory is sold on credit terms and the customer does not pay for, say 1 month, then the delay in getting the cash back in is even longer.

If the inventory is too low, this may show an overzealous application of the 'just-in-time' concept and consequential risks of running out of inventory. It may also indicate a company meeting a cash flow crisis by running down inventory levels. Inventory days needs to be compared to other companies and compared to previous years in the same company. Increasing inventory days may be investigated further by separately analysing raw materials (RM), work in progress (WIP) and finished goods (FG) to cost of goods sold. An increase in RM days may indicate mismanagement in the buying department; an increase in WIP may indicate production delays. If FG days increase, this may be a sign of decline in demand for the product and an increase in obsolete items.

The inventory ratio may also be expressed as the number of times an item turns over in a year – that is, how many times it is bought and sold during the year.

Inventory turnover is calculated as:

$$\frac{\text{Cost of sales}}{\text{Average inventory}} = \frac{8{,}799}{1{,}325} = 6.6 \text{ times}$$

You should note here that the word 'turnover' is being used to mean 'turn over' and is not referring to turnover, as in sales. This means that in order to meet the cost of sales for the period we will buy inventory costing \$1,325, 6.6 times or we could say if we buy inventory of £1,325 each time we purchase, we will need 6.6 purchases of inventory to meet the requirements for the cost of sales.

Test your understanding 4

A business has the following trading account for the year ending 31 May 20X8:

	$	$
Sales		45,000
Opening inventory	4,000	
Purchases	26,500	
	30,500	
Less: closing inventory	(6,000)	
		(24,500)
Gross profit		20,500

Its average inventory days for the year is: .... days.

Receivables days

This is a measure of the average time taken by customers to settle their debts. It is calculated by:

$$\frac{\text{Receivables}}{\text{Sales}} \times 365 = \frac{542}{23{,}636} \times 365 = 8 \text{ days}$$

Where details are available, credit sales only should be considered.

The sales figure will exclude sales tax but receivables will include sales tax, and so strictly speaking the figure is not comparing like-with-like. This sales tax on sales or receivables is not usually known and so this is inevitable. However, if the sales tax is known, then the figures should be adjusted so that both either include, or exclude, sales tax.

The result of this calculation should be compared with the number of days' credit normally allowed by the business to its customers. If it appears that customers are taking longer to pay than they should do, it may be necessary to take remedial action.

As with inventory days, a slowing down in the speed of collecting debts will have a detrimental effect on cash flow. On the other hand, it may be that the business has deliberately offered extended credit in order to increase demand.

Payable days

This is a measure of the average time taken to pay suppliers. Although it is not strictly a measure of asset efficiency on its own, it is part of the overall management of net current assets. It is calculated by:

$$\frac{\text{Payables}}{\text{Purchases}} \times 365 = \frac{1,086}{8,999} \times 365 = 44 \text{ days}$$

The purchases figure should exclude any cash purchases, if this information is available; where there is no purchases figure available the best alternative is to use cost of sales as the denominator. Similarly, payables should include only trade payables, not payables for expenses or non-current assets.

The purchases figure will exclude sales tax but payables will include sales tax, and so strictly speaking the figure is not comparing like-with-like. The sales tax on purchases or payables is not usually known and so this is inevitable. However, if the sales tax is known, then the figures should be adjusted so that both either include, or exclude, sales tax.

What does it mean?

The result of this ratio can also be compared with the receivables days. A firm does not normally want to offer its customers more time to pay than it gets from its own suppliers, otherwise this could affect cash flow. Generally, the longer the payables payment period, the better, as the firm holds on to its cash for longer, but care must be taken not to upset suppliers by delaying payment, which could result in the loss of discounts and reliability.

It is important to recognise when using these ratios that it is the trend of ratios that is important, not the individual values. Payment periods are longer in some types of organisation than in others.

Test your understanding 5

The annual sales of a company are $235,000 including sales tax at 20 per cent. Half of the sales are on credit terms; half are cash sales. The receivables in the statement of financial position are $23,500.

What are the receivable days (to the nearest day)?

.... days

Total working capital ratio

This measures the total length of time for which working capital is tied up in inventory, receivables and payables, before becoming available for use. It is the total of the number of inventories days, receivables days, less payables days. From the preceding three sections, you can see that this is:

Number of days – inventory	59
Number of days – receivables	8
Less number of days – payables	(44)
Total working capital days	23

This tells us that it takes, on average, 23 days in which to sell the inventory, receive payment from receivables and pay the payables. The total of 23 days may not seem too lengthy for a manufacturing business, but it does indicate the level of working capital needed in order to finance the ordinary activities of the business, which may result in the need for an overdraft or other sources of finance.

8 Capital structure ratios

Different firms have different methods of financing their activities. Some rely mainly on the issue of share capital and the retention of profits; others rely heavily on loan finance; most have a combination of the two.

The gearing ratio (or leverage ratio)

Gearing is a measure of the relationship between the amount of finance provided by external parties (e.g. debentures) to the total capital employed. It is calculated by:

$$\frac{\text{Debt}}{\text{Total capital employed}} \times 100 = \frac{4{,}500}{22{,}750} \times 100 = 20\%$$

You should recall from the discussion above regarding the return on total capital employed (ROCE), that total capital employed is equity plus debt ($18,250 + 4,500). This ratio has been calculated based on the capital employed at the date of the statement of financial position. An alternative would be to use the average capital employed and average loan capital during the year.

What does it mean?

The more highly geared a business, the more profits that have to be earned to pay the interest cost of the borrowing. Consequently, the higher the gearing, the more risky is the owner's investment. Remember that dividends do not have to be paid out if the directors decide not to declare them, so there is reduced risk with low-geared companies, especially in times when profits are falling. On the other hand, a highly geared company might be more attractive to shareholders when profits are rising, because there are fewer of them to share out those profits.

An alternative method of calculating gearing is known as the **debt:equity ratio.** In this case, the loan capital is expressed as a percentage of equity capital.

In this example, it would be:

$$\frac{\text{Debt}}{\text{Equity}} = \frac{4{,}500}{18{,}250} \times 100 = 25\%$$

Test your understanding 6

The draft statement of financial position of B Ltd at 31 March 20X0 is set out below.

Assets	$	$
Non-current assets		450
Current assets		
Inventory	65	
Receivables	110	
Prepayments	30	
		205
		655
Equity and liabilities		
Ordinary share capital		400
Retained earnings		100
		500
Non-current liability		
Loan		75
Current liabilities		
Payables	30	
Bank overdraft	50	
		80
		655

What is the gearing of the company?

.... per cent

Interest cover

Connected to the gearing ratio is a measure of the number of times that the profit is able to 'cover' the fixed interest due on long-term loans. It provides lenders with an idea of the level of security for the payment. The formula is:

$$\frac{\text{Operating profit}}{\text{Interest payable}} = \frac{9{,}100}{450} = 20 \text{ times}$$

This shows lenders that their interest is covered 20 times by the current profits. This would normally be a fairly comfortable level, but of course, it is future profits that will determine the actual level of cover.

Ratio analysis for sole traders

All of the above ratios can be calculated for sole traders, as well as for limited companies.

9 Chapter summary

This very important chapter is one worth spending time over. In a computer-based assessment, not only will you be expected to calculate ratios, but you may need to be able to do any or all of the following:

- explain what the ratio attempts to show;
- discuss the results of your calculations;
- suggest possible reasons for good/poor results or differences from previous years, other companies or expectations.

Although ratios are a useful additional guide to decision-making, they are also very difficult to interpret fully without additional information.

Before calculating any ratios the nature of the business should be considered. The following list of questions is a useful starting point:

- What is the nature of its business?
- Does it need a lot of assets to operate?
- How has it obtained its funding (shareholders' capital, loan capital or internally generated profits)?
- Does it have a high or low operating profit margin on its business?
- Does it have high or low turnover in relation to the amount of capital that is tied up in the organisation? (High-margin companies will normally have slower rates of sales/turnover because they usually charge higher prices and/or operate in premium segments of a market.)
- Does the company appear to be financially unstable (i.e. does it have excessive debts in relation to its assets)?
- Does the level of inventory or any other asset, or number of employees appear to be too high or too low to support the organisation's level of activity/sales?
- Is there any information to tell whether the business is more or less efficient/profitable than other competitors in the same industry?

The answers to these questions and to others that are naturally associated with them are key to understanding how an organisation is currently performing and how it is likely to perform in the future. Trends in these indicators are of interest to internal managers and accountants, and also to external users. Examples of external users are:

- investors and potential investors use this type of information to decide whether to buy, sell or hold shares in a particular company;

- lenders and suppliers wish to know about the solvency of an enterprise and its ability to repay loans or debts incurred in relation to the supply of materials or services;
- governments charged with the responsibility for framing fiscal policy or industrial policy in different sectors of the economy will find much of interest in them. Many of the accounting figures are used to compile national statistics on industrial output, gross national product (GNP), wage levels and inflation trends.

External sources of comparative information will usually be industry averages compiled by government agencies or independent industry groups. These are readily available on the Internet.

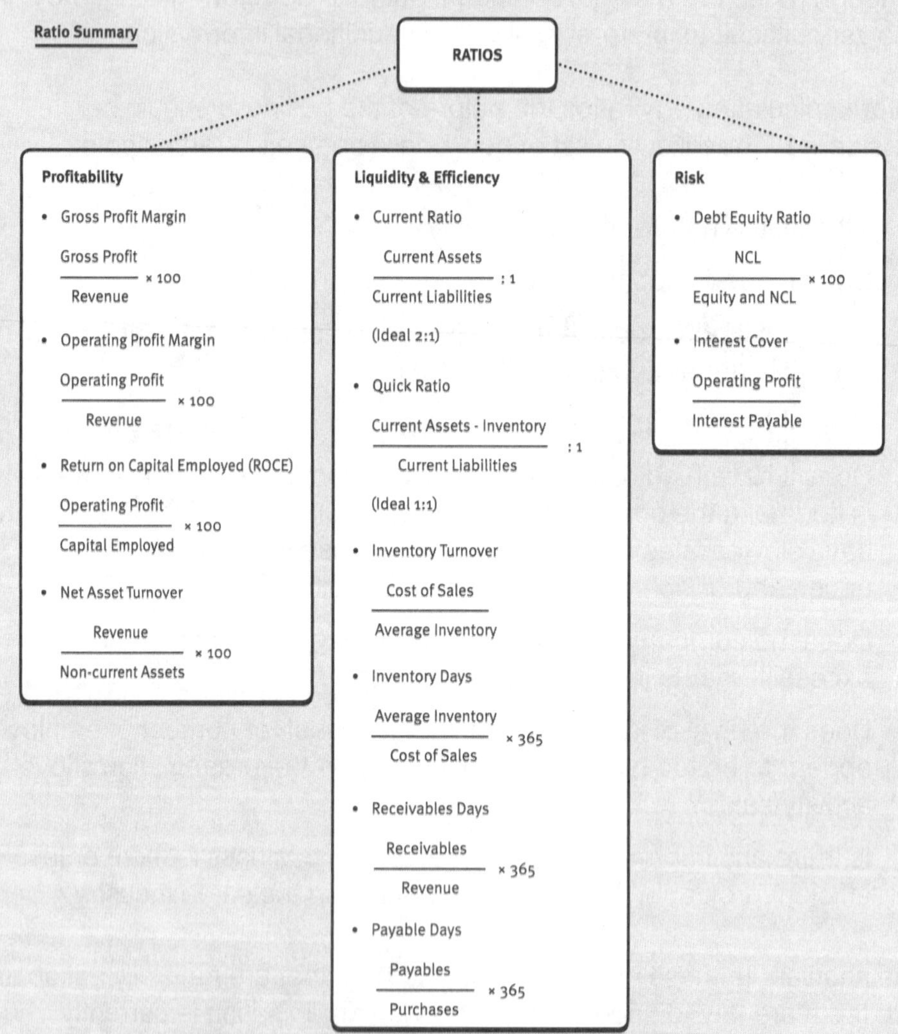

Test your understanding questions

Test your understanding 7

Sales are $110,000. Purchases are $80,000. Opening inventory is $12,000. Closing inventory is $10,000. Inventory days using average inventory is:

.... days

Test your understanding 8

A business commenced with a bank balance of $3,250; it subsequently purchased goods on credit for $10,000; gross profit mark-up was 120 per cent; half the goods were sold for cash, less cash discount of 5 per cent; all takings were banked. The resulting operating profit was:

$...............

Test your understanding 9

A company has the following details extracted from its statement of financial position:

	$000
Inventory	1,900
Receivables	1,000
Bank overdraft	100
Payables	1,000

Its liquidity position could be said to be:

A very well controlled, because its current assets far outweigh its current liabilities

B poorly controlled, because its quick assets are less than its current liabilities

C poorly controlled, because its current ratio is significantly higher than the industry norm of 1.8

D poorly controlled, because it has a bank overdraft

Test your understanding 10

The gross profit mark-up is 40 per cent where:

A sales are $120,000 and gross profit is $48,000

B sales are $120,000 and cost of sales is $72,000

C sales are $100,800 and cost of sales is $72,000

D sales are $100,800 and cost of sales is $60,480

Test your understanding 11

Your company's income statement for the year ended 30 September 20X8 showed the following:

	$000
Operating profit	1,200
Interest	(200)
Profit before tax	1,000
Income tax	(400)
Profit for the period	600

Its statement of financial position at 30 September 20X7 showed the following:

	$000
Share capital	8,000
Retained earnings	1,200
	9,200
10% debenture	2,000
	11,200

Return on average capital employed (ROCE) for the year ended 30 September 20X8 is:

.... per cent

Test your understanding 12

A sole trader made a loss during his financial year, but has more cash at the end of the year than he did at the beginning.

Which of the following could be a reason for this?

A The sole trader took more out in drawings this year than last

B Some non-current assets were sold during the year

C Receivables took longer to pay this year than last

D Prepayments were higher at the end of this year

Test your understanding 13

The inventory turnover ratio is six times where:

A sales revenue is $120,000 and the average inventory level at selling price is $20,000

B purchases are $240,000 and the average inventory level at cost is $40,000

C cost of goods sold is $180,000 and the average inventory level at cost is $30,000

D net purchases are $90,000 and closing inventory at cost is $15,000.

Test your understanding 14

An increase in inventory of $250, a decrease in the bank balance of $400 and an increase in trade payables of $1,200 would result in which of the following:

A a decrease in working capital of £1,350

B an increase in working capital of £1,350

C a decrease in working capital of £1,050

D an increase in working capital of £1,050.

Test your understanding 15

B made a return on capital employed of 25.5%. Its profit before interest and taxation amounted to $60,000. The asset turnover ratio (calculated as sales/capital employed) was 85%.

What was the value of sales revenue?

A $70,588

B $100,840

C $200,000

D $276,817

Test your understanding 16

The following trial balance has been extracted from the ledgers of JK Ltd at 31 March 20X3:

	$	$
Sales (all on credit)		647,400
Inventory(1 April 20X2)	15,400	
Trade receivables and payables	82,851	41,936
Purchases (all on credit)	321,874	
Carriage in	13,256	
Carriage out	32,460	
Electricity	6,994	
Local business tax	8,940	
Wages and salaries	138,292	
Postages and stationery	6,984	
Rent	14,600	
Sales tax control		16,382
Employees' income tax control		4,736
Motor vehicles		
At cost	49,400	
Cumulative depreciation		21,240
Bank deposit account	90,000	
Bank current account	77,240	
Ordinary shares of $1 each		50,000
Retained earnings		76,597
	858,291	858,291

The following notes are also relevant:

(i) Inventory at 31 March 20X3 was valued at a cost of $19,473.

(ii) Prepaid rent amounted to $2,800.

(iii) Accruals are estimated as follows:

Electricity	$946
Wages and salaries	$2,464

(iv) Depreciation on motor vehicles is to be calculated at 25 per cent per annum using the reducing-balance method.

(v) Accrued interest on the bank deposit account amounts to $7,200.

(vi) An accrual for income tax of $30,000 is to be made on the profits of the year.

Required:

(a) Prepare JK Ltd's income statement for the year ended 31 March 20X3.

(b) Prepare JK Ltd's statement of financial position at 31 March 20X3.

(c) Calculate the receivable days, payable days and inventory days.

Test your understanding 17

DWS Ltd prepares its financial statements to 30 September each year. On 30 September 20X4 its trial balance was as follows:

	Debit ($)	Credit ($)
Plant and machinery:		
Cost	125,000	
Acc. depreciation at 1 October 20X3		28,000
Office equipment:		
Cost	45,000	
Acc. depreciation at 1 October 20X3		15,000
Inventory at 1 October 20X3	31,000	
Purchases and sales	115,000	188,000
Returns inwards and outwards	8,000	6,000
Selling expenses	12,000	
Heat and light	8,000	
Wages and salaries	14,000	
Directors' fees	5,000	
Printing and stationery	6,000	
Telephone and fax	6,000	
Rent and insurance	4,000	
Trade receivables and payables	35,000	33,000
Allowance for receivables at 1 October 20X3		4,000
Bank	3,000	
Petty cash	1,000	
Dividend paid	2,000	
Ordinary shares of 50¢ each		100,000
Share premium account		8,000
General reserve		7,000
Retained earnings balance at 1 October 20X3		34,000
Suspense account	3,000	
	423,000	423,000

The following additional information at 30 September 20X4 is available:

(i) Closing inventory of goods for resale amount to $53,000.

(ii) Prepayments:

Telephone and fax rental	$1,000
Insurance	$1,000

(iii) Accruals:

Wages and salaries	$1,500
Directors' fees	2% of net turnover
Auditor's fees	$3,500

(iv) Irrecoverable debts to be written off amount to $3,000.

(v) Allowance for receivables is to be amended to 5 per cent of receivables, after adjusting for bad debts written off.

(vi) The following bookkeeping errors are discovered:

- The purchase of an item of inventory has been debited to the office equipment account, cost $1,200.
- The payment of $1,300 to a payable has been recorded by debiting the bank account and crediting the payable's account. Any remaining balance on the suspense account is to be added to prepayments or accruals, as appropriate, on the statement of financial position.

(vii) The figure in the trial balance for the bank balance is the balance appearing in the cash book, prior to the reconciliation with the bank statement. Upon reconciliation, it is discovered that

- unpresented cheques amount to $3,000;
- bank charges not entered in the ledgers amount to $4,000.

(viii) Depreciation of non-current assets is to be calculated as follows:

Plant and machinery	10% on cost
Office equipment	33.33% on the reducing balance at the end of the year

(ix) A final dividend of 1.5¢ per share was declared before the year end, but not paid until after the year end.
$10,000 is to be transferred to general reserves.
An accrual of $1,000 for income tax is to be made.

Required:

(a) Prepare the income statement for the year ended 30 September 20X4.

(b) Prepare the statement of changes in equity for the year ended 30 September 20X4.

(c) Prepare the statement of financial position at 30 September 20X4.

(d) Calculate the current ratio and the quick ratio.

Test your understanding 18

You are considering the purchase of a small business, JK, and have managed to obtain a copy of its financial statements for the last complete accounting year to 30 September 20X3. These appear as follows:

Income statement for the year to 30 September 20X3

	$	$
Sale		385,200
Less: cost of goods sold		
Opening inventory	93,250	
Purchases	174,340	
Less closing inventory	(84,630)	
		(182,960)
Gross profit		202,240
Less: expenses		
Selling and delivery costs	83,500	
Administration costs	51,420	
Depreciation	36,760	
		(171,680)
Net profit		30,560

Statement of financial position as at 30 September 20X3

Assets	$	$
Non-current assets		
Assets at cost	235,070	
Less accumulated depreciation	(88,030)	
		147,040
Current assets		
Inventory	84,630	
Receivables and prepayments	36,825	
Bank and cash	9,120	
		130,575
		277,615
Capital and liabilities		
Capital at 1 October 20X2		197,075
Net profit for the year		30,560
Proprietor's drawings		(12,405)
		215,230
Current liabilities		
Payables and accruals		62,385
		277,615

Required:

Calculate the following accounting ratios from the financial statements presented above:

(i) Net profit percentage

(ii) Return on capital employed

(iii) Current ratio

(iv) Quick (acid test) ratio

Test your understanding answers

Test your understanding 1

Mark-up is gross profit as a percentage of cost of sales, so a mark-up of 40 per cent will result in a selling price of 140 per cent of cost of sales. Thus, if the selling price is $350, this represents 140 per cent of the cost of sales, therefore 100 per cent would be 350/140 x 100 = $250 cost price.

This can be confirmed by checking that 40 per cent of $250 gives a mark-up of $100, and hence a selling price of $350.

A common mistake is candidates simply calculate 40 per cent of $350 to arrive at $140 as the mark-up (and hence $210 as the cost of sales); this is obviously incorrect as the mark-up is not 40 per cent of sales, but 40 per cent of cost of sales.

Test your understanding 2

Reconstruction of income statement:

	$	
Sales	2,400	(100%)
Cost of sales	(1,600)	(66%)
Gross profit	800	(33%)
Expenses	(680)	
Operating profit (120/2,400) × 100	120	(i.e. 5%)

Test your understanding 3

A

Current ratio	1,390:420 = 3.3:1	(i.e. high)
Acid test ratio	420:420 = 1:1	(i.e. ideal)

Test your understanding 4

Inventory days are:

$$\frac{\text{Average inventory}}{\text{Purchases}} \times 365 = \frac{[(4000 + 6000) / 2]}{24{,}500} \times 365 = 74 \text{ days}$$

Test your understanding 5

Receivables including sales tax/Credit sales including sales tax = \$23,500/ \$117,500 × 365 days = 73 days.

Test your understanding 6

Gearing = Debt/Debt + equity = 75/75 + 500 = 13% (alternative answer debt/equity = 75/500 = 15%)

Test your understanding 7

Inventory days are found by dividing cost of goods sold by average inventory and multiplying by 365. Average inventory is:

$$\left[\frac{12{,}000 + 10{,}000}{2}\right] = £11{,}000$$

Cost of goods sold is found as follows:

	$
Opening inventory	12,000
Purchases	80,000
	92,000
Less: closing inventory	(10,000)
Cost of goods sold	82,000

Rate of inventory turnover is therefore:

$$\frac{\$\ 11{,}000}{\$\ 82{,}000} \times 365 = 49 \text{ days}$$

Test your understanding 8

The answer can be found as follows:

	$
Cost of goods purchased	10,000
Cost of half the goods that have been sold	5,000
Gross profit mark-up on these goods = 5,000 × 120%	6,000
Therefore, selling price =	11,000
Cash discount given = 5% of $11,000	550
Therefore, operating profit = gross profit less discount	5,450

Test your understanding 9

C

The current ratio is current assets: current liabilities, that is 2,900:1,100 = 2.6:1. The quick ratio is current assets minus inventories: current liabilities, that is 1,000:1,100 = 0.9:1. The current ratio is high compared with the industry standard of 1.8:1, while the quick ratio is within acceptable limits of the 'norm' of 1:1. Without any evidence of the reason for the high inventory levels, its current ratio would appear to be higher than is required, and hence liquidity is poorly controlled.

Test your understanding 10

C

	$
Sales were	100,800
Cost of sales was	(72,000)
Gross profit	28,800

Gross profit mark-up = Gross profit/Cost of sales × 100 = 28,800/72,000 × 100 = 40%

Test your understanding 11

ROCE = Profit before interest and tax/Average capital employed 3 × 100

Average capital employed	= Opening capital + closing capital/2
Closing capital employed	= Opening capital plus profit for the year
	= 11,200 + 600 = $11,800
Average capital employed	= 11,200 + 11,800/2 = $11,500

Thus ROCE = 1,200/11,500 × 100 = 10.43%

Test your understanding 12

B

An increase in receivables (answer C) and prepayments (answer D) would result in a reduction in cash flow, not an increase. Drawings also reduce cash flow (answer A).

The sale of non-current assets, either at a loss or a profit, will bring cash into the enterprise, and could explain an increase in cash despite making a loss.

Test your understanding 13

C

The rate of inventory turnover is the number of times that inventory is used up during a year, and is measured as the ratio of the cost of sales to average inventory (at cost) during the year. The turnover ratio is 6 times when the cost of goods sold is $180,000 and average inventory is $30,000.

Test your understanding 14

A

	$
Increase in inventory	250
Decrease in cash	(400)
Increase in payables	(1,200)
Change in working capital	(1,350)

Test your understanding 15

C

Profit before interest and taxation = $60,000
Return on capital employed = 25.5%
Capital employed = $60,000/25.5% = £235,294
Asset turnover ratio = Revenue/capital employed = 85%
Revenue = 85% × $235,294 = $200,000.

Test your understanding 16

(a) **Income statement of JK Ltd for the year ended 31 March 20X3**

	$000	$000	$000
Sales			647,400
Opening inventory		15,400	
Purchases		321,874	
Carriage inwards		13,256	
Closing inventory		(19,473)	
			(331,057)
Gross profit			316,343
Carriage outwards		32,460	
Electricity	6,994		
Add: accrual	946		
		7,940	
Local business tax		8,940	
Wages and salaries	138,292		
Add: accrual	2,464		
		140,756	
Postage and stationery		6,984	
Rent	14,600		
Less: prepaid	(2,800)		
		11,800	
Depreciation of vehicles (49,400 – 21,240) × 25%		7,040	
			(215,920)
Operating profit			100,423
Interest receivable			7,200
Profit before tax			107,623
Income tax			(30,000)
Profit for the period			77,623

(b) **Statement of financial position of JK Ltd as at 31 March 20X3**

Assets	*Cost* *($000)*	*Acc. Depreciation*	*Carrying Amount*
		($000)	($000)
Non-current assets			
Motor vehicles	49,400	(28,280)	21,120
Current assets			
Inventory	19,473		
Receivables	82,851		
Interest receivable	7,200		
Prepayment	2,800		
Bank deposit account	90,000		
Bank current account	77,240		
			279,564
			300,684
Equity and liabilities			
Ordinary shares of $1 each			50,000
Retained earnings			154,220
			204,220
Current liabilities			
Payables	41,936		
Accrual for expenses (946 + 2,464)	3,410		
Income tax	30,000		
Sales tax	16,382		
Employees' income tax	4,736		
			96,464
			300,684

Workings

Retained earnings: $76,597 + $77,623 = $154,220

(c) **Receivables days:**

$$\frac{\text{Closing receivables} \times 365}{\text{Credit sales}} = \frac{82{,}451 \times 365}{647{,}400} = 47 \text{ days}$$

Payable days:

$$\frac{\text{Closing payables} \times 365}{\text{Credit Purchases}} = \frac{41{,}936 \times 365}{321{,}874} = 48 \text{ days}$$

Inventories days:

$$\frac{\text{Average inventories} \times 365}{\text{Cost of goods sold}} = \frac{(15{,}400 + 19{,}473)/2 \times 365}{331{,}057} = 19 \text{ days}$$

Test your understanding 17

(a) **Income statement of DWS Ltd for the year ended 30 September 20X4**

	$	$
Sales		188,000
Less: returns inwards		(8,000)
		180,000
Opening inventory	31,000	
Purchases (115,000 + 1,200)	116,200	
Returns outward	(6,000)	
Closing inventory	(53,000)	
Cost of goods sold		(88,200)
Gross profit		91,800
Selling expenses	12,000	
Heat and light	8,000	
Wages and salaries (14,000 + 1,500)	15,500	
Directors' fees (5,000 + 3,600)	8,600	
Printing and stationery	6,000	
Telephone and fax (6,000 – 1,000)	5,000	
Rent insurance (4,000 – 1,000)	3,000	
Auditor's fees	3,500	
Irrecoverable debts written off	3,000	
Change in allowance for receivables (see workings)	(2,400)	
Bank charges accrued	4,000	
Depreciation of plant and machinery	12,500	
Depreciation of office equipment	9,600	
		(88,300)
Operating profit		3,500
Income tax		(1,000)
Profit for the period		2,500

Statement of changes in equity of DWS Ltd for year ended 30 September 20X4

	Share Capital	Share Premium	General Reserve	Retained Earnings	Total
	$	$	$	$	$
Balance at the start of the period	100,000	8,000	7,000	34,000	149,000
Profit for the period				2,500	2,500
Dividends (2,000 + 3,000)				(5,000)	(5,000)
Transfer to general reserve			10,000	(10,000)	–
Balance at the end of the period	100,000	8,000	17,000	21,500	146,500

(b) **Statement of financial position of DWS Ltd at 30 September 20X4**

Assets	Cost ($)	Acc. Depreciation ($)	Carrying Amount ($)
Non-current assets			
Plant and machinery	125,000	(40,500)	84,500
Office equipment	43,800	(24,600)	19,200
	168,800	(65,100)	103,700
Current assets			
Inventory	53,000		
Receivables (32,000 – 1,600)	30,400		
Prepayments (3,000 + 1,000 + 1,000)	5,000		
Petty cash	1,000		
			89,400
			193,100

Equity and liabilities

Ordinary shares of 50c each		100,000
Share premium account		8,000
General reserve account (7,000 + 10,000)		17,000
Retained earnings		21,500
		146,500
Current liabilities		
Payables (33,000 - 2,600)	30,400	
Accruals (1,500 + 3,600 + 3,500)	8,600	
Overdraft (3,000 – 2,600 – 4,000)	3,600	
Income tax	1,000	
Declared final dividend	3,000	
		46,600
		193,100

(c) **Current ratio**

Current assets : Current liabilities
89,400 : 46,600 = 1.92:1

Quick ratio

Current assets less inventories : Current liabilities
(89,400 – 53,000) : 46,600 = 0.78:1

Workings

Re note (vi)

	$
Increase purchases by	1,200
Decrease office equipment by	1,200
Decrease bank by (2 x 1,300)	2,600
Decrease payables by	2,600

This leaves the $3,000 suspense account balance 'untouched'. Therefore, increase prepayments by $3,000 as instructed.

Re notes (iv) and (v)

	$
Receivables in trial balance	35,000
Irrecoverable debt written off	(3,000)
	32,000

Five per cent of $32,000 is $1,600; therefore decrease allowance by $2,400.

Depreciation calculations

Plant and machinery: (10% of $125,000) = $12,500

Office equipment: (($45,000 – $1,200) – $15,000) × 33.33% = $9,600

Director's fee accrual = 2% × 180,000 = $3,600

Dividend accrual = $100,000/0.5 = 200,000 shares × 0.015 = 3,000

Test your understanding 18

(i) Net profit/sales × 100
30,560/385,200 × 100 = 7.93%

(ii) Either
Net profit/average capital employed × 100
30,560/[(197,075 + 215,230)/2] = 206,152.5 × 100 = 14.82%
or
Net profit/closing capital employed × 100
30,560/215,230 × 100 = 14.20%

(iii) Current assets/current liabilities
130,575/62,385 = 2.09

(iv) Quick assets/current liabilities
45,945/62,385 = 0.74

chapter

22

Preparing for the Computer-Based Assessments (CBAs)

Chapter learning objectives

This section is intended for use when you are ready to start revising for your CBA. It contains:

- a summary of useful revision techniques;
- details of the format of the CBA;
- two mock CBAs.

These should be attempted when you consider yourself to be ready for the CBA.

1 Revision technique

Planning

The first thing to say about revision is that it is an addition to your initial studies, not a substitute for them. You should be studying and revising concurrently from the outset. At the end of each week, and at the end of each month, get into the habit of summarising the material you have covered to refresh your memory of it.

As with your initial studies, planning is important to maximise the value of your revision work. You need to balance the demands for study, professional work, family life and other commitments. To make this work, you will need to think carefully about how to make best use of your time.

Begin as before by comparing the estimated hours you will need to devote to revision. Prepare a written schedule setting out the areas you intend to cover during particular weeks, and break that down further into topics for each day's revision. To help focus on the key areas try to establish:

- which areas you are weakest on, so that you can concentrate on the topics where effort is particularly needed;
- which areas are especially significant for the CBA – the topics that are tested frequently.

Do not forget the need for relaxation and for family commitments. Sustained intellectual effort is only possible for limited periods, and must be broken up at intervals by lighter activities. And do not continue your revision timetable right up to the moment when you enter the assessment room: you should aim to stop work a day or even two days before the exam. Beyond this point the most you should attempt is an occasional brief look at your notes to refresh your memory.

2 Getting down to work

By the time you begin your revision you should already have settled into a fixed work pattern: a regular time of day for doing the work, a particular location where you sit, particular equipment that you assemble before you begin and so on.

You should have notes summarising the main points of each topic you have covered. Begin each session by reading through the relevant notes and trying to commit the important points to memory.

Usually this will be just your starting point. Unless the area is one where you already feel very confident, you will need to track back from your notes to the relevant chapter(s) in the Learning System. This will refresh your memory on points not covered by your notes and fill in the detail that inevitably gets lost in the process of summarisation.

3 Tips for the final revision phase

As the CBA approaches, consider the following list of techniques and make use of those that work for you.

- Summarise your notes into more concise form, perhaps on index cards that you can carry with you for revision on the way into work.
- Go through your notes with a highlighter pen, marking key conventions and definitions.
- Summarise the main points in a key area by producing a wordlist, mind map or other mnemonic device.
- On areas that you find difficult, rework questions that you have already attempted and compare your answers in detail with those provided in the Learning System.
- Rework questions you attempted earlier in your studies.

4 Format of the assessment

Structure of the assessment

The computer-based assessment is 2 hours and comprises 50 compulsory questions with one or more parts.
All questions should be attempted if time permits.

CIMA uses objective test questions in the computer-based assessment.
The most common types are:

- Multiple choice, where you have to choose the correct answer from a list of four possible answers. This could either be numbers or text.
- Multiple choice with more choices and answers, for example, choosing two correct answers from a list of eight possible answers. This could either be numbers or text.
- Single numeric entry, where you give your numeric answer, for example, profit is $10,000.
- Multiple entry, where you give several numeric answers, for example, the charge for electricity is $2,000 and accrual is $200.
- True/false questions, where you state whether a statement is true or false, for example, external auditors report to the directors is FALSE.
- Matching pairs of text, for example, the convention 'prudence' would be matched with the statement 'inventories revalued at the lower of cost and net realisable value'.
- Other types could be matching text with graphs and labelling graphs/diagrams.

5 Weighting of subjects

The current weightings for the syllabus sections are:

- Conceptual and regulatory framework – 20%
- Accounting systems – 20%
- Control of counting systems – 15%
- Preparation of accounts – 45%

In broad terms, the entire syllabus will be covered in each assessment.

chapter

23

Mock Assessment 1

Chapter learning objectives

This section is intended for use when you have completed your study and initial revision. It contains a complete mock assessment.

This should be attempted as an exam conditions, timed mock. This will give you valuable experience that will assist you with your time management and examination strategy.

Certificate in Business Accounting

Fundamentals of Financial Accounting

Illustrative Computer-based Assessment

Instructions: attempt all 50 questions

Time allowed: 2 hours

Do not look at or attempt this illustrative computer-based assessment until you have fully completed your revision and are about to sit your computer-based assessment.

Illustrative computer-based assessment 1: Questions

Test your understanding 1

The fundamental objective of an external audit of a limited company is to:

A give advice to shareholders

B detect fraud and errors

C measure the performance and financial position of a company

D provide an opinion on the financial statements

Test your understanding 2

A receives goods from B on credit terms and A subsequently pays by cheque. A then discovers that the goods are faulty and cancels the cheque before it is cashed by B.

How should A record the cancellation of the cheque in his books?

A Debit payables, credit returns outwards

B Credit bank, debit payables

C Debit bank, credit payables

D Credit payables, debit returns outwards

Test your understanding 3

The profit of a business may be calculated by using which of the following formulae?

A Opening capital – drawings + capital introduced – closing capital

B Closing capital + drawings – capital introduced – opening capital

C Opening capital – drawings – capital introduced – closing capital

D Closing capital + capital introduced – opening capital

Test your understanding 4

The turnover in a company was $3 million and its receivables were 5 per cent of turnover. The company wishes to have an allowance for receivables of 4 per cent of receivables, which would make the provision one third higher than the current provision. What figure would appear in the income statement?

Debit/Credit	$

Test your understanding 5

Which of the following should be accounted for as capital expenditure?

A the cost of painting a building

B the replacement of windows in a building

C the purchase of a car by a garage for resale

D legal fees on the purchase of a building

Test your understanding 6

A business purchases a machine on credit terms for $18,000 plus sales tax at 15 per cent. The business is registered for sales tax. How should this transaction be recorded in the books?

		Dr	Cr
		$	$
A	Machinery	18,000	
B	Payables		18,000
C	Machinery	20,700	
D	Payables		20,700
E	Sales tax	2,700	
F	Sales tax		2,700

Test your understanding 7

Which of the following statements most closely expresses the meaning of 'a fair presentation'?

A There is only one fair presentation of a company's financial statements

B Fair presentation is determined by compliance with European Union directives

C Fair presentation is determined by compliance with company law

D Fair presentation is largely determined by reference to international financial reporting standards

Test your understanding 8

On 1st May 20X0, A Ltd pays a rent bill of $2,400 for the period to 30th April 20X1. What is the charge to the income statement and the entry in the statement of financial position for the year ended 30th November 20X0?

Test your understanding 9

S Ltd exchanged inventory for a delivery vehicle with T Ltd. The inventory had cost S Ltd $12,000 and the normal selling price was $14,000; the delivery vehicle had cost T Ltd $11,000 and the normal selling price was $15,000.

How should S Ltd value the vehicle in its statement of financial position?

$...............

Test your understanding 10

Z's bank statement shows a balance of $1,650 overdrawn. The bank statement includes bank charges of $100 which have not been entered in the cash book. There are unpresented cheques totalling $950 and deposits not yet credited of $1,200. The bank statement incorrectly shows a direct debit payment of $320 which belongs to another customer.

The figure in the statement of financial position should be:
Overdrawn

$...............

Test your understanding 11

There is $200 in the till at the year end at F Ltd but the accountant suspects that some cash has been stolen. At the beginning of the year there was $100 in the till and receivables were $2000. Total sales in the year were $230,000. Receivables at the end of the year were $3,000. Cheques banked from credit sales were $160,000 and cash sales of $50,000 have been banked.

How much cash was stolen during the year?

$..................

Test your understanding 12

A car was purchased for $10,000 on 1st April 20X0 and has been depreciated at 20 per cent per annum on straight-line basis. The company policy is to charge depreciation, once a year at the end of the year, on the cost of an asset in use at the year end. Assume there is no residual value. The car was traded in for a replacement vehicle on 1st August 20X3 for an agreed figure of $4,900. What was the profit or loss on the disposal of the vehicle for the year ended 31st December 20X3?

Profit or Loss	$

Test your understanding 13

A company includes in inventory goods received before the year end but for which invoices are not received until after the year end. Which concept is this in accordance with?

A Historical cost

B Accruals

C Consistency

D Materiality

Test your understanding 14

I Ltd operates the imprest system for petty cash. On 1st July there was a float of $250. During July the petty cashier received $50 from staff for using the photocopier and a cheque for $100 was cashed for an employee. In July, cheques were drawn for $600 for petty cash. It was decided to increase the cash float to $180 from 1st August. How much cash was paid out by the petty cashier in July?

$..................

Test your understanding 15

Which of the following sentences does not explain the distinction between financial statements and management accounts?

A Financial statements are primarily for external users and management accounts are primarily for internal users

B Financial statements are normally produced annually and management accounts are normally produced monthly

C Financial statements are more accurate than management accounts

D Financial statements are audited by an external audit and management accounts do not normally have an external audit

Test your understanding 16

When there is inflation, the historical cost concept has the effect of:

A overstating profits and understating statement of financial position values

B understating profits and overstating statement of financial position values

C understating cash flow and overstating cash in the statement of financial position

D overstating cash flow and understating cash in the statement of financial position

Test your understanding 17

When reconciling the payables ledger control account with the list of payables ledger balances of M, the following errors were found: the purchase daybook had been overstated by $600 and the personal ledger of a supplier had been understated by $200.

What adjustment must be made to correct these errors?

Control Account		**List of Payable Balances**	
Debit or Credit	$	Increase or Decrease	$

Test your understanding 18

B is a builder with a staff of ten employees. In April 20X0, he paid the following amounts:

Net salaries after employees' income tax and social security tax	$16,000
Employees' income tax and employees' social security tax for March 20X0	$7,000
Employer's social security tax for March 20X0	$3,000

He owes $8,000 for April's employees' income tax and employees' social security tax and $3,500 for April's employer's social security tax. What is the correct expense to be included in April's income statement?

$..................

Test your understanding 19

The following information relates to M Ltd:

	At 30th September	
	20X1	20X0
	$000	$000
Inventory of raw materials	70	50
Work in progress	60	70
Inventory of finished goods	100	90
For the year ended 30th September 20X1		
Purchases of raw materials	$165,000	
Manufacturing wages	$30,000	
Factory overheads	$40,000	

The prime cost of production in the manufacturing account for the year ended 30th September 20X1 is:

$ ....

Test your understanding 20

Are the following statements TRUE or FALSE?

A When valuing inventory at cost, inward transport costs should be included.
TRUE/FALSE ....

B When valuing inventory at cost, production overheads should be included.
TRUE/FALSE ....

Test your understanding 21

On 30 June 20X0 an electricity ledger account had an accrual of $400 and a credit balance was brought down on 1 July 20X0. During the financial year electricity invoices totalling $5,000 were paid. In July 20X1 an invoice for $900 was paid for the quarter ended 31 August 20X1

What is the income statement charge for electricity payable for the year ended 30 June 20X1?

$..................

Test your understanding 22

The allowance for receivables in the ledger of B Ltd at 31 October 20X0 was $11,000. During the year ended 31 October 20X1 irrecoverable debts of $7,000 were written off. Receivable balances at 31 October 20X1 were $140,000 and the company policy is to have an allowance for receivables of 5 per cent.

What is the charge for irrecoverable debts and change in the allowance for receivables in the income statement for the year ended 31 October 20X1?

$..................

Test your understanding 23

The following is an extract from the statement of financial position of IAS plc for the years ended 31 July 20X0 and 20X1.

	20X1	20X0
	$000	$000
Inventory	40	90
Receivables	55	10
Payables	45	30
Accruals	15	20

What figure would appear in the statement of cash flows of IAS plc for the year ended 31 July 20X0 as part of the cash generated from operations?

Test your understanding 24

The inventory at SOR Ltd were valued at $14,000 and excludes goods returned by a customer on the last day of the month. The goods were purchased by SOR Ltd for $4,000 and were invoiced at a mark-up of 25 per cent.

The value of inventory at SOR Ltd should be:

$..................

Test your understanding 25

A trial balance does not balance. Which of the following errors may be the cause of this failure to balance?

A The purchase of a machine had been debited to the machine repairs account

B A cheque received from a customer was banked but no ledger entry was made

C The sale of goods on credit was debited to receivables and sales

D The depreciation charge on machinery had been credited to the cost of machinery account

Test your understanding 26

S is employed by T Ltd. His payroll details for January and February are as follows:

January:	Gross Salary $2,200;	Tax $500;	Social security $100;	Net pay $1,600.
February:	Gross Salary $2,500;	Tax $550;	Social security $110;	Net pay $1,840.

Tax and social security are payable to the government one month after they are deducted from employees' salaries.

How much cash did T Ltd pay out in February in connection with S's wages?

$..................

Test your understanding 27

When a company produces a statement of comprehensive income, which of the following items is included in 'other comprehensive income'?

A Profit on sale of a non-current asset

B Interest received

C Government grant

D Net gain on property revaluation

Test your understanding 28

N plc purchased a machine for $18,000. The transportation costs were $1,700 and installation costs were $500. The machine broke down at the end of the first month in use and cost $400 to repair. N plc depreciates machinery at 10% per annum on cost, assuming no residual value.

What is the carrying amount of the machine after one year, to the nearest dollar?

$..................

Test your understanding 29

Which of the following might explain the debit balance on a purchase ledger account?

A The company took a cash discount to which they were not entitled and paid less than the amount due

B The company mistakenly paid too much

C The bookkeeper failed to enter a contra with the sales ledger

D The bookkeeper failed to post a cheque paid to the account

Test your understanding 30

In a period of inflation, which of the following methods of charging inventory issues to production will give the lowest profit figure?

A Average cost

B LIFO

C FIFO

D Replacement cost

Test your understanding 31

Which of the following provides the best explanation of the objective of an internal audit?

A The objective is to assist the directors of a company in the effective discharge of their financial responsibilities towards the members

B The objective is to provide support to the external auditor

C The objective is to detect fraud and error

D The objective is to audit the financial statements

Test your understanding 32

The following information at 5 January 20X2 relates to a club which has a year end of 31 December 20X1.

	$
Subscriptions for 20X0 unpaid at January 20X1	400
Subscriptions for 20X0 paid during the year ended 31 December 20X1	550
Subscriptions for 20X1 paid during the year ended 31 December 20X1	7,000
Subscriptions for 20X2 paid during the year ended 31 December 20X1	2,000
Subscriptions for 20X1 unpaid at 31 December 20X1	850

It is the club's policy to write off overdue subscriptions after 1 year.

What amount should be credited to the income and expenditure statement for the year ended 31 December 20X1?

$..................

Test your understanding 33

Extracts from the financial statements of ASB Ltd are set out below.

Income statement for the year ended 31 December 20X1

		$000
Turnover		400
Cost of sales		(175)
Gross profit		225
Profit on sale of non-current asset		80
		305
Expenses	35	
Depreciation	40	
Operating profit		(75)
		230

	31st December 20X0 $000	31st December 20X1 $000
Inventory, receivables, current liabilities	50	65

What figure would appear in the statement of cash flows of ASB Ltd for the year ended 31 December 20X1 for cash generated from operations?

Test your understanding 34

The correct ledger entries to record the issue of 200,000 $1 Ordinary Shares at a premium of 20% and paid by cheque is:

	Dr	Cr
	$	$
A Bank	240,000	
B Share capital		200,000
C Share premium		40,000
D Share premium		240,000
E Share capital		240,000
F Bank	200,000	
G Share capital		160,000

Test your understanding 35

M plc's trial balance did not balance at 31 May 20X1. The following errors were discovered: insurance of $700 prepaid at 31 May 20X0 had not been brought down as an opening balance on the insurance account; wages of $6,000 had been incorrectly debited to the purchases account; the bookkeeper had failed to accrue for the telephone invoice owing at 31 May 20X1 of $400.

What was the difference on the trial balance?

$.................

Test your understanding 36

S is a builder who has numerous small items of equipment. He calculates his depreciation using the straight-line method of 20%. At the beginning of his financial year the equipment had a carrying value of $11,475; he bought equipment costing $4,362 and he sold equipment with a carrying value of $3,257 for $4,000. What is his depreciation charge on equipment for the year?

$.................

Test your understanding 37

The operating profit margin in a company is 9% and the asset turnover ratio is 3.

What is the return on capital employed?

.... %

Test your understanding 38

The accounts for SPA plc are set out below.

Income statement of SPA plc for the year ended 30 November 20X2

	$000	$000
Turnover		6,000
Opening inventory	200	
Purchases	3,100	
Closing inventory	(400)	
Cost of sales		(2,900)
Gross profit		3,100
Operating expenses		(400)
Operating profit		2,700
Interest		(200)
Profit for the period		2,500

Statement of financial position of SPA plc as at 30 November 20X2

Assets	$000	$000
Non-current assets		3,500
Current assets		
Inventory	300	
Receivables	900	
Bank	50	
		1,250
		4,750
Equity and liabilities		
Share capital		2,200
Retained earnings		2,100
		4,300
Current liabilities		
Trade payables		450
		4,750

The return on capital employed in SPA is:

.... %

Test your understanding 39

The asset turnover ratio in SPA using the total capital employed at the year end is:

.... :1

Test your understanding 40

The quick ratio in SPA is:

.... :1

Test your understanding 41

A credit balance of $800 brought down on X Limited's account in the books of Y Limited means that

A X Limited owes Y Limited $800

B Y Limited owes X Limited $800

C Y Limited has paid X Limited $800

D Y Limited has overpaid X by $800

Test your understanding 42

Match the following user groups with their responsibilities.

A	The government	1	Appointing directors
B	The shareholders	2	Ensuring that all accounting transactions are properly recorded and summarised in the accounts
C	The internal auditors	3	Collecting statistical information useful in managing the economy
D	The directors	4	Reporting to the directors on internal systems

Test your understanding 43

The following information relates to a company at its year end:

	$
Inventory at the beginning of the year	
Raw materials	22,000
Work in progress	4,000
Finished goods	63,000
Inventory at the end of the year	
Raw materials	25,000
Work in progress	1,000
Finished goods	72,000
Purchases of raw materials	220,000
Direct wages	300,000
Royalties on goods sold	45,000
Production overheads	360,000
Distribution costs	70,000
Administration expenses	290,000
Sales	1,400,000

The cost of goods manufactured during the year is:

$...............

Test your understanding 44

Your sales ledger control account has a balance at 1 November 20X1 of $30,000 debit. During November, credit sales were $67,000, cash sales were $15,000 and receipts from customers, excluding cash sales, and after deducting cash discounts of $1,400 were $60,000. Sales returns were $4,000.

The closing balance on the sales ledger control account was:

$...............

Test your understanding 45

In a not-for-profit organisation, the accumulated fund is:

A non-current assets plus net current assets less non-current liabilities

B the balance on the general reserve

C non-current assets plus working capital

D non-current liabilities plus current liabilities minus current assets

Test your understanding 46

Your company's bank statement at 31 July 20X1 shows a favourable balance of $10,300. You subsequently discover that the bank has dishonoured a customer's cheque for $500 and has charged bank charges of $150, neither of which is recorded in your cash book. There are unpresented cheques totalling $1,700. You further discover that a receipt from a customer of $400 has been recorded as a credit in your cash book.

Your cash book balance, prior to correcting the errors and omissions, was:

$..............

Test your understanding 47

Inventory is valued using FIFO. Opening inventory was 12 units at $4 each. Purchases were 60 units at $5 each, then issues of 18 units were made, followed by issues of 23 units.

Closing inventory is valued at:

$..............

Test your understanding 48

A book of prime entry is one in which:

A transactions are entered prior to being recorded in ledger accounts

B ledger accounts are maintained

C the rules of double-entry bookkeeping do not apply

D memorandum accounts are kept

Test your understanding 49

Sales are $310,000, purchases are $165,000, opening inventory are $21,000, closing inventory are $18,000.

Inventory days are:

$ ....

Test your understanding 50

Which two of the following statements are true?

A Sales less factory cost of goods completed equals gross profit

B Prime cost is recorded in the trading account

C Factory cost of goods completed is recorded in the trading account

D Closing work in progress is not included in the statement of financial position

E Royalty payments on goods manufactured are included in prime cost

F Trade discounts on the purchase of raw materials are included in prime cost

Test your understanding answers

Test your understanding 1

D

Test your understanding 2

C

Test your understanding 3

B

Test your understanding 4

Turnover \$3 million × 5% gives receivables of = \$150,000
Allowance for receivables is 4% × \$150,000 = \$6,000
Existing allowance is \$6,000 × 3/4 = \$4,500
Change in allowance to income statement = debit \$1,500

Test your understanding 5

D

Test your understanding 6

A, D and E

Test your understanding 7

D

Test your understanding 8

$2,400 for one year is $200 per month		
Charge to income statement	7 × $200 =	$1,400
Prepaid in statement of financial position	5 × $200 =	$1,000

Test your understanding 9

$14,000

Test your understanding 10

		$
Bank statement balance	overdrawn	(1,650)
Unpresented cheques		(950)
Outstanding deposits		1,200
Bank error		320
Cash book – credit balance		(1,080)

Test your understanding 11

Sales ledger control

	$		$
Opening receivables	2,000	Cheques banked credit sales	160,000
Credit sales (balancing figure)	161,000	Closing receivables	3,000
	163,000		163,000

Cash account

	$		$
Opening balance	100	Cash banked	50,000
Cash sales ($230,000 – $161,000)	69,000	Cash missing	18,900
		Closing balance	200
	69,100		69,100

Cash missing is $18,900.

Test your understanding 12

1st April 20X0 Cost		10,000
Depreciation charge at 20%		
20X0	2,000	
20X1	2,000	
20X2	2,000	
		(6,000)
Carrying amount 1 August 20X3		4,000
Proceeds 1 August 20X3		4,900
Profit		900

Test your understanding 13

B

Test your understanding 14

Cash Account

	$		$
1st July bal b/d	250	Cash cheque	100
Photocopying	50	Cash paid out (balancing figure)	620
Cash from bank	600	31st July bal c/d	180
	900		900

The answer is: cash paid out $620.

Test your understanding 15

C

Test your understanding 16

A

Test your understanding 17

Control Account		**List of Payable Balances**	
Debit or Credit	$	Increase or Decrease	$
Debit	600	Increase	200

Test your understanding 18

	$
Net salaries for April	16,000
Employees' social security and tax for April	8,000
Employer's social security	3,500
	27,500

Test your understanding 19

	$
Prime cost is direct materials and direct labour	
Opening inventory of raw materials	50,000
Purchases	165,000
Closing inventory of raw materials	(70,000)
Raw materials consumed	145,000
Manufacturing wages	30,000
	175,000

Test your understanding 20

Include Inward Transport Costs	Include Production Overheads
True or false	True or false
True	True

Test your understanding 21

Electricity Account

		$			$
30 June 20X1	Invoices	5,000	1 July 20X0	bal b/d	400
30 June 20X1	Accrual – $900 × 1/3	300	30 June 20X1	IS	4,900
		5,300			5,300

The answer is: $4,900

Test your understanding 22

	$
Receivables ($140,000 × 5%)	7,000
Allowance for receivables at 31 October 20X0	(11,000)
Change in allowance	(4,000)
Irrecoverable debts written off	7,000
Income statement	3,000

Test your understanding 23

	$000
Inventory	50
Receivables	(45)
Payables	15
Accruals	(5)
Cash generated from operations	15

Test your understanding 24

	$
Inventory at valuation	14,000
Goods on sale or return at cost	4,000
Inventory valuation	18,000

Test your understanding 25

C

Test your understanding 26

	$
Net pay February	1,840
Tax January	500
Social security January	100
	2,440

Test your understanding 27

D Net gain on property revaluation.

Items A, B and C would be recorded in the 'income statement' part of a statement of comprehensive income.

Test your understanding 28

	$
Cost of machine	18,000
Transportation	1,700
Installation	500
	20,200
Depreciation at 10%	(2,020)
Carrying amount	18,180

Test your understanding 29

B

Test your understanding 30

D

Test your understanding 31

A

Test your understanding 32

	$
Subscriptions paid for 20X1	7,000
Subscriptions owing for 20X1	850
	7,850

Test your understanding 33

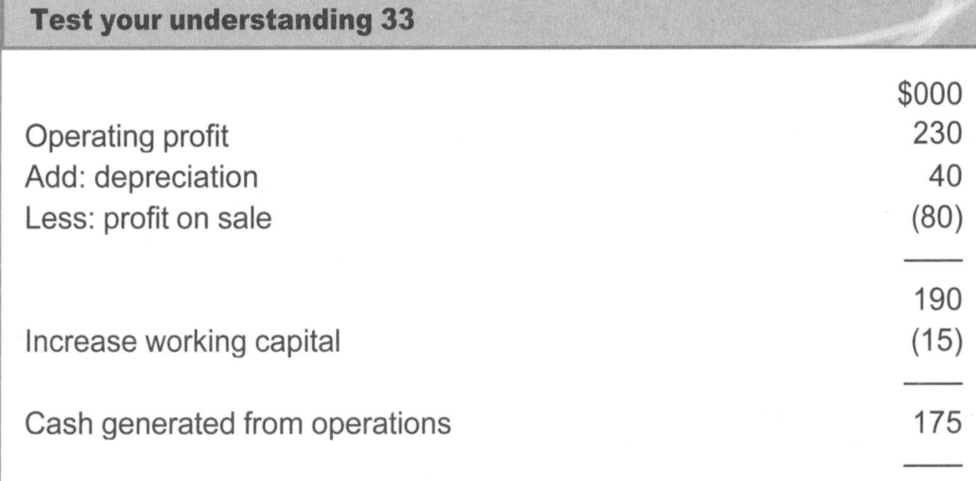

	$000
Operating profit	230
Add: depreciation	40
Less: profit on sale	(80)
	190
Increase working capital	(15)
Cash generated from operations	175

Test your understanding 34

A, B and C

Test your understanding 35

Insurance balance omitted	$700
Wages mis-posted – not affect trial balance	Nil
Accrual omitted – not affect trial balance	Nil

Answer is $700

Test your understanding 36

	$
Carrying value at the beginning of the year	11,475
Purchases	4,362
Disposals	(3,257)
	12,580
Depreciation at 20%	2,516

Test your understanding 37

Operating profit margin % × asset turnover : total capital employed = ROCE 9% × 3 = 27%

Test your understanding 38

$$\frac{\text{Operating profit}}{\text{Total capital employed}} = \frac{\$2,700,000}{\$4,300,000} \times 100 = 63\%$$

Test your understanding 39

$$\frac{\text{Turnover}}{\text{Total capital employed}} = \frac{\$6,000,000}{\$4,300,000} = 1.39 : 1$$

Test your understanding 40

$$\frac{\text{Receivables + Bank}}{\text{Current liabilities}} = \frac{\$900,000 + \$50,000}{\$450,000} = 2.11 : 1$$

Test your understanding 41

B

Test your understanding 42

(A3) (B1) (C4) (D2)

Test your understanding 43

	$000
Inventory at beginning of year – raw materials	22,000
Purchases	220,000
Inventory at end of year – raw materials	(25,000)
Direct wages	300,000
Production overheads	360,000
Inventory at beginning of year – work in progress	4,000
Inventory at end of year – work in progress	(1,000)
	880,000

Test your understanding 44

Sales ledger control account

		$			$
1 Nov 20X1	Balance b/d	30,000		Bank	60,000
	Credit sales	67,000		Cash discounts	1,400
				Sales returns	4,000
			31 Nov 20X1	Bal c/d	31,600
		97,000			97,000

Test your understanding 45

A

Test your understanding 46

Bank reconciliation	$
Balance at bank 31 July 20X1	10,300
Unpresented cheques	(1,700)
	8,600
Opening balance in cash book – balancing figure	8,450
Dishonoured cheque	(500)
Bank charges	(150)
Error ($400 × 2)	800
	8,600

Test your understanding 47

	units	unit $	Total $
Opening inventory	12	4	48
Purchases	60	5	300
Issue	(12)	4	(48)
Issue	(6)	5	(30)
Issue	(23)	5	(115)
Closing inventory	31	5	155

Test your understanding 48

A

Test your understanding 49

Average inventory is opening inventory $21,000 + closing inventory $18,000 = $39,000/2 = $19,500

Cost of goods sold is opening inventory $21,000 + purchases $165,000 – closing inventory $18,000 = $168,000

Inventory days is ($19,500 × 365)/$168,000 = 42 days

Test your understanding 50

C and E

chapter

24

Mock Assessment 2

Chapter learning objectives

This section is intended for use when you have completed your study and initial revision. It contains a complete mock assessment.

This should be attempted as an exam conditions, timed mock. This will give you valuable experience that will assist you with your time management and examination strategy.

Certificate in Business Accounting

Fundamentals of Financial Accounting

Illustrative Computer-based Assessment

Instructions: attempt all 50 questions

Time allowed: 2 hours

Do not look at or attempt this illustrative computer-based assessment until you have fully completed your revision and are about to sit your computer-based assessment.

Illustrative computer-based assessment 2: Questions

Test your understanding 1

A business is normally said to have earned revenue when:

A an order has been placed

B a customer is legally obliged to pay for goods delivered

C cash has been received

D goods have been manufactured and placed in inventories

Which concept does this comply with?

Concept ....

Test your understanding 2

The following information relates to NI Ltd at 30 June 20X6.

	$
Balance per cashbook – credit balance	5,200
Unpresented cheques	1,100
Bank charges not entered in the cash book	400
Receipts not yet credited by the bank	1,700
Dishonoured cheques not yet entered in the cash book	600

The balance shown on the bank statement at 30 June 20X6 was:

$ ....

Test your understanding 3

The following information relates to NBV Ltd for the year ended 31 July 20X5.

	$000
Prime cost	370
Carriage outwards	90
Depreciation delivery vehicles	50
Factory indirect overheads	560
Increase in WIP	65
Decrease in inventory of finished goods	40

The factory cost of goods completed for the year ended 31 July 20X5 is:

$ ....

Test your understanding 4

An external auditor carried out the following tests:

A Enquiries regarding internal systems of control

B Walkthrough test

C Inspecting a purchase invoice

D Inspecting a non-current asset

Which of the above are compliance tests?

Test your understanding 5

The following information relates to CT plc.

Machinery	$000
Cost at 1 January 20X4	90
Additions	30
Disposal	(20)
Cost at 31 December 20X4	100
Accumulated depreciation at 1 January 20X4	20
Depreciation charge	5
Disposal	(3)
Accumulated depreciation at 31 December 20X4	22

The profit on disposal of a machine was $3,000.

The cash flow from investing activities of CT plc for the year ended 31 December 20X4 would include:

$ .... inflow/outflow ....

Test your understanding 6

The accountant at SL Ltd is preparing quarterly financial statements for the quarter ended 31 July 20X3. The last quarterly gas bill, payable in arrears, received by SL Ltd was dated 31 May 20X3 and amounted to $2,800. The accountant, when preparing the quarterly financial statements for the quarter ended 30 April had expected the May gas bill to be $2,100. The accountant expects the gas bill for the quarter ended 31 August 20X3 to be $3,900. Gas bills are paid on the day they are received. All under/over estimates on accruals are charged within the period.

The charge to the income statement for gas in the quarter to 31 July 20X3 should be:

$..................

Test your understanding 7

IT plc has a policy that all items of equipment which cost less than $1,000 are charged to an expense account rather than a non-current asset account. This is an example of the concept of:

A money measurement

B prudence

C going concern

D materiality

Test your understanding 8

Internal auditors report to the:

A government

B external auditors

C shareholders

D management

Test your understanding 9

KP Ltd is preparing financial statements for the year ended 30 June 20X3. Rent is payable quarterly in advance on 1 February, 1 May, 1 August and 1 November. The annual charge for rent was $3,600 and $4,800 for the year ended 31 January 20X3 and 20X4, respectively. The financial statements should show:

Rent expense = $ .... Accrual = $ ....

Prepayment = $ ....

Test your understanding 10

DOB Ltd purchased a machine costing $20,000 on 1 August 20X2. The company estimated that the asset had a useful life of 4 years and an expected residual value of $2,000. The company uses the straight-line method of depreciation. The company's financial year end is 30 November. It is the company's policy to charge a full year's depreciation in the year of purchase and none in the year of disposal. On 1 November 20X5 the asset was sold for $5,500. The profit or loss on disposal in the year ended 30 November 20X5 was:

$ .... Profit/loss ....

Test your understanding 11

The following information is an extract from the financial statements of FWD plc for the years ended 31 August 20X2 and 20X3.

	20X3	**20X2**
	$000	$000
Inventory	22	16
Receivables	18	20
Bank	14	12
	54	48
Payables	(14)	(18)
	40	30

The statement of cash flows of FWD plc for the year ended 31 August 20X3 should include in the cash flow from operations:

$ .... inflow/outflow ....

Test your understanding 12

Which of the following entries would not affect the totals in the trial balance agreeing?

A An invoice for $250 for rent has been omitted from the ledgers

B A cash sale has been recorded as debit cash sales, credit cash

C An invoice for vehicle expenses has been charged to the vehicle non-current asset account

D A payment received from a customer has been posted to the sales ledger control account account twice

Test your understanding 13

Which of the following are not intangible non-current assets?

A Goodwill

B Trademark

C Investment

D Patent

E Brand

F Leasehold property

Test your understanding 14

ASB Ltd bought computer equipment on the 1 January 20X1 for $32,000 and estimated that it would have a useful life of 5 years and would have a residual value of $4,000. ASB Ltd uses the straight-line method of depreciation. On the 31 December 20X2 it now considers that the remaining life is only 2 years and that the residual value will be nil.

The depreciation charge for the year ended 31 December 20X3 and 20X4 should be:

$ ....

Test your understanding 15

A company has a quick (acid) test ratio of 2:1. Current assets include inventory of $12,000 and trade receivables of $4,000. Trade payables are $8,000.

The bank balance is:

$ .... Debit/credit balance ....

Test your understanding 16

Which one of the following does not help in the prevention of fraud and errors?

A Reconciliations

B Suspense accounts

C Organisation of staff

D Authorisation procedures

Test your understanding 17

The FRC cycling club started in January 20X2 and the following fees were received in the years ended 31 December 20X2 and 20X3.

	20X2	**20X3**
	$	$
Joining fees	11,000	13,000
Annual fees	8,000	10,000
Life membership fees	7,000	5,000
	26,000	28,000

Joining fees are recognised over a period of 4 years and life membership fees are recognised over 10 years.

The total amount of fees in the income and expenditure statement for the year ended 31 December 20X3 should be:

$ ....

Test your understanding 18

IAS plc declared a final dividend of 5% for the year ended 28 February 20X3. The nominal value of the shares is 25¢. X bought 800 shares at a price of $5 in December 20X2 and the shares were valued at a price of $8 on 28 February 20X3.

X will receive a final dividend of:

$ ....

Test your understanding 19

The internal financial statements of GH Ltd value inventories in line with IAS 2, i.e. lower of cost or net realisable value. The warehouse manager has produced the following schedule for the values of the three items (X1, X2 and X3) in inventory at the year end.

	First in/first out	**Net realisable value**
	$000	$000
X1	15	25
X2	10	6
X3	14	16
	39	47

At what value should the inventory be stated in the statutory financial statements?

$ ....

Test your understanding 20

The job descriptions of staff in the credit control department are normally segregated because:

A work is completed more efficiently

B lower salaries can be paid

C it motivates staff to perform better

D it facilitates internal control

Test your understanding 21

The management accounts within a limited company are determined by:

A the directors

B the shareholders

C company law and accounting standards

D company law

Test your understanding 22

When the historical cost concept is applied, the capital of an entity is measured in terms of:

A money

B money, adjusted for inflation

C fair value

D operating capability

Test your understanding 23

If work in progress increases during an accounting period, then:

A prime cost will increase

B prime cost will decrease

C the factory cost of goods completed will increase

D the factory cost of goods completed will decrease

Test your understanding 24

The following information was extracted from the pay slip of JS, who received her net salary in cash, for the month ended 31 January 20X5.

	$
Gross salary of	5,000
Tax deducted	500
Employer's social security tax	400
Employee's social security tax	350
Employer's contribution to pension fund	190
Employee's contribution to pension fund	210
Voluntary deduction for payment to charity	30

Tax, social security tax, pension fund contributions and payments to charity are all payable in February 20X5.

The charge to the income statement, the balance on the payroll control account and the net pay for JS's salary for January was:

Charge to income statement	Balance on payroll control account	Net pay
$.................	$.................	$.................

Test your understanding 25

In January 20X4, JR began trading as a car valeting service. He introduced small items of equipment with an estimated cost of $3,600. During the year ended December 20X4, he purchased new items of equipment for $1,700 and sold some items for $300 with an original cost of $700.

Using the straight-line method at 10%, the depreciation charge for the year ended 31 December 20X4 was:

$ ....

Test your understanding 26

After the income statement for EH Ltd had been prepared, it was found that accrued expenses of $1,500 had been omitted and that closing inventories had been overvalued by $500.

The effect of these errors is an:

overstatement/understatement of profit .... $..................

Test your understanding 27

A sales ledger control account at 1 June had an opening balance of $20,000. During June, sales were $180,000, being credit sales of $170,000 and cash sales of $10,000. Total receipts from cash and credit customers was $165,000. During the month, it was recognised that $3,000 of receivables were bad and that a further $5,000 may not be paid. During the month, there was a contra of $2,000 between the sales and purchase control accounts and customers returned goods at a value of $6,000.

The balance on the sales ledger control account at 30 June was:

$..................

Test your understanding 28

Which of the following would you expect to see in a statement of changes in equity?

	Yes	No
Dividends		
Profit for the year		
Directors' salaries		
Revaluation of property		
Taxation		

Test your understanding 29

CAD Ltd uses the weighted average cost formula for valuing inventory. On 1 April there were 80 units in inventory valued at $17 each. On 6 April, 30 units were purchased for $19 each; and on 20 April, 45 units were purchased for $20 each. On 25 April, 100 units were sold for $3,000. The value of the closing inventory at 30 April was:

$ ....

Test your understanding 30

The following information related to M plc for the year ended 31 July 20X9:

	$
Prime cost	164,000
Factory overheads	227,000
Opening work in progress at 1 August 20X8	82,000
Factory cost of goods completed	342,000

The closing work in progress at 31 July 20X9 was:

$ ....

Test your understanding 31

VIP Ltd is registered for sales tax and received an invoice from a legal firm for $6,000 plus sales tax. The rate of sales tax on the services was 20%. The correct journal entries are:

Account	Dr	Cr
	$	$

Test your understanding 32

E Ltd received an invoice for the purchase of non-current asset equipment which was credited to the correct supplier's ledger account but debited to the equipment repairs account instead of the equipment account. The effect of not correcting this error on the financial statements would be:

A profit would be overstated and non-current assets would be understated

B profit would be overstated and non-current assets would be overstated

C profit would be understated and capital would be overstated

D profit would be understated and non-current assets would be understated

Test your understanding 33

The accountant at URP Ltd is preparing the annual financial statements. The company is in dispute with one of its suppliers which is currently the subject of a court case for a claim against the company for $300,000. URP Ltd has also made a claim against its insurance company for $200,000 and is waiting to hear if the insurance company will pay up. The accountant has decided to accrue for the legal claim for $300,000 but to ignore the insurance claim of $200,000.

The accounting concept which underlies these decisions is:

.... concept

Test your understanding 34

The return on capital employed for ETC plc is 22% and the net asset turnover ratio is 4 times.

The operating profit margin is:

.... %

Test your understanding 35

Which of the following would not help detect errors in a computerised accounting system?

A Control accounts

B Passwords

C Batch processing

D Coding systems

Test your understanding 36

The total cost of salaries charged to a limited company's income statement is:

A cash paid to employees

B net pay earned by employees

C gross pay earned by employees

D gross pay earned by employees plus employer's social security tax contributions

Test your understanding 37

The trading account for SUV Ltd for the year ended 31 July 20X8 was:

Trading Account for the year ended 31 July 20X8

		$000
Sales		300
Opening inventory	25	
Purchases	125	
Closing inventory	(30)	
Cost of goods sold		120
Gross profit		180

The trade payables at 31 July 20X8 was $28,000.

The trade payables days at 31 July 20X8 was:
.... days

Test your understanding 38

The following is the aged receivables analysis for Z Ltd at 30 April 20X3.

Age of debt	Less than 1 month	1–2 months	2–3 months	Over 3 months
Amount ($)	18,000	30,000	14,000	12,000

The company makes an allowance for receivables as follows:

Allowance	0%	1%	10%	30%

The allowance for receivables at 1 May 20X2 brought forward was $6,000.

The entry for the allowance for receivables in the income statement for the year ended 30 April 20X3 and the net receivables figure in the statement of financial position at that date should be:

Income statement	Statement of financial position
$.................. debit/credit..................	$..................

Test your understanding 39

The following information relates to companies X plc and Y plc, who are competitors selling carpets.

	X plc	**Y plc**
Gross profit mark up	25%	20%

Which of the following are possibly true based on the information provided?

A X plc has a selling price of $100 and profit of $25

B X plc has a selling price of $125 and a profit of $31.25

C Y plc has a selling price of $120 and a profit of $20

D Y plc has a selling price of $100 and a profit of $20

Test your understanding 40

Which of the following are accounting concepts and which are qualitative characteristics of financial statements?

	Accounting concept	Qualitative characteristic
Timely		
Material		
Relevant		
Objective		
Complete		

Test your understanding 41

On 1 October 20X6, LED Ltd owed a supplier $1,300. During the month of October, LED Ltd:

- purchased goods for $1,800 and the supplier offered a 4% discount for payment within the month.
- LED Ltd returned goods valued at $170 which had been purchased in September 20X6.
- sent a cheque to the supplier for payment of the goods delivered in October.

The balance on the supplier's account at the end of October 20X6 is:

$..................

Test your understanding 42

The main advantage of using a sales ledger control account is that:

A it ensures that the trial balance will always balance

B it helps with credit control

C it helps in detecting errors

D double-entry bookkeeping is not necessary

Test your understanding 43

The following information relates to B Ltd for the year ended 31 August 20X7.

	$
Retained profit for the year	25,000
Net cash inflow from operating activities	23,000
Dividend paid	2,000
Profit on sale of non-current assets	500
Proceeds on sale of non-current assets	6,000
Taxation paid	1,000
Interest paid	3,500
Payments for non-current assets	7,000
Issue of debentures	4,000

The statement of cash flows will show:

decrease/increase .... in cash of $ ....

Test your understanding 44

The property in Credit Crunch Ltd has been revalued from $300,000 to $400,000, and the tax on the gain is $25,000.

Complete the following items to enter the above information.

Amount included in total comprehensive income	$
Amount included in statement of changes in equity	$
Property in statement of financial position	$
Revaluation reserve	$
Non-current liabilities	$

Test your understanding 45

DRP Ltd operates an imprest system for petty cash. On 1 May the float was $325. It was decided that this should be increased to $400 at the end of May.

During May, the cashier paid $15 for gardening, $120 for stamps and $175 for repairs. The cashier received $40 from staff for the private use of the telephone and $70 for a cash sale. The amount to be drawn from the bank account for petty cash at the end of May is:

$..................

Test your understanding 46

An audit trail in a computerised accounting system is:

A a history of all transactions on a ledger account

B information regarding all transactions in a period

C a list of all transactions automatically posted from day books to ledgers

D a list of all transactions checked by the internal auditor

Test your understanding 47

The following are extracts from the financial statements of RSVP plc for the year ended 31 March 20X8.

	$000
Issued ordinary shares of $1	450
Share premium account	75
Income statement reserve	40
Debenture	50
Profit before interest for the year ended 31 March 20X8	85

The return on total capital employed is:

.... %

Test your understanding 48

There was a fire at the premises of NGO Ltd during the year ended 30 November 20X9 and the accounting records were partly destroyed. The accountant is trying to prepare the financial statements from these incomplete records. She discovers that the electricity account was overpaid by $400 on the 1 December 20X8 and that there was $300 owing on 30 November 20X9. During the year, electricity payments totalled $3,000.

The charge to the income statement for electricity for the year ended 30 November 20X9 is:

$ ....

Test your understanding 49

In order to confirm that financial statements show a true and fair view (fair presentation), the external auditor should ensure that the financial statements comply with:

A internal procedures as specified by the directors

B the stock exchange listed company regulations

C the accounting conventions

D international financial reporting standards

Test your understanding 50

CO Ltd purchased equipment for $60,000 on 1 July 20X5 with an estimated residual value of $4,000. The company's accounting year end is 31 December. It is CO Ltd's policy to charge a full year's depreciation in the year of purchase. CO Ltd depreciates its equipment on the reducing balance basis at 25% per annum.

The carrying amount of the equipment at 31 December 20X8 should be:

$..................

Test your understanding answers

Test your understanding 1

B Concept: Realisation

Test your understanding 2

	Cash book	Bank statement
	$	$
Balance per cash book/bank statement	(5,200)	(6,800)
Unpresented cheques		(1,100)
Bank charges	(400)	
Receipts not credited by bank		1,700
Dishonoured cheques	(600)	
	(6,200)	(6,200)

Answer: $6,800

Test your understanding 3

	$000
Prime cost	370
Factory indirect overheads	560
Increase in WIP	(65)
Factory cost of goods completed	865

Test your understanding 4

A and B

Test your understanding 5

		$000
Additions		(30)
Asset disposal – cost	20	
– depreciation	(3)	
– carrying amount	17	
Profit on disposal	3	
Proceeds on disposal		20
Cash outflow		(10)

Test your understanding 6

Gas account

		Dr $	**Cr** $
20X3			
May 1	Bal b/f ($2,100 3 2/3)		1,400
May 31	Bank	2,800	
Jul 31	Accrual ($3,900 3 2/3)	2,600	
Jul 31	Income statement		4,000
		5,400	5,400

Test your understanding 7

D

Test your understanding 8

D

Test your understanding 9

Rent account

		Dr	Cr
		$	$
1 Jul 20X2	Bal b/f ($900 × 1/3)	300	
1 Aug 20X2	Bank	900	
1 Nov 20X2	Bank	900	
1 Feb 20X3	Bank	1200	
1 May 20X3	Bank	1200	
30 Jun 20X3	Income statement		4,100
30 Jun 20X3	Bal c/d ($1200 × 1/3)		400
		4,500	4,500

Rent expense = $4,100 Accrual = $nil Prepayment = $400

Test your understanding 10

	$
Cost machine	20,000
Expected residual value	(2,000)
	18,000
Annual depreciation charge	
$18,000/4	4,500
Cost machine	20,000
Depreciation charge 3 years ($4,500 × 3)	(13,500)
Carrying amount	6,500
Proceeds	(5,500)
Loss on disposal	1,000

Test your understanding 11

	$000
Inventory	(6,000)
Receivables	2,000
Payables	(4,000)
Cash outflow	(8,000)

Test your understanding 12

A, B and C

Test your understanding 13

C and F

Test your understanding 14

	$
Cost machine	32,000
Expected residual value	(4,000)
	28,000
Annual depreciation charge	
$28,000/5	5,600
Cost machine	32,000
Depreciation charge 2 years ($5,600 × 2)	(11,200)
Carrying amount	20,800
Depreciation charge 20X3 & 20X4	
($20,800/2)	10,400

Test your understanding 15

	$
Receivables	4,000
Bank	12,000
	16,000
Payables	8,000
Quick (acid) test	2:1

Test your understanding 16

B

Test your understanding 17

Fees – year ended 31 December 20X3

	$
Annual fees	10,000
Joining fees $(11,000 + $13,000)/4	6,000
Life membership fees $(7,000 + $5,000)/10	1,200
	17,200

Test your understanding 18

800 shares at 25¢	$200
Dividends 5%	$10

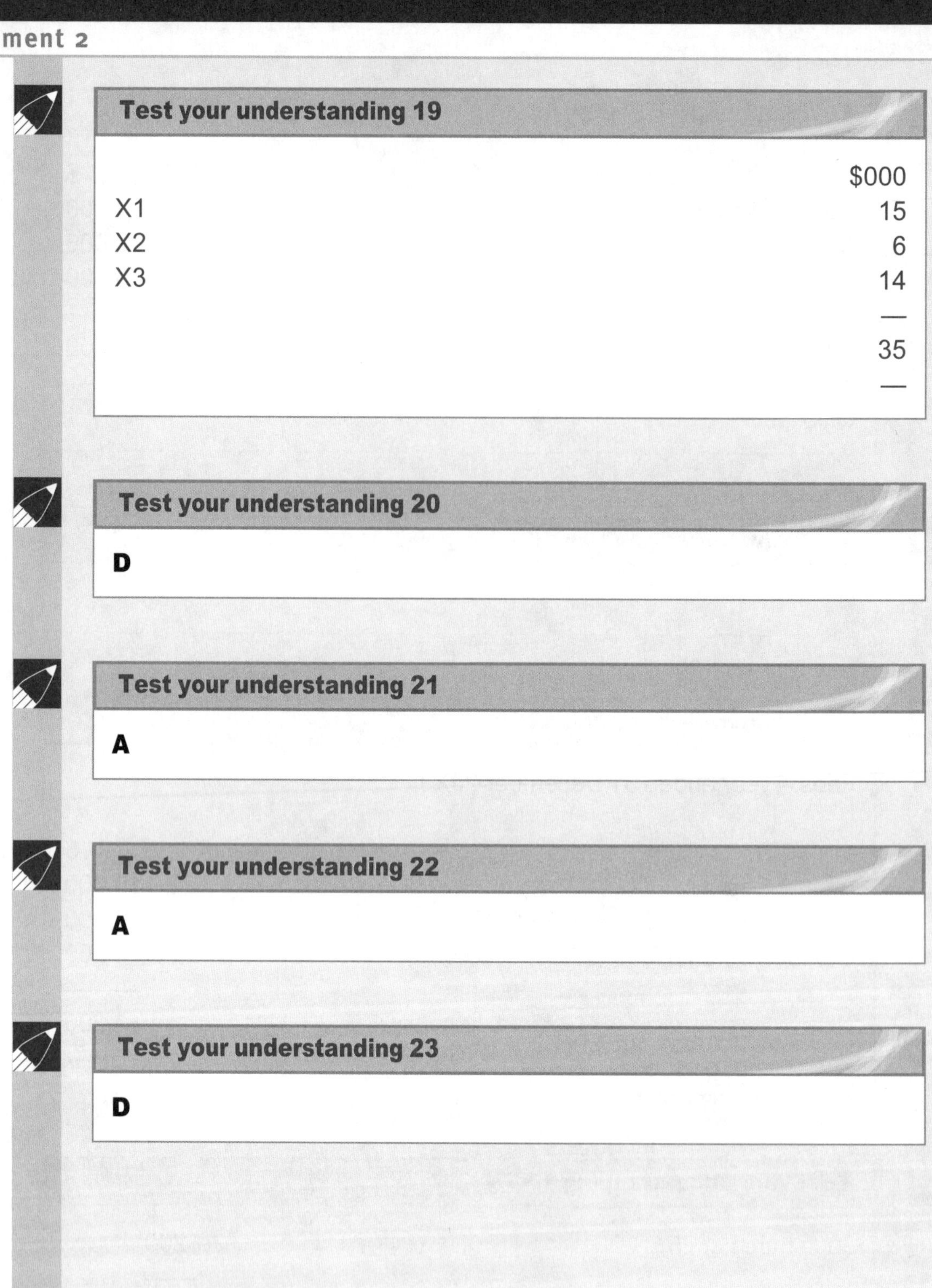

Test your understanding 19

	$000
X1	15
X2	6
X3	14
	—
	35
	—

Test your understanding 20

D

Test your understanding 21

A

Test your understanding 22

A

Test your understanding 23

D

Test your understanding 24

	Income statement	Payroll control	Net pay
Gross salary	5,000		5,000
Tax deducted		(500)	(500)
Employer's social security tax	400	400	
Employee's social security tax		350	(350)
Employer's contribution to pension fund	190	190	
Employee's contribution to pension fund		210	(210)
Voluntary deduction for payment to charity		30	(30)
Net pay			
	5,590	1,680	3,910

Test your understanding 25

	$
Estimated cost equipment introduced	3600
Additional equipment	1700
Equipment sold	(700)
Carrying value of equipment December 20X4	4,600
Depreciation charge – year ended 31 December 20X4	460

Test your understanding 26

Overstatement $2,000

Test your understanding 27

Debit		Credit	
	$		$
Opening balance	20,000	Bank	155,000
Sales	170,000	Bad debts	3,000
		Contra	2,000
		Returns	6,000
		Closing balance	24,000
	190,000		190,000

Test your understanding 28

	Yes	No
Dividends	✓	
Profit for the year	✓	
Directors' salaries		✓
Revaluation of property	✓	
Taxation		✓

Test your understanding 29

Date	**Units**	**Average Price ($)**	**Total ($)**
1 Apr	80	17	1,360
6 Apr	30	19	570
	110	17.55	1,930
20 Apr	45	20	900
	155	18.26	2,830
25 Apr	(100)	18.26	(1,826)
30 Apr	55	18.26	1,004

Test your understanding 30

		$000
Prime cost		164
Factory overheads		227
		391
Opening work in progress	82	
Closing work in progress	(131)	(49)
Factory cost of goods completed		342

Test your understanding 31

Account	Dr	Cr
	($)	($)
Legal fees	6,000	
VAT	1,200	
Trade payable		7,200

Test your understanding 32

D

Test your understanding 33

Prudence concept

Test your understanding 34

ROCE		Operating profit margin		Net asset turnover
22%	=	5.5%	×	4

Test your understanding 35

B

Test your understanding 36

D

Test your understanding 37

$28,000 × 365/$125,000 = 82 days

Test your understanding 38

Statement of financial position	**Receivables $**	**%**	**Allowance for receivables $**
< 1 month	18,000	0%	0
1–2 months	30,000	1%	300
2–3 months	14,000	10%	1,400
> 3 months	12,000	30%	3,600
			5,300

Allowance $	**Allowance $**	**IS A/c $**
1 May 20X2 6,000	30 April 20X3 5,300	700 Credit
Income statement $700 credit		Statement of financial position $5,300

Test your understanding 39

C

Mark up means profit on cost. If mark up = 20% for Y plc, then selling price is 120%. $120/120 x 20 = $20

Test your understanding 40

	Accounting concept	Qualitative characteristic
Timely		✓
Material	✓	
Relevant		✓
Objective	✓	
Complete		✓

Test your understanding 41

		$
1 Oct 20X6	Opening balance	1,300
	Invoice	1,800
	Cheque	(1,728)
	Discount	(72)
	Goods returned	(170)
31 Oct 20X6	Closing balance	1,130

Test your understanding 42

C

Test your understanding 43

	$
Net cash inflow from operating activities	23,000
Dividend paid	(2,000)
Proceeds on sale of non-current assets	6,000
Taxation paid	(1,000)
Interest paid	(3,500)
Payments for non-current assets	(7,000)
Issue of debentures	4,000
Increase	19,500

Test your understanding 44

Complete the following items to enter the above information.

Amount included in total comprehensive income	$75,000
Amount included in statement of changes in equity	$75,000
Property in statement of financial position	$400,000
Revaluation reserve	$75,000
Non-current liabilities	$25,000

Test your understanding 45

		$
1 May	Balance	325
	Gardening	(15)
	Stamps	(120)
	Repairs	(175)
	Telephone	40
	Sales	70
		125
	Drawn from bank	275
31 May	Balance	400

Test your understanding 46

B

Test your understanding 47

$$\frac{\text{Profit before interest}}{\text{Capital}} \qquad \frac{\$85,000}{\$615,000} = 13.8\ \%$$

Test your understanding 48

Electricity Account

Dr	$	Cr	$
1 Dec 20X8 Bal b/d	400		
Bank	3,000		
		31 December 20X9 IS	3,700
31 December 20X9 Bal c/d	300		
	3,700		3,700

Test your understanding 49

D

Test your understanding 50

$60,000 × 75% × 75% × 75% × 75% = $18,984

Index

Index

E

F

G

I

J

L

M

N

Index

Index